The Message and the Kingdom

Richard A. Horsley and
Neil Asher Silberman

GROSSET/PUTNAM
A MEMBER OF
PENGUIN PUTNAM INC.
NEW YORK

The Message and
the Kingdom

How Jesus and Paul

Ignited a Revolution and Transformed

the Ancient World

Grosset/Putnam
a member of
Penguin Putnam Inc.
200 Madison Avenue
New York, NY 10016

Library of Congress Cataloging-in-Publication Data

Horsley, Richard A.
The message and the kingdom : how Jesus and Paul ignited a
revolution and transformed the ancient world / by Richard A. Horsley
and Neil Asher Silberman.
p.   cm.
Includes bibliographical references
ISBN 0-399-14194-4
1. Church history—Primitive and early church, ca. 30–600.
2. Christian antiquities.   3. Rome—Antiquities.   I. Silberman,
Neil Asher, date.   II. Title.
BR170.H67   1997   97-16218 CIP
270.1—dc21

Printed in the United States of America

1   3   5   7   9   10   8   6   4   2

This book is printed on acid-free paper. ∞

Book design by Kate Nichols
Maps by Jeffrey L. Ward

Contents

Acknowledgments

URING THE LONG PROCESS of research, writing, and revision of this book, we received much welcome practical and professional support from many colleagues and friends. Among them are Laura Whitney and the circulation staff at Andover-Harvard Theological Library; the circulation staff at the Episcopal Divinity School-Weston School of Theology Libraries; the staff of the Sterling Memorial Library of Yale University; and Susan Burdick and the staff of the Yale Divinity School Library, who all provided invaluable assistance in tracking down obscure bibliographical references and hard-to-find monographs. Our thanks also go to Ann DiSessa of the University of Massachusetts at Boston for her invaluable administrative efforts and to Marcus Aurin, Heather Kapplow, and Jane McIntosh, who provided painstaking research assistance. Jack Hitt, Rabbi Howard Sommer, and Neil Elliott all took the time to read earlier versions of this book and offered important comments and helpful criticism. Carol Mann once again proved herself to be the best literary agent and advisor that anyone could hope for. At Putnam, Timothy Meyer's deft copyediting smoothed and refined the final version of the text. Jeffrey L. Ward transformed a collection of raw data and sketches into graceful maps and charts. We also benefited from Joel Fotinos's experience and considerable skill in shepherding the book through the final stages of production and publication. He was ably assisted by Associate Editor

David Groff and Marketing Coordinator Maria Liu. Our thanks also go to Susan Petersen of Riverhead Books, who was an early supporter of this project. Finally, we want to express our continuing gratitude and appreciation to our editor, Jane Isay. Her unflagging enthusiasm, patience, wisdom, and insight made this book a reality.

R.A.H.

N.A.S.

May 5, 1997

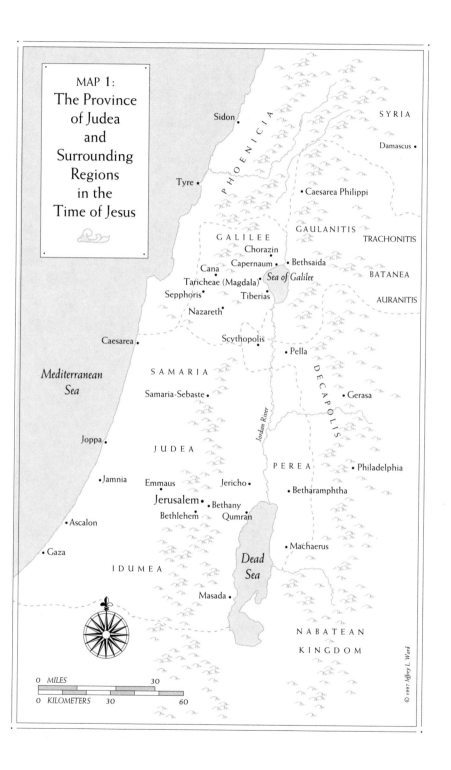

MAP 1:
The Province
of Judea
and
Surrounding
Regions
in the
Time of Jesus

Sidon

SYRIA

Damascus

Tyre

PHOENICIA

Caesarea Philippi

GAULANITIS

TRACHONITIS

GALILEE

Chorazin

Capernaum · Bethsaida

Cana

Taricheae (Magdala) · Sea of Galilee

BATANEA

Sepphoris · Tiberias

AURANITIS

Nazareth

Caesarea

Scythopolis

· Pella

Mediterranean
Sea

SAMARIA

Samaria-Sebaste ·

DECAPOLIS

· Gerasa

Joppa

JUDEA

Jordan River

PEREA

· Philadelphia

· Jamnia

Emmaus

Jericho ·

· Betharamphtha

Jerusalem ·

· Bethany

Bethlehem

Qumran

· Ascalon

· Gaza

IDUMEA

Dead
Sea

· Machaerus

Masada ·

NABATEAN

KINGDOM

© 1997 Jeffrey L. Ward

O   MILES   30

O   KILOMETERS   30   60

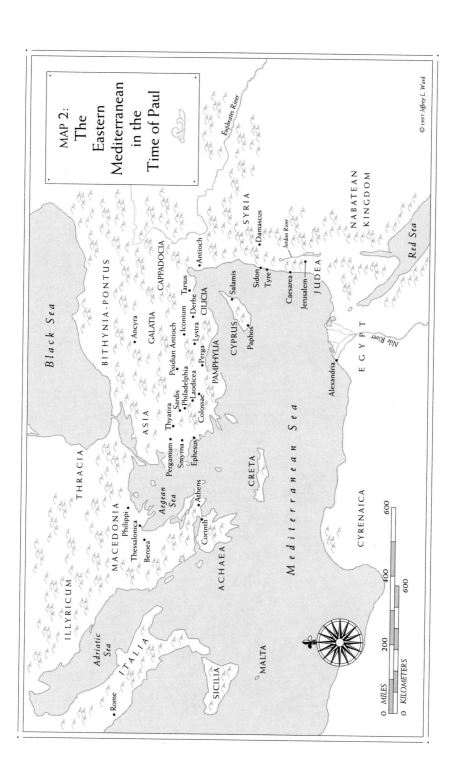

MAP 2:
The
Eastern
Mediterranean
in the
Time of Paul

© 1997 Jeffrey L. Ward

The Message and the Kingdom

Prologue

Searching for Jesus

IKE A PHANTOM LANDSCAPE rising from the rubble of long-buried villages, shantytowns, and market cities, the world of Jesus, Paul, and the earliest Christians is coming to life again. At dozens of archaeological dig sites in Israel, Jordan, Syria, Turkey, Greece, and Italy, excavators and New Testament scholars are piecing together the evidence of toppled columns, smashed pots, corroded coins, and fragmentary inscriptions to construct a dramatic new picture of the historical origins of Christianity—one that clashes disturbingly with more familiar, reverent images of Jesus, the disciples, and the peaceful hills and valleys of Galilee. In buried layers beneath the bustling streets of modern Mediterranean cities and at remote, out-of-the-way places whose names are difficult to pronounce and remember, archaeologists of many nations and religious persuasions are uncovering the evocative physical remains of an ancient society where unprecedented material splendor and luxury existed side by side with unprecedented suffering, hunger, and homelessness. As the dust rises and the diggers scrape away parched soil and collapsed stones from the streets, plazas, and buried floor levels of ancient cities and villages, they are bringing to life a long-silenced world of peasants, prophets, centurions, and Caesars, a world in which radical politics and membership in close-knit communities of "saints" were some of the most powerful ways that the earliest Christians sought to resist the power of foreign rulers and to assert their own dignity.

This book will attempt to reconstruct the social history of early Christianity from a wide variety of newly available evidence—drawn from recent studies of ancient Roman culture and from archaeological discoveries throughout the Mediterranean world. We, as authors, have come to this project of reassessment from quite different scholarly perspectives. Richard Horsley has devoted a significant part of his career to New Testament textual study, Judean history, and the search for the "Historical" Jesus. His earlier works were among the first to recognize that the public ministry of Jesus in first-century Galilee bore some striking similarities to other movements of peasant protest and resistance, as they have been described and observed by anthropologists all over the world. Neil Asher Silberman has written extensively on the modern political, religious, and ideological entanglements of Near Eastern archaeology. His recent study of the Dead Sea Scrolls led him to conclude that many modern scholars have greatly underestimated the political dimensions of apocalyptic expectation—in the case of the scrolls, they have perhaps overlooked their function as ideological protest against the hard realities of Roman imperial rule. The common theme of both our approaches is an appreciation for the close connections between ancient religion and politics. And in utilizing new sources of information to trace the earthly origins of Christianity, we will attempt to show that the world of John the Baptist, Jesus, the Apostle Paul, and the earliest Christians was not only a spiritual battleground but also a landscape of far-reaching economic dislocation, cultural conflict, and political change.

The early Roman Empire—as we will see in the chapters that follow—was a society where gleaming cities were rising in some places and children went hungry in others. It was a world where no luxury was enough for some great aristocrats and public celebrities, and where even the basic necessities of life lay beyond the grasp of the urban and rural poor. It was a world where dreams of limitless material wealth and technological progress danced in the heads of the great entrepreneurs and in the rhetoric of ambitious politicians—and where the looming nightmares of family break-down, crime, sudden loss of livelihood, and untreated and untreatable illnesses plagued the minds of the vast majority. It was, in short, a world that should seem ominously familiar—in which sweeping social and economic change was embraced by some and condemned by others, dramatically transforming the life of all the empire's people, from the wealthiest nobles in their palaces to the poorest shepherds wandering with their flocks in the hills. This is becoming increasingly clear because modern scholars have at last begun to explore the vast area covered by the rule and civilization of the Caesars to search for the lifestyles of *both* the rich and famous and the far larger, yet mostly hidden, world of the Roman have-nots, peasants, plebians, and slaves.

In the hills and valleys of the Galilee, recent excavations have revealed the remains of humble peasants' villages and market towns where Jesus' people lived and struggled for their daily existence. Digging through the thick mud of the shore of the Sea of Galilee, archaeologists have recovered the soggy timbers of a fisherman's boat submerged in the mud for more than two thousand years. It has offered a glimpse at the kind of vessel that might have been used by the fishermen-disciples Peter, James, and Andrew for hauling in their daily catch. Farther south, at the elegant palaces and public monuments erected by King Herod the Great at Masada, Jericho, and Jerusalem, scholars have documented the sheer scale and physical grandeur of Judea's ruling dynasty. On the Mediterranean coast, in the ruins of the ancient harbor city of Caesarea, the name of the notorious Roman governor Pontius Pilate has been found on a fragmentary Latin inscription. From the darkness of an ancient tomb just south of the Old City of Jerusalem archaeologists have retrieved an ornate ossuary inscribed with the name Joseph Caiaphas, who, according to the gospels, was the High Priest who presided over Jesus' trial. And the dramatic archaeological discoveries have shed new light on ideas as well as individuals: in the caves of the rugged wilderness of the Dead Sea region, thousands of tattered fragments of ancient Hebrew and Aramaic texts known as the Dead Sea Scrolls have revealed the deep messianic expectations gripping the People of Israel as they bridled under Roman rule.

Hundreds of miles to the north and west, in the mountains, valleys, and islands of modern Greece and Turkey, archaeologists have begun to piece together a very different aspect of Christianity's early history—one that intertwines with the social history of the Greco-Roman world. Digging through the ruins of temples, forums, and private houses in the cities of the Roman provinces of Galatia, Macedonia, Achaia, and Asia, expeditions have uncovered the material landscape across which the Apostle Paul traveled with his companions, preaching his distinctive gospel and establishing his first "assemblies of saints." As in Israel, some archaeological discoveries have offered tangible evidence for characters and places mentioned in the New Testament: the name of Lucius Iunius Gallio, the proconsul of Achaia who declared Paul innocent of charges brought against him (Acts 18:12–17), has been identified in an ancient inscription unearthed at Delphi, and in the excavations at Corinth and Ephesus archaeologists have begun to reconstruct the urban environment in which Paul and his followers lived. Yet in the finds recovered from individual excavations throughout Greece and Asia Minor and in the changing character of cities and settlements detected by region-wide surveys, we can see Roman civilization as far more than just a static backdrop. Archaeological finds are beginning to reveal the specific economic and political conditions to which earliest Christianity was a direct and power-ful response.

Modern teams of archaeologists tromping through the fields and across pastures, climbing through the thistles and into the gullies searching for and recording every tumble of building stones that might once have been a farmhouse or granary, or plotting every observed scatter of potsherds, have done nothing less than begin to rewrite the social history of the Roman Empire. In excavating the industrial quarters of ancient cities and docu-menting the ancient agricultural landscape through botanical analysis, photography of ancient field patterns, and satellite imagery of soil and water resources, archaeologists have already recognized some empire-wide patterns of social interaction between the Roman conquerors and the peoples whom they overran. In Galilee—the birthplace of Christianity—wide-ranging surveys have shown that a large number of small, rustic hilltop villages (some of them founded as early as 1200 B.C.E. and sup-ported over the centuries by a flexible mix of crops and herding) were coming under increasing economic pressure at the time of Jesus. The excavated finds and ancient sources indicate that the establishment of Roman rule and the incorporation of the region into the Roman economy caused a significant shift in the agricultural regime. And archaeological surveys conducted in such far-flung areas of the empire as southern Spain, Sardinia, Italy, Dalmatia, mainland Greece, Crete, and Cyprus have pro-duced a similar picture. The arrival of Roman armies, officials, and entre-preneurs in each new province brought about profound changes in agricultural methods, settlement patterns, and interregional links. Formerly autonomous regions, where traditional agricultural methods aimed at sub-sistence, not surplus, were drawn into an increasingly centralized economy where some people prospered mightily and others sank into helplessness and debt.

From Spain to the Euphrates, old patterns of independent farming, herding, and subsistence were gradually being replaced in the most fertile agricultural areas of the empire by more efficient and profitable agricultural methods, requiring far fewer independent farmers—yet many more tenant farmers and slaves. With traditional patterns of village life disrupted, many who could no longer find a place in the countryside flocked to the rapidly expanding cities. And once there, in the crowded streets, bazaars, and public forums, new forms of visual communication—classical architecture, statuary, coins, and public spectacles—offered the fragmented, dislocated population continual nonverbal reassurances that the New Roman Order was not only natural but had come to stay. Of course the incorporation of peoples, resources, and lifestyles into the empire did not happen all at once or at the same pace everywhere. And it was certainly not accomplished simply because some far-off government wanted it that way. Like the technological and economic revolutions of other times and places—the Renaissance, the Industrial Revolution, or even the present upheavals of the Information Age and deindustrialization—old-fashioned wisdom, skills, and work habits only gradually lost their value as a vast wave of institutional restructuring, labor migration, political instability, and market fluctuations ushered in a new order of relationships.

History has almost always been written from the viewpoint of those who build cities and conquer empires, but in the New Testament and the early Christian tradition we may be able to catch a rare glimpse at the hopes, dreams, and utopian visions of those who suddenly find themselves at the bottom of a new civilization's social heap. In this book we will argue that earliest Christianity was a movement that boldly challenged the heartlessness and arrogance of a vast governmental bureaucracy—run on unfairly apportioned tax burdens and guided by cynical special interests— that preached about "opportunity," "self-reliance," and "personal achieve-ment" while denying all three to the vast majority of men, women, and children over whom it presumed to rule. Christianity arose in a remote and poverty-stricken region of the vast Roman Empire, among the struggling farm families of a frontier province that could only be classed as "chron-ically underdeveloped" by modern economic criteria. Yet even after the movement's first great prophet was condemned as a threat to civil order and put to death for his preaching, his followers spread a coalescing gospel of resistance from the country to the city and from the eastern provinces of the empire to the far western edges of the Roman world. At the heart of this

movement was the dream of a down-to-earth Kingdom first enunciated by
the prophets of the tiny Land of Israel several hundred years before: "They
shall build houses and inhabit them; they shall plant vineyards and eat their
fruit. They shall not build and another inhabit; they shall not plant and
another eat. For like the days of a tree shall the days of my people be, and
my chosen shall long enjoy the work of their hands" (Isa. 65:21–22). And
that shared yearning for escape from powerlessness gave rise to new means
of religious expression, organization, symbols, and ritual that eventually
crystallized around the year 100 of the Common Era into an organized
form of belief and worship that we would recognize as Christianity.

There is no question that we now know more *about* the world of early
Christianity than any previous generation since the end of Antiquity. And
for many believing Christians, the finds unearthed in ancient Corinth,
Antioch, Jerusalem, and Capernaum over the last half century have been
regarded as nothing less than a godsend, offering the faithful potent new
affirmations of the historical reliability of church traditions and elucida-
tion for some long-obscure passages from the books of the New Testament. Through archaeology we can now plausibly begin to reconstruct
what it might have been like to grow up as a peasant child in first-century
Galilee, a bright young scholar in Tarsus, or a Christian martyr in Rome.
Yet we must also recognize that with all this archaeological abundance,
the challenge now facing historians of early Christianity is more than
simply and uncritically illustrating the gospels and epistles by archaeological evidence of the villages and cities Jesus and the apostles wandered through; the kinds of pottery and stoneware they used in
communal meals with their followers; the kinds of boats they used to
cross lakes and rivers; or the kinds of robes and sandals they wore. A truly
historical approach to the world of earliest Christianity must also attempt
to reconstruct the unspoken social, political, and economic background
for Jesus' miracles and teachings and must help us try to understand what
effect his message might have had on his listeners. It must also help us try
to understand why Paul's wide-ranging ministry took the particular course
that it did as he and his companions traveled through the cities of the
Roman Empire.

As we will try to show in the following chapters, the fallen stones and
buried ruins of the early Roman period can provide several simultaneous
levels of meaning. While some may regard the archaeological finds as
tangible illustrations of the historical veracity of the gospel stories, the

Book of Acts, and Paul's letters, they can also become building blocks of a parallel understanding of the life of Jesus, the career of Paul, and the rise of Christianity. For the movement that began two thousand years ago in the small region of Galilee at the eastern end of the Mediterranean, and which gradually spread out over the entire Roman Empire, can be seen not only as a unique moment in Western religious history but as a historical sequence of specific earthly actions, ideas, responses, and consequences that had—in their own right as human history—a profound impact on the social evolution of the Western world. Through the efforts of modern scholars, we are beginning to understand the lives and lifestyles of the earliest Christians from the perspectives of anthropology, sociology, economics, and political science. And from continuing archaeological exploration we now know enough about the everyday reality beyond the impressive splendor of the temples, triumphal arches, and sturdy aqueducts of the early Roman Empire to see that Jesus and his followers offered a powerful message of revival and renewal to people who were living through a time of stunning—often upsetting and dislocating—change.

The crucifixion of Jesus around 30 C.E. in Jerusalem profoundly altered the nature of the movement. Its message and organization would be further developed by Paul and the other apostles as they carried the name and memory of Jesus throughout the world. Theirs was an age when the powers-that-be did not look kindly on anyone who would challenge Roman authority and power, yet that is precisely what the followers of Jesus did when they built their far-flung network of communities of "saints." And in the following chapters, as we document the down-to-earth history of the Christian movement during its first century of existence, we will attempt to show that the continuing quest for the Kingdom of God by Jesus, Paul, and the earliest Christians should be understood as *both* a spiritual journey and an evolving political response to the mindless acts of violence, inequality, and injustice that characterized—and still all too often characterize—the kingdoms of men.

1

Heavenly Visions

WHO WERE THE STRANGE PEOPLE who called themselves "Christians"? What was the "Kingdom" to which they claimed allegiance? And why did they stubbornly refuse to offer the usual, patriotic sacrifices to Augustus Caesar and, in so doing, willingly go to their deaths? These were questions that most ancient Romans found hard to answer on the rare occasions when they came into direct contact with the unconventional sect of Christians, yet these subversive practices—the steadfast refusal to bow to false gods or pay homage to earthly powers—lay at the very heart of the early Christian faith. Emperor after emperor ordered campaigns of persecution against them. Roman authors branded them as the "notoriously depraved" adherents of a "deadly superstition" that represented a direct threat to the moral majority of imperial Rome. Christians were hunted down in the slums and back alleys of Rome and other provincial cities. They were rounded up, beaten up, and condemned to execution for atheism and treason—that is, failing to participate in the state-controlled cults of the gods of the Greco-Roman pantheon and abandoning honored family values of pagan society.

On the surface, at least, the Christians appeared to be quite harmless. "The sum and substance of their fault or error," observed the Roman jurist Pliny the Younger at the beginning of the second century C.E., after interrogating a number of suspected Christians, "was that they were accustomed to meet on a fixed day before dawn and sing responsively a hymn to

Christ as to a god, and to bind themselves by oath, not for any criminal purpose, but to abstain from fraud, theft, and adultery, and never make false promises or refuse to carry out a pledge when called upon to do so. When this ceremony was over, it was their custom to depart and to assemble again later to partake of food of an ordinary and innocent kind."

This was only a part of the story. In close-knit communities and weekly assemblies, in which the Spirit moved people to burst into strange tongues and shouts of praise to Jesus the Lord and God the Father, early Christians rejected conventional career hopes, social ladders, and civic honors. They fervently believed that the modern-day world of streets and market-places—the realm of tax collectors, loan agents, market inspectors, and imperial officials—could at any moment be rocked to its very foundations. All their hopes and energies were placed in expectations of the imminent return of the Risen Christ and His stunning demonstration of where the *real* power of this world lay. This was a Christianity without impressive churches, without authoritative clergy, without special outward trappings. Their hopes for a different kind of future for themselves and their children strengthened their faith in their impending redemption. Indeed, "Christianity" in its early decades was a network of poor people and marginal communities in both cities and rural areas that a government, even a modern government, would have had a problem recognizing as a "religion" at all.

Early Christianity was, in fact, a down-to-earth response to an oppressive ideology of earthly power that had recently swept across continents, disrupted economies, and overturned ancient traditions. And this triumphant ideology of progress and development was expressed in many media: in the elegies of Latin poets, in the grandeur of Roman architecture, in Roman lawcourts and statutes, in the technological triumphs of Roman engineering, and in the majestic, fatherly wave of every emperor's hand. At the beginning of the second century C.E.—just at the time when Christianity was crystallizing into a formalized, independent religion—a vast and growing public was being taught to cooperate in the construction of a new global system of economics, culture, and civil administration, in which the figure of the emperor had begun to take on the qualities of a single, supreme god. *That* was why the early Christians were viewed as so subversive, for anyone who refused to pay homage to Caesar was both atheist and traitor. In Roman eyes, the emperor—as the object of elaborate ceremonies of public veneration and the subject of wondrous tales of miraculous birth, charmed childhood, and divine ordination for imperial power—was the larger-than-life figure to whom all the empire's subjects were trained to look for guidance and to whom every knee was required to bend. His reign over the empire and everyone and everything in it was seen as a fact of nature, no less inevitable or divinely ordained than the yearly progression of the seasons or the heavenly cycles of planets and stars.

No believing Christian could possibly accept any of this Augustan propaganda. For them, Rome was the Beast, the Harlot, the Dragon, Babylon, the Great Satan. They knew that Rome's empire was made possible not by divine order but by the acquisition of vast territories through the deadly violence of the Roman legions and the self-serving acquiescence of their own local aristocracies. They knew that, step by step, the Romans had bullied, invaded, and eventually occupied all the lands around the Mediterranean, arrogantly assigning formerly independent peoples roles as clients or servants in their larger imperial schemes. The bloody path of Roman conquest had led from Italy to Sicily to Carthage, to Macedonia, southern Greece, Asia Minor, Syria, Judea, and Egypt. By the time of Augustus, the Romans were already masters of the entire Mediterranean, served by a growing bureaucracy of civil servants, garrison forces, and tax collectors who were dedicated to maintaining Roman domination. And as the world's riches flowed into Rome and into the treasuries of a select clique of Roman client kings and protégés, the Augustan promises of universal peace and prosperity for all the empire's subjects proved much easier to make than to keep.

Yet the Christian communities scattered across the eastern provinces of the empire in the early second century C.E. placed their faith in a different kind of universal dominion. It was embodied in the story of their own movement's origins and earliest history, a narrative that would ultimately prove far more influential than the *Aeneid* or the other pompous epics of Roman conquest. Circulating in at least four different versions—eventually ascribed to four Spirit-inspired scribes named Matthew, Mark, Luke, and John—the Christian narrative of the life of the founder of their movement created a community everywhere it was cherished and retold. It described the character and message of an immortal, world-redeeming figure who had been born in an obscure hill-country town of Judea—not in the imperial palace on the Capitoline Hill. In colorful sayings and parables, it described a different kind of Kingdom that would harbor no violence, inequality, or injustice—nor tolerate the arrogance of earthly emperors, rich men, and kings. The story took place more than a hundred years before, at a time when the mighty Augustus ruled in Rome, when a client king named Herod reigned in splendor and terror in a network of opulent palaces, and when a monumental Temple of the God of Israel crowned the skyline of the distant, Middle Eastern city of Jerusalem. The heroes of this story—for the most part, like themselves, poor people and peasants—harbored hopes that the brutal rule of the Caesars was just a passing trial and that the One True God of Heaven would reward them for their righteousness. And He would not fail to punish the wicked with fire and eternal damnation in a final Judgment Day. Decades passed, dynasties changed, and Rome retained its power, but as Christians gathered in small groups to read their sacred stories, to sing their hymns, and to partake of wine and bread in communal assemblies, they continued to believe in the coming day of judgment—and in the central role that they would play in the establishment of an eternal Kingdom of God.

IN DECLARING THEMSELVES to be the true heirs and beneficiaries of the promises of the One True God and Creator of the Universe, the members of early Christian communities throughout the Roman Empire adopted and adapted the tradition of a certain peculiar Middle Eastern people well known for their singular aversion to imperial authority. Indeed it is impossible to understand the historical development of the early Christian movement without understanding the contemporary economic and political situation of the Jews. At the time of Christianity's initial period of expansion, resident communities of Judeans or Jews—*Iudaioi*, in Greek, *Iudaei*, in Latin—were to be found in virtually every city and province of the empire. Since the time of Julius Caesar, they had been granted express sanction by the Roman authorities to live by their ancient customs and be excused from the requirement of offering sacrifices to idols—even idols of emperors. Centuries before, at a time when the Romans were still living among their swine in rustic stockades by the banks of the Tiber, the Jews—or, as they often preferred to call themselves, the "People of Israel"—were living in a small land at the eastern end of the Mediterranean and forming a unique tribal confederation of hill-country villages. Convinced that the swarming deities of neighboring peoples were nothing more than chimerical hobgoblins utilized by local strongmen, priests, and tyrants to exploit and terrorize their subjects, the People of

Israel resolved to establish a dramatically different kind of society. And in their self-supporting, kin-based communities of farmers, herders, and craftspeople, they lived out their heavenly visions in a down-to-earth existence of sowing, reaping, and sharing the fruits of the land.

To most outsiders, the Israelites' detailed code of laws, dietary regulations, and ethical standards—expanded and revised over the centuries—often seemed to be either a pious superstition or an elaborate excuse to avoid going along with majority customs, but the Israelite tradition had a direct impact on their character as a political community and on the way they led their day-to-day lives. The laws of their Torah, or "Teachings," with its legislation for tithes, offerings, Sabbaths, fast days, sabbatical years, and purity standards, enabled the People of Israel to maintain a stable system of social relations, economic welfare, and local autonomy. These were a people who refused to acquiesce in the dictates of pagan "gods" who somehow always seemed to demand crops and labor for the benefit of local princes and their idle retinues. And even though the Israelites' revulsion at their neighbors' cults and idols would later saddle them with a reputation for being xenophobic and clannish, its practical effect was to prevent their assimilation into the normal royal tributary systems of the ancient world. That was what made them so unusual. Through sacrifices, prayers, and psalms of thanksgiving, they celebrated their agricultural festivals, recalled the great events in their long march to freedom, and worshipped their God and Creator, whom they poetically depicted as the universe's only true "king."

Like most other peoples, the Israelites eventually found it necessary to adopt the institutions of a kingdom, and over the course of centuries, they suffered the same misfortunes of civil war, domestic upheaval, and conquest by foreign empires experienced by all the other earthly kingdoms of the ancient Near East. Yet in their response to those great national disasters, the People of Israel showed that they were unique. Instead of meekly accepting the verdict of history and abandoning their defeated deity— declaring that the foreign conquerors (and their gods) had proved themselves to be the victors—the People of Israel became convinced that their God was even more powerful than they had ever imagined: it was *He* who was directing all the events of human history. Their recent reverses and chastisements were the deserved punishment for the sins of the nation. The conquering nations were nothing more than God's pawns. And if they would observe the laws of the sacred Covenant and revere no power but

God the Creator, injustice, suffering, and imperial subjugation would someday perish forever and the earth itself would be transformed.

This expectation of God's eventual, direct intervention in human history in an act of redemption for the righteous was one of the most powerful concepts that the early Christians adopted from the People of Israel. The bitter misfortunes of the present could perhaps be more faithfully and patiently endured if they were seen as a necessary prelude for the glorious salvation to come. "For behold, I create new heavens and a new earth," God promised in the oracle of the prophet Isaiah, "and the former things shall not be remembered or come into mind. But be glad and rejoice forever in that which I create; for behold I create Jerusalem a rejoicing and her people a joy. I will rejoice in Jerusalem and be glad in my people; no more shall be heard in it the sound of weeping and the cry of distress. No more shall there be in it an infant that lives but a few days, or an old man who does not fill out his days, for the child shall die at a hundred years old and the sinner a hundred years old shall be accursed. They shall build houses and inhabit them; they shall plant vineyards and eat their fruit. They shall not build and another inhabit; they shall not plant and another eat; for like the days of a tree shall the days of my people be, and my chosen shall long enjoy the work of their hands" (65:17–22). In time, the apocalyptic visions of God's saving works became more vivid. Prophetic writings like the Book of Daniel offered cataclysmic descriptions of God's coming day of judgment on which all scores would be decisively settled, for both the living and the dead: "And many of those who sleep in the dust of the earth shall awake, some to everlasting life, and some to shame and everlasting contempt" (Daniel 12:2).

Christians would later adopt this vision of the general resurrection of the righteous, and they would link it with another vivid image drawn from the rich apocalyptic lore of the Jewish scriptures: that of a divinely dispatched redeemer who would suddenly burst upon the earthly scene and decisively alter the course of human history. The distinctive title of this heaven-sent savior figure—"messiah," *mashiach*, in Hebrew—was originally used in the Israelite scriptures to refer to anyone who was anointed, literally doused with the precious fragrant oil that conferred special status on priests, prophets, and kings throughout the ancient Near East. From the time of David, the anointment of the king of Israel had special significance, sanctifying his role as the guardian of Israel's very existence. But since the members of the royal house of Judah and the later Hasmonean kings had proved themselves utterly powerless to live up to the responsibilities of their office and defend the people of Israel against the relentless advance of foreign empires, a radically new vision of the character of Israel's *true* messiah arose.

The outlines of a potent messianic story were already evident in the prophetic oracles of Isaiah, Haggai, and Micah, but they reached a far more explicit form in the *Psalms of Solomon*, a text composed in Hebrew in Jerusalem in the first century B.C.E. and eventually translated into Greek and distributed widely throughout the Hellenistic world. It foretold the arrival of a messianic figure, a new son of David, who would finally lead Israel to regain its former glory and establish the Kingdom of God. This messiah would not be a normal political or military leader, but someone whom God had made "powerful in the holy spirit and wise in the counsel of understanding, with strength and righteousness" (17:37). Personally free from sin and compassionate to all the nations, he would "expose officials and drive out sinners by the strength of his word" (17:36). He would lead the righteous of Israel in a triumphant campaign to regain their land and their birthright; he would redistribute the land according to the ancient tribal allotments; and he would "judge peoples and nations in the wisdom of his righteousness" (17:29). And he would reign in glory in Jerusalem, making it into a truly holy city "for nations to come from the ends of the earth to see his glory, to bring as gifts his children who had been driven out" (17:31).

In the decades immediately preceding the birth of Jesus, a wide variety of messianic visions grew more fervent and vivid among the People of Israel, but the movement that eventually gave rise to Christianity actually began with the triumph of Roman arms and naked political ambition rather than the fulfillment of Israel's messianic hope. In the relentless advance of the Roman Empire through the eastern Mediterranean, the great general Pompey brought his legions into Judea in 63 B.C.E., imposed a new Roman-style system of administration on the country, and ousted the last of the native Hasmonean priest-kings. They also found themselves a dependable protégé in the person of a young man named Herod—the ambitious son of the converted Edomite who had served as chief adviser to the last Hasmonean priest-king Hyrcanus II—and who had proved his ability as an efficient royal administrator during brutal service as governor of the northern district of Galilee. Herod skillfully courted Roman leaders to gain for himself the crown of Judea. And during the next three decades of tyrannical dominion over an enlarged kingdom of Judea—which eventually

approached the size of the Solomonic kingdom—Herod "the Great," as he
came to be known throughout the Mediterranean, profoundly influenced
the earthly politics of the Land of Israel and created the repressive reign of
terror in which a number of new and powerful messianic movements arose.

IN A SINGLE VIVID CHAPTER in the Gospel of Matthew, Herod the
Great appears as a cruel and despotic ruler, always ready to utilize informers and violence to ensure the security of his rule. In the last days of his
reign—according to Matthew 2:1–16—when wise men from the East
followed a brilliant star to Judea to pay homage to Jesus as the newly born
"king of the Jews" in Bethlehem, Herod reportedly mounted a furious
search for his potential competitor, going so far as to order a general
"slaughter of the innocents" to ensure that no rival pretender to the throne
of Israel could possibly survive. Though the story of the slaughter is almost
certainly apocryphal (there is no reference to any such act of desperate
killing in the writings of the Jewish historian Flavius Josephus), most
scholars now agree that the chaotic last days of Herod the Great were the
authentic historical backdrop for the events of Jesus' birth and earliest
childhood years. If, as Luke 3:23 maintained, Jesus was around thirty years
old when he began his public ministry (sometime after the fifteenth year of
the reign of Tiberius Caesar), he would indeed have been born around the
time of Herod's death, which took place in 4 B.C.E. The later church
tradition that set the date of Jesus' birth at the year "0" was the result of a
simple but costly miscalculation by a sixth-century monk named Dionysus
Exiguus, who formulated the calendrical concept of "B.C." and "A.D." Yet
chronological considerations apart, the story of Herod's Slaughter of the
Innocents is no less powerful or vivid for its apparent lack of a literal
historical basis. In its gruesome details, it effectively echoes an earlier act of
tyrannical desperation well known from the Hebrew scriptures—Pharaoh's
murder of all the male children of Israel, and the miraculous survival of
Moses, who was destined to lead his people on their great Exodus (Exod.
1:15–2:10).

Indeed, to many of the common people he ruled in Galilee and Judea—
and for the generations that followed—King Herod must surely have
seemed like a latter-day pharaoh, both in the grandeur with which he
embellished the cities of his kingdom and in his shameless worship of
foreign gods. Long after his heirs had died or fallen from power, Herod was

remembered for his massive monuments and pagan constructions. In the former Israelite capital of Samaria, he raised an impressive temple to Augustus and renamed the refurbished city Sebaste, the reverent Greek word for "august." On the Mediterranean coast, he completely transformed the small Phoenician port of Strato's Tower into a bustling modern harbor city, which he named Caesarea Maritima, overseeing the construction of a spacious harbor complex that included warehouses, a theater, forum, royal palaces, and a magnificent temple overlooking the harbor dedicated to the worship of Roma and Augustus Caesar. Herod built equally impressive pagan monuments in distant places: Josephus reported that the Judean king gained great prestige throughout the Roman Empire for his generously donated theaters and public works in Phoenician and Syrian cities; for his huge contributions to the embellishment of the Greek city of Nicopolis, established by Augustus near the site of his decisive victory at Actium; for his donations to the people of Athens, Rhodes, and Sparta; and for his personal sponsorship of the Olympic games. Even at home he spared no expense in ensuring the splendor of a network of secure palace-fortresses and royal garrisons at Masada, Machaerus, Herodium, Jericho, and Jerusalem.

There was, of course, a price to be paid for this new pharaoh's extravagant spending. To support his building projects, lavish court life, and gifts to the imperial family, Herod laid a heavy burden of taxation on his subjects, which they met with only the greatest difficulty. Despite the threatening presence of his fortresses and his ruthless secret police apparatus, popular opposition to his rule simmered just beneath the surface. Large-scale revolts against his regime were just a matter of time. So by around 20 B.C.E., after two decades of pursuing a wholesale policy of Romanization, Herod began to realize that perhaps he should at least pay lip service to Israelite tradition in order to defuse the religious opposition to his rule. He thus began to court public support through a return to "traditional values." And he ironically did it by appealing to Israel's ancient hopes for redemption—and for the physical restoration of the national capital of Jerusalem—through the acts of a heaven-sent savior-king.

Posing as a new Solomon, Herod rebuilt and embellished the Jerusalem Temple on a scale of grandeur and opulence that made it one of the wonders of the ancient world. In its time, with its magnificent monumental entrances, royal colonnade built with towering Corinthian columns, spacious courtyards, gates, and central sanctuary structure, Herod's Temple made the previous Jerusalem temples seem like pitifully rustic little shrines. Herod's true genius lay in skillfully combining Israel's messianic legacy with Rome's ideology of empire. His patron, Augustus Caesar, in reconstructing the temples of Rome in the name of religious revival, had invented a new decorative grammar of Corinthian columns, enthusiastic geometric ornamentation, and lush floral decoration to symbolize the dawn of a new era of abundance and fertility under the peace and security of the Roman Empire. Can there be any doubt from the elaborate floral and geometric decoration of Herod's Temple described by Josephus and observed on fragments recovered in recent years by archaeologists around the Temple Mount that the same message was being issued in Jerusalem? Can there be any doubt that the golden vines with huge golden grape clusters that adorned the facade of the sanctuary—or the soaring golden eagle affixed to the main gate of the Temple enclosure—were symbols of the divinely ordained abundance and order of the Augustan Age?

How strange and significant it is therefore that just at the time when Matthew and Luke placed the birth of Jesus—born and proclaimed to be a new messiah-king of Israel—the issue of kingly succession had become a matter of paramount concern to the Herodian dynasty. During his thirty-six years of kingship, Herod had always been deeply afraid of princely intrigues and court conspiracies against him and had, one by one, ordered the execution of his three eldest heirs. So notorious was Herod's paranoia of potential rivals within his own family that Saturninus, a Roman governor of Syria under Augustus, cleverly quipped in Greek that he would much rather be Herod's pig (ὖς, "hus") than his son (υἱός, "huios"). And in his last year of life, Herod had repeatedly altered his royal will, finally deciding that his twenty-year-old, Roman-educated son Archelaus would be the best one to reign after his death. The decision proved to be a poor one. Archelaus made such a slight impression on later generations that he was mentioned only once in the gospels (Matt. 2:22). But that is not to say he had no historical importance. At the time of his accession, his utter misunderstanding and lack of sympathy for the traditions of his people had profound consequences for the course of subsequent events.

The atmosphere in Judea was explosive when word of Herod's death became public; in the last painful days of his fatal illness he had ordered the executions of several pious Jewish scholars and resistance leaders who had ripped down the golden eagle from the Temple's main portal—mistakenly believing that Herod was already dead. They were now widely seen as righteous martyrs, whose sufferings should be avenged. Archelaus had little sense of the depth of the public outrage. After leading the official period of mourning and public feast for his late father, he appeared in the Temple and explained to the crowd that before assuming the kingship, he would have to wait for official confirmation of his title by Augustus in Rome. This initial public act of obeisance to the Roman emperor—instead of the God of Israel—raised eyebrows. And when pilgrims from all over the country began to arrive in Jerusalem for the Passover festival, a more pointed political opposition began to crystallize. Widespread resentment of Herodian rule was becoming more evident, and indeed in his first public appearance Archelaus had agreed to lighten the people's tax load, free all political prisoners, and abolish the burdensome sales tax. Yet that act of concession merely intensified the hope in some quarters that Archelaus could be pushed further or even toppled from the throne. The crowded Temple courtyards became the center of intensifying opposition and Archelaus, "fearing that something dangerous might grow out of their fanaticism," according to Josephus, "sent a cohort of legionaries under a tribune to suppress the violence of the rebels before they should infect the whole crowd with their madness." The spark was thus tossed onto the tinder. When the infuriated crowd attacked the soldiers and drove them out of the Temple, Archelaus mobilized his cavalry forces, who returned to the Temple and killed thousands of pilgrims, scattering the survivors out into the countryside of Judea and forcing them to flee for their lives.

When news of the uprising in Jerusalem spread throughout the Land of Israel, messianic pretenders arose in every region, each one surrounded by a gang of tough young followers, and each aspiring to be proclaimed as the long-awaited redeemer-king of Israel. As would occur several more times through the history of the Roman Empire, the imperial authorities were caught off guard by the sheer depth of popular enthusiasm for the idea of freedom from Roman bondage and for the establishment of a Kingdom of God. In the district of Perea on the east bank of the Jordan, a former royal slave named Simon was proclaimed king by his supporters and led them on lightning raids against Herodian palaces and agricultural estates. In the villages of Judea, a former shepherd named Athronges assumed the role of a new David: assisted by four brothers, he proclaimed himself king, mounted attacks on Roman forces, and encouraged his followers to plunder Herodian property. And in Galilee, a local man named Judah, son of a famous Galilean bandit chief executed years before by Herod, led his followers on a rampage through the streets of the administrative capital of Sepphoris, breaking into its well-stocked armory and looting its governor's palace of treasure and luxurious furnishings.

The Romans reacted with expectable fury. Revolution against the civil order, no matter what its motivation, was a capital crime. The governor of Syria, Quintilius Varus, immediately proceeded southward from Antioch at the head of two legions, accompanied by the mobilized forces of the Hellenistic cities and of the region's other loyal client kings. By autumn, the Roman armies had swept through many of the towns and villages of the country, raping, killing, and destroying nearly everything in sight. In Galilee, all centers of rebellion were brutally suppressed; the rebel-held town of Sepphoris was burned to the ground, and all its surviving inhabitants were sold into slavery. In Perea, the rebel-king Simon was hunted down and beheaded by Herodian forces. And in Judea, Athronges, the shepherd-messiah, went into hiding and hundreds, if not thousands, of his followers were killed. Varus then proceeded to Jerusalem, ordering his soldiers to re-establish order in the city and to round up as many rebels as he and his soldiers could find. "Those who appeared to be the less turbulent individuals he imprisoned," wrote Flavius Josephus, "the most culpable, in number about two thousand, he crucified."

Those left living in the Galilee and the other regions of the Land of Israel in the wake of the bloody Roman campaigns of reconquest were surely not converted to enthusiastic support of the rule of Caesar by the violence of the legions. They were merely too frightened and vulnerable to make their true feelings known right away. This was the atmosphere of numbed sadness and fear of Roman repression in which the young Jesus and the other Galileans of his generation were raised. The Augustan ideal—the power of the king and the legacy of Herod—had at least temporarily triumphed as his son Antipas assumed rule over Galilee. For the foreseeable future, the Roman armies were too powerful to be defeated with the slingstones and captured spears and swords of a rag-tag peasant army led by local heroes and self-appointed messiahs—no matter what the prophetic oracles or omens might say.

Biblical scholars have long debated the reliability of the details of the gospel nativity stories and their relationship to contemporaneous events in Judea and Galilee. But for the purposes of reconstructing the social history of the early Christian movement, it does not really matter whether Jesus was born in Bethlehem (perhaps chosen symbolically by Matthew and Luke for its Davidic-messianic connections), or in his later hometown of Nazareth, as many scholars now believe. The massive uprising of the People of Israel after the death of Herod the Great would have left a deep impression on Jesus—and on all the members of his generation—wherever they lived. The dashed hopes of redemption and the horror of Roman repression seem to have intensified the faith of many of the farmers and townspeople of the Land of Israel in the reality and inevitability of the Kingdom of God. It forced them to seek other, creative ways to respond to Rome, its client kings, and its soaring ideology of empire without bringing the wrath of the Roman armies down upon themselves. In time, a new kind of search for redemption would spread from the Land of Israel to distant provinces and unfamiliar peoples. And in that respect, the gospels of Matthew and Luke are quite right in reporting that a unique heavenly vision arose among the People of Israel at the time of Jesus' birth. A new era had begun in the aftermath of the great uprising against Archelaus, yet—as we will soon see—it was not ushered in with glorious celestial omens or angelic songs. In fact, the roots of Christianity can be traced to a much more down-to-earth occurrence: the sudden elevation to power in Galilee of *another* ambitious Herodian prince who believed that he could be—and should be—king of the Jews.

2

Remaking the Galilee

THE SMALL BRONZE COINS minted by King Herod's son Antipas—the everyday pocket change that Jesus and his followers undoubtedly handled in Galilee's village squares and markets—are just mute pieces of corroded green-gray metal as they are sifted from the soil at modern archaeological digs. But when cleaned and carefully studied, those coins reveal a powerful juxtaposition of political symbols that earliest Christianity arose to contest. With a palm branch stamped on one side (calling to mind biblical descriptions of the fertility of the Land of Israel) and a Roman laurel wreath on the other (symbolizing the *auctoritas* and *dignitas* of the world-conquering Emperor Tiberius), the coins issued by Herod Antipas gave symbolic expression to his own political ambitions and messianic dreams. Circulating from hand to hand in an age when most people could read religious and political statements far more clearly in the insignia of kings than in the tight rows of letters inked on parchment or papyri—those coins of Antipas carried a cleverly mixed message that trumpeted his claim to possession of this part of the Land of Israel under the authority of the *corona civica*, or public crown, of the Roman emperor.

Although Herod Antipas may be just a walk-on player in the gospels, the story of his path to power over Galilee and the district of Perea east of the Jordan illustrates the important role that otherwise forgotten dynastic intrigues and Roman court politics played in creating the specific political and economic situation that John the Baptist, Jesus, and their followers faced. As the sixth son of Herod the Great, born around 20 B.C.E. to the Samaritan noblewoman Malthace, Antipas probably never set foot in Galilee during his childhood or ever knew much about its inhabitants' distinctive traditions. He had been raised as a pampered prince in the Herodian family and shuttled back and forth in a continual royal progress between the palaces at Jerusalem, Jericho, Masada, and Caesarea, until it was time— when he reached the age of ten or so—to be sent off for formal education in Rome. It was only at age sixteen, in 4 B.C.E., in the aftermath of his father's death and the great uprising against his older brother Archelaus, that political affairs in the Land of Israel began to affect him directly. In a bitter dispute over conflicting versions of Herod's will, (and Archelaus's ability to maintain order in Judea), the young Antipas argued boldly before the Emperor Augustus that *he*, not Archelaus or another brother named Philip, should be recognized as Herod's primary heir. Augustus declined the suggestion and decided to withhold the title of "king" from any of the brothers, dividing their father's kingdom between them—and thereby altering the Judean political landscape. Archelaus, the eldest, was demoted to "ethnarch," or communal leader, and granted rule over Judea, Samaria, and the southern district of Idumea. Philip, the next, was given the title "tetrarch," or territorial ruler, over the lands of Gaulanitis, Trachonitis, Batanea, and Paneas (covering the area of the modern Golan, northernmost Jordan and Israel, and southernmost Lebanon). And Antipas—though he had far greater ambitions— was also given the title tetrarch and installed as the Roman client-ruler over the districts of Perea and Galilee.

By Roman standards, Antipas's share was a disappointing inheritance, with its two, geographically separate, marginal districts, neither of which possessed modern cities, easily exploitable natural resources, or large royal estates. Perea was a narrow north-south strip of marginal farmland along the eastern bank of the Jordan River, deeply etched by a series of narrow valleys that snaked their way down from the highlands toward the arid Jordan Valley and the eastern shore of the Dead Sea. The land of Galilee, farther north, was more fertile and encompassed the northern and western shores of a large lake called Gennaseret, or the "Sea of Galilee," with its abundant supply of fresh water and rich fishing grounds. But the rugged, mountainous terrain of Galilee's northern regions produced no crops other than those grown by the hardy peasants who farmed its rocky upland valleys. And in the southern regions, where the hillsides rolled more gently and the terrain was more favorable for extensive plantations, farmers in villages like Nazareth, Cana, Japha, and Nain stubbornly clung to centuries-old agricultural methods, cultivating their own small vineyards, orchards, and family plots. Despite more than a hundred years of administration by Hasmonean and Herodian officials, the inhabitants of both "Upper" and "Lower" Galilee remained quite backward—at least from a Roman point of view. They had earned a reputation for being uncultured frontierspeople who resented the interference of outsiders. "The two Galilees have always resisted any hostile invasion," Josephus Flavius later observed of this territory and its people, "for the inhabitants are from infancy inured to war and have at all times been numerous; never did the men lack courage nor the country men."

Antipas quickly moved to impose Roman-style order. Among his first acts was the establishment of a modern administrative center from which security forces, market inspectors, and tax collectors could be easily dispatched. The former regional capital of Sepphoris lay in ruins as a result of the recent uprising, and Antipas ordered that it be reconstructed as a modern Roman city with a palace, treasury, archives, and forum. When it was completed, he brought in a new population of loyal functionaries and workers—to replace the former inhabitants who had been killed by Varus's legions or sold off into slavery. He named the new city Autocratoris—literally, "Imperial," or "belonging to the Emperor"—and this new city, situated on a commanding height, surrounded by villages and rich agricultural land, quickly became the Galilee's only true urban center, combining the functions of regional market, tax depot, and military command post. Recent excavations at Sepphoris have revealed evidence of Antipas's extensive rebuilding, offering a glimpse at some of the streets, squares, and impressive public structures (including a large Roman-style theater) that led Josephus Flavius to describe the city a few decades later as the "ornament of all Galilee." Yet Sepphoris-Autocratoris was not built as mere decoration. As the seat of the newly installed tetrarch and headquarters of the Roman-style government that Antipas had been taught to admire from his boyhood, it was a place from which the region's yearly revenues could be maximized through constant surveillance of the surrounding peasant population and through the intensification of taxation and trade.

About fifteen miles to the east—at the lakeside town of Magdala (the home of Mary Magdalene according to scriptural tradition)—other archaeological excavations have uncovered suggestive evidence of at least one way in which production may have been dramatically stepped up in Herodian Galilee. Although scenes of fishing on the waters of the Sea of Galilee in the time of Jesus are often bucolically portrayed in illustrated Bibles and Sunday-school textbooks, with images of solitary fishermen standing in their rowboats and peacefully casting their nets upon the waters, the pace and purpose of fishing on the Sea of Galilee may have taken on quite a different aspect by the time of Antipas. For thousands of years, fishing on the lake had been a highly localized, seasonal occupation, conducted by the farmers of the region in the relatively quiet period between sowing and harvest. Long-distance trade in fish was out of the question. After only a few hours out of the water, the catch—unless immediately cooked and eaten—would have begun to go bad. Yet all that began to change in the Hellenistic and Roman periods, when techniques were developed for salting and pickling fish on something approaching an industrial scale. And with the production process came a vast and growing market: urban populations throughout the Roman Empire grew to love the spicy, smelly fish sauces called *garum* and stews of salted fishheads and chopped pieces called *salsamentum*, both of which were highly valued as everyday condiments and all-purpose medicine.

By Antipas's time, Magdala had become such a famous center of this industry that it was commonly referred to as Taricheae, or the "Town of Salt-Fish." And anyone who thinks that fishermen on the Sea of Galilee in the time of Jesus were just picturesque peasants in rowboats does not appreciate the sheer weight of fish flesh that had to be hauled in every day and transported to Magdala's processing centers to be salted, pressed, fermented, and refined to produce even a modest output of *garum* and *salsamentum* for shipment overseas in heavy amphoras. This was an industry that apparently brought great wealth to some and great misery to others: the Magdala excavations have revealed a complex pattern of narrow urban streets, reservoirs, and buildings where the town's putrid business was conducted—and at least one spacious private villa, whose owner proudly announced the source of his fortune with a mosaic depiction of a boat and large fish installed on the floor of his entrance courtyard.

Yet the production of salted fish was only one entrepreneurial venture in an otherwise unbroken landscape of peasant villages, olive groves, vineyards, vegetable patches, and grain fields. Like most other client kings and local rulers of the time, Antipas had to rely on two basic methods to make the landscape more productive: intensified tax collection and more frequent use of conscripted peasant labor to carry out public works projects and to develop his privately held lands. By the terms of Augustus's division of his father's kingdom, Antipas was granted the right to collect taxes from his subjects in Galilee and Perea, a privilege that, according to Josephus, yielded an annual equivalent of two hundred talents (or about nine tons) of gold. Of course there was no *real* gold to be found in the hills and valleys of the tetrarchy—just wheat, barley, grapes, olives, vegetables, and livestock. Antipas therefore had to dispatch a veritable army of auditors, tax collectors, and soldiers to the groves, vineyards, and threshing floors of every village at harvest time to ensure that his share of the harvest (estimated by modern scholars to have amounted to as much as a third of the total crops and other agricultural products) was duly handed over to the Herodian authorities.

In earlier times, when the region was governed—and taxed—by distant empires or Jerusalem-based kingdoms, enforcement was apparently quite spotty. We know, for instance, that some of the more independent-minded inhabitants of the region reacted with violence or took to the hills when royal tax collectors arrived during the days of Herod the Great. But now, with Antipas dependent on Galilee as the main source of his income—and with his officials installed as permanent residents of Sepphoris-Autocratoris right there in the heart of the region—tax collection was going to be both frequent and heavy. It is therefore no accident or coincidence that the gospels abound with references to publicans, tax collectors, toll-takers, estate stewards, and shadowy "Herodians"— historical figures who cannot be dismissed as mere caricatures or scriptural villains. For at the time of Jesus, a growing bureaucracy closely connected to the court of Antipas played a crucial role in creating a crisis of debt and dispossession that touched and transformed the lives of nearly every peasant family in Galilee.

FOR JESUS and his Galilean neighbors and kinsfolk, Antipas's programs of city-building and tax collection were not simply dangerous threats to their livelihoods and time-honored techniques of farming and fishing: they posed an unprecedented attack on the very basis of the village culture that they and their ancestors had faithfully maintained for hundreds of years. Recent archaeological surveys of early Roman Galilee have shown the extent to which its landscape was entirely agrarian, how the hills and valleys in every direction were dotted with dozens—perhaps as many as two hundred—of small communities of farmers and herders living in clusters of rustic stone houses linked by open courtyards and surrounded by a patchwork of pastures and fields. Some of these villages had been in existence since the Iron Age and the birth of the Israelite nation; others were relatively recent, yet all shared the same basic layout of simple houses (with few structures ever exceeding any of the others in size or impressiveness) and the same mixed economy of dry farming, stock raising, and localized production of textiles, leather, and pottery. Indeed, the archaeological picture closely parallels the way of life described in some of the earliest legislation and social codes of the Bible: close-knit communities composed of kin-based extended families, grouped into larger clans and territorial tribes, who carried on a flexible system of small-scale cultivation that spread the risks of bad harvests from drought, warfare, or natural disaster over a wide range of agricultural products and crops.

Agrarian cultures like this one—in virtually every era and place where they have been closely studied by anthropologists and sociologists—are known to cherish one goal above all others: family survival on the land of their ancestors, with generation after generation preserving ancient customs and social institutions and faithfully passing them on. From the evidence we gain from the gospels, from rabbinic literature, and from the scattered descriptions of Josephus, we know that the Galileans, too, clung passionately to ancestral traditions, convinced that as members of the People of Israel they were heirs to the great promises given by God to their patriarch and forefather Abraham. And they were confident that if they remained faithful to their laws and traditions they would become a great people "as numerous as the stars of heaven and as the sand on the seashore" (Gen. 22:17) and forever retain their hold on the land that God had given to them. Their ancestral laws regarding social relations, property rights, personal morality, festivals, Sabbaths, and sabbatical years were—as we have already mentioned—not abstract religious dogma or standards of individual ethics. They offered the People of Israel, both as a nation and as local communities, a down-to-earth constitution, a code of conduct and handbook of instructions by which they could survive on the land in their families and villages and perhaps even prosper in a challenging—if not overly productive—physical environment.

Over the centuries, the villagers of Galilee—like their fellow Israelites in other parts of the country—had gradually learned to accept the burdens imposed upon them by kings and royal officials, producing enough to satisfy both the demands for royal tax and tribute and to feed themselves and their families. But royal taxes were not the only exaction. The villagers of Galilee (like all other members of the People of Israel) were instructed to set aside a significant portion of their produce for priestly tithes, first-fruits offerings, and various other sacred donations for the Temple in Jerusalem. By the first century, every Israelite male was required to make an annual contribution of a half-shekel to the Temple (and for villagers, that coin could be obtained only through the exchange of crops or agricultural products—in addition to the ten percent already required for the annual tithe). And even in seasons when drought or blight severely limited the harvest, the tax collectors and priestly representatives still turned up at the local threshing floors and olive presses to make sure that every family contributed their due. Penalties for nonpayment could be severe and violent when the farmers of a particular village or region did not willingly yield up the lion's share of their harvest to satisfy the demands of the official representatives of the Jerusalem Temple and Herodian state.

Historian Martin Goodman has drawn on archaeological and textual evidence to analyze the painful process of community disintegration going on in the same period in the villages of Judea—offering an uncanny parallel to the economic conditions described by the gospels in Galilee. Since the agricultural productivity of the Land of Israel was never exceptionally high even under the most favorable conditions, and since even the slightest reduction in crop yields made it impossible for many peasant families to produce enough for both taxes *and* family survival, an increasing number of farmers were forced to borrow against future harvests in order to be able to retain enough of their crops and animals to carry them over to the next year. Indeed, the evidence drawn from rabbinic literature and from legal documents of the period suggests that rural indebtedness dramatically increased throughout the Herodian period, with desperate farmers seeking loans from the officials of the Herodian administration and the priestly aristocracy. Yet this stop-gap measure soon had catastrophic consequences: once a peasant farmer pledged away an even *greater* proportion of the next harvest, it was unlikely that he could avoid sinking even deeper into debt in the following years. And since the only collateral that peasants could use to obtain loans was the land that had been farmed by their families for generations, their inability to repay mounting debts eventually resulted in foreclosure. In many cases, that legal action would have changed once-free villagers working the lands of their ancestors into permanently impoverished sharecroppers eking out a living on vast (and rapidly growing) aristocratic estates.

Had biblical law been strictly enforced, this situation could never have developed. For according to the explicit provision of Deuteronomy 15:2, in every seventh year each Israelite "creditor shall release what he has lent to his neighbor; he shall not exact it of his neighbor, his brother, because the Lord's release has been proclaimed." The Holiness Code of Leviticus further underlined the reason why debts had to be forgiven and the title to property returned to its original occupants: God was the only true owner of the Land of Israel, and "the land shall not be sold in perpetuity, for the land is mine; for you are strangers and sojourners with me" (Lev. 25:23). Yet the interpreters of the law in the Herodian period found a way to get around this otherwise unambiguous legislation in order to ensure the availability of loans to peasants who were struggling for survival—and to protect the interests of those with money to lend. With the acceptance by the religious and legal authorities of a maneuver known in rabbinic literature as the *prosbul*, private loans that were registered with local courts were declared to be enforceable, even if they were scheduled to come due during a sabbatical year.

Needless to say, with loans more readily available, the crisis of debt and dispossession grew deeper. Slowly the villages of the Land of Israel—once duly and solemnly distributed by God to the families, clans, and tribes of Israel—were passing into the hands of aristocratic families, who happened to have influence in royal or priestly circles or large reserves of disposable wealth. This was a horrible reversal of the familiar biblical stories of Exodus and the conquest of Canaan that were read about and talked about in the village assemblies when the scrolls of the Law were taken out to be read on Sabbaths and festival days. And here was the spiritual crisis that compounded the economic: countless villagers throughout the Land of Israel whose lives were impoverished and disrupted had to face the urgent question of how or why God could permit such a thing. Some turned to complex ritual explanations, seeing the people's problems as divine punishment for their failure to maintain the highest standards of ritual purity or by their shirking of the full complement of the tithes and offerings prescribed by the levitical code. Others ascribed the widespread suffering of everyday people to the work of demons or evil spirits, who, according to folk traditions, were fallen angels who took delight in sowing greed, discord, and misfortune among the People of Israel.

Yet others found solace in violent fantasies of retribution—looking forward to a time when God would cleanse this evil land and chastise the wealthy, the wicked, and the idolatrous just as He had done at the time of Noah's Great Flood. He would then establish His eternal rule over the simple, righteous People of Israel, when, as Isaiah predicted, "the meek shall obtain fresh joy in the Lord, and the poor among men shall exult in the Holy One of Israel. For the ruthless shall come to nought and the scoffer cease, and all who watch to do evil shall be cut off" (29:19–20). And for these people, the day of judgment loomed on the horizon. Subsequent events and descriptions make it clear that many of the people of Galilee—like their fellow Israelites in other parts of the country—nervously awaited signs of the coming events predicted so vividly in the apocalyptic scriptures. And they eagerly harkened to the voice of prophets who preached that it might still be possible for at least some of them to escape divine vengeance and inherit the promise of the Kingdom of God.

AROUND 28 OR 29 C.E. ("the fifteenth year of the reign of Tiberius Caesar" according to Luke 3:1), a unique leader and preacher gained fame throughout the Land of Israel by offering a new way for people in all walks of life to ensure their salvation on the coming day of judgment through a decisive commitment to alter the course of their lives. According to Josephus Flavius, this figure, widely known as "John the Baptizer," or "John the Baptist," was "a good man" who "exhorted the Jews to lead righteous lives, to practice justice toward their fellows and piety toward God, and so doing to join in baptism." As we will see, that ritual had far-reaching significance in the political context of the times. Dressed in the traditional garb of Israelite prophets—a hairy garment and leather girdle—and subsisting on a sparse diet of "locusts and wild honey" according to Mark 1:6, John reportedly attracted crowds from all over the Land of Israel with a message delivered in the ancient fire-and-brimstone style of Israelite prophecy. As he stood by the banks of the Jordan River that the People of Israel had once crossed so triumphantly in their God-driven wanderings toward freedom, he condemned the present-day leaders of Israel—as well as their compliant and weak-willed subjects—for their sinful failure to keep both the spirit of the Covenant and the letter of the Law.

Archaeology cannot verify or disprove any specific details of the life of John the Baptist. The overlapping accounts of his career found in both the gospels and in the writings of Josephus offer us the only evidence we possess for his existence as a historical character. Yet those accounts of John's words and actions mesh well with other historical data we have at our disposal. We know, for instance, that in the same era and in the same general area where Josephus and the gospels place the ministry of John the Baptist there were other figures and movements who had separated themselves from what they perceived as the iniquities of Judean society—and for whom the practice of immersion played a powerful and conspicuous role. Josephus himself boasted of a youthful apprenticeship with a well-known ascetic named Bannus, "the Bather," "who dwelt in the wilderness providing only such clothing as the trees provided, feeding on things that grew of themselves, and using frequent ablutions of cold water, by day and by night for purity's sake." The mention of Bannus's frequent bathing is significant, for immersion was not only prescribed for removing physical impurity, it was also seen as a metaphor for moral purification. As Isaiah instructed: "Wash yourselves; make yourselves clean; remove the evil of your doings from my eyes; cease to do evil; learn to do good; seek justice, correct oppression; defend the fatherless, plead for the widow" (Isa. 1:16–17).

Though we have no evidence that isolated figures like Bannus promoted any particular social agenda, the situation was quite different with another group of enthusiastic bathers in the lower Jordan Valley: the community of priestly purists who established a community at the site of Qumran at the northwestern shore of the Dead Sea—and whose peculiar beliefs and apocalyptic preoccupations are known to us from the Dead Sea Scrolls. This group had withdrawn from Judean society to protest the rule of people they saw as wicked priests and idolatrous political leaders—and had established strict rules of conduct and ritual to set them apart from those "sons of darkness" in order to ensure their redemption as the Elect of Israel at the coming end of days. Among the ruins of their settlement in this otherwise arid and desolate location, excavations have revealed a surprising number of stepped pools and reservoirs, fed by a sophisticated system of flood water channels, at least some of which seem to have been used for religious rites. As we know from the scrolls, the ritual immersion solemnly practiced by the members of the closed community at Qumran was not meant merely to remove physical impurities or to improve the character of the bather; it signified that a profound change in character and social commitment had *already* been made.

The Dead Sea text known as the *Rule of the Community* states that unless a member had fully committed himself to the ideals of the community and spurned all the ways of darkness "he will not become purified by acts of atonement, nor shall he be purified by the cleansing waters." But if the commitment to observe all the laws of God was honestly made and deemed legitimate by the community "his flesh is cleansed by being sprinkled with cleansing waters and being made holy by the waters of repentance." And the declaration of community membership, solemnly symbolized by the repeated ritual of baptism, meant that the bather had rejected the entire complex of economics, political institutions, and cultural expression that was being carried on in mainstream society. Indeed, Josephus—in his description of the practices of the pious Jewish sect of the Essenes (who were long connected with the Dead Sea Scrolls and are still identified by some scholars as the inhabitants of the Qumran Community)—offers another insight into the significance of baptism as *both* a rite of purification and a sign of membership in a sacred fellowship that vowed to "practice piety toward the Deity," "to observe justice to men," and forever to "hate the unjust and fight the battle of the righteous ones."

John the Baptist apparently gave the ritual of immersion a new form and a new meaning. Although some scholars have speculated on John's possible connection to Qumran (in theories ranging from suggestions of boyhood adoption to an explicit identification of John as one of the community leaders), his open-air preaching to large crowds of people from "Jerusalem and Judea and all the region about the Jordan" (Matt. 3:5) and his institution of a practice of public baptism for everyday people—not just ascetics or initiates in closed communities—clearly set him apart. Unlike the wandering hermit "Bannus" or the priestly separatists of Qumran, John promoted baptism as a highly visible, one-time ritual for anyone who would accept it. And while most other people of his generation regarded the act of immersion as self-motivated and private, John presided over highly public ceremonies of immersion at places where large crowds could gather to hear his preaching and to undergo the ceremony of baptism themselves. John's overarching message was one of apocalyptic expectation and preparation: "Repent, for the Kingdom of God is at hand" (Matt. 3:2). Yet in his incendiary visions of a coming day of judgment, John did not mention the rewards that would come to the righteous. He turned his focus, instead, on God's imminent destruction of those wicked nobles and arrogant leaders who would soon receive their just rewards.

In a series of powerful oracles repeated almost word for word by both the Gospel of Matthew and the Gospel of Luke—and believed by many scholars to be drawn from an early stratum of Christian tradition, perhaps even from the early followers of John the Baptist—John used images of village life to describe the coming judgment: "Even now the axe is laid to the root of the trees; every tree therefore that does not bear good fruit is cut down and thrown into the fire" (Matt. 3:10; Luke 3:9). Speaking of God's imminent, grim harvest, he warned his listeners that God's "winnowing fork is in his hand, and he will clear the threshing floor and gather his wheat into the granary, but the chaff he will burn with unquenchable fire" (Matt. 3:12; Luke 3:17). John preached that God's promises to the descendants of Abraham were in danger if they did not immediately commit themselves to a whole-hearted return to observance of the Covenant; and it did not matter if they were priestly aristocrats with long, distinguished genealogies preserved in the archives of the Temple or simple peasant farmers who traced their birth-rights all the way back through their families, clans, and tribal ancestors to the Patriarch Abraham. "Do not say to yourselves, 'We have Abraham as our father,' " John reportedly raged against the people who had gathered to listen to him on the rocky banks of the Jordan, "for I tell you, God is able to raise up children to Abraham from these stones" (Matt. 3:9; Luke 3:8).

John saw his mission to call the people out into the wilderness of purification and renewal, out to the Jordan across which they had entered the land that God had promised them in the first place, to renew their Covenant with Him. In the course of their daily lives, in an era of increasing economic tensions and apprehensions about the future, they had lost sight of the only way they could survive: a return to the observance of the Covenant that God had made with their forefathers at Sinai. And they would seal their renewed commitment to the laws and traditions of Israel with a single act of immersion—not the ice-cold baths of ascetic hermits or the repeated lustrations of sectarian acolytes—but a one-time public acknowledgment of a new, life-long commitment, administered in the flowing waters of the Jordan by John "the Baptizer" himself. John's speech preserved in Luke 3:10–14 may be, as many scholars maintain, a relatively late interpolation, but even so, it offers uncanny echoes of precisely the kinds of economic problems and legal abuses that characterized the Herodian administration, and indeed all Roman imperial regimes at the time of John's ministry. To "the multitudes" John reportedly instructed, "He who has two coats, let him share with him who has none; and he who has food, let him do likewise." To "tax collectors" he insisted that they "collect no more than is appointed you." And to "soldiers" who came to be baptized (apparently Jewish members of the security forces of the Herodian administration), he warned against extortion and plunder: "Rob no one by violence or with false accusation, and be content with your wages."

Despite the assumptions of most New Testament scholars that the teachings of John the Baptist were purely "religious" and that his visions of a coming day of judgment were apocalyptic fantasies rather than reformist ideals, we must remember that John's preaching and baptizing did not take place in a historical vacuum but were expressed in a specific historical context, with certain current realities in mind. And if we take into account the situation in the Land of Israel under Herodian and Roman domination—at the time when Bannus bathed alone and the Qumran community set itself apart from the Sons of Darkness—we can see how physical separation from the mainstream society and the act of symbolic, Covenant-renewing immersion can be seen as profoundly political statements of opposition to the religious and political situation in Herodiam-dominated Israel. John the Baptist was offering crowds of people who lived under the shadow of Rome and under the burden of Herodian control and taxation a new way to end the pain and uncertainty that plagued their daily lives. John's baptism was not a panacea but a symbol of something much more important: a personal pledge to return to the way of life that God had decreed for the People of Israel. In fact, Josephus Flavius knew only of John's practical teachings, not his apocalyptic visions, reporting—as already mentioned—that John was a good man who "had exhorted the Jews to lead righteous lives, to practice justice towards their fellows and piety towards God." And Josephus understood that John required a commitment from the people to whom he offered baptism, that "they must not employ it to gain pardon for whatever sins they committed, but as consecration of the body, implying the soul was already thoroughly cleansed by right behavior." That right behavior was a commitment to participate in a national revival of righteousness and renewal of the Covenant of Israel. And that, of course, meant a forthright and practical rejection of the new kind of world that Herod Antipas was trying to build.

A HEAD-ON CLASH between the tetrarch and the Baptist was therefore probably inevitable, since Antipas had quite a different idea of the way to redemption, drawn from some of the very same scriptural promises that John the Baptist evoked in his own fiery messages of righteous rage. The Herodian family had long associated itself both with the grandeur and glory of the House of David and the inheritance promised to the Patriarch Abraham (which was far easier to establish with its deep roots in Idumea and among the sons of Abraham's other son Ishmael and Jacob's son Esau), and before long Antipas began to act as if he believed that the divine promises to the People of Israel could best be fulfilled through *him*. In his first decade as tetrarch of Galilee, he had emerged as the rising star of the Herodian family—especially after his elder brother Archelaus proved utterly incapable of ruling Judea and was exiled in 6 C.E. to the distant Gallic town of Vienne on the Rhone. With Archelaus's vast inheritance of Judea, Samaria, and Idumea now ruled directly by a series of Roman officials with the title of "prefect," the Jewish people lacked a single, recognized leader and political patron. Antipas clearly longed to fulfill that function, and after the abrupt departure of Archelaus, he claimed for himself the exclusive use of the family's dynastic title, henceforth calling himself "Herod" or "Herod Antipas."

In a world of Roman power politics and ruthless competition between rival local leaders, Antipas believed that his people's best route to salvation was through aggressive economic development, not religious fundamentalism. The Jordan Valley might be a sacred wilderness of biblical associations to some of his subjects, but Antipas envisioned it as a busy, profitable highway. Since the beginning of his rule, Galilee had been only loosely linked with Perea on the eastern bank of the Jordan; the placement of the tetrarchy's administrative center at Sepphoris, far to the northwest, made economic development of the *entire* tetrarchy difficult. No less important was the fact that a booming caravan trade in precious goods from Arabia (swelling the coffers and ornamenting the tombs and temples of Petra, capital city of king Aretas IV of Nabatea) was passing through or just to the east of Perea, transitting the Greek cities of the Decapolis and heading north into the Roman province of Syria, without enhancing Herodian revenues. Years before, in an effort to encourage an alliance, or at least peace, between the Judean and Nabatean royal families, the Emperor Augustus had suggested that Antipas take a Nabatean princess as a bride. But that marriage did little either to resolve the longstanding rivalry between Judea and Nabatea or to calm Antipas's ambitions. For soon after Augustus's death in 14 B.C.E., Antipas announced plans to shift the administrative center of his government to a place from which *both* Galilee and Perea could be controlled.

It did not matter to Herod Antipas that the proposed location of his new capital city was the site of an ancient cemetery and that by Mosaic law this would render its inhabitants permanently ritually unclean. Nor did it matter much to him that his lavish, gilded palace in the tetrarchy's new capital was filled with statues and paintings of animals and was therefore a violation of the explicit Israelite prohibition of graven images. In the cosmopolitan imagery of contemporary Augustan art they undoubtedly symbolized the bounty and plenty that would soon come to both Perea and the Galilee. Antipas named his new city "Tiberias" in honor of Augustus's successor, Tiberius, and, according to Josephus, populated it with "a pro-miscuous rabble, no small contingent being Galilean, with such as were drafted from territory subject to him and brought forcibly" to fill the city's new residential quarters and take advantage of its modern facilities: a stadium, modern market, baths, and council hall. If anyone was seeking the Kingdom of God, Antipas was eager to show that the era of its fulfillment had arrived. He began to issue distinctive bronze coins in a conveniently wide range of denominations bearing the traditional palm branch of the Israelite nation and the laurel wreath of the Roman emperor. And it was certainly not without significance that in 18 or 19 C.E., Antipas officially established a new era for himself and his people, counting the years from the founding of Tiberias.

At the same time, Antipas made it clear that he was eager to take over his late father's role as a patron of the Jerusalem Temple and accept a royal-messianic destiny in Judea as well. In 26 C.E., after the arrival in Judea of a particularly arrogant new Roman prefect named Pontius Pilate, Antipas and his brother Philip intervened directly with the emperor to force Pilate to remove what the Judean public considered to be idolatrous shields from the Holy City of Jerusalem. Yet that was far from being enough to establish his royal credentials, for as the son of a Samaritan mother and tetrarch of only two rather marginal frontier districts of the Land of Israel, he needed some greater personal claim. And he found it in yet another act of Davidic mimicry. Just as the young David—the youngest of his brothers—had married Michal, daughter of King Saul, to propel him toward the throne over all Israel, Antipas resolved to aside his Nabatean consort and to wed a member of the Hasmonean clan.

How the fateful liaison between Antipas and Herodias, daughter of the

Hasmonean prince Aristobulus, was arranged is now lost in the mists of history, but there are some suggestive clues. It most probably took place in Caesarea Maritima, Herod the Great's model harbor city on the Mediterranean, at a time when Herod Antipas was about to embark on a sea voyage to Rome to pay his personal respects to the Emperor Tiberius. Josephus described the encounter this way: "When starting out for Rome, he lodged with his half-brother Herod, who was born of a different mother, namely the daughter of Simon the High Priest. Falling in love with Herodias, the wife of this half-brother—she was a daughter of their brother Aristobulus and sister to Agrippa the Great—he brazenly broached to her the subject of marriage. She accepted and pledged herself to make the transfer to him as soon as he returned from Rome." Despite the mare's nest of incestuous family relationships in which she lived, Herodias, in her mid-thirties by the late twenties of the first century, clearly relished the opportunity that marriage to Antipas offered. All her life she had been kept in the confines of the royal house, being betrothed to Herod's youngest and least consequential son while she was still an infant. She, like all the other Hasmonean heirs, was always in a dangerous position in the House of Herod, precisely because their family possessed a nostalgically patriotic—if wildly romanticized—image in certain Jewish circles for their descent from the family of Judah the Maccabee.

As such, the Hasmoneans were always potential rivals to the Herodians, and Herod the Great had done his best to lower the risks by murdering his Hasmonean wife Mariamne, her mother, and his two Hasmonean sons, Alexander and Aristobulus. And yet the public fascination with Hasmoneans, in both Judea and the diaspora, continued. Soon after the death of Herod, in fact, a young man popped up in the city of Sidon claiming to be the Hasmonean heir Alexander, who had miraculously escaped Herod's order of death and kept himself in hiding until his evil father was dead. At a time when the surviving Herodian brothers were arguing over their patrimony, this Alexander *redivivus* sailed off to Crete and then proceeded to Melos and then on to Rome, showered with gifts and enthusiastic acclamations of support by the local Jewish communities. Acclaimed as a king by the Jews of Rome, he was eventually unmasked by a suspicious Augustus and sent off to serve out the rest of his reign as a rower in the galleys. But the Hasmonean mystique endured. Thus the meeting of the minds and ambitions of Antipas and Herodias was to have enormous effect as a critical dynastic alliance, even though the marriage explicitly violated the levitical laws of incest. For Herodias's father Aristobulus was Antipas's half-brother and that made his marriage to Herodias an impermissible union between uncle and niece. To make matters worse, Herodias was married to Antipas's half-brother, Herod Philip, and, according to the laws of Leviticus, "uncovering your brother's wife's nakedness" was a sin. The Gospel of Mark 6:18 leveled this more specific and direct accusation against the tetrarch, identifying it as a public pronouncement of none other than John the Baptist: "For John said to Herod, it is not lawful for you to have your brother's wife."

It is thus clear how John the Baptist came to the attention of Antipas and quickly provoked direct retaliation. As a popular folk-prophet attracting crowds in the very wilderness that Antipas hoped to develop, John did not simply preach in generalities, leaving discreetly or politely unmentioned exactly whom he had in mind. Like Amos and Hosea and Jeremiah before him, he was a prophet engaged in a passionate critique of current political happenings, never afraid to point fingers or name names. And while the Roman-educated Antipas may have been familiar with the royal Davidic traditions of his own family, he apparently did not have a sufficient knowledge of his own people's scriptures to realize that there was more than one interpretation that could be put on his marriage to Herodias. While he hoped to be seen as acting out the role of a new David by taking the hand of a former king's "daughter," his subjects soon began to see him as a new version of the hated King Ahab wedding a new Jezebel.

To make matters worse, events were unfolding on the wider political stage that placed Antipas in a highly vulnerable political situation. When gossip about his impending matrimonial plans spread through court circles, Antipas's Nabatean wife (whose name was not recorded) fled to the Herodian family fortress of Machaerus on the eastern shore of the Dead Sea and from there southward with an armed guard, across seventy miles of rugged wilderness terrain to the safety of her father's fabled capital city of Petra, which lay hidden in the region's rose-red sandstone ravines. With the flight of his daughter, King Aretas was almost certain to renew hostilities against the Herodians and Antipas needed to get his own tetrarchy ready for war. That is presumably why Antipas "sent and seized John and bound him in prison for the sake of Herodias," according to Mark 6:17. For with the outright condemnation of Antipas's reign and incestuous marriage to a Hasmonean princess, John the Baptist's movement of direct and potent political protest posed a serious internal political threat. As Josephus described the situation, "When others joined the crowds about him, because they were aroused to the greatest degree by his sermons, Herod became alarmed. Eloquence that had so great an effect on mankind might lead to some form of sedition, for it looked as if they would be guided by John in everything they did. Herod decided it would be much better to strike first before his work led to an uprising than to wait for an upheaval, get involved in a difficult situation, and see his mistake."

It was already too late. In flocking out to see John the Baptist on the banks of the Jordan River in the wilderness frontier between Galilee, Samaria, Perea, and Judea, peasants and townspeople saw new vistas of people and places. They were also shown how the present reality of suffering and dispossession might be changed by their own actions and moral resolve. John's direct attack on the dynastic manuevers of Antipas came in the course of his continuing campaign against the injustice and arrogance of Herodian society. In demonstrating their opposition to Antipas's violation of Israel's ancestral laws and covenantal traditions, and in acting out their commitment to oppose those violations through the ritual of John's baptism, John's followers were already in open revolt. It did not matter that John the Baptist was arrested for sedition and kept permanently out of public circulation in one of the tetrarch's many fortresses. A growing number of the People of Israel were convinced that the Kingdom of God was indeed at hand and that the sufferings of the righteous would soon come to an end.

HERE, AT LAST, we come to the entrance of the main character who would have such a profound effect on subsequent events. In a crucial passage in the Gospel of Mark—followed with slight but significant textual changes in Luke and Matthew—the evangelist related that "in those days Jesus came from Nazareth of Galilee and was baptized by John in the Jordan" (1:9). With that act, the public career of Jesus began. Over the centuries, countless volumes of theological and historical commentary have been written to explain the meaning of Jesus' baptism and his personal relationship to John. Much of the debate has centered on the question of John's own understanding or awareness of the role that a messiah would play in God's coming judgment—and whether he identified Jesus as one who was destined to take up that role. But since our concern here is with

earthly history, we can say that the circumstances of Jesus' baptism by John
are relatively clear: at a time of rapid economic change and social dislocation in the territory of one of Rome's client rulers, a thirty-two-year-old
woodworker from a tiny agricultural village joined the crowds of peasants
and townspeople flocking out to an open-air revival meeting in the wilderness. Had the ruler of this small territory been less ambitious or more
sensitive of his people's feelings, such a gathering might never have occurred. In that case, the career of Jesus and the story of Christianity might
have unfolded in a very different way. Theology aside, we can say that the
baptism of Jesus took place within the context of a popular revival movement that was spreading among a predominantly rural population that was
being taxed, exploited, and regimented in new—and to their eyes—
extremely threatening ways.

In the specific case of Jesus, we can point to recent political and economic
changes that he could hardly have ignored. The construction of Antipas's
new capital at Tiberias would have further disrupted the lives and livelihoods
of the people of his home village of Nazareth. As long as the nearby city of
Sepphoris was the tetrarchal capital, there might at least be opportunities for
day labor and craftsmen's jobs. But with the shift of the capital fifteen miles to
the east on the lakeside, Sepphoris had declined in relative importance; Josephus later quoted a report that Antipas had explicitly intended that "Sepphoris should be subordinate to Tiberias." So while taxation continued—
and perhaps even intensified to defray the costs of the construction of Antipas's new city—the region around Sepphoris would have suffered a serious
economic downturn, as the old capital of Antipas's tetrarchy lost its luster in
the shadow of the new. And it is impossible to ignore completely the juxtaposition of the general economic background and these developments with
the first event in Jesus' life that we can be relatively sure of: that sometime
around 28 or 29 C.E., less than ten years after the establishment of Tiberias
and more than thirty years into the reign of Herod Antipas, Jesus traveled
from Nazareth out to the wilderness of the Jordan Valley to accept baptism
by John. It was both a political act and a demonstration of personal commitment. And although some scholars have recently insisted that the Historical
Jesus was a wandering Cynic teacher, tossing off clever aphorisms about
country life, blissfully unconcerned with the petty nationalistic politics of
his people, Jesus' early connection with John—the fiery preacher of anti-
Herodian, apocalyptic resistance—provides quite a different perspective on
the initial act of his public career.

A journey out to see John the Baptist in the wilderness would have taken Jesus—presumably in the company of other people from Nazareth—out across the fringe of the Jezreel Valley where they would have passed through other rural villages, meeting tenant farmers and migrant workers, and seeing, at least from the distance, the houses of the overseers and the great villas of the wealthy lords. Yet if the rural landscape of Antipas's realm was a world of carefully regulated oppression, closely guarded by soldiers, loyalists, and paid informers, there were places— desolate, lonely places—far from the cities and farmers' villages where people could, at least briefly, feel free. That was where John the Baptist was preaching. And for most Galileans, the wilderness of the parched Jordan Valley was a place where fearsome spirits ranged freely, the scene of earlier miracles and triumphs of the people in the days of Elijah, and before him, of Joshua, who led the People of Israel in their struggles to secure independence of the land. That is the most we can say of the immediate circumstances of Jesus' baptism. And of the ceremony itself, little can be said except that he presumably joined the assembled throngs (even a few hundred people gathered in the same place would have seemed like a throng to a life-long resident of a small village) making the public commitment—as Josephus described it—"to live righteous lives, to practice justice towards their fellows and piety towards God."

Many scholarly attempts have been made to reconstruct what precisely happened at the moment of Jesus' immersion in the cold, flowing water of the Jordan, when, according to Mark, coming to the surface "immediately he saw the heavens opened and the Spirit descending upon him like a dove; and a voice came from heaven, 'Thou art my beloved Son; with Thee I am well pleased' " (1:10–11). That reverent account of Jesus' baptism was written with a knowledge of all that came afterward throughout the rest of Jesus' career. But that is not to underplay the deep emotional effect that a sudden meeting with the famous prophet John, in front of a mixed crowd of friends and strangers, and of a sudden plunge in the Jordan's cold, flowing water, would have had. From that moment on—even after John the Baptist was hauled away to prison by soldiers—the power of Herod Antipas would have seemed empty to him.

As with so many other people in Judea, Galilee, Perea, and Samaria, Jesus had listened to John the Baptist's message of how personal action and commitment could fit into God's larger plan for history. Though Herod and his officers might invoke Roman law or the ideals of "progress and civilization" to lay claim to crops, livestock, and peasant labor—or to demolish or take possession of rustic stone houses and agricultural fields—theirs was illusory power. The time was quickly approaching when God would intervene directly in human affairs. At some point after his baptism by John, Jesus apparently became active in the anti-Herodian renewal movement; according to the Gospel of John 3:22, he began to baptize people himself. Matthew and Mark relate that soon after the arrest of John the Baptist by Herodian authorities, Jesus reappeared in Galilee filled with the conviction that the Spirit of the God of Israel was directing and empowering his actions—and that he must carry on the idea of the Renewal of Israel among the people in their towns and villages, not in the wilderness. Jesus' understanding of the Kingdom of God would ultimately prove far more influential than that of John the Baptist and far more powerful than that of Herod Antipas. For Jesus did not believe that the Kingdom of God would arrive with fire and brimstone. And he was convinced that he would not need aqueducts, palaces, coins, marble columns, or soldiers to utterly remake the Galilee.

3

Faith Healer

DESPITE THE DISTANCE, the times, the language, and the customs, there is much we would find familiar on a hot Sabbath morning in the lakeside village of Capernaum. The climate there would remind us of other hot, steamy places where life is hard and colonial regimes are common: not big cities with their chilly weather, busy streets, and impressive monuments, but villages of thatched-roofed houses with dirt floors and handmade mud ovens, where the shade of a tumble-down shanty or frayed awning is all there is to protect you from the merciless sun. We would recognize this place as the home of poor people—where scorching summertime winds rush down the parched hillsides to blow across the flat roofs of its houses, scattering the acrid smoke of kitchen fires and the stench of open sewers out over the tepid, murky waters of the nearby lake. And down by the water, we would hear the creaking of ropes, the lapping of worn wooden boats at the dockside, and the muffled laughter and gossip of local boys told to sit there by their elders—to make sure that no one pilfers the few poor possessions of pocket knives, fish-hooks, and cooking pots left aboard.

Along the docks, where the fishermen's nets are spread out to dry in the sunshine, we would smell the pungent aroma of a thousand and one nights' catches of sardines rising from the damp mass of woven cords and twine. Indeed, the smell of fish would be everywhere in this village: on hands, in houses, in the mud of the streets and open places, and in the rotting fins and fishheads left among the sherds of broken storejars, discarded from the hundreds sent off every day on donkeyback to the putrid *garum* factory at Magdala, just a few miles away. Yet today, on the Sabbath, no business would be transacted and no taxes collected. The narrow dirt streets of this village would be quiet, except for the murmuring of prayers in the weekly assembly—perhaps held in a courtyard or storehouse. The place where it met was less important than the sense of community it fostered. In both Hebrew and Greek, the assembly's name, *knesset/synagōgē,* meant "meeting" or "coming together." It was there that the village's fishermen, farmers, prostitutes, and bureaucrats could listen to the chanting of ancient scriptures, bless themselves and their children, and at least temporarily distance themselves from the misery and suffering that this modern world has forced them to bear.

Tiberius Julius Caesar Augustus now rules the empire, but the particular string of royal Latin names is not important. That far-off authority figure, whose grim profile is seen only on grasped coins in the marketplace and whose latest, verbose edicts are regularly mocked by the young men of the village, could be any distant king, emperor, or president—surely not the legitimate ruler of this village and the land to which it belongs. Nor is the true ruler of this village the emperor's compliant servant Herod Antipas, who lives with his illegitimate wife-sister-niece Herodias in their ghost-haunted capital of Tiberias, behind closely guarded palace walls. Centuries before, God bequeathed this territory to the tribe of Naphtali "according to its families," but in His own mysterious ways He has now temporarily given it into the hand of Tiberius, Antipas, and the various Herodian functionaries who build themselves grand villas by the Tiberias seashore, own the best agricultural land in the district, and hold all the residents of this village in a continuous state of poverty and uncertainty. Or, on second thought, perhaps the temporary rulers of this village are actually the gruff foremen who stand at the docks every morning and weigh the fish as they are poured into jars after a long night's hauling, or the loan clerks and scribes with their ledgers of last year's cash advance and this year's mortgage payment, or the tax collectors who come to take a large share of the peoples' grain, vegetables, olive oil, and mutton, meanwhile skimming off a fat portion for themselves. Or could it possibly be that the current tyrants of this frightening landscape of hunger and poverty are actually the weakness and isolation of the individual fishermen and peasants—who, not having any practical way to rebuild their lives, families, and sense of well-being, have tragically surrendered their dignity to the relentless pace of modernization and have allowed themselves and their families to become helpless pawns in other men's imperial dreams?

WE MUST CONTINUALLY REMIND OURSELVES in constructing a social and political history of the world of the New Testament that our story is not only about famous prophets and princes. The story of the grassroots movement of Galilean peasant protest that would, decades later, be transformed into the religion we call Christianity involved thousands of nameless people whose lives and hopes and fears for the future were never recorded in the chronicles of Church, Synagogue, or Imperial Rome. The people whom Jesus knew and grew up with lived on the very fringes of the empire (not in a geographical sense, of course, for Galilee and all of Judea were linked closely by road connections and sea lanes to the rest of the Roman Empire), but on the fringes of empire in the sense of their being part of the vast, marginal majority who lived permanently beyond the reach of Rome's empty promises that it could provide prosperity and hope to even the lowliest, degraded classes of women and men.

With the help of archaeology, ancient Jewish sources, social history, and insights drawn from the ethnohistory of peasant societies throughout the Mediterranean, we can at least make an attempt to reconstruct the human landscape at ground level when Jesus began his public ministry. We can suggest some of the reasons why his teachings and healings made such an indelible impression, and we can even speculate on the social effects that his sudden appearance, surrounded by a small group of disciples, may have had in various Galilean villages and towns. But it is impossible to construct a day-by-day or even month-by-month chronology for the public ministry of Jesus. Even though the gospels of Matthew, Mark, Luke, and John contain many of the same stories of Jesus' miracles, healings, and teachings, the order in which they are presented and the significance they are given in each of the gospels differ dramatically. John, for instance, reports that Jesus was deeply involved from the outset in the affairs of Judea, making repeated trips to Jerusalem during the course of his ministry. Matthew, Mark, and Luke, on the other hand, depict Jesus as remaining in Galilee and in the villages of Phoenica and southern Syria until he finally journeyed southward to Jerusalem for a climactic Passover pilgrimage in the last week of his earthly life. New Testament scholars since the eighteenth century have tried—and continue to try—to identify "earlier" and "later" strata of tradition in the texts of the various gospels, seeking to isolate the "authentic" sayings and actions of Jesus from later interpolations and insertions. But since there is still wide scholarly disagreement on many of the most basic questions, we might be wise to follow the advice of New Testament scholar John Meier and recognize that there is really no "before" and "after" in the career of Jesus as recorded in the gospels. The scriptural evidence is comprised of a complex web of progressively elaborated memories, stories, anecdotes, and quotations relating to the brief period of Jesus' public preaching—which by most accounts could hardly have lasted more than a year or two.

Thus as historians, rather than theologians, we must concentrate less on sacred biography and more on the social history of the local population as it can be reconstructed from a combination of gospel sources and external evidence. And although there is no way to confirm or document the gospel stories of Jesus' temptation in the wilderness or the precise route he used to return to Galilee after his baptism, we do have some solid information on contemporary conditions in the region where he spent much of his public career. At the time of Jesus' arrival, the lakeside towns of the Sea of Galilee—chief among them, Capernaum, "the village of Nahum," located just west of the Upper Jordan River on the northern coast—were experiencing some dramatic changes. Until the late Hellenistic or Roman period, the agricultural and fishing communities of the northern lakeshore would have been literal backwaters, offering few attractions for the travelers and merchants who passed through the area on the overland highway to Syria. But with the division of Herod's kingdom by Augustus, the region became a sensitive border area between the tetrarchies of Antipas and his brother Philip, where traffic was monitored and customs duties paid. The mention of a tax office in Capernaum (from which Jesus reportedly recruited his disciple Matthew [Matt. 9:9]) and the reported presence of a military officer (identified as a centurion in Luke 7:2) provide possible indications of heightened government involvement and surveillance. And the construction of Herod Antipas's new capital of Tiberias—only a decade or so before Jesus' arrival—with its transfer of jobs, civil and religious courts, market days, and alteration of transport patterns—would have gradually drawn all the villages around the Sea of Galilee into an intensifying whirlpool of taxation and trade.

Archaeological excavations at Capernaum have revealed that its first-century residents apparently maintained the traditional Israelite mode of village life, with houses grouped around common courtyards. Yet as we have seen in the evidence from Judea in the same period, that way of life was under considerable stress. We can also assume that the preaching of John the Baptist had recently aroused considerable public excitement, and that excitement must have reached a fevor pitch with the news of the Baptist's arrest. In the meantime, the daily grind of the region's farmers, craftspeople, and workers continued as they were forced to work harder than ever to meet their obligations for priestly tithes and for Herod Antipas's intensified collection of taxes. Even some of the lake's fishermen, whose daily hauls of silvery sardines and bottom-feeding carp had to provide both food for themselves and raw material for the nearby salt fish factories of Magdala, may have begun to question the system by which they were fishing less for themselves and more for the greater glory of Antipas. All these factors would likely have contributed to the appeal of an extraordinary young man from Nazareth who did not remain in the wilderness but actively sought to spread his message of relief and redemption among the villages of what was perhaps the most rapidly changing region in all of Galilee. And he soon found local people who were ready to help him. "Seeing Simon and his brother Andrew casting a net into the sea," Mark 1:16–17 reported of Jesus' arrival at the Capernaum lakefront, "Jesus said to them, 'Follow me and I will make you become fishers of men.' "

AS FAR AS WE KNOW, John the Baptist did not perform miraculous healings. His style was that of an ancient prophet warning the People of Israel of the impending threat of God's fiery vengeance, soon to rain down on the earth and incinerate the evil and the unrepentant like so much useless chaff. Jesus was different. Although he, too, seems to have urged his listeners to examine their lives and repent, for "the time is fulfilled and the Kingdom of God is at hand" (Mark 1:15), he usually spoke with kindness and good humor, occasionally confronting critics and doubters with provocative parables and amusingly pithy turns-of-phrase. At the same time, he possessed extraordinary skill as an exorcist and healer, attracting crowds of people who flocked to him for miraculous cures. The gospels contain a series of powerful and poignant descriptions of how in his travels from village to village Jesus offered long-sought relief to violent, wild-eyed young men who seemed to be possessed by demons. They tell of friends so eager to see a paralyzed neighbor walk again that they carried him for miles to a house where Jesus was staying just to get the man into Jesus' presence; of a village elder who presided in the local assembly and came begging Jesus to come heal his sick daughter; of a desperate woman, racked by illness, who forced her way through a crowd just to touch Jesus' garment hem.

Although we have grown skeptical of modern faith healers—with their shouted biblical verses and joyous, dancing disciples suddenly throwing away their crutches and leg braces—we must be careful not to reduce Jesus' exorcisms and healings to mere scriptural metaphors for deeper spiritual healing. In the first century, exorcisms and spontaneous cures were, in themselves, not considered impossible or even unusual. We know from the esoteric and magical texts of the period, for instance, that many people believed the world was inhabited by spirits of both good and evil and that every event, every action, and the well-being and inner workings of the bodies of all of God's creatures were affected by that ongoing—and largely invisible—struggle between darkness and light. As long as God withheld His final judgment over the earth and his creatures, both angels and demons would continue to range widely, variously helping or hurting humankind. Those spirits were the hidden causes of both good fortune and demonic possession, and their sudden removal was usually less a matter of "miracle" than technique. In many cases, the painful symptoms of illness were subject to cure through personal atonement, a prayer of supplication to God, or the contribution of a free-will offering to the Temple in Jerusalem. Sometimes, the demonic infestation was harder to deal with and only the services of a skilled professional healer (whose amulets or spells invoking the power of God or the names of His various angels) could force the unwelcome spirits to flee. Most difficult of all were the evil spirits that many people believed were drawn to earth by the collective sins of the entire nation of Israel, in their failure to remain true to the Covenant. And since *those* pervasive evil spirits would linger until God finally brought about the end of days and ushered in a new era of redemption, many people simply resigned themselves to live with the horrible sights that no folk healer could deal with: the wild-eyed young men who lived as wandering outcasts and madmen in the villages and who could suddenly fly into rages and seizures; the helpless infants and children who fell victim to sudden rashes and fatal fevers; the farmers and fishermen who became blinded or crippled in the course of their daily struggle for existence; and the teenaged girls destined to become the wives and mothers of a new generation of Israel, who began to hemorrhage uncontrollably at puberty and were unable to conceive.

Today's medical historians and public-health experts can offer us precise clinical diagnoses of many such serious mental and physical disabilities that are still tragically common in inner cities and in impoverished areas of the developing world. A great many were undoubtedly caused by unchecked infection and viruses spread from poor hygiene or unsanitary conditions, while others—no less severe in their symptoms or debilitating effects—may have been caused by what psychologists call conversion or somatization disorders, related to intense psychological conflict, chronic depression, or stress. That is certainly not to minimize the reality of the suffering: we who live under drastically different circumstances may have difficulty understanding the feelings of helplessness experienced by people eking out a bare existence in a region undergoing profound economic transformation—with their traditional family structures rapidly crumbling and with no alternative health facilities available to them. Anthropological studies of other times and places have shown how the strained, bruised hands and arms of migrant farm workers and sharecroppers can gradually become withered or disabled, as malnutrition, uncertainty about the future, and brutal working conditions combine to create a deep sense of futility. We might also find that many of the deaf-mutes and demon-haunted young men we repeatedly hear about in the gospels may have been people whom we would today describe as "the homeless"—those troubled sons and daughters who found it impossible to cope with the realities of life around them and drifted away from their families, living on the alms of others and acting out their pain and physical frustrations in unpredictable ways. Although we do not have enough information to suggest clinical reasons for the success that Jesus of Nazareth had in dealing with these kinds of people, something undeniably powerful happened when he appeared back in Galilee. For far from being just another disciple of John the Baptist who merely echoed his mentor's oracles, Jesus uniquely touched and transformed the lives of many. And his healing power was something that contemporary observers—both those who followed him and those who dismissed him—considered to be somehow different from the norm.

Indeed, had Jesus' initial acts of exorcism and healing been merely haphazard miracles and wonders aimed solely at individuals, he would never have gained such great attention. Had he arrived back in his boyhood home of Nazareth or appeared suddenly in the lakeside town of Capernaum to hang up his shingle as just another Galilean shaman or folk-doctor, he would almost certainly have been viewed as unwelcome competition by the local village healer—and would, sooner or later, have been forced out of town. Yet Jesus' acts of healing, as they are portrayed in the gospels, were not the usual works of sorcery or folk medicine. We never get any sense that he resorted to the use of charms, symbolic amulets, or complicated incantations. There is no evidence in his recorded words or actions, or in the accusations of his accusers, that he had undergone professional training as a shaman, or ever charged a fee for his services. Jesus, instead, seemed filled with a powerful spirit. The restorative and creative energy he shared with others (and which many of his followers believed was divine) was not aimed solely at individuals but served as a way of transforming wider community life. And the remarkable resonance that Jesus' words and actions seemed to have with certain people led many Galileans to believe that the Kingdom of God that John the Baptist had preached about was not merely imminent but was *already* at hand.

The sudden wave of healings was an unmistakable sign of God's presence, since the ancient Israelite prophets' descriptions of the coming Kingdom of God had often told how the People of Israel would be restored to *physical* health. Isaiah had looked forward to the day when "the eyes of the blind shall be opened and the ears of the deaf unstopped; then shall the lame man leap like a hart and the tongue of the dumb sing for joy" (35:5–6). Psalm 146 spoke of God's power to restore sight and heal even the most crippled of bodies (v. 8). And the prophet Elijah, empowered by God, had been able to raise people from the dead (1 Kings 17:17–23) and his protégé Elisha knew how to cure leprosy (2 Kings 5:10–14). Much closer to the time of Jesus, one of the Dead Sea Scroll documents—known to scholars as 4Q521, or "The Messianic Apocalypse"—combined several of the most familiar scriptural expectations of miraculous healing into a single poem about the imminent intervention of God in the world. Making His presence known to the poor and the pious, He would "release the captives, make the blind see, raise up the downtrodden." He would also "heal the sick, resurrect the dead, and announce glad tidings to the poor." For many people in Galilee, Jesus offered that kind of alternative to John's vision of fire and brimstone. He preached that the evil and unjust would certainly be punished in God's vengeance, yet Jesus also offered stunning evidence that God's power was already manifest and available to the long-oppressed rural population of the Land of Israel.

We cannot be sure where Jesus' initial acts of healing happened—the gospels of Mark (1:23–27) and Luke (4:33–36) report that Jesus' first exorcism took place in the Capernaum synagogue assembly; neither Matthew nor John identify a specific place. Yet once those initial healings happened, we have no reason to doubt that the sight of one person's sudden relief from affliction would have encouraged others to come forward. And once people heard of life-giving power flowing through Jesus, excited reports of healing in one village would have kindled the hopes of people in distress in other villages: if only they could reach Jesus, they, too, could have access to God's Kingdom—right here and now. The intense desire to be well again would have caused news about Jesus to spread like wildfire and "at once his fame spread everywhere throughout the surrounding region of Galilee" (Mark 1:28). And if we can begin to grasp the specific social and political context—if not fully understand the biological mechanisms—we can see how Jesus could have become a touch point where dispossessed rural people could tap into a source of powerful, positive energy and, in effect, begin to heal themselves.

Many other folk-prophets and healers would pass through this region in the decades and centuries that followed, but none of them would make the impression that Jesus of Nazareth did. Although it is impossible to know what proportion of the village population actually responded to Jesus' message and actions, at least some of those who *did* seem to have undergone a permanent, life-transforming change. And here is our main historical hypothesis about the Galilean phase of Jesus' public career: he directly addressed the painful specifics of peasant life under the rule of Herod Antipas, offering his listeners far more than just generalized promises or threats. He showed them that they were not condemned to be powerless victims. This was not political protest in the sense of making overt, anti-government speeches or secretly plotting armed rebellion, but it was political in a far more powerful way. In Jesus' presence or under his influence, people who had been previously paralyzed or crippled by forces beyond their control began to piece their lives back together, for he offered them both a new feeling of community and a new personal confidence. While John the Baptist languished on death row in one of Herod

Antipas's prisons for his "seditious" preaching, Jesus of Nazareth returned to Galilee to recognize that much of his people's suffering lay in their resignation and passive acquiescence to the economy and power of the new regime.

Jesus' healings and exorcisms were, in fact, merely part of a larger program. For just as the Prophet Elijah, seized by God's Spirit in the course of a wider campaign of political and economic renewal, had summoned rain clouds (1 Kings 18:41–45), multiplied the pitifully small supply of grain and oil possessed by the hungry widow (1 Kings 17:12–15), and miraculously parted the waters of the Jordan (2 Kings 2:7–8), this new prophet named Jesus, who was also seemingly possessed by divine power, was remembered for turning water into wine at a village wedding, stilling the Sea of Galilee's angry waters, and multiplying the loaves and the fishes for the hungry multitudes. His miracles were seen not so much as bizarre natural curiosities but as additional signs that God had once again chosen to intervene in the earthly history of Israel. And this time, Jesus asserted, it was for the permanent establishment of God's Kingdom on earth. The gospels of Matthew and Luke preserve a telling anecdote that so closely mirrors the expectations of the Dead Sea Scroll "Messianic Apocalypse" that it may reflect widely shared understandings of what signs the people should look for at the onset of the end of days.

According to the story, the imprisoned John the Baptist sent some of his disciples to question Jesus about his possible identity as the prophet sent by God to usher in the messianic era. For his part, Jesus did not respond directly but merely pointed to the events that were causing such excitement in the villages of Galilee: "Go and tell John what you see," he replied to the Baptist's disciples. "The blind receive their sight and the lame walk, lepers are cleansed and the deaf hear, and the dead are raised up and the poor have good news preached to them" (Matt. 11:4–5; Luke 7:22). That would have been enough to indicate what was *really* happening. An era of spiritual—as well as social, political, and economic—renewal was dawning, right under the nose of Herod Antipas, the faithful client of imperial Rome. Yet the pervasive impact of Rome, in the villages of Galilee and throughout the rest of the Land of Israel, could not be unbuilt in a day. The next step for Jesus would therefore be to move beyond healing and wonder-working and suggest some practical ways by which the people's suffering under the reign of Herod Antipas might be reversed and then permanently overcome.

FROM THE TIME of his arrival back in Galilee's villages, Jesus had continued to proclaim John the Baptist's urgent and overarching message: "The time is fulfilled; the Kingdom of God is at hand" (Mark 1:15). For centuries, church leaders and biblical scholars have speculated and argued about the meaning of that phrase as an abstract theological concept and how Jesus' understanding of that concept might have been quite different from John's. Even today, many ecclesiastical traditions suggest that the "Kingdom of God" refers either to the blessed, heavenly state of all those who accept Jesus as a personal savior, or to the sacred domain of the True Church as it stands holy and eternal in an otherwise wicked world. The very different idea that the coming of the Kingdom of God referred to frightening, physical changes soon to overtake all of creation was stressed early in this century by the influential New Testament scholars Albert Schweitzer and Rudolf Bultmann, who interpreted Jesus' message of the Kingdom (like John the Baptist's fiery preaching of impending judgment) in the context of contemporary Jewish apocalyptic writings that described a coming "cosmic catastrophe," which would utterly destroy and transform the world. And they believed that Jesus, when placed in proper historical context in the traditions of second-temple Judaism, should not be understood as a mild-mannered teacher and healer but an uncompromising prophet of doom and destruction who really believed that the world as he and the other members of his generation knew it was about to pass away.

Yet it is hard to reconcile that grim understanding with the joyful, life-affirming message that the former carpenter from Nazareth announced in the people's midst. As we have already mentioned, traditional Jewish prophetic and apocalyptic language (as used in the gospels, as well as in the Dead Sea Scrolls, other apocryphal Jewish texts, and the New Testament Book of Revelation) need not be understood literally as a nuclearlike destruction of the world and all its inhabitants but rather as a vivid, if hyperbolic, way of speaking about dramatic historical change. We might even suggest that the only "cataclysm" that either John or Jesus would have expected would be the coming humbling and humiliation of those Herodian magnates and grandees who had abandoned traditional Israelite values for the seductive ideology of Rome. In both John's and Jesus' preaching, the coming of the Kingdom of God meant a revolution in the way people behaved toward each other and their recognition that they should have no Caesars, tetrarchs, centurions, or other overlords above them except for the one God and Creator of the world. In practical terms, that meant rejecting the rule of all powers and returning to the pure covenantal system under which Israelites—and indeed all peoples—would be considered to be brothers and sisters under God. In modern political terms, that might be called a revolution, but for Jesus and the people of his time, it was nothing more nor less than Israel's ancient legacy. And like earlier Israelite prophets whose public role he reenacted, Jesus taught that Israel's non-kingly Kingdom could already be present and functioning in the land's fields, towns, and villages—if only people recognized its sanctity and reoriented their community life accordingly.

As the power moved through Jesus to restore the lame, deaf, blind, and demon-possessed, Jesus stressed the close connection between the energy displayed in his healings and the spirit energizing the larger Renewal of Israel: "If it is by the finger of God I am casting out demons, then the Kingdom of God has come upon you" (Luke 11:20). God was certainly controlling events, but He did not need armies or weapons of war to carry out His will. In contrast to those among the People of Israel who eagerly looked forward to an impending celestial battle between the Sons of Light and the Sons of Darkness to bring on the Age of Redemption, or those who advocated direct military action against the Romans and the Herodian mercenary forces (a path that could only result in another bloody repression against the poorly armed, poorly trained bands of guerrillas), Jesus suggested that God was establishing His Kingdom by creating an alternative society.

What kind of a society was it? In the message that accompanied his healings and exorcisms, Jesus addressed the distress of the people directly. Under the pressure of Herodian taxation and land dispossession, they had slipped away from a traditional village spirit of mutual cooperation: divisiveness and mutual recrimination had to be stilled. It was not that the Galilean village had been idyllic or peaceful before the coming of the Hellenistic kingdoms or the Roman Empire; the life of peasant farmers eking out a living—with little or no surplus to protect them from the effects of drought, war, and disease—could never have been easy. But the

People of Israel had always maintained the social codes and standards of community behavior deeply ingrained in the Mosaic law. Unfortunately, under the pressure of debt and taxation, Roman legal standards, not the Torah, began to take precedence. Villagers who may previously have felt a responsibility to help their neighbors in times of shortage were no longer under legal obligation to do so, especially since they were themselves now debtors, hard-pressed to provide their own children with food to eat. Local feuds which could have been easily resolved in normal times now often erupted into insults, fistfights, and family feuds. Land or goods taken as loan collateral—that should have been returned to its original owners by the law of the sabbatical year—now became the big-city creditors' permanent property. The simple fact was that the People of Israel were badly divided. Villagers who could have cooperated in their own liberation were at each others' throats. Jesus' healings and teachings must be therefore seen in this context, not as abstract spiritual truths spoken between stunning miracles but as a program of community action and practical resistance to a system that efficiently transformed close-knit villages into badly fragmented communities of alienated, frightened individuals.

"I tell you who can hear," Jesus is quoted in an early saying, "love your enemies, do good to those who hate you, bless those who curse you, pray for those who abuse you. To him who strikes you on the cheek offer the other also" (Luke 6:27–29). This was not mere pacifism or meekness, but the first step in the reconciliation and renewal of the People of Israel. As the admonition in Leviticus 19:18 had instructed: "You shall not take vengeance or bear any grudge against any of your people, but you shall love your neighbor as yourself." The scribes and teachers of Israel had always tried to reinforce traditional covenantal teaching of mutual aid among households with the sabbatical year laws and the strict prohibitions against usury and debt slavery. In fact, the Book of Sirach, also known as Ecclesiasticus and written in the early second century B.C.E., eloquently expressed the feeling that the essence of the Israelite tradition was communal solidarity: "The merciful lend to their neighbors; by holding out a helping hand they keep the commandments" (Sir. 29:1). Jesus restated and expanded the tradition. "If anyone would sue you and take your cloak," he reportedly said of the symbolic repossession of collateral for a loan, the debtor should embarrass the lender by giving him "your tunic as well" (Matt. 5:40). "If someone pleads for a loan, do not refuse. Do good and lend" (Matt. 5:42). Such cooperation and mutual assistance were precisely what the age-old covenantal tradition had fostered and articulated, and we must see these teachings as a practical response to the contemporary political and economic situation of the people of Galilee under Herodian rule.

Against the defensive mutual hostility of everyone looking out for his or her own interest—since all were hungry and mutually indebted—Jesus insisted on practical action to renew the Covenant, thereby restoring the promised blessings of God. The words of the Lord's Prayer—so familiar to us in their spiritualized, otherworldly reading—can also be understood in a way that evokes the hope that many first-century Galilean peasants may have harbored of overturning an oppressive system of taxation and land dispossession that produced only hunger and mounting debt. "Our Father, who art in heaven, hallowed be Thy name. Thy kingdom come, Thy will be done, on earth as it is in heaven. Give us this day our daily bread; and forgive us our debts as we also have forgiven our debtors; and lead us not into temptation, but deliver us from evil" (Matt. 6:9–13). This kind of hope of an earthly kingdom ruled only by God, without violence or economic inequality, might have seemed to many—then as now—a chimerical ideal. But it also could have served as an impetus to action for discouraged and indebted peasants who had lost control of their land.

The Kingdom of God was indeed at hand if they believed it—not a dream, not a vision of heaven, not a spiritual state, but a social transformation here and now in the very fields they plowed and the very villages they lived in, if only they rejected injustice and heeded the commandments of God. Recalling the visions of ancient Israelite prophets that peace, prosperity, and well-being would come to the House of Israel when the laws of the Covenant were finally observed and justice honored, the hungry peasants and landless laborers of Israel looked toward the glorious period of God's restoration in terms of abundance, celebration, and feasting. Isaiah had, after all, promised that "the Lord of Hosts will make for all people a feast of fat things, a feast of wine on the lees, of fat things full of marrow" (25:6). And as if to proclaim that the glorious time of redemption was even now dawning, Jesus gathered his followers with what little food they had in the empty places around the Sea of Galilee, far from the surveillance by the watchful eyes of Herodian officials and tax collectors on the roads and in the towns. In gospel stories of the miraculous multiplication of a handful of loaves and fishes, we can understand Jesus' references to "banqueting in the kingdom"—where the power of God was enough to feed a hungry multitude. And when Jesus repeated his evocative images and parables of wedding feasts and "great suppers," there was a contemporary allusion intended alongside the biblical. He could have been understood to be mocking the lavish palace celebrations of Herod Antipas, at which court advisers and officers feasted sumptuously on foods that they and their fellow peasants had raised and quaffed fine wines from royal vineyards that used to be their fields.

Thus through healings, preachings, and banquets, Jesus began to catalyze a movement that envisioned the independence of Israel in its village communities. The people of Israel—the heirs to God's promises of redemption if they would be true to the Covenant he had forged with them—were free to refuse to be faceless cogs in the great mill of Roman prosperity. They could remain within their villages, freely and willingly sharing, rather than allow themselves to become beasts of burden to build theaters and forums, to plow and harvest fields now owned by others, or bring to the palaces of the high and mighty the first-fruits of the land. This was powerful preaching, made even more stunning by the acts of divine power that made Jesus famous. Yet it was also sedition of the highest order. In that sense, Jesus himself may have been well aware of the strong reaction his movement was bound to evoke sooner or later from Herodian officials who could only feel threatened by the idea of an alternative society. There might even be violent confrontation within individual families about the radical path he had shown. "Do you think that I have come to give peace on earth?" Jesus reportedly asked his closest disciples. "No, I tell you, but rather division; for henceforth in one house there will be five divided, three against two and two against three; they will be divided father against son and son against father, mother against daughter and daughter against her mother, mother-in-law against her daughter-in-law and daughter-in-law against her mother-in-law" (Luke 12:51–53).

JESUS' SWEEPING PROGRAM of community renewal could never be accomplished by a single person, and from the very beginning of his public career, we can perceive the vague outlines of an organizational strategy. In sending apostle-envoys like Peter, Andrew, John, and James the Capernaum fishermen into the villages of Galilee and surrounding territories, Jesus chose to spread the message of the Kingdom through the efforts of those who took on the role of the ancient "sons of the prophets"—that wandering guild of Spirit-fired preachers and miracle workers whose righteous acts and teachings among the people of the northern Kingdom of Israel were recorded in the Books of Kings. This, too, was an ancient tradition, not an innovation. Just as the prophet Elijah had spearheaded a movement of individual and national renewal against the abominations of the evil Israelite king Ahab, helped by the sons of the prophets, so, too, did Jesus work for the redemption of Galilee from the predations of Antipas, aided by his own corps of prophet preachers whom he had instructed to leave their homes and families. Their job would be to work among the villages in places that Jesus himself did not or could not manage to get to, preaching the reality of the Kingdom of God and manifesting its already-present powers in healings and exorcisms.

The mission of Jesus' disciples was an ambitious yet down-to-earth attempt to overturn the accepted order through a revolution in the people's behavior; it was not a program of purely spiritual conversion or even a well-intentioned tour of backcountry peasant villages by alienated young idealists seeking to do good and find meaning in their lives. Despite the well-publicized contention of some contemporary New Testament scholars, particularly those associated with the Jesus Seminar, that the Historical Jesus was a Galilean guru of nonpolitical, countercultural wisdom and that his wandering followers were simply peasant versions of the itinerant Cynic philosophers of the Greco-Roman world (who preached to people on the street corners of ancient Hellenistic cities, urging them to abandon the hollow values and respectable conventions of the dominant Greco-Roman culture) the cross-cultural comparison is valid only in a very general sense. If we can cautiously assume that the specific *details* of Jesus' recorded instructions to his envoys (Mark 6:8–11; Matt. 10:9–10; Luke 10:4) contain characteristic elements of material culture that would have been meaningful in his time but unimportant to later ecclesiastical editors, we can see that they would never have been identified as Cynic preachers by any of their contemporaries. While a Cynic preacher was recognizable in the Hellenistic cities by his tattered cloak, walking staff, and hanging purse in which he held the handouts he collected, Jesus explicitly instructed those he sent into the villages to carry *no* purse, *no* knapsack, *no* sandals, and not to talk to people along the way. Far from being beggars on the move, tossing off pithy sayings to anyone who would listen, they were instructed to work for a certain period of time in each village, staying in the household of their host and eating whatever was put before them. Like "the sons of the prophets," these Spirit-filled envoys or "apostles" of Jesus served as mediums of God's positive spirit, nurturing local solidarity and cultivating a renewal of community. Far from being a band with a purely spiritual mission of individual moral improvement, they were dispatched to promote a community-oriented political-religious program of renewal throughout the villages of Galilee.

That is certainly not to say that every Galilean villager responded enthusiastically to the apostles' calls to join Jesus' movement. The very absence of any historical references outside the literature of the New Testament to the career of Jesus in Galilee suggests that it was an extremely local phenomenon among the Galilean villages—either unknown or, more probably, deemed unworthy of mention by contemporary chroniclers or the official scribes of the Herodian court. Even within the gospel tradition (which, as we will see, retrospectively concentrates much of the opposition to Jesus in the shadowy figures of "the scribes and Pharisees"), we get a sense of the kind of general hostility and skepticism that Jesus faced. In a tense and pressure-filled time, when most people would have been reluctant to risk their lives or their family's survival on idealistic, visionary notions, it is not hard to understand why many Galileans would have shunned Jesus and his followers, fearing that their presence might provoke repressive actions against their village by the authorities. And those whose lives and livelihoods depended directly on Antipas's bureaucracy or the collection of tithes for the priests of the Jerusalem Temple would have considered his preaching dangerous and tried to discredit him in various ways. Just as they had apparently ridiculed John the Baptist, the fiery preacher of covenantal repentance, as having been "possessed by a demon" (Matt. 11:18; Luke 7:33), they now sought to demean Jesus' celebration of the Kingdom in "banquets" with destitute peasants and foul-smelling fisherfolk by calling him "a glutton and a drunkard, a friend of tax collectors and sinners" (Matt. 11:19; Luke 7:34).

Another serious threat that Jesus apparently faced was the accusation that he was a witch who was empowered by the very evil spirits he was supposedly driving out: "He is possessed by Beelzebul, and it is by the prince of demons that he casts out the demons" (Mark 3:22). Others, among the still-faithful followers of John the Baptist, may have regarded

Jesus with resentment, seeing him as an ambitious young man now trying to upstage the true prophet, now that he was languishing in jail. Indeed, entire villages seem to have greeted his news of the coming Kingdom of God with cold disinterest, preferring to try to survive under the current difficult conditions the best they could. For his part, Jesus was under no illusions that everyone would joyously enter the renewed Covenant of Israel, and just as he was sometimes filled with the Spirit of healing, he could sometimes become filled with prophetic rage. "Woe to you, Chorazin! Woe to you, Bethsaida!" Jesus intoned against the lakeside villages, "for if the deeds of power done in you had been done in Tyre and Sidon, they would have repented long ago in sackcloth and ashes! But I tell you, it shall be more tolerable on the day of judgment for Tyre and Sidon than for you" (Matt. 11:21–22; Luke 10:13–14). At times even the people of the village he chose as his headquarters seemed unwilling to accept his prophetic message: "And you, Capernaum, will you be exalted to heaven? You shall be brought down to Hades" (Matt. 11:23; Luke 10:15).

Yet Jesus' most dangerous opponents were not timid villagers or low-level functionaries but high government officials. For from his palace in Tiberias, Herod Antipas and his administration kept a close watch on the nearby villages and were prepared to deal quickly and decisively with even the slightest hint of sedition or civil unrest. Even though the gospels have all but forgotten about the tetrarch's dominating role in the events of the era (in their theological preoccupation with the meaning of Jesus' subsequent crucifixion and resurrection in Jerusalem), it is likely that Antipas would have been aware of the disturbance that Jesus was causing among the Galilean peasantry and would have wanted to take action immediately. He had apparently learned from his father the wisdom, perhaps necessity, of maintaining a network of local informers; so developed, in fact, was the paranoia and security apparatus of the Herodian dynasty that it merited mention by Josephus: "Both in the city and on the open roads there were men who spied upon those who met together. And they say that even Herod himself did not neglect to play a part in this, but would often put on the dress of a private citizen and mingle with the crowds by night, and so get an idea of how they felt about his rule."

Thus the Herodians could quickly respond to potential unrest with sheer power and military coercion. But sometimes their hand could be overplayed. Such was apparently the case with John the Baptist, whose message was carried on even after his arrest. We do not know the precise circumstances of John's imprisonment and eventual execution in the royal fortress of Machaerus in Perea, for Josephus mentions only Herod Antipas's nervousness about widespread unrest in the region brought on by John's "eloquence" and reports only that John "was brought in chains to Machaerus, and there put to death." Mark 6:17–29 and Matthew 14:3–12 present far more elaborate stories, describing how Antipas's wife Herodias sought to have John executed for having publicly condemned her marriage, and how her daughter Salome's salacious dance at Antipas's birthday banquet finally persuaded him to put John to death. From a purely historical perspective, it is impossible to know if John the Baptist's head was actually brought before Antipas on a platter—as Salome reportedly requested—yet the request, the dance, and the platter have been the motifs of grotesquely vivid paintings and manuscript illuminations from early Christian times to today.

But if Antipas thought he had finally rid himself of a prophetic nuisance on the chopping block at Machaerus, another had now arisen in Galilee. The chronological sequence of events at this point is only approximate, for we cannot be sure how long John remained in prison before his execution, or when during Jesus' public career that execution occurred. But some time after the violent death of John the Baptist in the remote fortress of Machaerus, Antipas learned through his informers of the excitement going on in the villages of Galilee. According to the tradition preserved in Mark 6:14–16 and echoed in both Matthew 14:1–2 and Luke 9:7–9, he received ominous, conflicting reports about the healing and preaching activities of Jesus: "Some said, 'John the Baptist has been raised from the dead; that is why these powers are at work in him.' But others said, 'It is Elijah.' And others said, 'It is a prophet, like one of the prophets of old.' " Antipas, with his own royal-messianic aspirations, knew enough about Israelite traditions to identify Jesus as a danger. And although scholars have long debated the significance of Antipas's reactions to these reports, the implications are clear that he saw in Jesus far more than some local hero and faith healer who would soon be exposed as a fraud and simply fade away. Jesus' healings and exorcisms, his open-air "banquets" and prophetic declarations were dangerous provocations that undermined the new order and the rules of cold power, logic, and fiscal calculation on which it was based. The wave of sedition in the countryside that had begun with John the Baptist was apparently growing. And thus there may have been more of a touch of ironic political humor than credulous belief in reincarnation in Antipas's words quoted in Mark 6:16 that "John, whom I beheaded, has been raised."

JESUS, FOR HIS PART, was preparing for a confrontation with Herod Antipas, though at first he seems to have avoided it. There may be more than the traditional symbolism of Exodus and wandering before liberation in the fact that during the initial period of his ministry, Jesus is shown often meeting with his followers in desolate, wilderness places, far away from Galilee's closely watched villages and towns. But with the movement spreading, it could not be kept secret forever. And whoever the characters were who are identified variously in the gospels as the scribes, Pharisees, and Herodians, who conspired to "entrap" Jesus, it seems clear enough that at some point Herod Antipas had heard enough about Jesus that he resolved to do to him what he had done to John. Yet in Luke 13:31, where Jesus was reportedly informed by "some Pharisees" of Antipas's intentions to kill him, and was advised—for his own good—to flee the realm of the tetrarch like some common criminal, he reacted with defiance. "Go and tell that fox," he instructed, " 'behold I cast out demons and perform cures today and tomorrow, and the third day I finish my course.' "

The logic of the Kingdom of God was leading to Jerusalem and to a more direct prophetic demonstration than John the Baptist had ever been able to perform. During the months preceding his final journey, Jesus initiated his movement of community renewal, dedicated to restoring reciprocity and cooperation in the spirit of the dawning Kingdom of God. Yet his movement of revival of village life could not become just another separatist movement, withdrawing from confrontation and seeking the shelter of obscurity in the backcountry valleys and remote mountainous areas of Galilee. However ambivalently the Galileans may sometimes have felt about it, Jerusalem was still the traditional capital of Israel; it had been a significant site since the time of Abraham's meeting with Melchizedek; it had been the first capital of a united Israel; it was there that Solomon's great Temple stood. In Jerusalem's streets and public squares the political history of the People of Israel had been enacted, from Abraham to David to Ezra to the Maccabees. In the courtyards and forecourts of the Temple, the ceremonies and sacrifices were conducted to ensure the well-being of Israel. Yet those tithes and offerings were now somehow ineffective, for the People of Israel now found themselves in bondage with a client prince ruling in Galilee and a Roman prefect in Judea itself. The festival of Passover was rapidly approaching, and fired by the Spirit of God—and convinced that the Renewal Movement in the Galilean villages meant that God's Kingdom was indeed at hand—Jesus would embark on a Passover pilgrimage to Jerusalem to proclaim the reality of God's new deliverance of the People of Israel from bondage to a latter-day pharaoh. Like Elijah, he would deliver God's oracles of judgment to the nation's political leaders and ruling institutions. Like Jeremiah, he would demonstrate the imminence of divine judgment in the very courtyard of the Temple, where the Passover pilgrims would see him and carry the message of liberation back to the villages and out to the scattered communities of Israelites all over the Roman world.

The tradition of Jesus' journey to Jerusalem is so central and pervasive in all later variants of the Christian historical tradition—and in the few non-Christian references to him—that it is clear that by the end of the Galilean phase of his ministry, he had come to envision his prophetic role in national rather than regional terms. Ironically, it may have been Herod Antipas's increasing interest in the Temple as a tool to enhance his own power that inspired Jesus' actions. The only legitimacy that Antipas could claim for his wider royal ambitions was, after all, his patronage of the magnificent Temple that his father had built. In the rising plumes of smoke from the Temple's great altar, in the offerings of the time-honored sacrifices prescribed in the Torah, and in the pomp and circumstance of their own lavish pilgrimages to the Holy City, Herod Antipas and his Hasmonean wife Herodias believed they could display their piety and beneficence to the People of Israel at the same time as they reassured their imperial overlords that they could shepherd their people into a permanent state of obedience and loyalty to Rome.

Jesus sought to turn the People of Israel away from that Herodian vision toward the tradition of an independent Israel, and it is significant, in this connection, that the gospel traditions stress "twelve" as the number of the core group of disciples, with Jesus proclaiming that his twelve closest followers were commissioned with establishing justice for all the twelve tribes of Israel (Matt. 19:28; Luke 22:29–30). That would mean spreading his message to every region of the land that God had promised as an eternal inheritance for the children of Abraham and the twelve sons of Jacob. It would mean spreading the message of renewal into every village of the Promised Land. Yet no mere territorial definition was enough to encompass the entire People of Israel, for Israel existed wherever village communities or urban synagogue assemblies gathered to remember God's great acts of deliverance, to celebrate the annual festivals, or to hearken to the obligations of the Mosaic covenant. Since at least the time of the Assyrian conquest more than seven hundred years before, a great part of the Israelite people had been scattered. Even during Jesus' own lifetime, he had witnessed Galilean villagers taken away into distant slavery by Roman soldiers; he had undoubtedly heard about other villagers who had voluntarily abandoned their impoverished homeland for the better prospects of life in Jewish communities elsewhere in the Mediterranean world. Those people, too, were the "lost sheep of Israel," who would soon be redeemed. Though living far away from the Promised Land and in cities, mines, and work camps—not only villages—they were potential members of the Renewed Israel. And even though Antipas was making serious efforts to become their official protector, Jesus envisioned a different reality, one in which the scattered, harried people of Israel would finally abandon all hope in the seductive appeal of a Herodian-style kingly messiah and "come from east and west and sit at table in the kingdom of God" (Luke 13:29).

For those who followed Jesus, the time for the Renewal of Israel—so long expected and prayed for—had finally come. Yet the hard, historical consequences of Jesus' decision to travel to Jerusalem would be as unexpected as they were fateful. Living all his life in Galilee, Jesus clearly underestimated the power of another pharaoh, not of the House of Herod, but of the great City of Rome. Herod Antipas might have hoped someday to rule from Jerusalem, but for the time being the Romans were there. As a result, the outcome of Jesus' decision to mount a defiant prophetic demonstration in Jerusalem, before the eyes of the entire Jewish people, would be unexpectedly violent. And that tragic, violent outcome would lead at least some of Jesus' original Galilean followers down the path to Christianity.

4

Power and Public Order

I N THE SPRING of the year of creation 3790 by the reckoning of the
Jewish sages (the sixteenth year of the reign of Tiberius Julius Caesar
Augustus to most other civilized people), there were things on the
Imperial Prefect's mind far more important than crowd control for the
Passover festival in the city streets, public squares, and private courtyards of
Jerusalem. In Rome, the world's only *truly* Holy City, where Marcus Vincius
and Gaius Cassius Longinus now served as consuls, the age of the "new men"
had apparently dawned at last. A career officer named Lucius Aelius Sejanus,
who served as Praetorian Prefect—commanding the imperial guards and
overseeing all domestic security matters—had won the complete confidence of the emperor. Old Tiberius, now spending most of his time away
from Rome at his island retreat at Capri, had left the day-to-day affairs of the
empire largely to him. Rumors had it that Sejanus, though only of knightly
rank, aspired to the purple. And if an *eques* like Sejanus could aspire to the
world's highest office, his success would expand the horizons and possibilities of many a faithful imperial servant—not least among them the
Imperial Prefect of Judea, an ambitious, dedicated man named Pontius
Pilate, now serving in this particularly thankless and difficult posting at the
very edge of the civilized world.

Ever since the humiliating exile, more than twenty years before, of
Herod's heir Archelaus, Judea had been administered as the emperor's
private possession by a series of no-nonsense colonial officials who knew

that riots, rebellions, or persistent deficits would be highly deleterious to the subsequent course of their careers. And for the previous four years, since around 26 C.E., Pilate had faithfully carried out the twin responsibilities of his office: taming and Romanizing this parched rump of the late Herod's larger kingdom and enriching his coffers and Romanizing his public persona. For Pontius Pilate had ambitions like every other civil servant who dreamed of being back in the Roman Forum, of rising to acknowledge the adulation of the crowd and—who knows—perhaps even sitting at the right hand of his patron Sejanus, who might someday become emperor himself. Judea, the Jews, and Jerusalem were not important in themselves but only as stepping stones to greater glory. And Pilate seems to have recognized early on that the keys to success in this age of ambition and political positioning were balancing the books, keeping public order, and keeping his ears and eyes open for potentially significant changes in the ruling echelons in Rome.

Despite his latter-day fame as one of the main characters in the stories of the passion and crucifixion of Jesus, however, Pontius Pilate (or Pontius Pilatus, as his name was spelled in Latin) is a rather shadowy historical figure whose personal origins and eventual fate are unknown. The only identifiable archaeological remains of his ten years' service in Judea are a series of bronze coins (bearing a mixture of religious and imperial symbols) and a single badly damaged Latin inscription from Caesarea discovered in the early 1960s that records his dedication in Judea's main harbor city of a "Tiberieum" or sanctuary to the imperial cult. This is in perfect accord with what we know of Pilate from the few brief mentions he received in the writings of Tacitus, Philo of Alexandria, and Josephus. For Pilate was apparently an aggressive promoter of Roman power and the imperial cult. Early in his administration he reportedly dispatched his troops from their winter quarters in Caesarea up to Jerusalem, marching with their battle standards raised proudly, and with their golden eagles and other imperial insignia glinting brightly in the sun. All previous Roman prefects had understood that the Jews—with their superstitious fear of images of gods, humans, and animals—could become unruly at the sight of imperial standards, so they felt it wise to avoid trouble and equip their forces with specially fashioned standards with all idolatrous images removed. But Pilate was not one to make special concessions. It was only when angry crowds of Jewish townspeople and villagers descended on Caesarea, and— in the face of Roman soldiers with their swords bared—proved that they were ready to die rather than allow graven images to be brought into the Holy City of Jerusalem, that Pilate was finally forced to swallow his pride and order the offending standards withdrawn.

And then there was the matter of the Temple treasury, which in Pilate's eyes represented a large concentration of valuable resources that were simply going to waste. The city of Jerusalem, steadily growing since its massive rebuilding and expansion by Herod the Great, was badly in need of a new water supply. Located high in the hill country, far from any lake or river—and having only rainwater cisterns and a single spring to supply it—Jerusalem was a public health disaster just waiting to happen. Even though advanced Roman aqueduct technology could solve the city's water problems and funds were available in the Temple, the priests who controlled the treasury of tithes and offerings gathered from all the People of Israel refused to allow even a portion to be handed over to the Roman authorities. So Pilate simply took matters into his own hands, to force the Judeans to do what simple common sense dictated they should. He sent soldiers into the Temple compound, confiscated the funds in question, and ordered the construction of a proper aqueduct. And when crowds of Judeans massed in Jerusalem to protest the project, Pilate was ready. Soldiers armed with clubs and dressed in civilian clothing mixed with the protesters. At a prearranged signal they violently and bloodily scattered the crowds.

So thanks to Pilate, Jerusalem now had a modern water supply— despite what he considered to be the militant, self-destructive backward- ness of its inhabitants. Even if he had to back down on the matter of the battle standards and—later—in an attempt to decorate his Jerusalem residence with ornamental shields bearing not images but merely Latin *inscriptions* to the divine status of the emperor, he had reason to be optimis- tic about the long-range prospects of his term in Judea, even though there were some clear pitfalls along the way. The most notable of these obstacles was the unique, not to say unseemly, status of the local dynasty of client kings, who had been lowered in status by Augustus but not yet completely deposed. Those bothersome Herodians, with their international reputation and powerful connections, were not to be taken lightly. The ambitious tetrarch Herod Antipas, after all, would have liked nothing more than to demonstrate that he could rule Judea far more peaceably and profitably than a mere prefect. Pilate therefore had to be ever vigilant to guard against civil unrest anywhere in Judea, lest unfavorable news or unpleasant gossip about his own performance be spread by Herodian supporters among the ruling circles in Rome.

Jerusalem at festival times was the most dangerous potential source of political embarrassment, for the tens of thousands who gathered there for each of the three major pilgrimage festivals could be a source of disorder and violence. Whatever Pilate may have known about the substance of the celebrations—commemorating events in the history of the independent People of Israel and its liberation from tyranny—he was clearly aware that the festivals provided occasions for arriving peasants, far from home and the restrictions of community, to let off some steam. Young men and women came to Jerusalem from all over the Land of Israel, and indeed from the entire diaspora, to breathe the air of freedom, have fun, make trouble, and give vent to the pain of their narrowly circumscribed lives. Of course there were many wealthy, respectable people among the pilgrims, and at the center of it all were the solemn ceremonies in the Temple courts of purification and dedication, firstfruits and free-will offerings, sin offerings, peace offerings, and live sacrifices offered by the linen-robed priests. Yet the festivals permitted even the most humble of the pilgrims to forget their daily problems. Tenants and workers were released for a few days from the demands of landlords and nobles. The harsh realities of debt and dispossession took a backseat—at least for a while—to the sight of smoke rising from the altar and the stories of the ancient liberation of the People of Israel by God.

That year, Jerusalem was preparing for the usual, massive influx of Passover pilgrims. With tens of thousands of peasants from all over the country now filling up the inns and courtyards of the city and the surrounding villages, paying their copper coins for admittance to the ritual baths to purify them of their spiritual and cultic impurity and buying sheep and sacrificial birds from authorized dealers for offering in the Temple, it would be all Pilate's few hundred men could do to prevent a drunkard's rage or a fistfight between strangers from exploding into a riot resulting in the death of soldiers or the destruction of imperial property—news of which would undoubtedly get back to Rome. Such incidents would not look good when the time came for his superiors to review his record and recommend him for promotion. So if things got out of hand, Pilate would waste no time in calling out the troops to take care of any troublemakers, "mingling their blood with their sacrifices," as he reportedly did with a group of anonymous Galilean pilgrims described in the Gospel of Luke 13:1. Pilate knew that his twin goals in Judea were to pacify and Romanize the province and to advance his own political ambitions. The two were inextricably combined. And whether in symbols of imperial power minted on coins, technological innovations like aqueducts, or quelling civil disturbances, he would use all the means he had at his disposal both to transform Judea into a modern province and to defeat the unruly forces that were dedicated to keeping it, in his eyes, stubbornly uncivilized.

JESUS' FATEFUL TRIP to the Passover festival of 30 C.E. with his closest circle of followers has always been seen as the defining moment in the history of Christianity. Symbolically reenacted every year in Christian churches the world over, the events of Holy Week begin with the commemoration of Jesus' triumphant, messianic entry into Jerusalem on Palm Sunday, continue with the remembrance of his "casting out of the money changers" from the courtyards of the Temple, and culminate in the solemn rituals related to the Last Supper on Holy Thursday, his trial and crucifixion on Good Friday, and his Easter Sunday resurrection from the tomb. Yet the Passion Narratives in the gospels—which have always been the main narrative sources for this yearly observance—offer a complex web of conflicting details, chronological discrepancies, and theological interpretations that greatly complicate any definitive judgment on the historicity of any of the individual incidents. The most that modern historians are willing to agree on is that Jesus went to Jerusalem with a close circle of followers; that he performed some sort of disruptive demonstration in the Temple; that he was accused of blasphemy and sedition by the priestly authorities; and that he was crucified as a rebel against the imperial order by soldiers of the Roman garrison.

That sequence of events would have been tragically familiar to anyone in first-century Jerusalem, a place where, as Josephus described, sometimes with almost bored indifference, the grim fates awaited a long procession of folk-prophets, would-be messiahs, and self-appointed wonder workers who roused the crowds or created disturbances in the Temple at festival times. But what set Jesus of Nazareth apart from all these other countercultural figures? And what are we to make of the extraordinarily detailed tradition that grew up around his final, climactic visit to Jerusalem? For some modern scholars, truth is indeed in the details. Raymond E. Brown, in his massive, thoroughly documented study *The Death of the Messiah*, insists that there is a sound basis for many of the specific events described in the Passion Narratives. For him, the gospel stories are "history remembered"—remembered vaguely and perhaps incorrectly in some cases, but history nonetheless. Other scholars dismiss the story of Jesus' last week in Jerusalem as a pious fiction—inspirational, moving, and heartfelt—but fiction nonetheless. For them, the Passion Narratives are "prophecy historicized," to use the words of the leading Historical Jesus scholar John Dominic Crossan. According to Crossan's perspective, the later followers of Jesus, with deep faith in his messianic identity, carefully combed the Hebrew scriptures for messianic themes and allusions and wove them into a highly symbolic story of Jesus' last week on earth. Their intention was to understand and explain why he came to Jerusalem, what happened to him there, and why his arrest and crucifixion was far different from that of a common criminal.

There is no question that the gospel writers were deeply concerned with prophetic fulfillment; at certain points in each of their stories they very pointedly cited specific biblical passages in Greek translation—showing how ancient prophecies were precisely fulfilled in the events of Jesus' death. But which came first, the event or the interpretation? In many cases, it is impossible to tell. And to complicate the issue—and to allow history to be considerably more complex than true-or-false, black-and-white academic categories of "history remembered" or "prophecy historicized"—we have to recognize that the significance of the events might have been bitterly contested soon after they happened, even by people who had witnessed or participated in them themselves. As we have seen, certain biblical prophecies could be used to bolster hopes in a royal messianic tradition like that cherished by the Herodians, while others were quoted to support an anti-kingly ideal. Thus both Jesus and his Herodian and priestly opponents, in acting out certain traditional "scripts" deeply embedded in Israelite culture, may *already* have been attempting to actualize conflicting prophetic expectations in public by their intentionally symbolic words and actions in Jerusalem's Temple courtyards and city squares.

Although only the Gospel of Luke mentions Antipas's presence in Jerusalem on this particular Passover (23:6–16), the pilgrimage festivals were the perfect occasions for displays of Herodian prestige and power, and the appearance of Herodian families there had become something of a routine. Jerusalem had itself become something of a monument to the

Herodian dynasty, with their royal history inscribed on the very walls of the city, where the looming towers Phasael, Hippicus, and Mariamne preserved the names of a brother, friend, and wife of Herod the Great. Herodian prestige was also visible in the monumental palace in the Upper City where the Roman prefects now resided; it could be seen in the tomb of David in the Lower City, lavishly embellished by Herod himself. The massive Temple was, of course, the centerpiece. Herod the Great had been so deeply associated with its conception, building, and maintenance that it was recognized the world over almost as a Herodian family shrine. Thus despite the ruling of Augustus that had restricted Herod Antipas's territorial sovereignty to the Galilee, he had particular political reasons for making a grand appearance in Jerusalem during this particular Passover festival: having recently beheaded a popular prophet, he would have had good reason to emphasize his pious public image as generous patron of the Temple and protector of world Jewry. And his ceremonial entry into the city before the festival would have been orchestrated in appropriate regal style—with a large entourage and with obligatory acclamation by Jerusalemites dependent for their livelihoods on the Temple's vast bureaucracy and associated service industries.

We know this because Josephus repeatedly mentions the Herodian fondness for public spectacles; indeed, the traditional Christian celebration of "the triumphal entry" into Jerusalem on Palm Sunday stands squarely in the tradition of Herodian messianism in its unabashed imperial mode. Herod the Great was famous for his ostentatious entrances into cities he visited, and just eight years after this particular Passover—in 38 C.E.— Herod's grandson (and Antipas's nephew) Agrippa passed through the streets of Alexandria in a grand procession "accompanied by bodyguards in gleaming armor of silver and gold," according to the account of Philo. That spectacle made such a deep impression among the increasingly anti-Jewish population of the city that some young Greeks reportedly crowned a local simpleton as a mock king and greeted him with false adulation, shouting out the Aramaic word *marin*, "our lord." That anecdote may offer us a new understanding of the meaning of Jesus' entry into Jerusalem—both of the visual form of royal processions of this period and in the mock-royal parades that they could provoke. For centuries—even today—in the solemn, ritualized Palm Sunday processions that wind their way down the Mount of Olives toward the walled Old City of Jerusalem, high-ranking priests and prelates of many distinct denominations and ancient church traditions, dressed in garments of brocade and gold mitres, commemorate Jesus' entrance into the Holy City with all the trappings of royalty. Yet the "prophecy historicized" by Jesus and his followers in his "triumphal procession" would appear rather to have been an intentional and skillful political parody. If we strip away the layers of ecclesiastical tradition and attempt to reconstruct the situation in first-century Jerusalem, we may see that Jesus was not seriously claiming royal honors but bitterly mocking the messianic pretensions of the Herodian family.

Centuries before, the Judean prophet Zechariah—exposing the empty braggadocio of the Davidic dynasty, whose last princes were powerless, orphan heirs—had articulated an appropriate "script" for the parody that Jesus now enacted. At a time when real-life kings strutted their arrogance and rode through the city gates on handsome chargers in full royal regalia, Zechariah personified the figure of Israel's true redeemer in a much more modest way. "Lo, your king comes to you! Triumphant and victorious is he, humble, and riding on an ass" (Zech. 9:9). Yet the gospel accounts do not grasp the irony of either Zechariah's oracle or its performance by Jesus as street theater. The crowd's acclamation of the prophet Jesus riding into the Holy City has been taken at face value not only by the evangelists but by later Christian commentators, who believed that the crowd identified Jesus of Nazareth as the true Davidic king. Yet it is clear that—with his donkey and tattered peasant clothing—Jesus was parodying the kind of procession that would have been familiar to the people of Jerusalem. How much clearer those royal symbols must have been for the people and pilgrims of Jerusalem when the peasant-prophet Jesus entered the city to the ostensible acclaim of the crowd. Even though Matthew tried to make sure that his readers did not miss the source of the prophecy by quoting the words of Zechariah (Matt. 21:4–5), the true power of Jesus' demonstration, like so many other public acts he had performed since the start of his ministry, made the prophetic point more vividly in its visual symbolism than quoted scripture could ever do.

Could there be anything but ridicule of Antipas when the followers of Jesus called out in acclamation to their donkey-riding "king" and covered his path with the same messianic palm fronds that Herod Antipas so conspicuously inscribed on his coins? It is significant that Luke (19:39) reported that some Pharisees in the crowd approached Jesus and sternly told him, "Teacher, rebuke your disciples." But were they to be rebuked for sedition or sarcasm? It is inconceivable that Jesus—the tireless preacher against the evils of wealth and royal power—would have taken upon himself the mantle and trappings of the Davidic dynasty: that was precisely the kind of royal thinking that he had fought against so powerfully in the villages and towns of Galilee. And it is extremely unlikely that he now suddenly abandoned his vision of the kingless Kingdom. For as we will see, Jesus' subsequent prophetic demonstrations in the Temple and against Jerusalem's ruling institutions were all perfectly consonant with his larger vision of a Renewed Israel.

JESUS' PRINCIPAL PROPHETIC FOCUS was the Temple, now filled with Passover pilgrims. That monumental edifice created a powerful visual impression on the many visitors, both Jewish and Gentile, who have left universally admiring descriptions of its appearance in antiquity. Rising above the close-packed quarters of the city, its massive podium and surrounding colonnades sheltered the inner courts of the Temple complex, within which stood the Sanctuary. Through the recent excavations along the southern wall of the Temple compound and detailed examination of the physical remains around the present area of the Dome of the Rock and the al-Aqsa mosque—combined with the ancient descriptions—the physical appearance and layout of the Temple is becoming increasingly clear. Most ancient visitors, ascending a monumental staircase on the southern side of the Temple platform, would have passed through underground tunnels to emerge on the broad plaza to the south of the Temple itself. There, in the surrounding shaded colonnades and opulent royal stoa built by King Herod, were all the services needed by the arriving pilgrims: facilities for the purchase of ritually pure doves, oil, and flour for offering; ritual baths for purifying immersion and places to exchange normal clothing for the white robes of the Temple worshippers; and bankers' tables set up to serve the pilgrims by exchanging the countless coins of the Roman world's many kingdoms, provinces, tetrarchies, and principalities into currency acceptable to the Temple's treasury. Beyond the main entrance plaza, the Temple compound loomed like a raised island of even greater sanctity, whose entrances were jealously supervised by Temple officers called Levites— hereditary clans of service personnel. The admittance to these inner courts was restricted to Israelites who had undergone ritual purification, and that sanctity of participation in Temple worship was enforced stringently. Fragments of two ominous stone inscriptions that were affixed to the low wall around the inner courtyards have been recovered, with their carefully chiseled letters highlighted with red paint. Their Greek texts (clearly intended for those pagan visitors to Jerusalem who might have been unwitting, innocent tourists) read: "No foreigner is to enter within the forecourt and the balustrade around the sanctuary. Whoever is caught will have himself to blame for his subsequent death."

Inside that balustrade lay a series of courts entered through imposing gates, aligned from east to west, and oriented toward the Sanctuary structure of the Temple. In the first courtyard, the so-called "Women's Court," the worshippers assembled for communal occasions and could use the services of the wood and oil stores and the chambers for ritual purification. Beyond lay the inner court of the Temple, entered through the massive Nicanor Gate with its towering bronze doors and flight of fifteen semicircular steps. This area served as a stage for public readings of the Law and performances of the Temple musicians and singers, who were also drawn from the clans of the Levites. At times of festivals and public worship, the doors remained open and even those Israelites not directly connected with the worship could see the priests solemnly sacrificing on the huge main altar in that inner courtyard. Every day, a contingent of priests chosen by lot would offer up live sacrifices on behalf of the entire people and then bring to the altar the many private offerings brought by individuals for the fulfillment of purification rituals, various religious obligations, and personal vows. Still farther inward were the open doors of the Sanctuary structure in which could be seen—though perhaps only dimly in the darkness—the golden altar of incense, the golden table of offerings, and the golden menorah, which came to symbolize the entire Temple cult. No one but the High Priest ever entered the innermost chamber, the Holy of Holies, at the rear of the Sanctuary. But it was there, on the Day of Atonement, that he represented the entire People of Israel in a moment of direct contact with the presence of God.

How strange and impressive and intimidating this complex of marble and gold, of incense, blood, and solemn ritual must have seemed to peasants, day laborers, and fishermen who were making their first pilgrimage from the Galilee. It wasn't just a matter of the three-day journey and the expenses that staying in Jerusalem would have cost them. It wasn't just the sight of the structures that soared into the sky like mountains, the magnificent appearance of the priests and the great Jewish nobles who had come from the four corners of the world to participate in the festivals, and it wasn't even the frightening press of tens of thousands of people (to villagers for whom population was counted in the dozens and where everyone, good and bad, was known by name and family affiliation) that made it so strange. And it wasn't just that the Temple was a distant Jerusalem institution existing far from the daily grind of peasant lives. Over the centuries since the destruction of Solomon's Temple by the Babylonians, the rural population of Judea, and later of Galilee as well, had gone back and forth in its allegiance to the Temple—ranging from what seems to have been wholehearted identification at times of external threat (as during the Maccabean rebellion) to widespread passive resistance and evasion of the growing burden of tithes, offerings, and taxes that were required of them. Its official representatives and most energetic supporters were to be found all over the country—in the families of the twenty-four priestly "divisions," most of whom served in Jerusalem for only short periods, and in the "scribes and the Pharisees" mentioned often in the gospels, who apparently served in the villages as experts in the Law and religious functionaries. Their presence among the rural population would have been conspicuous, especially at the times of firstfruits and harvest, when they supervised the collection of offerings and tithes. And despite their assurances that the Temple and its elaborate sacrificial cult were meant for the benefit of all Israel, the real sacrifices seemed to be those made by the already overtaxed and hard-pressed peasantry.

In short, the vast ritual of hierarchical holiness and strictly divided spaces appeared to be the very antithesis of the covenantal ideals of those hilltop communities of fiercely independent Israelite men, women, and children who insisted that they had no lord to rule over them except God. Thus we come to the great paradox of the Temple: in order to enshrine the idea of the Covenant directly between the people and God, a huge bureaucratic organization had arisen at the central cult place, maintained by a vast civil service of scribes, administrators, accountants, service personnel, Temple officers, and high priestly families who were all dependent on the Temple revenues for their support. According to the Torah, the Temple tithes and offerings were meant to ensure God's blessing for the country's agricultural bounty. Yet they also placed a significant economic burden on the rural population when other taxes and tribute were also in place. And when the priestly hierarchy was seen living in luxury and passively acceding to the demands of the ungodly Romans by authorizing a daily sacrifice for the well-being of the emperor (as was the practice since the beginning of direct Roman rule in Judea), there must have been a question in the minds of many of the People of Israel about which of the Temple's aspects—the covenantal or the oppressive—was the dominant one.

It is against this historical background that we must view the actions of Jesus in Jerusalem. He arrived in the city as a traditional prophet of Israel who came to pronounce God's judgment against the ornate, Roman-style Temple—precisely at a time when God's kingless Kingdom was being realized in the rural communities' Renewal of Israel. This, in itself, was nothing new in the Israelite tradition. The classical prophets had repeatedly indicted the Temple, along with its sponsoring monarchy, for undermining the village life of the people and for violating rather than reinforcing the Covenant's basic social ideals. Even Isaiah, who had experienced a stunning vision of the heavenly Temple (6:1–5), had pronounced God's absolute condemnation of the Temple rituals and offerings that drained the economic life blood of the people: "What to me is the multitude of your sacrifices? says the Lord; I have had enough of burnt offerings of rams and the fat of fed beasts; I do not delight in the blood of bulls, or of lambs, or of he-goats" (1:11). Rather, Isaiah insisted, speaking in the name of God, "Bring no more vain offerings, incense is an abomination to me. New moon and sabbath and the calling of assemblies—I cannot endure iniquity and solemn assembly. Your new moons and your appointed feasts my soul hates; they have become a burden to me, I am weary of bearing them" (1:13–14). What was important was the fulfillment of the Commandments with the recognition of their real purpose, and in a passage we have already quoted, Isaiah reminded the people to "remove the evil of your doings from before my eyes; cease to do evil, learn to do good; seek justice, correct oppression; defend the fatherless, plead for the widow" (1:16–17). Likewise, the prophet Jeremiah from the village of Anatoth had pronounced the end of God's patience with the priestly establishment in Jerusalem because they had perpetually broken the Covenant—stealing, murdering, swearing falsely—but still supposed that they could successfully appease God in their observance of the Temple cult. Echoing the words of Micah, Jeremiah proclaimed that God was about to destroy the Temple: "Zion shall be plowed as a field; Jerusalem shall become a heap of ruins, and the mountain of the House, a wooded height" (26:18).

The Temple was meant to be a means to the end of the redemption of Israel, not an end in itself. The prophets focused rather on the security and sufficiency of the people, the true "Zion" or "Mountain of the Lord." The "new heaven and new earth" they envisaged (Isa. 65:17) would not come as a result of some cataclysmic transformation of the world as they knew it but would dawn as an earthly era of social justice and peaceful, shared prosperity, just as had been promised for the People of Israel, secure in their villages and tribal inheritances, in the original vision of the Mosaic Covenant. Although the gospels relate that those who testified that Jesus had pronounced ominous curses against the Temple were "false witnesses" (Matt. 26:59–61; Mark 14:56–59), the multiple traditions of Jesus' threat to destroy the Temple (Mark 13:2; 15:29) and the pains taken in John's Gospel to explain such a tradition away by claiming that he was merely "speaking of the 'temple' of his body" (2:21) strengthen the solid historical basis on which they rest. It was a true prophet's obligation to speak out against injustice. And no less powerful in that respect were Jesus' symbolic actions in the Temple's very courtyards. The theological interpretations of his "casting out of the moneylenders" have long pictured Jesus as a religious reformer fired by righteous indignation at the corruption he found in the Temple, or as one who was purifying the Temple of base (Jewish) rituals and monetary dealings in order to prepare it for the purer worship that would come with the inclusion of the Gentiles in a transformed mode of worship of the God of Israel. But this bold demonstration must be seen against the background of an Israelite prophetic past, not a Christian future: in the vivid memories of overturned tables, coins scattered on the pavement, and the fluttering of sacrificial doves suddenly freed from their pens are echoes of earlier prophetic demonstrations. Thus Ahijah the Shilonite ripped up a new garment into twelve pieces to symbolize the imminent disintegration of David's kingdom (1 Kings 11:29–39) and followed it with a pronouncement of God's judgment against the Davidic dynasty. And the prophet Jeremiah appeared in Jerusalem's Valley of Hinnom in the presence of "the elders of the people and some of the senior priests," smashing a pottery jar and crying out with God's threat that "so will I break this people and this city, as one breaks a potter's vessel, so that it can never be mended" (19:11).

The action of Jesus in the Temple, when taken together with his mockery of the kingly arrogance of Antipas, can thus be understood as a dramatic prophetic performance of the divine action he believed was imminent. With the inauguration of a new era in the history of his people, Jesus was not rejecting the traditions or divine election of Israel. Far from it;

in healing withered limbs and casting out demons from possessed Galilean peasants, fishermen, and workers, Jesus was acting as a prophet to help the People of Israel regain control over their lives and livelihoods. He had come to Jerusalem to announce the coming of God's Kingdom and to pronounce God's verdict against all those who remained part of the problem and refused to dedicate themselves to the solution. The booths of money changers and dove sellers were not important in themselves but had become part of a vast cultic system supported by peasants' sacrifices and offerings that siphoned off resources which could otherwise have kept families and whole villages viable. Whether or not Jesus understood exactly how profitable the Temple services were for the few families that controlled them; whether he understood the tangled history of the priesthood under Herod the Great and the extent of their subservience to the Romans, he gave voice to the frustrations of every faithful Israelite who wondered if the rebuilt Herodian Temple with its massive bronze gates and Corinthian columns was really the true House of the God of Israel. There might have been many in the crowd of pilgrims in the outer courtyard of the Temple who would have dismissed Jesus as just another peasant agitator and would have disagreed with his conclusions. But few would have mistaken what he was doing. As he smashed tables and scattered silver coins across the pavement, the voice of God seemed to possess him with a peasant prophet's fiery oracle that the Kingdom of God was at hand.

FROM THEIR ELEGANT VILLAS in the Upper City overlooking the Temple, the several high-priestly families, who had been exalted to their position of power by Herod the Great, should have felt uneasy. They were perched in a dangerous position between the masses of the Israelite population and the coldly imperious officials of Rome. Ever since the vast expansion of the Temple structures and institutions, these high-priestly families and families of priestly officers in charge of the Temple's treasury, workshops, storerooms, and supply facilities had amassed considerable fortunes, passing down their particular responsibilities and privileges—and wealth— from fathers to sons. Unlike the members of the twenty-four priestly courses who lived throughout the country, these priestly officials were permanent residents of the Holy City, and the impressive archaeological remains of their Jerusalem residences show how elegant their lifestyle had become. In spacious structures unhesitatingly dubbed "mansions" by the archaeologists who uncovered them in the 1970s, we can get a glimpse of a lavish life in mosaic-floored reception rooms and dining rooms with elaborate painted and carved stucco wall decoration and with a wealth of fine tableware, glassware, carved stone tabletops and other interior furnishings, and elegant peristyles. The discovery of an incised depiction of the Temple menorah on the wall of one of the houses and an inscribed weight bearing the name of Bar Katros, one of the high-priestly families, make the connection with the Temple aristocracy particularly clear. Their wealth and prominence in Judean society has been further underlined by the elaborate family tombs which they built on the outskirts of the city. One such tomb, recently discovered about a mile and a half south of the Old City, contained a carved stone ossuary, or ceremonial bone container, bearing an Aramaic inscription reading "Yehoseph Bar Kayyaf"—identified by scholars as the final resting place of the remains of Joseph Caiaphas, the High Priest at the time of Jesus' last pilgrimage to Jerusalem.

Beyond the fascinating recovered relics, however, lies a more sobering historical reality. For it is quite clear that the continued wealth of the high-priestly families and their political fortunes were dependent on the Roman authorities. Piety and righteousness had long since ceased being the main criteria for a High Priest's successful term in office; ever since the deposition of Archelaus, the High Priests had been the *de facto* representatives of the Judean people to the Roman authorities and they were saddled with the responsibility of maintaining order in Jerusalem. Roman officials could— and did—appoint them to office or depose them at will. Thus the High Priest and his high-ranking assistants, who were nominally in charge of the Temple and enjoyed considerable benefits from the booming pilgrim offerings and revenues, did not act from a position of strength. In fact, they—as much as the Romans—were held hostage by the festival throngs, hoping against hope that the explosive mix of God, freedom, money, and celebration and the city streets would not detonate the appearance of public order, which in the best of times was a brittle veneer. They were even held hostage to the actions of the lower priesthood, those lesser men from the countryside brought to serve in their appointed courses for weeklong stints and festival duty in the Temple. For if these country priests were ever to declare that the behavior of their wealthy superiors was incorrect or ritually invalid, who knows what would happen to the rule of the Temple— and, more important, to the Judean people's acceptance of the rule of Rome?

It is impossible to know whether or how much the high-priestly officials learned about the spectacle of Jesus' "messianic" entry into Jerusalem, but they surely could not have been unaware of the disturbance he caused within the Temple precincts. In addition to the constant patrols of Levite guards and watchmen within the Temple compound, a permanent garrison of Roman auxiliaries was stationed in the massive Antonia Fortress at the northwestern corner of the Temple enclosure, and at festival times they patrolled back and forth along the flat roofs of the overlooking colonnades, always on the watch for some tumult or seditious action on the part of the pilgrim crowd. They need not have acted immediately. More than once we hear from Josephus of uproars in the courtyards that were allowed to run their course—for at least a little while. But once the people had been allowed to let off a little steam or if the disturbance threatened to spread to other parts of the city, the Temple authorities stepped aside as the army stepped in. Through the first century, in fact, there were apparently so many popular demonstrations and riots that it is almost impossible to say with absolute certainty how the authorities may have reacted in a particular case. The gospel stories were written decades later, apparently based on oral traditions and theological interpretations of the meaning and significance of Jesus' death. No eyewitness or official of the administration was likely to have been available for interviewing. And although countless scholars have combed through rabbinic legislation and Roman administrative annals to find suitable precedents for the gospel episodes concerning the arrest and trial of Jesus, no abstract principle of policy or precedent of imperial administration is likely to be much help in understanding this particular chain of events.

Just imagine the situation from the perspective of the Temple authorities: the city was filled to the brim with pilgrims and the Roman authorities were in no mood for nonsense. Pontius Pilate had learned from the hard experience of the incidents of the standards and the aqueduct that administering this province and its quarrelsome people must be done forcefully yet quietly. Herod Antipas was greatly complicating the situation in Judea by his ambitious pursuit of a more prominent position and, presumably, by his very presence in the city for the festival. And here, all of a sudden, comes a peasant prophet (apparently already well known in the villages of Galilee) attracting attention by staging a mocking "triumphal" entry into the city and then making his way into the Temple plaza with his followers, overturning tables and destroying Temple property. No civil or ecclesiastical authority—then or now—would ever tolerate this kind of behavior; it threatened the kind of order and respectability that they stood for, and their support of the Roman authority on which their power now depended. And then, as now, there must undoubtedly have been procedures in place to take care of rabblerousers and madmen who stirred up the crowds at festival times. As we will see several decades later in the arrest of Paul in the Temple and in the many cases reported by Josephus, the security personnel in the Temple and the soldiers in the Antonia Fortress knew precisely what to do. If the disturbance was serious enough and access to the Temple court was possible, they intervened immediately to arrest and interrogate the suspect.

In other cases, they would wait until the pilgrims' excitement had cooled and the city was quiet before decisively eliminating the source of the threat. And that is what seems to have happened with Jesus: whether by a tip provided by an informer or by their own investigation among those present in the Temple courtyard, the authorities apparently learned of Jesus' whereabouts and ordered him arrested. After a last supper with his followers, he was taken into custody and questioned. And assuming that, like Elijah or Jeremiah before him, he defiantly refused to abandon his prophetic mission and disown his actions and oracles, his fate was sealed by the executive decisions of fairly low-level security officers whose names we will never know. In his analysis of the Passion Narratives, John Dominic Crossan frames the situation succinctly, explaining why an intricate analysis of the details of the highly embellished gospel accounts would be pointless: "There would be no need to go very high up the chain of command for a peasant nuisance nobody like Jesus, no need for a formal interrogation before Caiaphas, let alone a detailed trial by Pilate. In the case of Jesus, there may well have been Arrest and Execution but no trial whatsoever in between."

Had Jesus of Nazareth been merely a lone mouthpiece of the Spirit-pronouncing oracles, he would probably have been simply thrown out of Jerusalem after a sound thrashing as happened to another Jesus, the son of Ananias, somewhat more than thirty years later, in 62 C.E. "Four years before the war," related the historian Josephus Flavius, "when the city was enjoying profound peace and prosperity, there came to the feast at which it is the custom of all Judeans to erect tabernacles to God, one Jesus, son of Ananias, a rude peasant, who, standing in the temple, suddenly began to cry out, 'A voice from the east, a voice from the west, a voice from the four winds; a voice against Jerusalem and the sanctuary, a voice against the bridegroom and the bride, a voice against all the people.' Day and night he went about all the alleys with this cry on his lips. Some of the leading citizens, incensed at these ill-omened words, arrested the fellow and severely chastised him. But he, without a word on his own behalf or for the private ear of those who smote him, only continued his cries as before. Thereupon, the magistrates, supposing, as was indeed the case, that the man was under some supernatural impulse, brought him before the Roman governor; there, although flayed to the bone with scourges, he neither sued for mercy or shed a tear, but, merely introducing the most mournful variations into his ejaculations, responded to each stroke with 'Woe to Jerusalem!' When Albinus, the governor, asked him who and whence he was and why he uttered these cries, he answered him never a word, but unceasingly reiterated his dirge over the city, until Albinus pronounced him a maniac and let him go."

Yet Jesus of Nazareth was a far greater threat than Jesus, son of Ananias, and he could not be safely sent away with mere cuts and bruises. He was not a lone "madman" but the leader of a growing movement of rural villagers and, now in Jerusalem, he compounded his general prophetic demonstration against Antipas and the Temple with some carefully aimed condemnations of the evils and injustices of the present regime. Even the Synoptic Gospels, which are demonstrably skittish about emphasizing the intensity of Jesus' assault on the ruling authorities, portrayed him in a series of sharp confrontations with the various ruling groups in Jerusalem. The Synoptic Gospels' parable of the "wicked tenants," for example (Matt. 21:33–46; Mark 12:1–12; Luke 20:9–19), pointedly fit the context of first-century Judea and Galilee in its detailed description of tenant farming in an atmosphere of tension and open violence between the sharecroppers and the collection agents of the absentee landlord. But at the same time, Jesus cleverly showed how the great landowners among the priestly and Herodian aristocracy who had transformed the rural landscape were themselves only tenants. Since God was the only true "proprietor" of the Land of Israel, He would surely strip them of their "tenancy rights" if they continued to shirk their obligations to faithfully cultivate God's vineyard or to respect the rights of the legitimate heirs.

And then there is the telling anecdote about the coin to be rendered to Caesar. In Mark 12:13–17 (paralleled in Matt. 22:15–22 and Luke 20:20–26), "some of the Pharisees and some of the Herodians," seeking to entrap

Jesus in a treasonable statement, ask him whether it was "lawful to pay taxes to Caesar or not." In Judea, under the direct rule of Rome since the ouster of Archelaus more than two decades earlier, the issue of imperial taxation had led to widespread agitation and public resistance. For the People of Israel to pay heavy taxes to their own kingly overlords was one thing; to have to pay them directly to a pagan emperor who claimed to be divine was both extortion and a direct violation of the Mosaic laws against idolatry. And even if Judeans and Israelites had, centuries before, given indirect tribute to the Assyrians, Babylonians, and Persians through the revenues of the king or the Temple, the people of the countryside had never before been subjected to such a direct and continuous assault by the corps of auditors, census takers, bookkeepers, and tax farmers sent out by the Romans. And there is no reason to believe that the deep-seated popular opposition to Roman taxation showed any signs of fading away.

Yet taxation was everything to the Romans; it was the very raison d'être of their empire. To oppose publicly their right to collect it was tantamount to a declaration of war. And so we come to the story of Jesus' famous phrase "Render unto Caesar . . ." with an understanding both of what he may have intended and how his listeners would have understood what he said. That means we should be under no anachronistic illusions that there could have been any distinction between "Church and State" or between "temporal" and "spiritual" kingdoms. Jesus merely sought to evade a trick question posed by his opponents: Is it lawful to pay taxes to Caesar or not? The tribute to Rome was based on the presumption that the emperor was the supreme owner and savior of the world. No such acknowledgment could ever be made by a true member of the Covenant of Israel. But Jesus took what was posed as an incriminating question and answered it in a way that proclaimed a sweeping condemnation of illegitimate Roman political power over Israel.

Jesus called for a coin bearing the imperial image and asked the questioner, "Whose likeness and inscription is this?" We have already seen in connection with the coinage of Herod Antipas what an important role imperial symbols played in circulating ideas of power among the general populace. Those coins were both the advertisement for kingly power and the currency in which proper political subservience had to be paid. Thus, in producing the coin or perhaps simply by repeating the phrase about it, Jesus skillfully reminded his listeners that Caesar's rule was arrogant, evil vanity. And then, as the story portrayed, Jesus spoke over the heads of the ostensible listeners to his followers and the people in general: "Render to Caesar the things that are Caesar's and to God the things that are God's." Could anyone have been in any doubt what things belonged to God—and what to Caesar? Since God had created the earth and everything in it, Jesus would have made it perfectly clear by his cryptic statement that nothing could legitimately be owed to Caesar at all.

The authorities in Jerusalem—priestly, Herodian, and prefectural—knew all too well the cost of excessive lenience when it came to a matter of popular unrest. To ignore the kind of an outburst that Jesus had made in the Temple and to ignore his dangerous teachings would only encourage others to follow his example. To allow him to get off with a simple scourging would only make him a hero in the eyes of his followers. It would be far more prudent to act quickly and decisively, to make an indelible impression on the assembled pilgrims who might otherwise have foolishly believed that this Jesus was a genuine prophet of God. Although the power of capital punishment was the sole prerogative of the Roman governor, he had no less an interest in maintaining the public order—and his reputation as a good administrator—than the Temple authorities.

Thus there is no need to speculate on how or why a cabal of High Priests would have wanted to frame Jesus or why in the world Pilate would have gone along with their conspiracy, even though, in the words of Luke's blatant apology in 23:4, he found "no crime in this man." The stories of Pilate washing his hands of the matter and the bloodthirsty screams of the rabble who chose Barabbas over Jesus are all the work of later Christian writers who—unlike Jesus—were desperately intimidated by the Romans and turned the blame on the Jews to divert accusations of disloyalty or rebellion away from themselves. In Jerusalem, the situation was clear-cut and would not have required extensive deliberations. Neither the High Priest, nor Herod Antipas, nor Pontius Pilate could allow themselves to be humiliated in public by a peasant prophet who spoke defiantly of their impending destruction and roused the populace to resist their rule—nonviolently. In the recent, celebrated case where John the Baptist had aroused the public "to the greatest degree by his sermons," Herod Antipas had decided "that it would be much better to strike first and be rid of him." Execution by beheading was the way that John the Baptist was dealt with. But that was too respectful a punishment for a troublemaking villager from Galilee. With Jesus in custody, utterly unrepentant, and persisting with his visions of a Redeemed Israel freed of the overlordship of the Romans, there was only one order that Pontius Pilate, the prefect of Judea and faithful servant of Tiberias Caesar, could possibly give. The people of Judea needed to be shown the terrible price of resistance. And for the good of the public order and as an exercise of imperial power, this Galilean "prophet" would have to be put to death in Jerusalem in the most painful, humiliating, and public way.

THERE SHOULD BE NO QUESTION or mystery about the brutality of Roman crucifixion. Were we not so familiar with the stylized image of Jesus on the cross and were we not so thoroughly programmed from our earliest schooldays to admire the grandeur, majesty, and technological sophistication of the Roman Empire (and so subtly trained to acquit a heartless imperial commandant like Pontius Pilate of his crimes and to blame the victims), we might be able to see this oppressive, genocidal, imperial mode of torture for what it was. All over the Mediterranean world, north to Gaul and across the Channel to Britain, Roman emperors, governors, prefects, and procurators had the power, and even the responsibility, to inflict unspeakable pain and physical suffering on any person whom their officers grabbed from the fields or the streets and identified— rightly or wrongly—as a threat to private property, public order, or state security. The horrible, prolonged process of crucifixion was described in detail by Cicero, Livy, Tacitus, and Seneca the Younger, so we have abundant independent evidence of its ghastliness, quite apart from the Passion Narratives. The condemned person would be stripped naked and humiliated in public and scourged soundly by soldiers with metal-tipped leather lashes. Then, forced to carry a heavy transverse beam, or *patibulum*, to the place of execution, the victim was brutally hung up on the vertical post. And he would remain there, guarded by soldiers, for as long as it took to die of his wounds or succumb to the asphyxiation caused by the sagging weight of his exhausted body—which was bound to the rough wooden cross with ropes or affixed there with jagged iron nails.

Although we are used to seeing the familiar images of the crucifixion of Jesus, with his arms outstretched and nailed at the palms to the crossbar, there was no single particular way that crucifixion was always done. In the only case where the remains of a crucified person have ever been recovered, archaeologists in Jerusalem excavated a tomb containing the bones of a young man whose arms had apparently been tied to the top of the crossbar and whose ankles had been nailed to the sides of the upright. The only object was pain and humiliation. In fact, Josephus Flavius reports that at the time of the Jewish Revolt against the Romans—some forty years after the execution of Jesus—the Roman soldiers on crucifixion detail had become so numbed to the violence and embittered against rebellious Judeans that they "nailed up their victims in different postures as a grim joke."

Thus, no less than the other powerful forms of visual communication used by the Romans, crucifixion was meant to convey a message—and such it was surely meant to be in the case of Jesus of Nazareth. The stench, screams, and horrible sights of the public places of execution on the outskirts of every Roman city offered a grotesque counterimage to the elegance and architectural splendor of the temples, forums, and plazas within. The cross and the Corinthian column were the two sides of the Roman experience. One offered shade and shelter to all those who would accept the Roman world's logic and structures of power; the other systematically transformed anyone branded as an enemy of the Roman order from a living, breathing person into a bruised, bloated, almost unrecognizable corpse. Crucifixion was as much communal punishment and state-sponsored terrorism as it was judicial vengeance against a particular crime. The crosses planted outside the cities warned potential rebels, runaway slaves, and rebellious prophets of what could happen to *them*.

In most cases, as we've said, there was not much in the way of formal proceedings. When the Roman governor Varus crucified two thousand Judeans in the summer of 4 B.C.E., there is little possibility that there were *any* formal proceedings. The point of crucifixion was precisely the fear of its sudden, merciless application; it was one of the purest forms of official, governmental violence. Thus, as so many exegetes and scholars have pointed out, the fact that Jesus of Nazareth was crucified is as eloquent a testimony as any to the depth and the clarity of the threat that he posed. This Galilean prophet could have been beaten like the later Jesus, he could have been beheaded like John the Baptist, or stoned as one who blasphemed the sanctity of the Temple. But this was a much more public matter, in which the power of the Roman administration and the public order of Jerusalem were at stake. We can have little doubt that after his arrest and a brief interrogation, this self-proclaimed Jeremiah was paraded, powerless, in front of the people. Mocked, scourged, and bound to a cross at Jerusalem's public place of execution, Jesus was left there to die a slow and painful death under the sagging weight of his bruised, naked body. The good news of the Kingdom of God would now have to be spread by others. His prophetic demonstration against the powers-that-be in Jerusalem had come to an end.

5

Preaching the Word

THE DREAM SEEMED TO FLICKER OUT with Jesus' painful, humiliating execution, but there was something about the idea of reviving the glory of Israel through a revitalization of its traditional village life that simply refused to die. In the decades that followed the crucifixion, several distinctive variations of the Renewal Movement crystallized around the memories of Jesus held by various groups of his followers. While these followers still saw themselves as being entirely within the Israelite tradition, they began the process of gradual differentiation that would eventually result in the emergence of a new religion—though still retaining many local variations of Israelite belief and ritual—known as Christianity. But the process was a slow one, deeply affected by local conditions and events. Far from Jerusalem, in the hard-pressed towns and villages of Galilee where people had been touched by Jesus' personality and message, the news of his death would have slowly spread from the returning pilgrims and then would have traveled by word of mouth through the courtyards, markets, and fields. Many people would undoubtedly have viewed his death as a tragedy, yet another example of the tragic destiny that awaited all true prophets of Israel under the continuing reign of terror of the Romans and Herodians. Others might have just shaken their heads sadly, with their basic skepticism of Jesus' message of effecting the Renewal of Israel merely confirmed. But it is unlikely that any of those Galilean peasants, fisherfolk, and workers learning about the crucifixion of

Jesus in Jerusalem would have heard the now-familiar stories of Good Friday and Easter Sunday. The empty tomb and the resurrection would not become prominent themes until much later. In fact, it is quite possible that the close circle of Galilean followers who accompanied Jesus to Jerusalem for that fateful and tragic Passover pilgrimage may not have had any idea at all of the exact location of Jesus' burial place or even the final fate of his mortal remains.

As John Dominic Crossan has so powerfully pointed out in his studies of the gospel Passion Narratives and their importance in early church traditions, it is important to realize just how horrifying Jesus' execution must have seemed at the time. One of the cruelest aspects of Roman crucifixion was the way it robbed its victims of even their post-mortem existence, for in most cases, the bodies of the victims would be left hanging on their crosses long after they died—to be slowly picked apart by crows or scavenging dogs. That was an essential part of the punishment meted out to any slave, peasant, or rebel who dared to challenge Roman authority. In some cases, the body would eventually be taken down and buried by Roman soldiers, irreverently and shallowly, but certainly not in a respectable family tomb. Only in those highly exceptional circumstances, where the crucified victim's friends and family were prominent enough, wealthy and savvy enough to bribe the proper officials, or secure enough in their public positions not to fear open identification with a condemned criminal, could they claim the body from the authorities and see that it was properly laid to rest.

The general archaeological situation in Jerusalem seems to confirm the rarity of proper burial for those who were crucified. Josephus explicitly mentioned the crucifixion of almost ten thousand individuals in Jerusalem in the course of several widespread rebellions against the Romans, and we can safely assume that many more people were nailed to crosses in times of relative tranquility (at least in the eyes of the Romans) as punishment for individual acts of murder and robbery or solitary protests. And despite the fact that hundreds of family tombs—and the bones of thousands of individuals—from first-century Jerusalem have been excavated in a broad swath of cemeteries ringing the southern, eastern, and northern outskirts of the ancient city, only a *single* skeleton bearing the signs of crucifixion (with a jagged iron spike driven through the victim's ankle bone) has ever been identified. The remains of the thousands of other crucified victims of Rome's quest to impose brutal order on the people of Judea have simply disappeared from the archaeological record, apparently exposed to the elements or scavenging animals. And for their families and survivors back in the first century, the loss of the physical body would have signified a horrible, restless fate for the departed soul. That was crucifixion's final, cruel humiliation. Crossan and other scholars have therefore suggested that the gospel stories of the intervention of the wealthy Joseph of Arimethea in retrieving Jesus' body from Pilate and making sure that it received a proper burial may have been later idealizations of a much grimmer historical reality—and the stories were told, retold, and embellished over the coming decades precisely because Jesus' fate at the hands of the Romans was so ignominious.

This, of course, is a very modern, skeptical way of looking at Good Friday and Easter Sunday. For centuries, the burial of Jesus and the miracle of the empty tomb were unhesitatingly considered to be historical events. The only real question about them was where they took place. The location of Jerusalem's public place of execution seems to have survived in folklore and popular tradition for centuries—and those folk memories apparently proved invaluable in the search for Jesus' tomb that was mounted in the early fourth century C.E. by Queen Helena, mother of the first Christian emperor, Constantine. Reportedly also guided by divine inspiration, the visiting empress became convinced that her Jerusalem workmen and diggers had found not only the tomb of Jesus, but also the nearby hill of Golgotha and the remains of the True Cross. No expense was spared in the subsequent construction of the Church of the Holy Sepulchre to commemorate and preserve Christendom's holiest sites. And from that time onward, the ever-expanding complex of chapels, domes, columns, and bedrock outcroppings served as the spiritual and physical objective for the quests of Crusaders and pilgrims, and was revered all over the Christian world. Even persistent nineteenth-century Protestant doubts about the Holy Sepulchre's authenticity (it was located in the *middle* of the city after all—an impossible place for both corpses and tombs in light of ancient Jewish purity laws!) did nothing to shake the general belief in the historical reality of Jesus' crucifixion and resurrection. The rejection of the icon-laden Church of the Holy Sepulchre by many Protestants merely paved the way for their own identification and veneration of the burial place of Jesus in a quiet, parklike spot to the north of the walled city that they called "The Garden Tomb."

Ironically, the current scholarly consensus about the location of

Golgotha and the tomb of Joseph of Arimethea has, after so much dispute
and dissension, concluded that the site of the Holy Sepulchre might be the
genuine one after all. The extensive archaeological excavations carried out
among the ruins, open spaces, and beneath the streets of the Old City of
Jerusalem since 1967 have revealed Jerusalem's city walls followed an
unpredictably irregular circuit in the early Roman period. Most archaeologists now agree that the site of the Church of the Holy Sepulchre was
located *outside* one of the city walls' zigzags at the time of Jesus—and that
area could indeed have served as an extramural place of execution by the
Roman authorities. Add to that the evidence of the remains of several typical
first-century chamber tombs that have been discovered beneath the floors of
some of the Church's chapels (suggesting that the area was used for burials),
and it seems that the Holy Sepulchre's historical reliability can no longer be
entirely dismissed. A case can—and is—made by some scholars for the
basic historicity of the gospel stories of the crucifixion, the intercession of
Joseph of Arimethea, and perhaps the vigil of some of Jesus' closest followers
around the tomb. But for the immediate purposes of the story we are telling,
the precise details of Jesus' passion and burial in Jerusalem had little impact
on the further dramatic developments of his movement. For despite the
gruesome martyrdom of its first great proponent, the quest for the Kingdom
of God through the renewal of the Covenant of Israel went on without
interruption in the towns and villages of Galilee.

THE DISTURBING NEWS of Jesus' death may indeed have passed
quickly northward to Galilee and then spread throughout the surrounding
region, and it was there in Jesus' home region that one of the most
important and longlasting variants of the Renewal Movement lived on.
While some of Jesus' early followers were undoubtedly discouraged and
abandoned the movement, others apparently had their faith and commitment confirmed. Indeed, the Renewal Movement seems to have gone on
substantially as before—without a change in any of its main goals or the
introduction of any new rituals. We know this because the earliest collection of traditions about Jesus (of which we have any evidence) makes no
reference to Jesus' crucifixion, resurrection, or divine status. It does not
mention Jesus' miraculous appearances to a select group of apostles, instructing them to "go therefore make disciples of all nations, baptizing
them in the name of the Father and of the Son, and of the Holy Spirit"

(Matt. 28:19). It is, instead, a collection of pithy, colorful, and provocatively short speeches about the Kingdom of God, with each set of sayings dealing with a special concern of the movement: how covenantal relations might be restored in village communities; how new communities might be brought into the movement; and how individual members should act toward their oppressors and enemies.

This is the famous "Q" Sayings Gospel, named for the German word *Quelle*, or source, that was initially recognized by nineteenth-century biblical scholars, who carefully catalogued the passages in the gospels of Matthew and Luke in which the wording was almost identical. As a result of their painstaking textual comparison, they theorized that the authors of the gospels of Matthew and Luke had both utilized an earlier source containing a collection of the sayings of Jesus which they each wove together—in their own characteristic ways—with the concise narrative that had been provided by the Gospel of Mark. The fact that an independent collection of Jesus' sayings—lacking a narrative, biographical structure—could have existed was confirmed by the discovery in Egypt in 1945 of a similar "Sayings Gospel of Thomas" among the long-lost Nag Hammadi texts. But as an apparent source of Matthew and Luke, "Q" is considered to be much earlier and offers a unique glimpse at the mindset of the Galilean followers of Jesus, who are depicted in the gospels as coming in crowds to be healed by him, to be fed by him, and to listen to his preaching but who mysteriously disappeared from the gospel picture once he left for Jerusalem.

The speeches in Q offer some important clues about the kinds of issues and concerns that gripped those first followers of Jesus. And the fact that their collection of traditions was preserved for decades, circulating for a considerable time as an oral tradition before being set down in writing and used by Luke and Matthew, suggests that it represented the cherished beliefs and memories of living communities that survived for many years. Who they were is another matter. Some scholars who have studied Q more in the context of wider Greco-Roman cultural currents have likened the people who preserved the Q sayings to the Cynics of the Greek world— free-thinking vagabond philosophers who spoke out brazenly in public places, contesting the conventional wisdom and preaching a counter-cultural lifestyle of radical individualism, free of property, parents, and propriety. The scholars of the modern "Cynic school" of interpretation have tended to read Q as a compendium of individualistic ethics without reference to a concrete social context, and have characterized some of the most famous sayings of Jesus as more playful than prophetic. In their view, Jesus was a provocative sage, adept at clever repartee. In his declarations that "blessed are you poor, for yours is the kingdom of God" (Matt. 5:3; Luke 6:20), Jesus was remembered as the sage teacher who advised his followers to "love your enemies, do good to those who hate you, bless those who curse you, pray for those who abuse you" (Matt. 5:43–44; Luke 6:27–28), and "don't judge and you won't be judged" (Matt. 7:1–2; Luke 6:37). According to this historical perspective, the mission of those who joined in this enterprise would be, like first-century flower children, to abandon normal routines of life and "leave the dead to bury the dead; but as for you go and proclaim the Kingdom of God" (Matt. 8:22; Luke 9:60).

In our earlier chapter on Jesus' Galilean ministry we argued that the sayings of Jesus were not abstract ethical injunctions but powerful political prescriptions—integral expressions of ongoing political, economic, and religious revitalization among the towns and villages of Galilee. We do not see Jesus' teachings as free-floating, intoxicating puffs of countercultural wisdom, attractive to individuals who, like the ancient Cynics, were alienated from, but still very much a part of, the dominant culture. Quite to the contrary, we see the teachings and sayings of Jesus as a powerful communal response to the very real conditions of poverty and oppression that prevailed among the villages of Galilee both before and after Jesus' brief public ministry. The "Cynic" characterization of Jesus and his early followers reduces his movement to an individualistic culture-criticism, which would hardly have generated any lasting community institutions or group consciousness. First-century Galilee was a place where class differences were real and painfully visible on the landscape, where elite culture was an instrument of control and oppression, and where traditional ethnic identity, however vaguely remembered or stretched across political boundaries, was an embattled, last bastion of communities striving to retain at least some measure of autonomy.

All too often, comfortable modern scholars fail to grasp the profound inequalities built into the very structure of Greco-Roman society, strictly segregating those who enjoyed the fruits of technology and cultural expression from those less civilized natives who paid the bill. Many modern commentators believe that the new archaeological evidence of the spread of Greek language, the establishment of cities "proud of their Hellenistic institutions, including theaters, sporting arenas (*gymnasia*), and schools," proves that "Hellenistic culture was taken for granted" by everyone and could serve as the medium through which the countercultural tenets of Cynic philosophy spread even among the peasantry. That assumption of equal access for all who would wish to climb the social ladder demeans the repeated protests of those Galileans who recognized that the new styles and new logic of the Greco-Roman world provided their rulers with the instruments of their own oppression and shaped the landscape of the power that took away their identity. No run-of-the-mill Galilean peasant would ever have been allowed to mingle with the wealthy and witty urbanites in the theaters, sporting arenas, or schools of Sepphoris and Tiberias where Cynic philosophy was supposedly taught and discussed.

The "Q" Sayings Gospel does, in fact, offer us a glimpse of the Renewal Movement in Galilee after the death of Jesus, but it is a movement still deeply rooted in an independent Israelite identity, using the symbols of Covenant and community to battle a continuing Herodian threat. The speeches in Q clearly include political assertions that are not in the least playful. They include Jesus' respectful references to the fiery preaching of John the Baptist, who had been martyred by Herod Antipas (Matt. 11:9–11; Luke 7:26–28); his curses against the villages of Bethsaida, Chorazin, and Capernaum, whose people have apparently refused to join the movement of resistance (Matt. 11:21–24; Luke 10:13–15); predictions of the imminent humbling of the high and mighty (Matt. 8:11–12; Luke 13:28–30); and reassurances of the power of the Law of Moses and the role of his followers as leaders of a movement of national liberation—"judges" after the manner of the biblical heroes Gideon, Samson, and Deborah, whose "judging" was, in fact, charismatic leadership over the twelve tribes of Israel (Matt. 19:28; Luke 22:28–30). These more militant, Israel-oriented sayings have been ascribed by some scholars to a later layer of tradition within Q, when opposition and political change forced the Q people to abandon their carefree Cynicism. But this theory of progressive divergence from the original ideals of an edenic group of countercultural pranksters springs from its own preconception with the primacy of pure cultural critique in the Jesus Movement. It is thought to have embodied a refreshingly cosmopolitan aversion to narrow provincialism and to have been driven by freewheeling individualism. That may be a pleasing modern way to think of the earliest followers of Jesus, but it has little to do with what was going on in the Galilee.

Although it is difficult to date archaeological layers with the precision of less than a decade, we do know from the frequency of new coin-types minted by Herod Antipas that the late 20s and early 30s was a time of exceptionally intense economic and political activity in his tetrarchy. By that time, his new capital city of Tiberias by the shore of the Sea of Galilee would have been fully constructed, with its markets and civic institutions fully functioning. Antipas may also have intensified his activities on the east bank of the Jordan: at the site of the ancient town of Betharamphtha he established or expanded a modern city named Julias. This apparently took place sometime soon after 29 C.E., to commemorate the death and deification of Augustus's widow Livia, now known by her dynastic name Julia. No less important was Antipas's growing interest in the wider Mediterranean world and in his continuing patronage of Jewish Diaspora communities. Dedicatory inscriptions mentioning the benefactions of Herod Antipas (styled as "Herod, son of Herod the King") have been discovered at the great healing center at the Temple of Asclepius on the island of Kos in the Aegean and the Temple of Apollo and commercial center of Delos, both places that are known to have had large Jewish communities that had been extensively patronized by Herod the Great. And from Josephus's descriptions of Antipas's lavish banquets with his family in the coastal city of Tyre, it is more than likely that he continued his father's tradition of beneficence to the Hellenistic cities of Phoenicia and Syria—in the form of funds to erect roads, aqueducts, and impressive public buildings, and of course in making conspicuous personal appearances in those cities, presenting himself as the kind of thoroughly Romanized kingly figure that he wanted to be.

All this activity took financial resources and there was really only one place that Antipas could get them: through continuing and even intensified taxation of the rural inhabitants of his land. Those who might describe the Q community in this period as "dancing to the pipes," as the New Testament scholar Burton Mack puts it, minimize or even ignore the very real hardships, social dislocation, and disintegration of families that continued as before. Jesus offered the people of Galilee a way to respond to the threat of the new order, and we see, in addition to the prophetic speeches in Q, other kinds of memories of Jesus' brief ministry in the region that served as the watchwords and vivid, symbolic images that kept alive his activist program for the Renewal of Israel. In addition to the familiar collections of sayings, story-tellers repeatedly retold the tales of Jesus' prophetic acts of power, his healings and exorcisms, and his fearless confrontations with the representatives of the ruling authorities. It is going too far to suggest that every cluster of textual tradition that later found its way into the gospels represented a separate group of Jesus' followers, each with a different understanding of who he was and what he intended. But it can certainly be said that in the year or so that he moved through the Galilee, and perhaps into the surrounding territories, Jesus made a profound impression—so profound, in fact, that stories, embellished legends, and poetic descriptions continued to circulate as both a guide to effective resistance and as powerful expressions of the legacy of Israel.

The so-called "pronouncement stories," for instance, later incorporated in the Gospel of Mark, cover a wide range of subjects of particular concern to the people of Galilee. His followers remembered his unforgettable phrases: "It is easier for a camel to go through the eye of a needle than for a rich man to enter the Kingdom of God" (Mark 10:25). Or when asked why he and his hungry followers gathered grain from the fields and thereby violated the Sabbath, he was remembered to have responded, "The Sabbath was made for humans, not humans for the Sabbath" (Mark 2:27). It is easy to imagine how these memorable sayings might have become familiar proverbs—attributed to Jesus—and repeated again and again when the appropriate situation arose. From this period, too, we can perhaps trace the spread of the stories of the miracles of Jesus and see how they expressed the basic message of the liberation and Renewal of Israel. The tales of Jesus walking on water, calming the storm, and feeding the multitudes from a handful of loaves and fishes take on their full significance when they are seen as echoes of Israel's great saga of independence. The waves of the Sea of Galilee might not exactly be the Red Sea and the loaves and fishes might not be exactly manna, but the point was succinctly and symbolically made that Jesus was leading Israel on a new Exodus from the bondage of another tyrannical pharaoh, right now in current times. And just as Moses had conveyed a precious law code to the people, Jesus—as a new Moses—was restoring the essence of the Covenant. And the stories of the new Exodus miracles eventually began to combine with the stories of Jesus' Elijah-like performances and healings. And despite the mixed scriptural metaphors and allusions, the growing collections of sayings and stories about Jesus served as a means of remembering the powerful and persuasive message that Jesus enunciated so clearly: pay no allegiance to earthly kings and tetrarchs; reach out to friends and neighbors; renew the timeless Covenant of the People of Israel and enter the kingless Kingdom of God!

How far this message traveled, transmitting the wit of Jesus' clever sayings or the amazing stories of healings and natural wonders, is impossible to know. The rugged hill country of Upper Galilee rolled imperceptibly northward into the rugged hill country of southern Phoenicia. The eastern lakeshore district of Antipas's territory was just a short walk or boat ride from the tetrarchy of his brother Philip. And from there, the villages extended northeastward toward the city of Damascus and the Roman province of Syria. The movement inspired by Jesus and carried on in his name after his execution was clearly identified with the traditions of Israel, but in this rural region and in this period of history, the distinction between "Jew" and "Gentile" was sometimes both fuzzy and unclear. Though educated scribes could consult genealogies and literary traditions to carefully delineate where the northern tribal divisions of Zebulun, Issachar, Asher, Dan, and Naphtali began and ended, the ties of family, landholding, and marriage between people in adjoining villages could carry the feeling of being *connected* to the House of Israel far beyond the scriptural boundaries. Relatives and in-laws linked communities and traditions in a living sense of community that transcended geographical definitions or facile criteria of Israelite ethnicity. In the shared past were cherished ancestors and epics. And all the villagers of this region now suffered under the same economic and social pressures that Jesus sought to address.

Membership in the movement begun by Jesus wasn't a matter of sudden conversion to the transcendent belief in a crucified and resurrected messiah. The faith and hope he inspired were much more down to earth than that. The sayings of Jesus—as remembered or imagined—offered a set of quite specific instructions about the way that people should act in public and treat each other in order to bring the ancient community of Israel to life again. Some villagers may have reacted to it as a social experiment to be enacted quietly and in private; others may have seen the message of Jesus as a direct political program to challenge the rule of Herod Antipas and his ilk. Jesus of Nazareth might have been put to death to preserve the public law and order in Jerusalem during a particular Passover festival, but what he did and how he died in Jerusalem was far less important in the years that immediately followed his execution than the spreading impact of the movement he founded in the hill country towns and lakeside villages of Galilee.

WHAT ABOUT Jesus' famous disciples? So far we have only briefly mentioned the role played in his ministry by that close circle of followers who are first identified as the "Twelve" in the Gospel of Mark 3:14–19. Multiple gospel traditions indicate that Jesus delegated the preaching of the Kingdom and its manifestation in healings and exorcisms to many others. Those remembered by name, including the Galilean fishermen Simon Peter, his brother Andrew, and James and John, the sons of Zebedee, were apparently prominent in the leadership of the movement after Jesus' crucifixion. There is no reason to doubt that they had been central figures in the movement during the Galilean ministry, spreading the message of the Renewal of Israel in villages and towns that Jesus may never have visited himself. The number twelve associated with this group clearly referred to the twelve tribes of Israel, but that number may well be only a symbolic one. Moreover, the use of the less specific terms "disciples" and "apostles" suggests that there was a far wider group of traveling preachers and healers who recognized Jesus as their mentor and carried the word to the villages and towns of the Land of Israel. That group, moreover, was almost certainly not exclusively male but included women, such as Mary of Magdala.

The Twelve—as a group and as individuals—play a particularly conspicuous role in the gospels. Peter, James, and John appear often in private conversations with Jesus, asking questions, receiving rebukes and instructions, witnessing the Transfiguration, and accompanying him to Jerusalem. One of the Twelve, Judas Iscariot, is blamed for betraying him. At the time of the arrest of Jesus, all of the Twelve reportedly fled. The historical reliability of these events and descriptions remain the subject of intense debate between scholars. And archaeology and social history are, in this case, clumsy tools to verify the specific actions of these individuals. As we have seen, we can talk easily about the wider village Renewal Movement in its first-century context or about the social effects of violent repression within the Roman Empire, but how particular individuals would have acted when their prophet-leader was arrested, publicly humiliated, and cruelly executed by the forces of civil order is impossible to tell. What is clear is that the small group of early Galilean followers of Jesus known as the Twelve played an increasingly important role in the movement for the

Renewal of Israel *after* the crucifixion. For whether or not the events of Good Friday and Easter unfolded exactly as they were described in the gospels, the *memory* of those events established the Twelve in a unique position of authority.

Later Christian tradition recognized the Twelve as followers who had a direct and immediate encounter with Jesus after the crucifixion, though the precise details—or even general character—of that encounter are variously retold. The Gospel of Mark 16:1–7 relates that Mary of Magdala, Mary the mother of James, and Salome, upon discovering Jesus' tomb was empty, were told by a mysterious young man, dressed in white and sitting inside it, that they should "go, tell his disciples and Peter that he is going before you to Galilee; there you will see him as he told you." Chapter 28 of the Gospel of Matthew also tells the story of the women (now only the two Marys) going to the empty tomb on Sunday and receiving instructions (now from an angel, not a young man). Yet verse 16 of this gospel adds the details of the subsequent appearance of Jesus, appearing directly to "the eleven disciples" (minus the treacherous Judas Iscariot) and commissioning them to "go therefore and make disciples of all nations." In yet another story, the Gospel of Luke 24 describes how Jesus appeared to two otherwise unidentified disciples as they walked on the road to the Judean village of Emmaus; how he appeared again to Peter; and once again in the presence of the Eleven in Jerusalem. And the Gospel of John—which contains the most elaborate resurrection stories of all—has the risen Jesus appear to Mary of Magdala; the Twelve in Jerusalem; again, eight days later in Jerusalem, to show his wounds to doubting Thomas; and then finally to his disciples "by the Sea of Tiberias."

In whatever way these diverging stories are reconciled as versions of the same events (or explained by scholars as spiritual epiphanies, hallucinations, or spirit possession), one thing seems quite clear from the letters of Paul, which were written only about twenty years later. By the mid-30s, there was in the city of Jerusalem a group of Jesus' Galilean followers famous both for their devotion to the memory and teachings of Jesus, and for having had direct contact with him after his death. Those post-crucifixion contacts convinced the Jerusalem community that they had a unique, divine mandate to speak in the name of Jesus. And that was something that the scattered Q village communities to the north, with their continuing traditions of Jesus the prophet —with their conspicuous silence on the matter of his death or resurrection—either did not agree with or knew nothing about. In fact, it might legitimately be asked why, if Jesus had been so singlemindedly devoted to the practical ideal of the renewal of the villages of Israel through the egalitarian devotion of its peasants to their covenantal tradition, did a core group of fishermen and farmers want to abandon the hills, lakeshore, and valleys for the crowded, noisy, and chaotic city of Jerusalem? If Jesus had merely come to Jerusalem to condemn the ruling establishment and pronounce prophetic condemnations of the messianic aspirations of the Herodians and the top-heavy Temple bureaucracy, why in the world wouldn't all of the members of his closest circle of followers return to Galilee to carry on his work in the regions where it had the greatest impact and thereby help bring on the Kingdom of God?

Surely the establishment of a permanent community of the Renewal Movement in Jerusalem represented a dramatic departure from the agrarian origins of the movement. Over the last quarter century, the series of intensive, large-scale archaeological excavations undertaken in Jerusalem has offered us a glimpse at just how different the urban landscape in the alleyways, gates, and public spaces of Jerusalem was from those of first-century Galilee. Sepphoris and Tiberias were, despite Herod Antipas's pretensions, just the small administrative centers of an out-of-the-way tetrarchy. Jerusalem was a city with an empire-wide reputation. We have already mentioned the opulent residential quarter that occupied the Upper City, where the priestly and secular aristocracies built their palatial villas overlooking the Temple compound and the monumental platform and entrances to the Temple itself, with the royal stoa and the outer courtyards, lined with the stands of the dove-sellers and the tables of the money changers, eager to offer their services to the throngs of visitors. We have also described the large-scale crafts industries and supply facilities that ensured the smooth running of the Temple throughout the year. A large corps of Temple accountants kept track of the tithes and contributions, and hospices and inns throughout the city catered for the thrice-yearly influx of pilgrims. But there was more, much more, than the priestly establishment and the Temple-related industries to first-century Jerusalem.

From ancient descriptions and modern archaeological findings, we know that the bazaar-stalls throughout the city were filled with the fruit of the labor of countless workers and tradesmen: jewelry, wrought iron, spun and dyed textiles, shoes, sandals, incense, bread, cakes, oil, soap, fresh meat, pottery, perfumes, stone vessels, and glassware were only a few of the products hawked on the streets and in Jerusalem's shopkeepers' stalls. And down the steep slope of Jerusalem's Lower City, the thin spine of hillside that had served as the main urban area in the times of David and Solomon had now become the crowded living and working quarters for the Jerusalemites who made everything else possible. Though the recent excavations of the City of David have not uncovered much more than the badly eroded remains of close-packed houses, cisterns, and ritual baths from the time of Jesus, we know from Josephus and from later rabbinic literature that this part of the Lower City and the adjoining slopes of the Tyropoeon, or "Cheesemakers," Valley was the principal residence of the tradespeople and day laborers who made up the bulk of Jerusalem's poor.

These people, too, were the lost sheep of Israel, brought into the city over the decades—simultaneously pushed out of the rural areas through dispossession of family holdings and lured to the city by the attractions of work in construction or in the thousand and one other jobs that could be had in Jerusalem. For landless peasants, the prospect of steady employment in the construction of the Temple must have been an offer too good to refuse: Josephus later reported, "If anyone worked but for one hour of the day, he at once received his pay for this." And scores of references in rabbinic literature to wood cutters, porters, watchmen, bathhouse attendants, tanners, fullers, dung collectors, messengers, butchers, donkey drivers, barbers, and dyers suggest just how commonplace and essential wage laboring had become. In fact, the problems of rural debt and tenant farming that Jesus had confronted in Galilee could be seen from another perspective in the streets and bazaars of Jerusalem. The swelling urban population there was part of the same economic transformation from traditional peasant agriculture to empire-wide commerce that had spread throughout the Land of Israel and to communities throughout the diaspora.

What was to be done about it? How could the utter dependence and bitter competition of everyday people for daily wages be exchanged for the ideals of sharing and cooperation of the village life of the Covenant? And how could the establishment of a community of Jesus' closest followers in Jerusalem bring it about? We have only the evidence of the Book of Acts and a few brief references in Paul's letters to help us reconstruct the character and history of the earliest Jerusalem community. Yet there are some clear hints that its organization represented a fateful step away from a purely rural movement to one in which the Kingdom of God slowly became a metaphor. The Book of Acts makes no mention of any return by the disciples to Galilee but rather describes the explicit directive by the Risen Jesus to the apostles to "be my witnesses in Jerusalem and in all Judea and Samaria" (1:8). And in whatever way we read the subsequent sequence in Acts describing the election of a new member of the Twelve to replace Judas; the conspicuous leadership of Peter; and the fiery gift of the Spirit to the assembled community at Pentecost, Acts 2:44–47 offers a striking description of the distinctive kind of alternative community set up by this group of disciples in Jerusalem. "And all who believed were together and had all things in common; and they sold their possessions and goods and distributed them to all, as any had need. And day by day attending the temple together and breaking bread in their homes, they partook of food with glad and generous hearts." The description is given slightly more detail in 4:34–35: "There was not a needy person among them, for as many as were possessors of lands or houses sold them, and brought the proceeds of what was sold and laid it at the apostles' feet; and distribution was made to each as any had need."

There is a tendency among scholars to see these descriptions as retrospective idealization, written decades later by a Greek-speaking evangelist who was more at home with the Greco-Roman philosophical ideals of communal living than with the egalitarian laws of the Israelite Covenant. In seeking comparisons to the Jerusalem community's primitive communism with the high praise offered in writings of Plato and Aristotle to those in the Greek world who would undertake the selfless sharing of private property, they overlook—as the New Testament scholar Brian Capper has noted—the distinctively Judean practice of donating all individual wealth and personal possessions to a communal treasury that is so clearly documented in the literature of the Dead Sea Scrolls. At precisely the same time and in the same small province of Judea, another group who condemned the evils of Roman society and opposed the present priestly leadership of the Temple had organized themselves into a community in which admission to full membership entailed handing over all individual earnings and private property.

Josephus's description of the widespread communities of the Essenes (whose connection with the Dead Sea Scroll community is still debated) suggests an underlying ideal: "Riches they despise, and their community of goods is truly admirable; you will not find one among them distinguished by greater opulence than another. They have a law that new members on admission to the sect shall confiscate their property to the order, with the result that you will nowhere see either abject poverty or inordinate wealth; the individual's possessions join the common stock and all, like brothers, enjoy a single patrimony." This is all quite reminiscent of how the Book of Acts describes the Jerusalem community. And even if the colorful story in the Book of Acts 5:1–11 about the doomed couple Ananias and Sapphira who joined the community but secretly held back some of their assets is understood as a late, moralistic legend, the phenomenon of property sharing at this time and place is not at all alien to a first-century Judean context. More than that: the principle of creative economic cooperation and sharing between neighbors—as a practical technique of survival, not simply as an ethical virtue—was one of the cornerstones of Jesus' teachings about the way that the Kingdom of God might be gained.

Just as the traditions of the Q Community remembered Jesus' sayings about the difficulty of rich people entering the Kingdom of God and the virtue of selling all one's possessions as the key to separating from the injustices of the Roman economy and returning to the ideals of the clan-based Israelite villages, so too can the shared treasury of the Jerusalem community be seen as a conscious attempt to create a "village" in the streets and slums of the city—which had become the new home of so many former Israelite peasants who had been forced off their land. In their encounter with the harsh social reality of Jerusalem, a group of Jesus' followers—who may or may not have been considered by all his followers to be the most prominent or most natural heirs of his movement—began to interpret Jesus' message in this wider way.

Although the gospels and the later Christian tradition identified Peter, John, James, and nine other disciples as the core and guiding leadership of the movement, we must be careful of retrospective judgments about what form the program of renewal preached by Jesus was destined to take. What began as a rural movement, whose language was that of fishermen, peasants, and debtors—expressed in pithy sayings about barns, oxen, threshing floors, birds' nests, mustard seeds, and lilies of the field—would also become a campaign of outreach to the lost sheep of Israel everywhere. At this point in the unfolding historical picture, we cannot be sure of precisely what the founders of the Jerusalem community believed or what rituals they engaged in, beyond a fervent belief in the necessity for establishing a kingless Kingdom of God. Though many commentators have seen the reference in Acts 2:46 to the community's "breaking bread in their homes" and partaking of food "with glad and generous hearts" as an early reference to the ceremony of the Eucharist, there is no need to see this as anything but a continuation of the custom of banqueting to celebrate the joys of the Kingdom that was so much a part of Jesus' Galilean ministry.

The problem posed by empire for the continued survival of the People of Israel was far more sweeping than tenant farming, excessive taxation, or the arrogance of Herodian client kings. For Galileans, Judeans, and Jewish communities throughout the Mediterranean, a way had to be found to maintain sacred, ancestral traditions of Covenant and community without abandoning the unique social vision they contained. Now, at a time of rapid economic change and political subservience to the Roman Empire, a powerful, many-faceted prophetic movement had begun. Even as the memory of Jesus' plan for the Renewal of Israel was being preserved in collections of his sayings circulating in the villages of Galilee and adjoining regions, a slightly different set of memories and ideals was being crystallized in Jerusalem. And as subsequent developments would show, this community's ideology was far more dangerous to the authority of the priestly aristocracy and the ambitions of the Herodian House than the bucolic dreams of peasants. For if the renewal and liberation of Israel could be furthered with the establishment of a "village" in the metropolis of Jerusalem, then the ideal of a covenantal village-in-the-city might prove successful in establishing economic autonomy and resistance to the empire *everywhere* in the Jewish world.

We have no reason to believe that the first Jerusalem community of the Renewal Movement was regarded as either heretical or blasphemous by the majority of Jerusalemites. So long as its members maintained a fairly low profile and did not—as their late prophet Jesus did—disturb the public order with flamboyant demonstrations of passion and moral outrage—they were regarded as just another shade in the ideological spectrum of Israelite belief. While the intervention on their behalf by the famous Pharisaic Rabbi Gamaliel described in Acts 5:34-39 is probably not reliably historical (but based on later polemics with the early rabbis), Josephus confirms the contention of Acts that the Jerusalem community was still stable and thriving a full three decades after the crucifixion. More than that: Josephus observed that the later judicial execution of James, the brother of Jesus who had risen to the leadership of the Jerusalem community, offended "those of the inhabitants of the city who were considered the most fair-minded and who were strict in observance of the law." Thus we can reasonably assume that the community of Jesus' followers distinguished itself not by its antinomian religious dogma but by its unique social vision. And as we will see, that social vision could be powerfully translated to address the concerns and preoccupations of diaspora Jews as well.

IN ITS STORY of the steady, outward progress of the Jesus Movement from Judea to the farthest reaches of the Roman Empire, the Book of Acts stresses its immediate, powerful appeal not only to Galileans and Judeans but to pilgrims from all over the world. As the years passed, the appeal of the Jesus Movement to people *outside* Judea would become an increasingly significant factor in the course of its independent development. In Acts's vivid description of the descent of the Holy Spirit on the first Pentecost after the crucifixion—and the first instance of spontaneous "speaking in tongues" by the disciples—the people who suddenly understood the message of Jesus were many: "Parthians and Medes and Elamites and residents of Mesopotamia, Judea, and Cappadocia, Pontus, and Asia, Phrygia and Pamphylia, Egypt and the parts of Libya belonging to Cyrene, and visitors from Rome, both Jews and proselytes, Cretans and Arabians" (2:9–11). Soon afterward, the community of Galileans gained new members from far-flung places who would become important actors in the unfolding drama: among them Barnabas from Cyprus, Nicolaus from Antioch, Stephen, Philip, Prochorus, Nicanor, Timon, and other individuals who comprised a large and influential faction known in Acts as the "Hellenists." There has long been a debate among New Testament exegetes and scholars whether these "Hellenists" were Jews, Jewish converts, unconverted sympathizers, or perhaps even transient pagan visitors to Jerusalem. But the prominent New Testament scholar Martin Hengel has made a persuasive case for seeing them as Greek-speaking Jews (in distinction to the Aramaic-speaking Galileans and Judeans) who, for various reasons, had settled in Jerusalem and maintained separate communal identities based on their places of origin and their continued use of their Greek mother tongue. Nothing is necessarily implied by the term "Hellenist" about their religious outlook or attitude toward the Temple and the Law.

It was all a matter of group cohesion. The Book of Acts enumerated some of the many groups of foreign-born Jews who settled in Jerusalem and organized themselves into clearly delineated communities: "those who belonged to the assembly [*synagōgē*] of the Freedmen (as it was called) and of the Cyrenians and of the Alexandrian and of those from Cilicia and Asia"

(6:9). And archaeological evidence substantiates the existence of such groups of resident Greek-speaking foreigners. An inscribed block of limestone recovered from the slope of the Lower City of Jerusalem records, in Greek, the donation by Theodotus, son of Vettenus (a Latin-sounding name that may indicate a Roman origin), of a "synagogue for the reading of the law and instruction in the commandments; also the lodging, the guest room, and the water system to provide for those in need coming from abroad." Then as now, the motives for Jewish philanthropy and physical return to Zion could be many—prestige, pride, family ties, religious devotion—yet the pressure of active anti-Jewish persecution and the psychological burden of permanent minority status in the diaspora have always been among the most important incentives for a return to the Land of Israel. Many New Testament scholars have overlooked this political motivation for the presence of diaspora communities in Jerusalem—and, by extension, have not grasped the political orientation of the early Hellenist members of the Jerusalem Jesus community. Reduced to its simplest formulation, diaspora Jews came to Jerusalem to proclaim, practice, support, and preach their devotion to *ioudaismos*—a term that is usually translated "Judaism" or "Jewishness" (with its many unspoken modern associations of Torah-observance, dietary laws, and purely religious ritual) but which can perhaps be more accurately understood in the Roman period as a new, militant ideology of political solidarity and cultural autonomy for Jewish communities throughout the empire.

Over the centuries, as Judeans, Galileans, and other Israelites had gone into exile as slaves, mercenaries, prisoners of war, or voluntary expatriates, they formed local communities to preserve the main outlines of their customs and covenantal traditions, in whatever places they settled and in whichever form their customs were remembered or maintained. We have widely divergent archaeological and epigraphic evidence of scattered diaspora communities in Egypt, Cyrenaica (modern Libya), Asia Minor, and Greece. Their community councils and communal study-and-prayer gatherings were largely autonomous; yet at times of political crisis in Judea— such as the Maccabean Revolt—many diaspora communities acted simultaneously, if not in concert, to come to the aid of the Temple in Jerusalem. With the gradual unification of the Mediterranean under the Hellenistic kingdoms and with the establishment of more regular means of communication, a general Jewish Diaspora consciousness began to arise. Beginning first with the struggle against *hellenismos*, or the Hellenistic styles, logic, and economy that threatened traditional Jewish existence both in the diaspora and the Land of Israel, the political implications of subsequent Roman expansion throughout the Mediterranean sharply focused the practical goals of *ioudaismos*.

Economic survival, civil rights, and communal security became the most pressing issues as Jewish communities in the various Hellenistic cities and kingdoms came under the rule of a single Roman Empire. Although Roman leaders like Julius Caesar and Augustus guaranteed the Jewish communities extensive rights and powers of self-government as a semi-independent people, the civic elites in many of the major Hellenistic cities, perhaps smarting under their own loss of independence as Rome asserted its dominance—and certainly suspicious of the semi-independence of the alien elements in their midst—periodically tried to deny many of those Rome-guaranteed Jewish community rights. The anti-Semitic scenarios played out in the first century in the cities of Egypt, Cyrenaica, and Asia Minor are ominously familiar: scurrilous charges of disloyalty and xenophobic hatred against "the Jews" gradually gave way to officially sanctioned discrimination and, eventually, to mob violence against Jewish life and property.

For some Jews and Jewish communities, the solution to this threat lay in wholehearted support for the Herodian family, in the hope that Herodian power in Judea and their influence in the highest circles of Roman society would offer political protection to otherwise isolated Jewish communities. As Herod the Great and his sons gained fame for their lavish gifts of public buildings and monuments to cities throughout the Mediterranean (and as those high-visibility benefactions by the King of Judea bolstered the prestige of the local Jewish communities), a sense began to grow that Jews everywhere had a stake in the kingdom of Judea and the Temple in Jerusalem. They were no longer helpless, scattered communities of refugees looking back in sorrow to a lost homeland but a worldwide people whose identity did not depend on living in the Land of Israel. Yet overt political support for the Herodians and devotion to the Temple were not the only ways that *ioudaismos* could be expressed. The diaspora also included countless poor laborers, craftspeople, military veterans, former farmers, and freed slaves who looked homeward to Zion with a prophetic, rather than a kingly, sensibility. Although we tend to homogenize the religious and political attitudes of ancient peoples, it is not unreasonable to suppose that at least some of the many diaspora Jews who returned to

Jerusalem for briefer or longer periods—like the "needy" mentioned in the Theodotus inscription—might have shared the widespread resentment against the economic injustice of Herodian and Roman Judea and the self-interested exactions of the Temple aristocracy. And in the literary tradition of the period we can trace a radical diaspora tradition that rejected the resort to client kingship or accommodation with the ruling powers in a distinctive literature of struggle and martyrdom.

The earliest occurrence of the term *ioudaismos* is, in fact, contained in a history of the Maccabean Revolt of the 160s B.C.E. written in Greek by Jason of Cyrene in North Africa, widely read and circulated among Jews of the Hellenistic diaspora, and known to later generations in its abridged form as The Second Book of Maccabees. In this work and in the texts that expand on its basic themes and stories, we can begin to see what kind of impact the ideal of martyrdom for the Renewal of Israel might have had on at least some diaspora Jews. In recounting the successful revolt led by Judah the Maccabee against the Seleucid Empire, a special importance is given to the place of righteous Judeans who died for the cause. Those martyrs' shining example of steadfast obedience to the laws and traditions of Israel—despite political oppression and physical suffering—served as models for the ongoing attempts of embattled diaspora Jewish communities to defend themselves, resist local persecutions, and reestablish rights of self-government. Most prominent are the figures of Eleazar, an aged, righteous sage, and seven heroic brothers who suffered public humiliation and eventual death by torture for their refusal to violate the laws of the Covenant—in this case, eating swines' flesh at the command of an imperial officer. The martyrs all readily acknowledged that the misfortunes of their people were due to their own sins, but as we have stressed in our description of Jesus' sayings, those "sins" are not to be understood as arbitrary, individual ethical or moral failings but specific violations of covenantal law. The failure of the People of Israel to carry out the divinely mandated regulations, social responsibilities, and communal obligations had—it was fervently believed—always brought on terrible consequences for which even the righteous had to suffer.

Yet the torture, pain, and martyrdom suffered by the righteous had a positive spiritual value. On the one hand, the martyr provided a role model for Jews everywhere who were faced with the grim choice of apostasy or death. The aged Eleazar chose the torture wheel, according to 2 Maccabees 6:28, "to leave the young a noble example of how to die willingly and nobly for the sacred and holy laws." And there was a further role for the martyr that was expressed clearly in Fourth Book of Maccabees, another Hellenistic Jewish work apparently produced in the early first century C.E. The martyr's death sounded a clarion call for repentance and renewal of the entire people. For if the misfortunes of Israel were caused by the sins of the nation—in their disregard of the covenantal laws of Sabbaths and festivals, social welfare, moral codes, and egalitarian social relations—those misfortunes would end once the Law was obeyed. As 4 Maccabees 18:3–4 put it: "Those men who surrendered their bodies to suffering for piety's sake were in return not only admired by mankind but were also deemed worthy of the divine portion. And it was because of them that our people enjoyed peace—they revived the observance of the law in their land and repulsed the enemies' siege." The great Maccabean victory over Antiochus Epiphanes was therefore ascribed not only to bravery or good generalship but to the recognition of the entire people—witnessing the death of the martyrs—that they must return to faithful observance of the Law.

IN THE CROWDED, bustling streets of Jerusalem—and in the great cities from which diaspora Jews came to Jerusalem as pilgrims or new immigrants—there could be no talk of a return to village life, except in its use as poignant metaphorical language of estate owners, tenants, servants, and harvests that would turn the hearts of the People of Israel back to the tradition of the Covenant. Peter, John, and James and the other members of the Twelve of the Jerusalem community presumably looked back upon the tragic death of Jesus at the hands of the Romans as an impetus to press on with the movement he had initiated, and to live out and preach out the word of the Renewal of Israel among all the lost sheep of Israel in the city of Jerusalem and beyond. And intentionally or unwittingly, their stories of the crucifixion and the appearances of Jesus to them meshed perfectly and powerfully with the idea of righteous martyrdom as understood in the diaspora. For just as God was believed to have granted the Maccabean martyrs the right "to stand beside the divine throne and live the life of the age of blessing," so would the stories of Jesus' appearances to his closest disciples serve as proof to some of his divine vindication as a latter-day saint of the People of Israel. It is impossible to determine when the community of Galilean followers of Jesus first began to attract the attention and sympathy of Jews from the diaspora, but the Book of Acts reports that within just a few years of the crucifixion, the growing community of the Renewal Movement in Jerusalem contained significant numbers both of Aramaic-speakers ("Hebrews") and Greek-speakers ("Hellenists").

To what extent they organized themselves into separate communities is only hinted at in the narrative of Acts 6:1, where a dispute between the Hebrews and the Hellenists over the allocation of community funds for the support of widows led to the appointment of "seven men of good repute" to oversee the distribution of food to the community's poor. This group of seven became, in the Acts account, the nucleus of the Hellenists' subsequent mission to the Gentiles. But there is serious reason to doubt that this group was really devoted only to table-service, or that its members ever intended to reach beyond the People of Israel. The Hellenists' "Seven" can be seen as a symbolic scriptural number, much like the Galileans' "Twelve," who were meant to judge the twelve tribes of a Renewed Israel. The appointment of the Seven is fully consistent with the first-century practice of appointing seven magistrates in every Judean town and village, which was drawn from the Deuteronomic injunction to "appoint judges and officers in all your towns which the Lord your God gives you" (16:18). Josephus preserved a more specific tradition in which every city of Israel was to have "seven men long exercised in virtue and in the pursuit of justice." Thus the appointment of the seven deacons may be seen as a further development of the Galilean leadership's original idea of a village-in-the-city—taking the traditional ideal of the Israelite village as a model for the establishment of a Jesus community in Jerusalem and for the later establishment of Jesus communities all over the world.

With the appointment of its officials and the emergence of the idea that each community constituted an "assembly" (ekklesia, in Greek, usually translated as "church," actually refers to an assembled community or civic council, as does its synonym synagōgē), the Renewal of Israel could really get under way. Certain eclectic innovations in ritual and religious expression were probably to be expected. Quite early on in their discussions and interactions with Jesus' original followers the Hellenists in Jerusalem may have adapted the Galileans' practice of conducting festive banquets to celebrate the coming of Kingdom and fused this with the contemporary Greco-Roman practice of holding tableside symposia in honor of favorite teachers or deities. But the shared veneration of both "Hebrews" and "Hellenists" for Jesus as a martyr for the cause of the Renewal of Israel would certainly not have had the trappings of the worship of a divinity. In adding the Greek word *Christos*, the "anointed one," to the name of Jesus, the Hellenists were unambiguously declaring that the life and death of the Galilean prophet, with his calls for a kingless Kingdom and a return to the independent traditions of Israel, was inspired by divine anointment or election. Jesus was surely a prophet and a vindicated martyr, but not a god. What remains something of a puzzle is how and why at least some of the Jesus communities so quickly symbolized his vindication in messianic terms, as the heavenly enthronement of one to whom royal titles should be ascribed. An obvious possibility is that they believed that their prophet-martyr had been vindicated as the *true* messiah precisely in opposition to the pretensions of Herodian messianism that both imitated and accommodated itself to the power of empire.

In any case, by the mid-30s, a polished, poetic epitome of the *kerygma*, or sacred proclamation, of the Renewal of Israel movement had already been formulated. As later stated by Paul in his First Epistle to the Corinthians 15:3–7, it declared "that Christ died for our sins in accordance with the scriptures, and that he was buried, he was raised on the third day in accordance with the scriptures," and that he first appeared to Peter, then to the Twelve, then to more than five hundred brethren, then to James, the brother of Jesus, and then to all the apostles. Seen in the context of the martyrdom ideal of militant *ioudaismos* and the continuing resistance of the People of Israel to imperial subjugation, the power of this statement is clear. The anointed prophet of the Renewed Israel had died (in the tragic fashion of earlier martyrs) because of the sins of the nation—the "sins" of widespread abandonment of the fundamental laws of the Covenant. It was the lapse of the people's devotion to the hillcountry Israelite village tradition that had brought down the wrath of God upon them in the form of evil emperors, unjust prefects, corrupt priests, and ambitious client kings.

Like the holy martyrs of the Maccabean period who effected the miraculous downfall of the powerful Seleucid oppressors, the suffering sacrifice of Jesus of Nazareth—it was surely hoped—would bring about a national triumph again. Just as the shocking spectacle of the deaths of the Maccabean martyrs on the torture machines of the Seleucids had once upon a time roused the nation to return to the Law and thereby defeat the evil designs of their oppressors, the death of Jesus on the cross of the Romans might make the People of Israel come to their senses again. Even though Pilate still ruled from Caesarea, the Temple still stood at the center of a massive and well-funded bureaucracy, and Herod Antipas still pressed on with his political program, the movement for the Renewal of Israel that Jesus had so forcefully initiated steadily gained new members and new understandings of its mission in the world. The villagers throughout the northern regions, the community around the Galilean leadership of the Twelve in Jerusalem, and the Hellenists with their idea of alternative town assemblies were all determined in their own distinctive ways to reestablish the glory of Israel as a coalition of autonomous, egalitarian communities. And although Jesus had come to be known to the Greek-speaking congregations as *Iesous Christos*, the prophet-martyr who had been designated as "anointed" by God at his vindicating ascent to heaven, the meaning was not yet much different than that of the prophet-martyr of the Q communities, who had died for the cause of the Renewal of Israel.

The challenge was now to spread the word of Jesus' martyrdom and vindication among the People of Israel not as a tragedy or travesty of justice but as a spur to action and liberation from Rome's ideological and political yoke. As the author of 2 Maccabees 6:12, when recounting the stories of earlier martyrs, had put it, "I beseech those who read this book not to be cast down by such misfortunes but to consider that these punishments were meant not for the destruction of our people, but for their correction." Of course, many Judeans, Galileans, and diaspora Jews must have scoffed at the very idea of being corrected in their ways of life by the homilies and comical demonstrations of a Galilean peasant prophet-martyr. For many, it would have seemed that the world-conquering power of Rome could not be successfully challenged without armies, without weapons, or without the direct intervention of God. Others preferred to place their faith for Jewish survival in the influential political connections of the Herodians or in the delicate *modus vivendi* worked out between the Roman prefects and Jerusalem's priestly aristocracy. And yet others, committed to the Mosaic laws as they were interpreted by the priests and scribal sages in Jerusalem, would have insisted that redemption would come only through a scrupulous payment of tithes, offerings, and pledges—and through meticulous observance of the purity laws.

The Book of Acts 6:9 depicts the Hellenist leader Stephen being charged with blasphemy by other diaspora Jews in Jerusalem—"some of those who belonged to the Synagogue of the Freedmen (as it was called), and of the Cyrenians, and of the Alexandrian, and of those from Cilicia and Asia." Standing boldly before the High Priest, the narrative of Acts has him announce what amounted to a declaration of independence from the increasingly bureaucratic Temple cult. Quoting freely from Amos, Isaiah, and Jeremiah, Stephen asserted that "the Most High does not dwell in houses made with hands" (7:48). This is all highly reminiscent of the kind of prophetic demonstration that Jesus had made just two or three years before. And the results were not dissimilar. Although the details of the Book of Acts 7:54–60 are confusing in their sudden shift from an orderly trial before the High Priest to the frenzy of an angry mob who stone Stephen to death, this story may preserve an authentic tradition about a violent dispute between two groups of diaspora Jews resident in Jerusalem. Although the Book of Acts makes Stephen the first Christian martyr and his death the beginning of worldwide Christian mission, we must see this conflict—symbolically if not historically—as a clash between two Jewish ideologies. One group identified the Temple and the central institutions of Israel as the bedrock of survival; the group represented by Stephen saw the fulfillment of God's promises to the People of Israel coming through less centralized, less hierarchical means.

Despite the opponents and the skeptics, the word of the kingless Kingdom went out from Zion, carried in the hearts and minds of men and women whose names we will never know but may have included names like Stephen, Philip, Prochorus, Nicanor, Timon, Parmenas, and Nicolaus. These people believed that the time had come to tell of the martyrdom of Jesus and preach his gospel of renewal to all the cities of Israel, to bring about a return to what they considered to be the genuine covenantal tradition and put an end to this ungodly age. Theirs was not an otherworldly or surrealistic apocalyptic vision, based on the clash of heavenly armies or the sudden, miraculous descent of a New Jerusalem. It was a vision of a world in which Israelites would treat each other as brothers and sisters, not slaves, beasts of burden, or saleable commodities. And as they fanned out to spread the word of the Kingdom of God in the Jewish communities of their home cities of Egypt, Greece, Italy, Asia Minor, and Syria, they fervently believed that this new world did not lie in the distant future but was already a dawning reality.

6

Reviving the Nations

SLOWLY THE WORD of the Kingdom of God went out to all the
world's nations, carried by the apostles of Jesus as they traveled on
foot and on horseback along the empire's great highways and
sailed across the Mediterranean aboard merchant galleys and passenger
ships. Their main destinations were Rome, Alexandria, Tyre, Ephesus, and
Antioch, where large Jewish communities struggled to maintain an autonomous existence, instructing their children in the lore and customs of
their ancestors, celebrating their distinctive fasts and festivals, and maintaining their faith in the eventual redemption of Israel. Like their co-
religionists in Galilee and Judea, many Jews of the diaspora shared a
vibrant apocalyptic tradition of messiahs, heavenly councils, angelic
hosts, and divine timetables, through which they envisioned that God
would bring about the final defeat of evil and the triumph of the forces of
good. Their hopes had often been disappointed as the sudden appearance
of comets and other celestial omens in the heavens, or news reports from
the East of tumults and miracles, proved to be just passing sensations. Yet
now, in the waning days of the reign of Tiberius, a new flurry of excitement arose as the prophets and teachers of the Renewal Movement
returned to their home communities. In describing the events that had
taken place just a year or two before in Jerusalem, they proclaimed that
those events were unmistakable proof that God had at last begun to
intervene on behalf of the righteous men and women of Israel.

In weekly synagogue assemblies, in impromptu streetcorner sermons, and in family gatherings, the followers of Jesus tirelessly spread the powerful teachings of economic justice and social cooperation that the Jerusalem community of the Twelve had preserved. Yet the factor that set the apostles' message apart from other reformist creeds within contemporary Judaism were the stories they told of Jesus' resurrection. In an era when chilling tales of ghosts, phantoms, and wandering specters had enormous influence on people's lives and perceptions, the descriptions of Jesus' physical triumph over the humiliation and ignominy of Roman crucifixion had an extraordinarily powerful emotional effect. The apostles reported that even though Jesus had been mocked in public and nailed to a cross in Jerusalem by the Romans (in the same grisly ritual that was all too familiar—and final—to the residents of every Roman city), and even though his crucified body had been scourged, pierced, and broken, he had risen from the dead. And this was no hazy, primeval legend about the miraculous ascent to heaven of ancient seers like Enoch and Elijah; the unforgettably vivid appearances of the Risen Jesus in both Galilee and Jerusalem—witnessed by hundreds of reliable people—lay in the realm of stunning current events. Indeed, the earliest proclamations about Jesus emphasized the frequency and reality of these post-crucifixion appearances—to Peter, to James, to all Twelve of the central disciples, to all of the apostles, and to "five hundred brethren at one time, most of whom are still alive" (1 Cor. 15:5–7). And in whatever rationalistic or theological way we may today seek to account for these early stories of the Risen Jesus, they clearly carried the conviction—at least to some of the first-century listeners—of thoroughly believable eyewitness accounts. Told and retold throughout the diaspora, they convinced many people that God had demonstrably taken the first step in bringing about the *general* resurrection of Israel's righteous martyrs and freedom fighters that was expected to occur at the End of Days.

As belief in the significance of Jesus' resurrection spread among particular Jewish communities—perhaps confirmed or intensified by demonstrations of miraculous healings and exorcisms performed by Spirit-fired apostles—local *ekklesiai* or communities of "saints" or followers of "The Way" of Jesus were formed. This process of gradual differentiation of a discrete group from a wider synagogue population should not be understood as a "conversion" *away* from Judaism to a new religion but as the awareness of "election" *within* the People of Israel. For just as the members of the Qumran community came together in the wilderness and immersed themselves in ritual baths to mark their designation as the remnant of Israel who would inherit God's Kingdom, and just as the devotees of John the Baptist underwent the public ceremony of baptism in the Jordan River to announce their renewed personal commitment to the Covenant, the followers of Jesus practiced their own initiation ceremony, immersing their naked bodies in ritual baths, in flowing streams or rivers, or by sprinkling on the head by a Spirit-inspired apostle to signify their own admission to the Kingdom of God. And in contrast to other Jewish apocalyptic groups, the focus of the followers of Jesus was firmly on the present. While the Qumran community looked to the future for signs of the End of Days and John the Baptist spoke of the *coming* Kingdom, the followers of Jesus believed that his vindication by God on the cross in Jerusalem—in the face of both Roman brutality and the political impotence of Judean leaders—had *already* inaugurated the era of the salvation of Israel.

Their festive banquets likewise celebrated the living presence of the Kingdom. Once a sufficient number of local people had been baptized in the name of Jesus, they would begin to meet regularly for prayer, praise, and sustenance, following the custom of "feasting for the Kingdom" that had been initiated by Jesus himself in Galilee. Other Jewish groups also celebrated special meals of prayer and thanksgiving: the Pharisaic fellowships, or *havurot*, held communal meals as a central feature of their movement, and the "messianic banquet" of the Qumran sect described in the Dead Sea scroll *Rule of the Community* was important as a sacred rehearsal for the feast of bread and wine that would be enjoyed by the righteous remnant of Israel at the End of Days. In the earliest Christian communities, the institution of the Lord's Supper, or as it came to be known, the "Thanksgiving," or *eucharistia* for the members' inclusion in God's Kingdom, also relied on traditional Jewish formulas with Jesus placed in a traditional prophetic role. The Didache, a Christian text of the late first century, instructed the celebrants to raise their chalice to thank God "for the holy vine of David, which thou hast made known through thy servant Jesus," and to break bread together so that just "as this broken bread, once dispersed over the hills, was brought together and became one loaf, so may thy *ekklesia* be brought together from the ends of the earth into thy kingdom." Addressing the "God of David," they gave thanks for "the knowledge and faith and immortality, which Thou hast made known unto us through Thy servant Jesus." And their most fervent wish was that "grace" would come "and the present world pass away."

These early Christian rituals gave voice to the distinctive apocalyptic tradition of the People of Israel announced by Israel's divinely inspired prophets, but before long the movement began to attract adherents from other nations as well. Quite independent of the scriptural stories of the Apostle Philip's conversion and baptism of the Ethiopian eunuch (Acts 8:26–39) and the Apostle Peter's baptism of the centurion Cornelius at Caesarea (Acts 10), there are indications that within just a few years of the crucifixion of Jesus, increasing numbers of Greek-speaking pagans were joining the close-knit communities of Jesus' Jewish followers, sharing in the solemn sacrament of baptism and celebration of the Lord's Supper, and joyfully looking forward to the advent of the Kingdom of God. It is unclear whether Jesus himself ever addressed his message to pagans. In two cases where he was reported to have performed healings for people identified as non-Israelite—the Syro-Phoenician woman of Mark 7:24–30 and the "centurion" at Capernaum of Matthew 8:5–13—the gospels record his pointed comments to his followers that the larger and apparently main aim of his movement was the restoration of *Israel*. Yet whether these are authentic quotations or whether Jesus had originally envisioned an out-reach to all the world's peoples, it seems clear that within a few decades of his crucifixion, the appeal of the movement that carried his name and message had considerably widened from its original Galilean and Judean base. As Flavius Josephus reported in a single paragraph about Jesus in his many volumes of writings, Jesus was "one who wrought surprising feats and was a teacher of such people as accept the truth gladly. He won over many Jews and many of the Greeks."

To understand the attraction of the Jesus Movement among non-Israelites, we must stress—once again—that "religion" in the ancient world was not a matter of individual choice or personal theological reflection that could be neatly separated from an individual's "secular" life. A person's adherence to the cult of a certain god or goddess represented membership in a particular nation, ethnic group, tribe, clan, professional association, or station in life. The cults of Dionysos, Apollo, Adonis, Aphrodite, Atargatis, or Augustus Caesar in any Greek or Roman city—with their priesthoods, benefactors, yearly festivals, and sacrificial rituals—created and cultivated communities of shared identity and interests as well as promoting particular economic and political goals. To worship a particular god was to pledge allegiance to something. Thus we must see in the scriptural stories of the first Gentile conversions performed by the Apostles Philip and Peter not sudden theological triumphs but symbolic narratives of a more gradual and complex process by which pagan men and women, who were alienated from or uncomfortable with their former social identities in the day-to-day life in the Roman Empire, found the *ekklesiai* of the Jesus Movement to be desirable alternative *communities*.

How and why they felt that way are questions that have been addressed by such sociologists of early Christianity as Wayne Meeks, Gerd Thiessen, and John Gager—each with slightly differing results. Yet there was a precedent for such a shift of social allegiance from the pagan mainstream to a monotheistic minority: over the previous centuries, many pagans throughout the Mediterranean had abandoned the worship of the various official gods and goddesses to associate themselves with the monotheistic message and supportive community life of Israel. Despite the great pains with which later theologians attempted to portray the Jews of New Testament times as a xenophobic, purity-obsessed people who would have little or nothing to do with outsiders, there is abundant historical evidence from various parts of the diaspora of how close and how frequent the religious contact between Gentiles and local communities of Jews could sometimes be. In many of the major cities of the Mediterranean, weekly synagogue assemblies with their public reading and exposition of scripture attracted large numbers of sympathetic pagans who were impressed with the power of monotheism and the underlying social ideals of the Mosaic law. Some became so admiring of Israel's traditions that they underwent the formalized rituals of conversion, including the ritual of circumcision for men. Others remained devout at a distance, popularly known in Greek as *theosebeis*, or "Godfearers." The phenomenon was apparently widespread. In Rome, satirists like Horace and Juvenal noted the susceptibility of so many of their countrymen to foolish and very un-Roman Jewish "superstitions." In Alexandria, we hear of the "multitudes" of non-Jews who joined the annual pilgrimage to the island of Pharos (where, according to legend, the Bible was first translated into Greek) "both to do honor to the place in which the light of that version first shone out, and also to thank God for the good gift so old yet ever new." In Damascus, many wealthy pagan matrons had been attracted to Judaism to the extent of undergoing formal conversion. And farther north, in the Syrian capital of Antioch, Josephus reported that the Jews of that city—the third largest in the empire after

Rome and Alexandria—"were constantly attracting to their religious ceremonies multitudes of Greeks, and these had in some measure incorporated
with themselves into their community."

The mixed Jewish-Gentile *ekklesiai* of Jesus throughout the eastern
Mediterranean were thus part of a larger phenomenon of sympathy and
awareness by pagans of the current Jewish scriptural concepts of judgment,
messiah, and God's rule on earth—which was, in fact, the only conceptual
framework in which the gospel of Jesus, in its expectation of God's imminent intervention in history, could possibly have made sense. It is hardly
surprising, therefore, that some Gentiles who were already sympathetic to
Judaism would have welcomed the excited reports from the East that the
physical resurrection of a crucified prophet-martyr of Israel in the Holy
City of Jerusalem signaled the start of the long-awaited time of redemption. The same conditions of poverty and powerlessness that attracted
some Jewish peasants and townspeople to seek relief and escape in the
expectation of God's Kingdom through membership in the Jesus Movement, attracted Godfearers and sympathetic pagans and motivated them to
undergo baptism and join in the celebration of the Eucharist. These
unofficial ceremonies, conducted for the most part in private houses,
expressed shared apocalyptic excitement, and there is no indication that
Jewish ritual law insisted on a strict separation between Jews and Gentiles
in their celebrations of the Kingdom of God any more than it did in the
weekly synagogue services where Jews and pagans frequently mixed. Although we can never be sure where or when Gentiles first responded to the
Jesus Movement (whether in Judea as the Book of Acts suggests, or in the
diaspora), their Spirit-filled response to the message and resurrection of
Jesus was itself seen by some of Jesus' original Jewish followers as yet
another powerful omen. Hadn't Isaiah declared that at the time of redemption all the world's peoples would recognize the One True God's power and
glory? Anyone well versed in the scriptures surely knew that the prophet
had solemnly predicted that at a time when "darkness shall cover the earth,
and thick darkness the peoples," the glory of God would arise upon Israel
"and the nations shall come to your light" (60:2–3).

THE PARTICIPATION of Gentiles in the *ekklesiai* of the various cities of
the diaspora may have been a cause for praise and celebration by members
of the Jesus Movement, but it was soon viewed with alarm by the leaders of

at least some Jewish Diaspora communities. The attendance of Godfearers and sympathetic pagans at the weekly synagogue assemblies of the entire community was one thing, but their enthusiastic acceptance of the teachings of a radical minority—that joyfully proclaimed the imminent, fiery demise of Rome and the glorious establishment of an alternative Kingdom—was the kind of extremist ideology that could bring down the wrath of both Rome and the local authorities on the heads of the entire Jewish community. For those pragmatic Jewish leaders who were primarily concerned with communal survival, the outspoken anti-imperial gospel of Jesus posed a clear political danger. And although it is impossible to know from the surviving sources if the local leadership of every diaspora community reacted in the same way to the preaching and organizing efforts of the apostles of Jesus, both the Book of Acts and Paul's Letter to the Galatians report that within just a few years of Jesus' crucifixion, his followers in the Syrian city of Damascus became the victims of an aggressive campaign aimed at silencing them. According to Acts, this effort to uncover cells of the Jesus Movement was spearheaded by a young man named Saul, who had been born in the prosperous Jewish community of Tarsus in southeastern Asia Minor and brought up in Jerusalem as a protégé of the famous Pharisaic sage Gamaliel. After reportedly making a name for himself as a noted persecutor of the Jesus communities in Judea, Saul was dispatched to Damascus by the High Priest in Jerusalem to locate and arrest followers of Jesus, so that "if he found any belonging to the Way, men or women, he might bring them bound to Jerusalem" (Acts 9:2).

As a growing number of scholars have noted, we must be careful in taking all these biographical details at face value, for in his own later letters, Saul—or "Paul," as he soon came to be known—was completely silent on the matter of his birthplace, his place of education, and his connections to the Jerusalem establishment. Although it is possible that Saul, then a man in his twenties, possessed informal links with the Temple hierarchy in Jerusalem through its Damascus representatives, it is now regarded as highly unlikely that he was dispatched from Judea as a special agent with the powers of arrest. The High Priest of the Jerusalem Temple would have been taking an extraordinary risk in violating the judicial sovereignty of the Roman Governor of Syria, who was not only the supreme authority in Damascus but who exercised general supervision of affairs in Judea as well. No less important was Paul's own claim that he was "not known by sight to the churches of Christ in Judea" (Gal. 1:22) until many years later—a detail that would tend to contradict the extent of his notoriety as a persecutor there. Far more likely is the possibility that by the early 30s, Saul—known by the resident Jews there as "the man from Tarsus"—was the son of Jewish immigrants living and working in Damascus as a low-level official or self-appointed representative of the local leadership, intent on defending what he saw as the best interests of his community. And there can be little doubt of Saul's devotion to the traditions of Israel: he later recalled how he "advanced in *ioudaismos* beyond many of my own age among my people, so extremely zealous was I for the traditions of my fathers." As we have seen, *ioudaismos* was not merely a matter of religious observance but a movement of political activism and autonomy by diaspora Jews. And it was to the end of ensuring community solidarity and security in Damascus that Saul "persecuted the church of God violently and tried to destroy it" (Gal. 1:13).

As New Testament scholar Paula Frederikson has persuasively argued, Saul's campaign of persecution against the Damascus Christians—whether it was inspired and initiated by Temple officials in Jerusalem or by the local leadership of the Damascus community—was therefore not motivated primarily by religious objections to the Damascus Christians' ritual observances or their close relationship with Gentiles, but to the specific political threat that they posed to the larger Jewish community. There is compelling evidence that the political position of the Jews in first-century Damascus was, in fact, extremely delicate. Despite the prosperity of some of the prominent Jews in the city—and despite the conversion to Judaism of highborn Damascene women—the Jews were vulnerable targets. Less than forty years later, at the time of the outbreak of the revolt against the Romans in Judea, all the Jews of Damascus were rounded up on a blanket charge of sedition and confined in the local gymnasium, where, "within one hour," according to Josephus, their local captors "slaughtered them all with impunity." An atrocity like that bespoke decades of tension and anti-Jewish hatred; it is not difficult to see why some of the local Jewish leaders in Damascus would have done almost anything to prevent accusations that they were harboring or perhaps even encouraging dangerous revolutionaries. But something went terribly wrong in the course of one particular campaign to silence the followers of Jesus. Saul of Tarsus suddenly, inexplicably went over to the dissidents. Acts 9:3–6 described it as an unforgettable moment of spiritual pyrotechnics: "Now as he journeyed he approached Damascus, and suddenly a light from heaven flashed about him. And he fell to the ground and heard a voice saying to him, 'Saul, Saul, why do you persecute me?' And he said, 'Who are you, Lord?' and the voice said 'I am Jesus, whom you are persecuting; but rise and enter the city and you will be told what you are to do.' "

For centuries, theologians, poets, painters, sociologists, psychologists, and psychiatrists have all tried their hand at interpreting Saul's "conversion" on the road to Damascus, attempting to explain why a hardline proponent of *ioudaismos* could suddenly become an apostle of Jesus. Indeed the very phrase "on the road to Damascus" has come to signify in our culture a sudden change of heart, commitment, or behavior through a singular moment of revelation and clarity. Traditional Christian interpretation has usually portrayed Saul's transformation as a sudden acceptance of Jesus Christ as his personal savior and a change of religion from "Judaism" to "Christianity." But an interpretation divorced from its Israelite roots obscures the distinctive nature of Paul's experience, which was a fairly well-known phenomenon among first-century Jews. Only when we recognize the rich and deeply rooted tradition of sudden, divine revelation among virtually all strains of Jewish belief in the first century, will we be able to comprehend how a well-educated proponent of *ioudaismos* like Saul understood what had happened to him. Having been trained in the traditions of his people and undoubtedly well versed in the vivid Hebrew and Aramaic descriptions of miraculous heavenly ascents and divine encounters that were such a prominent part of first-century Jewish literature, Saul would never have regarded himself as a sudden convert to a new religion. His miraculous light-filled conversation with a heavenly figure would not have changed his basic scriptural outlook but would have merely shown him previously unknown *details* of God's unfolding plan for Israel's salvation at the End of Days.

Just as the Israelite prophet Micaiah ben Imlah received a new prophetic commission when he "saw the Lord sitting on his throne and all the host of heaven standing beside him on his right hand and on his left" (1 Kings 22:19); just as Ezekiel first perceived the details of the End of Days when he was granted a vision of "the likeness of a throne, in appearance like sapphire and seated above the throne was a likeness as it were of a human form" (1:26); and just as Daniel had glimpsed the momentous events of redemption with a vivid image of "one like a son of man" coming on the clouds of heaven, Saul's own brilliant celestial vision of the Risen Jesus offered him a stunning apocalyptic vision. It confirmed that God had indeed begun to inaugurate a new age for Israel—just as the followers of

Jesus had so passionately and joyously claimed. Here, suddenly appearing before him, was the figure whom the Romans had reportedly put to death in Jerusalem, now transfigured in glory like one of the heavenly figures known in the scripture as *bene elohim*, or "sons of God." The fact that Saul of Tarsus had never met or seen the earthly Jesus was not important. He may even have heard—and callously dismissed—the secondhand stories of Jesus' post-crucifixion appearances in Galilee and Jerusalem. But now that he had experienced his own direct encounter with the Risen Christ, Saul became convinced that Jesus' earlier incarnation as a poor Galilean peasant was merely a prelude to his revelation as Israel's messianic redeemer, spoken of in the scriptures he had studied from his youth. What is more, he came to believe that the security concerns of the Jews of Damascus were soon to become completely irrelevant when Jesus returned to earth as Israel's messiah, completing the establishment of the Kingdom of God by bringing about the conquest of evil and the vindication of the forces of good. It is pure speculation to assume that Saul's revelation came as the result of a personal crisis or painful realization that his relentless persecution of a few poor peasants and townspeople in Damascus did nothing to advance the salvation of Israel. Yet it is understandable that when faced with a personal crisis or disillusionment with his role in the Damascus community, Saul's personal transformation would have taken a form appropriate to his educated background: a sudden, divine commission to preach the *true* path to Israel's redemption, in the tradition of generations of righteous Israelite prophets, scribes, and seers.

"Saul" thus became "Paul" in his experience of a private mystical revelation that completely transformed his outlook on both the future and the present state of the world. Whether or not he immediately recognized that his commission was to convey the gospel of the risen-and-soon-to-return Jesus among all the world's peoples; whether he received the sacrament of baptism and was initially brought into the fellowship of the Damascus *ekklesia* (as reported in Acts 9:18 but not mentioned in his own letters); or whether the change of name from the Hebrew Saul to the Latinized Paul took place at this moment (or later, in his subsequent missionary travels, as indicated by the sudden shift at Acts 13:9), Paul's apocalyptic vision brought about a far-reaching transformation in his life. Instead of continuing to serve the established institutions of the Jewish community in Damascus and the Temple hierarchy in Jerusalem—and thereby passively accepting the rule of Rome as the will of God and a fact of nature—he looked forward to a new era of human existence, in which life on earth would be transformed. Leaving behind his old life in Damascus, he went off for a period of solitary exile to sort out his thoughts and ponder the future. "I did not confer with flesh and blood, nor did I go up to Jerusalem to those who were apostles before me," he recalled in his later Letter to the Galatians, "but I went away to Arabia" (1:17).

Paul's three-year journey through the kingdom of Nabatea—in the rugged territory of modern south Jordan and northwestern Saudi Arabia—apparently provided him with further visible confirmation of the reality of the dawning Kingdom of God. We must not visualize Saul's sojourn in Arabia as a lonely wandering in a desolate wilderness, or as a mission to "convert" the Nabateans. It was a period of self-imposed exile and reflection in which he traveled through a landscape of caravan cities, market towns, and rural villages whose inhabitants were themselves undergoing profound political change. If we are justified in dating the crucifixion of Jesus, as many scholars now do, to the spring of 30 C.E. and the personal transformation experienced by Saul in Damascus some three or four years later, we would have to conclude that he traveled through Nabatea precisely at the time when the political rivalry between King Aretas IV and his former son-in-law Herod Antipas of Galilee and Perea had risen to the point of open war. Archaeological finds show that by this time Aretas had raised his kingdom to unprecedented levels of splendor and prosperity. The spectacular tomb monuments, temples, cult places, and theater of his capital city of Petra—all carved from the golden pink sandstone of the bluffs and ravines that conceal and envelop the city—were material testaments to the Nabateans' careful and skillful control of the traffic in precious commodities like incense, spices, gold, pearls, and rare medicines that wound their way along the caravan routes from southern Arabia and the Persian Gulf.

Yet historical events were unfolding in the political life of the region that must have seemed like heaven-sent omens to those attuned to seek evidence of divine intervention in human affairs. We know from the later accounts of Josephus that in this period Herod Antipas was increasingly focusing his attention on the growing power and wealth of the Nabatean kingdom. Mobilizing a private, Roman-trained army, he began to expand the area of his territorial control southward from Perea into the region southeast of the Dead Sea. His eventual occupation of the land around Gabalis—a village provocatively close to King Aretas's capital city of Petra—was the spark that set off an unexpectedly portentous chain of events. In 35 or 36 C.E., King Aretas, who had long been yearning for revenge against the indignity imposed upon his daughter by Antipas, staged a surprise attack on the newly established Herodian enclave near Gabalis, utterly routing and destroying the Herodian mercenary forces, which had been recruited with such effort and at such great cost over the previous years. As a result of this victory, Aretas became the most powerful client king in the region, soon expanding his influence as far north as Damascus. And Antipas, for his part, suffered the bitter fate of one who had gambled everything and lost. The public humiliation he suffered in the same desert region where King David had won his celebrated victories against the Moabites—combined with the serious financial blow he suffered in the destruction of his well-equipped mercenary army—spelled the end of his quest to become Israel's new messiah-king. Within two years, a badly shaken Antipas had fallen out of favor with the Roman imperial authorities, was stripped of his lands and his title, and was exiled with his Hasmonean wife Herodias to the distant city of Lugdunum (modern Lyons) in Gaul. That Herodian political collapse was seen by many as due primarily to God's displeasure. As Josephus later noted in his description of the Battle of Gabalis, "To some of the Jews the destruction of Herod's army seemed to be divine vengeance, and certainly a just vengeance for John who was called the Baptist. For Herod had put him to death, though he was a good man."

In the defeat of the hated Antipas in Nabatea, the followers of Jesus could also have seen vindication; the clanging of swords and the whoosh of arrows in the highlands of Nabatea could be perceived as yet another sign of the imminent advent of the Kingdom of God. This was precisely the time that Paul—as we know from his own later letters—finally left the territory controlled by the victorious Nabateans, escaped from Damascus, and made his way to Jerusalem, where he spent two weeks in the company of Jesus' original Galilean followers. But Paul's stay in Jerusalem was not meant to be permanent; this was not the community he would join. Throughout his career he would cling to the belief that his Damascus revelation bestowed upon him a unique commission from the Risen Jesus, no less potent or meaningful than the visitations granted to Peter, James, and the rest of the Twelve. Paul now believed that time was quickly running out before the return of Jesus as the Judge of the world and Messiah of Israel. And the word of that world-transforming fact had to be preached far beyond the farms, towns, and salt-fish factories of Jesus' ministry—and far from the familiar courtyards, squares, and Temple of Jerusalem. The righteous remnant of humanity had to be warned of God's impending judgment and offered an opportunity—through faith in the gospel of the crucified Jesus—to be saved. "Then I went to the regions of Syria and Cilicia," Paul recalled in Galatians 1:21, describing his departure from Jerusalem to the area around Tarsus in the northeastern corner of the Mediterranean, where his family origins reportedly lay. And once there, committed to spreading the word of Jesus to all who would listen, Paul would play a crucial role in the birth of a new faith.

ALMOST THREE HUNDRED MILES to the north, across desert, mountains, farmland, and river valleys, lay the vast metropolis of Antioch-on-the-Orontes, where a revolutionary new version of the gospel of Jesus was already being formed. Antioch might not have been able to boast the antiquity or biblical associations of either Damascus or Jerusalem, but for anyone living in the eastern Mediterranean in the first century, it was the "big city" to which ambitious people gravitated and all eyes turned. As the capital of the Roman province of Syria, nestled in a broad, fertile valley between the mountains and the coast, Antioch served as a regional market, tax-collection center, and final way station for the overland trade routes from the Persian Gulf and Mesopotamia and from the distant spice-and-incense-producing lands of the Arabian peninsula. Over the previous few decades, it had grown into a sprawling megalopolis, the third largest city in the empire, with a population as high as 500,000 by the mid-first century. There, in the marketplaces and colonnades of the greatest city of the Roman East, fortunes could be gained or squandered; forbidden vices could be tasted; and new philosophies and radical ideologies were constantly being born. With a huge, polyglot urban population of Parthians, Arabs, Cappadocians, Persians, Armenians, Greeks, Jews, and native Syrians, newly established clubs, guilds, and cultic associations proliferated, offering the highly mobile, constantly interacting urban population novel forms of social identity and community life.

The general religious atmosphere in Antioch—unlike the situation in conservative Alexandria and other smaller Roman cities—was both fluid and permissive. Besides the well-known attraction that Judaism held for Antioch's Godfearers and sympathetic pagans, the official worship of Roman and Greek gods and goddesses in Antioch was deeply influenced by

Near Eastern traditions and ceremonies. Among the people of the city, Near Eastern gods like the Phoenician Adonis, the Egyptian Osiris, and the Phrygian Attis became centerpoints of novel mystical sects in which initiates were promised physical well-being, extraordinary powers, and even personal immortality through the practice of secret rites. Indeed, Syria became notorious in early imperial times—at least in the eyes of self-appointed protectors of Roman virtues and values—as a dangerous breeding ground for "atheistic" mystery religions that placed the interests of the *individual* adherent ahead of the more proper, patriotic veneration of the gods of the empire. In an era of big-city life, disintegrating community networks, and increasing personal alienation, the appeal of such new age cults was enormous. New Testament scholar Dieter Georgi has stressed how the appeals of traveling missionaries of the new pagan mystery religions—often accompanied by public healings and exorcisms—convinced many to join sacred fellowships and thereby gain the promise of personal salvation through communion with a particular deity.

The followers of Jesus, arriving in Antioch from Jerusalem, readily found a place for themselves in this dynamic religious landscape. The Book of Acts, woven together decades later from venerated traditions, legends, and personal recollections, offers a vivid narrative of the arrival of the first apostles of the Jesus Movement in Antioch, who had gradually made their way northward from Jerusalem, "speaking the word to none but the Jews. But there were some of them, men of Cyprus and Cyrene, who on coming to Antioch spoke to the Greeks also, preaching the Lord Jesus. And the hand of the Lord was with them, and a great number that believed turned to the Lord" (Acts 11:19–20). It is unlikely that all these initial Greek converts to the gospel of Jesus in Antioch were already Godfearers or otherwise associated with the city's large Jewish community, for the scriptural emphasis on the uniqueness of this preaching "to the Greeks" of the city suggests that Antioch was long remembered as the place where a direct appeal to a large pagan audience was first made. Yet at the same time—as we know from subsequent developments—the followers of Jesus actively preached among the Jews of the city, who were estimated to number as high as 65,000 and whose synagogue assemblies, scattered in both poor city quarters and wealthy suburbs, ranged in orientation from fierce nationalism to more thoroughly assimilated, Hellenistic ideals. It is significant that no persecution of the followers of Jesus by the local Jewish leadership of Antioch is recorded in the Book of Acts, a source that regularly emphasizes such occurrences. Antioch's sheer size and cosmopolitan atmo-sphere apparently provided unique circumstances in which a small group of Spirit-filled preachers and prophets was able to organize fellowships among *both* Jews and Gentiles. For the new Jewish followers of Jesus in Antioch, his martyrdom and resurrection confirmed longstanding apocalyptic expecta-tions. For the pagans, Jesus Christ was seen as a universal, heaven-sent redeemer figure, whose Israelite origins and scriptural associations offered a time-honored religious background that may have offered an attractive alternative to the myths of the pagan mystery gods. Thus the potential power of the Jesus Movement in a large city like Antioch was its broad appeal to the public as a unique composite ideology of individual salvation and the communal, historical expectation of Jewish apocalyptic belief.

The decade extending from the mid-30s to the mid-40s is one of the most obscure periods in the history of early Christianity, for we possess only a few vague details about the composition of the newly formed communities of Jesus followers in Antioch during this period, and only a few fragmentary scriptural glimpses at their evolving theology. On the evidence of the Book of Acts 13:1, we learn that the *ekklesia* at Antioch was led by an eclectic and socially diverse group of "prophets and teachers," including a wealthy Cypriot Jew named Joseph nicknamed "Barnabas" (or "son of encourage-ment," according to the loose translation of Acts 4:36); "Symeon who was called Niger" (whom the New Testament scholar F. F. Bruce once theorized was an African); Lucius of Cyrene from the coast of Libya; and Manaen (a Graecized form of the Hebrew name Menahem), who was known as a childhood friend and former member of the court of Herod Antipas. We have no idea of the political reactions of this community to the turbulent political events of this period—from the death of Tiberius and the accession of Caligula in the spring of 37; to Caligula's mad plan to set up a colossal image of himself in the Jerusalem Temple in 39–40; to the assassination of Caligula and the accession of his uncle Claudius in January 41 C.E. But there is at least one indication that they were increasingly recognized as members of a new religious movement, rather than just another reformist Jewish sect. Just as the acolytes of the imperial cult were known as *Augustiani*, and just as the adherents of the various mystery religions were known by the name of the patron deities who were invoked in their secret, communal meals and ceremonies, the faithful followers of Jesus in the city—both Jews and Greeks—came to be known as *Christianoi*, or "Christians," to the people of Antioch (Acts 11:26).

It is also clear that by this time the Antioch *ekklesia* considered itself something more than just another alternative village-in-the-city restricted to the salvation of the righteous in Antioch and its immediate vicinity. In later church tradition, the Antioch community was remembered as a dynamic congregation with a special commission of outward preaching, and the Antioch Christians seem to have gradually expanded their activities into the hinterland of Antioch and around the broad Bay of Alexandretta to the neighboring cities of Cilicia. During this era of expansion, according to Acts 11:25, Barnabas encountered Paul in the Cilician city of Tarsus, where he was working as an independent apostle, and invited him to join the Antioch community. In his own letters, Paul makes no mention of such an encounter, but in whatever historical circumstances he first came to the city, Paul clearly became one of Antioch's most energetic and outspoken organizers. Though younger and apparently still subordinate to Barnabas in the leadership of the community, he played a central role in widening its missionary horizons. Off to the west was the island of Cyprus, then as now a meeting place of peoples from the entire Mediterranean basin, with fertile farm land, rich copper mines, and bustling cities inhabited by Greeks, Anatolians, Phoenicians, Syrians, and Jews. To the northwest was the rich coastal plain of Pamphylia, with its prosperous harbor cities and large Jewish population. And beyond that coastal plain lay a range of mountains through which highways led into the interior of Asia Minor—a vast continental expanse of cities, peoples, and tribes. The Book of Acts describes the decision of the Antioch community to expand its missionary outreach as the result of a sudden burst of divine guidance: "While they were worshipping the Lord and fasting, the Holy Spirit said, 'Set apart for me Barnabas and Saul for the work to which I have called them.' Then after fasting and praying they laid their hands on them and sent them off" (13:2–3).

As always, we must keep in mind that behind the unique and admittedly powerful events described in the scripture often lay far more complex—if less dramatic—social realities. The imperative for outward mission could not have been entirely sudden, unexpected, or restricted entirely to the divine commission of Barnabas and Paul. The Christians of Antioch had already begun to reach out to new peoples beyond the "lost sheep of Israel," and since we know from Paul's report in Galatians 2:1 that his work in Syria and Cilicia went on for over a decade, we must assume that the Antioch community's sense of outward mission—and recognition of the possibilities of success in various regions—must have developed gradually with a steadily widening network of contacts and personal reconnaissances. We might therefore suppose that Acts's subsequent narrative of Barnabas and Paul's joint missionary adventure (often called "Paul's First Missionary Journey" and described in chapters 13–14) can be viewed as both a commemoration of the efforts of two of the community's most extraordinary leaders and the distilled recollection of the efforts of many unrecorded individuals from the Antioch community as they fanned out to preach and organize in the surrounding regions over the course of several years. Like the gospels' differing accounts of Jesus' Galilean ministry, Acts's account of this initial journey may be less a chronological narrative than a powerful montage of vivid anecdotes and evocative biblical images played out on a familiar geographical landscape for the peoples of Syria and Asia Minor. Thus setting sail from Antioch's Mediterranean port of Seleucia, Barnabas, Paul, and their young companion named John Mark from Jerusalem sailed westward to Cyprus, where Paul appeared before the Roman governor, Sergius Paulus, and bested "a Jewish false prophet named Bar-Jesus" in a contest of magical power (highly reminiscent of Moses and Aaron's victory over the Egyptian magicians in Genesis 7:8–12 and Elijah's victory over the prophets of Baal in 1 Kings 18:20–40). Then departing on a northbound ship from Cyprus bound for the port city of Perga in Pamphylia, they parted company with John Mark and headed off alone into the interior of Asia Minor, visiting and preaching in quick succession in the cities of Pisidian Antioch, Iconium, Lystra, and Derbe, where they encountered intense hostility from local Jewish communities yet gained many pagan supporters, thereby opening "a door of faith to the Gentiles" (Acts 14:27).

The itinerary of Paul and Barnabas in Cyprus and southern Asia Minor follows the route of well-known imperial highways and sea lanes, yet the historical reliability of several of its specific details has become the subject of scholarly dispute. No conclusive proof has been found for the tenure of a proconsul named Sergius Paulus on Cyprus at the time of Paul's visit (Acts 13:7), and direct archaeological evidence is lacking for the presence of Jewish communities in Pisidian Antioch and Iconium before the second or third century C.E. The Acts narrative nonetheless remains an important historical source in its portrayal of the general trend of many years of preaching and traveling by presenting a few representative stories, in which Paul and Barnabas—representing the outward spread of the Jesus

Movement from Antioch—begin to change the focus of their message and gain an increasing number of adherents from the pagan populations of Cyprus, Pamphylia, and southern Galatia. In those regions, the Antioch apostles encountered countless righteous suffering men and women, who—though born and brought up as pagans—responded with passion and devotion to a new movement that offered both spiritual regeneration and the apocalyptic hope that the world was about to undergo a miraculous change. We might imagine that the description of Jesus' martyrdom and message had to be tailored to suit the cultural background and limited (or non-existent) familiarity of the people with the detailed apocalyptic time-tables and imagery of the Israelite scriptures. Yet the economic and social conditions of these regions, relatively recently incorporated into the Roman Empire, offered a fertile field for early Christian mission. The inexorable disintegration of time-honored local traditions in the competitive, increasingly regimented imperial economy provided a powerful impetus for people to seek both individual spiritual solace and a sense of belonging to a self-supporting, alternative community. We cannot be sure where or even if Paul, Barnabas, or any other members of the Antioch community attempted to establish permanent *ekklesiai* in these regions, but at least an initial foothold was made. And from the standpoint of Israelite apocalyptic tradition, that was no mean achievement. Isaiah had declared that God's faithful servant Israel was meant to be "a light to the nations, to open eyes that are blind, to bring prisoners from the dungeon, from prison those who sit in darkness" (42:6–7). And as the years passed and the End of Days inexplicably tarried, the leaders of the North Syrian branch of the Jesus Movement saw their work among the restless workers and displaced peasants of the pagan population of the surrounding territories as an essential part of God's plan for fulfillment. For if they kept up their faith and intensified their efforts, they fervently believed that the steady, Spirit-filled outreach to the Gentiles—in combination with the inward renewal of the People of Israel—would properly inaugurate the Kingdom of God.

AT THIS TIME of great missionary success, a serious confrontation was looming. Back in Judea, the character of the original Jerusalem community was slowly changing, affected by the death or departure of some of its original leaders, by altered local conditions, and by changing internal priorities. A great deal had changed in the years since Jesus had called a few young men away from their fishing boats, their nets, and their old lives on the docks of Capernaum. Now, as an economically independent group in the midst of the city—and no longer a spontaneous, Spirit-filled movement of Galilean peasants—the community of Jesus' followers had to adapt themselves to life in the spiritual and political capital of the People of Israel. If we take the narrative of Acts 1–11 as a general portrait of this group in transition, we can see that the group of "Twelve" who had originally composed Jesus' inner circle gradually changed its membership and function. With the death or departure of some of the original members, new apostles were chosen (Acts 1:15–26). And since the needs of the community, supplied from the common treasury of the village-in-the-city, required long-term administration, a new body of leaders, called "the elders" (Acts 11:30) began to regulate the community's economic affairs. Antipas was no longer on the scene and both the unpopular prefect Pontius Pilate and the long-serving High Priest Joseph Caiaphas had been ousted from office by the Roman governor of Syria. Yet the larger goal of participating in the final establishment of Israel's kingless Kingdom still awaited fulfillment, since the priestly hierarchy of the Temple continued to bow to the demands of the Roman imperial administration, and the surviving heirs of the Herodian house clung to their messianic fantasies. Thus through the late 30s—at a time when the Antioch community was increasingly turning its attention outward—the Jerusalem community of the Jesus Movement became increasingly preoccupied with political developments within the Land of Israel. And the most dramatic challenge to their goal of the Renewal of Israel came with the rise of a new Herodian pretender. Chapter 12 of the Book of Acts unmistakably mimicked the words of Exodus 1:8 in describing the ominous rise to power of an evil, new pharaoh: "About that time Herod the king laid violent hands upon some who belonged to the church."

It is unlikely that Jesus or his closest followers ever heard of Marcus Julius Agrippa, but if any of them had, they would probably have heard his name mentioned—in passing—as a bored prince of the Herodian family, who had once held the office of *agoranomos*, or market inspector, in the Galilean capital of Tiberias. Back in the late 20s, at a time when the urban economy of Herod Antipas's newly established city was expanding—to the delight of the local aristocracy and to the detriment of the surrounding rural population—Prince Agrippa had been entrusted with oversight of the city's commercial activity, the integrity of its weights and measures, and its export-import balance sheet. As a grandson of Herod the Great and the great-great grandson of the Hasmonean king Hyrcanus II, brought up in Rome as a pampered young royal in the household of Augustus, Agrippa clearly had much grander ambitions than municipal government. The death of Tiberius in the spring of 37 therefore came to him as a godsend: Agrippa's old friend, the new emperor Caligula, bestowed upon him the territories in the Upper Jordan Valley—Gaulanitis, Trachonitis, and Batanea—that had been ruled by his late uncle Philip. And Caligula crowned this imperial favor by granting Marcus Julius Agrippa the largely ceremonial title of "king." Kingship and its messianic implications were, of course, themes of the utmost significance to the People of Israel no matter what the Romans might think. No member of the Herodian or Hasmonean House had held a royal title since the death of Herod the Great more than forty years before, and in the summer of 38, on his way back from Rome to Judea, Agrippa received a wildly enthusiastic greeting from the Jews of Alexandria, who viewed him as a potential political savior in their continuing conflicts with the city's militant Greek majority. The celebrations continued upon Agrippa's arrival in Jerusalem. And in the coming years, Agrippa proved to be a skillful—and lucky—navigator through the uncertain currents of imperial favor. After Caligula ordered the exile of Antipas and Herodias to distant Gaul, Agrippa curried the emperor's favor to gain rule over Galilee and Perea. And in the chaos after Caligula's assassination, Agrippa's early and skillful support of the next emperor, Claudius, ultimately won him the prize sought by every Herodian heir since the death of Herod. In 41 C.E., Agrippa was granted the crown of Greater Judea—including Samaria and Idumea—placing him on the throne of a realm that embraced the entire Land of Israel.

For many Judeans, divine favor seemed to be guiding the spectacular political rise of King Agrippa I, who quickly established a position as the most important client king in the region. Aretas of Nabatea had, in the meantime, been succeeded by a weaker younger brother, and a resurgent Judea once again dominated local affairs. Within the Land of Israel, the collection of taxes—which had been carried out separately in Galilee and Judea for more than a generation—was now consolidated and used to support an enlarged army and an ambitious program of public works, especially in Jerusalem. On an ideological level, messianic symbolism was once again utilized to marshal public support for the Herodian regime. The ceremonies and splendor of the Jerusalem Temple—with all their prestige in the eyes of Jews in the Land of Israel and throughout the Roman Empire—became objects of Agrippa's direct patronage, and he assiduously cultivated his public image as Israel's divinely sanctioned king. Centuries later, rabbinic literature preserved memories of Agrippa's great devotion to the Temple and conveyed at least a hint of the deep impression he made. In its discussion of the ancient custom (and apocalyptic hope) that a divinely ordained king of Israel should read the Torah scroll in the Temple at the end of every sabbatical year, the Mishnah (*Sotah* 7:8) provided a moving description of Agrippa's public reading of the Law in the Temple courtyard at the end of the feast of Tabernacles. Standing before the assembled throng of pilgrims and reading from the Book of Deuteronomy, Agrippa reportedly paused at the passage at 17:14–15, which had always been regarded as the central proof text for those who looked forward to the redemption of Israel through the reign of a righteous king.

"When you come to the land which the Lord your God gives you," the passage stated, "you may indeed set as king over you him whom the Lord your God will choose. One from among your brethren you shall set as king over you." According to the Mishnah, Agrippa's "eyes flowed with tears" when he reached this passage, presumably fearing that his tangled Herodian ancestry would disqualify him from the kingly role. Yet many of those who were assembled in the Temple courtyards were ready to accept him: "Do not fear, Agrippa!" the Mishnah reported that they shouted. "You are our brother! You are our brother! You are our brother!" And during the rest of his reign Agrippa indeed enacted the role of a king who would build up "the fallen booth of David." Although the archaeological remains of Agrippa's greatest building project in Jerusalem can now be traced only with difficulty in empty lots and open spaces a few hundred yards north of the northern wall of the Old City, the massive, weathered stones of his unfinished fortification wall represent his ambitious plan to expand and defend David's ancient capital. And to emphasize the significance of his royal actions, Agrippa emblazoned the ancient Near Eastern symbol of the sacred canopy of the Great Kings of Assyria, Babylonia, and Persia on his widely distributed bronze coins.

Yet the adulation enjoyed by Agrippa was far from universal. His majestic bearing and court splendor could only have outraged all those committed to the time-honored Israelite ideal of a kingless Kingdom of God. And if the Jesus Movement, in particular, had begun in protest against the arrogance and emptiness of the messianic pretensions of Herod Antipas, how much more outspoken would be their condemnation of this new Herodian pretender—who had actually achieved all that Antipas had sought. Little wonder, then, that the Jerusalem community of the Jesus Movement soon became the objects of repressive action: two of the Twelve seem to have been targeted directly by King Agrippa's security forces. According to Acts 12:2, James, the son of Zebedee (who with his brother John and with Peter had been among the earliest followers of Jesus among the fishermen of Capernaum), was arrested and executed, and Peter barely escaped a similar fate. The standard explanation of this persecution of the Jerusalem community has always been religious: the followers of Jesus were hunted down and killed by the new king for their refusal to observe the traditional laws of purity and offerings for the Temple—and for their tendency to consort with Gentiles. Yet once again a political explanation appears more plausible. As historian Daniel Schwartz has pointed out in his exhaustive analysis of the reign of Agrippa, there is not the slightest hint in the account of Acts 12 that ritual laxity had anything to do with the crackdown on the leaders of the Jerusalem community of the Jesus Movement. Indeed, the mention of James being put to death "with the sword" (rather than stoning, which was more usual for religious crimes) and the strange absence of the Temple authorities in the legal proceedings suggest that this was an explicitly *political* witchhunt. And if we read the account of Acts against the background of Agrippa's efforts to impress the populace of Judea with his own messianic credentials, it becomes clear that Agrippa's security forces moved against the followers of Jesus as dangerous antiroyal agitators, not as nonobservant Jews.

The ideology of the Jesus Movement in Judea during this period seems to have evolved in direct response to Agrippa's challenge, combining traditional apocalyptic expectations of the coming End of Days with a more symbolic interpretation of the Temple cult. It has always been something of a mystery how and why during this period James, the brother of Jesus, appeared so suddenly as one of the "pillars" of the community— especially since he was not included in the original Twelve. The fact that he was *not* one of the Twelve may have made him a less obvious target for Agrippa, yet it is also possible that James may have risen to prominence by responding to the messianic pretensions of Agrippa in a powerful, if indirect, way. The scriptural designation of James as one of the "pillars" of the Jerusalem community may conceal a clear symbolic allusion of the self-understanding of the Jerusalem community as an *alternative* to the Temple.

Another dissident group, in the wilderness of the Dead Sea shore, also envisioned themselves as a substitute "Temple," poetically identifying the various parts of the ideal Temple described in Isaiah 54:11-12—stones, gates, towers, and wall—with its ruling council and leadership. This closely parallels the use of architectural metaphors in early Christian literature suggesting that Jesus was "the stone that the builders had rejected"; that Peter was the "rock" (*Petros*, in Greek, *Cephas*, in Aramaic) on which the church was built (Matt. 16:18); that the apostles are the "foundations" (Ephesians 2:20); and that the "pillars" were the community's guiding leadership (Gal. 2:9). The second-century church historian Hegesippus described James, in particular, as the "Rampart of the People," and it may be that this emphasis on the human—rather than physical—components of the Temple cult was a direct response to Agrippan propaganda and public works rather than an abstract spiritual ideal. Just as his brother Jesus had confronted the political pretensions and godlessness of an earlier generation of Herodians and their supporters, James was gradually recognized in Judea as the leader and prophet of a renewal movement that would bring about the salvation of the People of Israel.

King Agrippa's messianic campaign, in the meantime, burned out in a blaze of self-promotion. Like his grandfather before him, Agrippa began to style himself as the King of the Jews throughout the Roman Empire, and his regional ambition lured him to underwrite public festivities and impressive monuments in the pagan cities of Caesarea and Sebaste in the Land of Israel, Berytus and Heliopolis-Baalbek in Phoenicia, and even in Athens, the cultural capital of the Greek world. By 43 C.E., at a time when the hostile intentions of the Parthian Empire across the Euphrates had once again become a source of concern to Roman policy planners, Agrippa convened a conclave of fellow client kings in Antipas's old lakeside capital in Tiberias. The invited guests included nearly all of the Roman-educated eastern princes who had been given their thrones by either Caligula or Claudius—Antiochus of Commagene, Sampsigeramus of Emesa, Polemos of Pontus, Cotys of Armenia Minor, and Agrippa's own brother Herod, who had become the ruler of Chalcis, a tiny principality in the mountains of Lebanon. This group assembled by Agrippa represented a confederation of local rulers who, if united, might sway the balance of power between Rome and Parthia. Not surprisingly, the Tiberias conclave was perceived by the emperor's inner circle as a potentially deadly threat to the interests of the empire. When viewed against the background of Agrippa's grandiose public appearances in Jerusalem and his unauthorized attempt to expand the fortifications of his capital city, the Romans concluded that the Judean king had outlived his usefulness. Yet always with a flair for the dramatic, Agrippa's exit proved to be as grand as his entrance. Josephus described his appearance in Caesarea in 44 C.E. to attend an imperial festival, "clad in a garment woven completely of silver," which, reflecting the rays of the morning sun, "was wondrously radiant and by its glitter inspired fear and awe in those who gazed intensely upon it." This was not the costume of a humble client king but a royal messiah, and Josephus went on to report how Agrippa's "flatterers raised their voices—though hardly for his good— addressing him as a god." The Book of Acts 12:21–23 preserved a similar story, telling of Agrippa's royal appearance in Caesarea and the cries of the people who had assembled before him, assuring him that his was "the voice of a god, not a man." The outcome of this messianic pretention was expectable: whether by Roman poison, stroke, heart attack, or smiting by an angel of God (as suggested in Acts 12:23), Agrippa's reign ended as miraculously—and as suddenly—as it had begun.

With Agrippa dead, a grim feeling of powerlessness must have gripped the People of Israel. The expanded Kingdom of Judea was brought under direct control of a succession of imperial procurators, who clearly had only their own—and the empire's—interests in mind. In the coming decades, a succession of Spirit-fired prophets would arise repeatedly in Jerusalem and gather crowds of eager supporters with the claim that God's Kingdom was dawning and that the power of Rome would suddenly crumble. But as far as we know, none of these popular movements had an organizational struc- ture or long-term support system equal to that of the community of the followers of Jesus, now led by his brother James. Although James plays a relatively minor role in the traditional histories of early Christianity, the independent testimony of Josephus indicates that he became a well-known and well-respected figure in Jerusalem. The church historian Hegesippus described him as a pious, priestly figure who wore garments of linen and was often found in the Temple "on his knees beseeching forgiveness for the people, so that his knees grew hard like a camel's from his constantly bending them in the worship of God." Whatever the historical reliability of this later description, we know from subsequent developments that he gave renewed voice to the original idea of the restoration of the kingless Kingdom and to his deep and abiding commitment to Israel's Covenant with God. Sometime in the late 40s, word may have reached the Jerusalem community of the far-flung missionary activity of the Christians of Antioch, with their appeals to the pagans of the surrounding territories. The Book of Acts 11:27–30 preserves memories of contacts between the two communities, and at least one instance of monetary support sent from Antioch to Jerusalem. Missionary outreach to the pagans was a daring and delicate challenge. For the followers of Jesus in Jerusalem—especially after the fall of the apostate "messiah" Agrippa and the return of direct Roman domination—the Renewal of Israel was of prime, urgent importance and they were convinced that observance of the laws of the Mosaic Covenant was the irreducible rock on which the dawning of the Kingdom of God and the mission to the nations would have to be built.

SO THE WORD WENT OUT once more from Zion and the missionary independence of the Antioch community was suddenly shaken to its core. If the Greeks, Syrians, Cypriots, and Galatians who had been attracted to the Renewal Movement through the tireless preaching of the apostles wanted to become full-fledged members of God's holy people, they were free—and even blessed—to do so. Yet, in the opinion of some outspoken followers of Jesus who were intent on keeping the Renewal of Israel in the forefront of the movement, there were certain basic obligations that had to be observed by anyone who would hope to share in the Kingdom of God. According to Acts 15:1, a bitter confrontation erupted in Antioch when "some men came down from Judea and were teaching the brethren, 'Unless you are circumcised according to the custom of Moses, you cannot be saved.'" This demand for circumcision—and the wider observance of Israelite ritual laws it implied—has often been viewed by New Testament commentators as a narrow-minded retreat from universalism, but it can perhaps be better understood, in its specific historical context, as a call for solidarity. In the wake of Agrippa's death and the resumption of direct imperial rule in Judea, many believed that the observance of the Mosaic law, with its distinctive calendar, festivals, life-cycle celebrations, and social regulations, was the only effective way left to the People of Israel to resist Rome's culture of idolatry and inequality. Jesus' resurrection may indeed have signaled the start of the age of redemption, but all the relevant scriptural references suggested that the redemption would be of a renewed, purified, and ultimately expanded *Israel*, in which and through which righteous Gentiles would also be saved. Thus the "men that came down from Judea" to Antioch—perhaps with the support of a local faction of the movement—did not necessarily disavow the universal scope of the movement or of Antioch's mission to the Gentiles but rather sought to reinforce a common vision and purpose for them all.

Yet in the late 40s, no single faction—whether locally formed or arriving from Jerusalem—could easily impose its scriptural interpretations on those who held different ideas. Well over a century would pass before Christianity would, in any sense, be recognizable as an institutionalized religion, with a uniform organizational structure, standard ecclesiastical offices, or an orthodox theology. At this time, the Jesus Movement was still a diffuse network of prophets, teachers, missionaries, village communities, and urban assemblies—spread throughout the Land of Israel and in the major diaspora centers—in which there were many divergent understandings of the significance of Jesus' resurrection and earthly ministry. In a huge city like Antioch, many small house-assemblies were scattered throughout the various quarters and suburbs, and *general* meetings attended by all the Christians in the city would have been either unprecedented or rare. But this new debate, spreading throughout the Antioch community, was apparently bitter, and opinions on both sides of the issue were strong. Opponents of the demand for circumcision of Gentile members could point to the long-standing precedent of the attendance of Godfearers and sympathetic pagans at synagogue assemblies, with the requirement of circumcision never automatically being imposed on them. The Jerusalem community nonetheless had a certain spiritual authority, and the views of its members could not be rejected out of hand. So, according to Acts 15:2, "when Paul and Barnabas had no small dissension and debate with them, Paul and Barnabas and some of the others were appointed to go up to Jerusalem to the apostles and elders" to see if their doctrinal differences could be resolved. With that decision, a turning point had been reached in the history of the movement: the Spirit-fired faith of the Antioch apostles now had to contend with Jerusalem's growing concern with the movement's ideological coherence in a time of apocalyptic confrontation with Rome.

Once again we should recognize that the dispute in Antioch and its eventual outcome, depicted in the scriptures as the clash of towering personalities (Paul and Barnabas against James and the other Jerusalem "pillars"), may also reflect a general transformation in the relationship between the two communities. Paul's later description of the decision to go to Jerusalem—like Acts's account of the decision of the Antioch community to undertake its first foreign mission—avoided the mention of any outside influences or internal discussions, declaring that this fateful step was suggested "by revelation" to him (Gal. 2:2). Years later, when he was writing his letter to the Galatians, Paul sought to emphasize how divine inspiration, rather than personal or political considerations, had directed the course of his career. He believed that he had been commissioned by God to fulfill the role of the faithful servant in Isaiah whom God "had called from the womb" to preach to the non-Israelite peoples (Isa. 49:1; Gal. 1:15). This prophetic figure was destined to face many hardships and obstacles, not the least of which was the fear that he "had labored in vain" (Isa. 49:4). Thus even though it is reasonable to assume that Paul traveled to Jerusalem as a member of a larger delegation from the Antioch community of which the older and more well-established Barnabas was the leader, Paul framed the episode as a personal quest for validation: "I went up again to Jerusalem with Barnabas," he noted in Galatians 2:1, to defend "the gospel which I preach among the Gentiles lest somehow I should be running or had run in vain."

Paul's claim notwithstanding, the vision of righteous Gentiles fulfilling ancient prophecy by harking to God's glory and entering His Kingdom in the final age of redemption was hardly a theological innovation. The concept had long been a powerful and persuasive element of mainstream Jewish prophetic imagery, figuring prominently in the oracles of Isaiah, Jeremiah, Micah, Zephaniah, and Zechariah, as well as in more recent works like the books of Tobit, Enoch, and Jubilees. For most Jews, the prospect of widespread Gentile conversion was a distant expectation, but within the Jesus Movement—due largely to the efforts of Paul's circle in the Antioch community—the word of Israel's God and the impending Day of Judgment was being preached in distant places and among peoples who had no connection with synagogue communities. But the leadership of the Jesus Movement now had to face some important practical questions that the traveling apostles—in their apocalyptic fervor—had neglected to address. How was anyone to know if spirit-filled Gentiles who had been roused by the apostles' preaching were really possessed by *God's* Spirit? What was to be their relationship to the law-observant People of Israel? How could the depth or endurance of their commitment to the Kingdom of God be judged? Some way had to be found to regulate or at least verify the commitment of outsiders in whatever time remained before the coming day of judgment. In an effort to achieve the same objective, other Jewish groups had developed various initiation procedures and classification techniques. The rigid rules of the contemporary Essenes and the Qumran community required that initiates from the outside successfully pass through a series of ever-more-demanding ceremonies and obligations before they were admitted to full membership in the eschatological community. Yet even then, all were not subject to the same level of strictness. According to Josephus, the celibate Essenes made provisions for an associated order of married members who would follow slightly different rules. Likewise, in the Pharasaic movement, there were several levels of training and observance that potential members were required to pass through before admission to full membership.

The Jesus Movement seems to have adopted a parallel procedure in which former pagans might be officially admitted as members of its fellowship. Until the dispute at Antioch, there is no evidence for formal entrance procedures (except perhaps for the ritual of baptism) or membership classes within the movement, but Acts 15:19–21 preserves the text of a detailed ruling reportedly handed down by James in the presence of the Antioch delegation (which some scholars claim was drafted some time later) that set a minimum standard of behavior for believing Gentiles. They would henceforth be required to observe four basic laws: "to abstain from the pollution of idols, and from unchastity, and from what is strangled, and from blood." By the ancient code of Leviticus (Lev. 17:8–9, 10, 13; 18:26), those laws identified them as "sojourners in the midst of Israel"—a class of outsiders who had accompanied the People of Israel in their Exodus wanderings, yet who did not take upon themselves the full burden of the Law. Yet that was apparently only a minimum requirement; as Paul's later letters to the Galatians, Corinthians, and Philippians reveals, many outspoken apostles of Jesus would continue to urge believing Gentiles to undergo circumcision as a formalized ritual of conversion—and thereby to become full members of a Renewed Israel. In the meantime, however, a schism in the movement was averted by the establishment of a legally recognized category of Gentile believer who would not be *compelled* to undergo circumcision. Paul later recalled his satisfaction at the decision, for he had brought along a young man named Titus, to demonstrate the righteousness and faith of Antioch's non-Israelite Christians. The demonstration was apparently effective. As Paul noted, "even Titus, who was with me, was not compelled to be circumcised, though he was a Greek" (Gal. 2:3).

The Jerusalem conference seems to have concluded with a new sense of shared fellowship and purpose in a movement that included both Jews and Gentiles—and that feeling was manifested in an extraordinarily down-to-earth way. Paul's final reminiscence of the meeting recalled how the Jerusalem leadership had requested that they "remember the poor, which of course I was eager to do" (Gal. 2:10). Traditional scholarship has usually interpreted this phrase as a reference to a voluntary, personal vow made by Paul to send occasional monetary contributions to "the poor" of the Jerusalem community (with the "poor" being a purely spiritual or poetic designation for the leadership). Yet the phrase may well refer to a broader agreement by the Antioch community—rather than just Paul and Barnabas—to help support the destitute men, women, and children in the Jesus Movement generally. We have already seen how the Jerusalem community had established a unique communal living arrangement in the city, pooling all their private resources and providing for the distribution "to each as any had need" (Acts 4:35). It is reasonable to assume that at least some of the diaspora assemblies of the Jesus Movement, founded by apostles from Jerusalem, were based on a similar principle of sharing—and the viability of such utopian villages-in-the-city would have been difficult if not impossible to maintain in the competitive, hierarchical economy of the Roman Empire. Thus, the Antioch delegation, in reaching a meeting of the minds with the Jerusalem leadership on a doctrinal matter, may have agreed to cooperate in a program of economic support for the material survival of the movement. Indeed, Paul would later consider the raising of a "collection" for the assemblies of Judea to be an important demonstration of Christian solidarity.

So the Antioch representatives returned northward, linked by a new series of agreements with the Jerusalem community. But new issues of dispute were not long in arising. If non-circumcised, non-Israelite converts were to be considered "sojourners" rather than true Israelites, should any distinction be made between them in the many house-congregations of Antioch where Jews and Gentiles, living together in crowded city quarters, freely mixed? Once again we have a scriptural story about a clash between well-known personalities that may signify a more complex, community-wide change. According to Galatians 2:11–13, Peter, the Galilean fisherman-turned-apostle, arrived in Antioch on a visit shortly after the Jerusalem conference and willingly joined in a mixed Jewish-Gentile celebration of table fellowship. Yet he was severely rebuked by arriving representatives from Jerusalem ("certain men from James" according to Gal. 2:12) who demanded that Gentile and Jewish members celebrate their meals separately. Their arguments were apparently persuasive, for Paul later reported that not only Peter but Barnabas and "the rest of the Jews" of the Antioch community drew back and separated themselves (Gal. 2:13). Antioch's scattered Christian house-congregations were thus at least temporarily divided between assemblies of Torah-observant members (both Jews and full Gentile converts)—and assemblies of "sojourners" who, though ritually distinct, together comprised a new People of God. The extended residence in Antioch of the Apostle Peter, closely connected with the original movement for the Renewal of Israel and long remembered in church tradition as the first "bishop" of the city, may reflect this change of affairs. Meanwhile, active missionary outreach continued. Acts 15:39 suggested that Barnabas set off again to spread the word of Jesus in his native island of Cyprus, and other first-century sources report that Antioch continued to be one of the most important and energetic centers of early Christianity.

Yet there was at least one member of the Antioch community who refused to go along with the new organizational arrangement. Paul adamantly clung to the belief that the Kingdom of God was already dawning and that, whatever anti-Roman political agenda the Judeans might harbor, his vision of a completely Spirit-driven, Law-free mission to the Gentiles was divinely inspired. Although the post-crucifixion appearances of Jesus to Peter, James, the Twelve, and the other brethren in Jerusalem had become legendary throughout the movement, Paul considered himself no less an apostle—for on the road to Damascus "last of all, as to one untimely born, he appeared to me" (1 Cor. 15:8). Paul had been active for years in preaching the gospel of Jesus as he understood it, and he was convinced that the joyful singing and praying of Gentiles for the advent of the Kingdom—in their own way and on their own terms, without ritual requirements or special categorization—was an essential part of the ongoing redemption of the world. Had not Isaiah insisted: "Let not the foreigner who has joined himself to the Lord say, 'The Lord will surely separate me from his people'; and let not the eunuch say 'Behold I am a dry tree' " (56:3). Though perhaps only gradually recognizing his prophetic destiny as a uniquely commissioned Apostle to the Gentiles in the course of his proselytizing travels, Paul felt betrayed by his colleagues and passionately believed that the establishment of the Kingdom of God—through the ingathering of Spirit-filled Gentiles—now depended on him. The day of judgment was quickly approaching and Paul was intent on spreading the word of Jesus freely, no matter what the authorities in Antioch and Jerusalem believed. Paul therefore turned his back on Antioch and set off on his own into unfamiliar regions and among distant peoples, as if to fulfill the words of Isaiah: "It is too light a thing that you should be my servant to raise up the tribes of Jacob and restore the preserved of Israel; I will give you as a light to the nations, that my salvation may reach to the end of the earth" (49:6).

7

Assemblies of the Saints

EYOND THE HIGH RANGE of the Taurus Mountains, stretching
northward for hundreds of miles across the sun-baked highlands of
Galatia to the islands and jagged coastlands of the Aegean, lay a
vivid patchwork of ethnic groups, regions, and peoples whose proud
histories and ancient traditions were being slowly and painfully destroyed
by the Roman Empire. From the perspective of the Hellenistic cities of
Syria and Cilicia from which Paul set out on his independent mission, those
regions beyond the mountains were the far-flung lands of myths, monsters,
and heroes—of Greeks, Macedonians, Thracians, Trojans, Amazons, Phry-
gians, and assorted other Anatolian peoples—who had been celebrated in the works of classical historians, poets, and artists for hundreds of
years. But from the perspective of imperial balance sheets and provincial
administration, those fabled lands and peoples had now been conquered
and carved up into four vast and entirely artificial provinces—Achaia,
Macedonia, Asia, and Galatia—each ruled by a Roman governor with a
military garrison and small staff of accountants, retainers, and scribes.
Those provincial structures existed for only one reason: to ensure that each
region be economically developed and efficiently exploited, providing a
continuous flow of resources, crops, crafts, commerce, and—most of all—
tax revenues toward Rome. To that end, new roads were built and
new cities established at strategic points along the main trade routes,
with Roman-style administrative buildings, marketplaces, theaters, and

impressive temples to the emperors sprouting up among the shrines to local deities. Yet for the vast majority of the population (perhaps as much as nine-tenths of the total), who struggled to survive from farming and herding in the surrounding rural territory, those tiny islands of marble rising across the provincial landscape in the midst of the plowed fields, pasture land, and scrubland could not be regarded as much more than the police stations and tax-collection centers of the new political and economic order. And for at least some of those countless Galatians, Macedonians, and Achaians who felt more pain than pleasure from the rule of the Caesars, the gospel that Paul brought to the region provided a reinforced sense of community and the prospect of eventual freedom from Rome.

For almost a decade—from about 48 to 56 C.E.—Paul ranged widely over the provinces of Galatia, Macedonia, Achaia, and Asia, sometimes alone, often accompanied by two or three companions, preaching tirelessly about the impending changes that he believed were about to sweep over the world. He traveled through rural areas where hard-pressed peasant populations responded with joy to the prospect of a coming day of judgment when their burdens would be lifted and when ambitious landlords and cold-hearted estate stewards would finally receive their just rewards. He preached in crowded urban streets and workshops where day laborers, slaves, and indentured craftspeople dreamed of regaining control of their own futures—assuring them that they would live to see the current imperial regime of power and economic inequality crumble before their eyes. Yet in order to reconstruct the history and development of Paul's movement, with its far-reaching implications for the subsequent religious history of Europe and the Mediterranean region, we must recognize both the value and the limitations of our two main scriptural sources: the collection of Paul's letters preserved in the New Testament and the connected narrative of the Book of Acts. As we noted in the last chapter, the Book of Acts offers a fascinating tale, filled with exciting adventures and stirring speeches, that traces Paul's career along a winding geographical course from Tarsus to Damascus to Arabia to Jerusalem to Antioch through Asia Minor, to Macedonia, Achaia, and Asia, and, after a final fateful return to Judea, to Rome. Moving from one vivid scene to another, its text glosses over long journeys and stretches of time with just a few words of transition; reports of intensive missionary activities in cities like Philippi, Thessalonica, Corinth, and Ephesus are reduced to a few specially selected anecdotes mentioning only a handful of individuals by name.

This literary approach has obvious power: the Book of Acts is a histori-cal pageant of epic proportions, in which the listing of specific names and places is far less important than the deeper spiritual lesson being conveyed. In retelling the story of the wide-ranging journeys of Paul and the earliest apostles, Acts vividly personalizes a long, complex process by which the original Judean and Galilean Renewal Movement began to take on a worldwide scope. To regard it as a literal, journalistic chronicle account of what actually happened to Paul in each of the regions he passed through is to misunderstand its value as a poetic expression of the author's faith in the divinely ordained triumph of Christianity.

Yet if Acts is a biblical epic, spanning continents and oceans, Paul's epistles are extracts from the handwritten journal of a revolutionary work-in-progress—a collection of passionate notes from the underground. In their web of scriptural references and complex argumentation about the meaning of Christ's crucifixion and resurrection, about the nature of salva-tion, faith, law, and history, the epistles convey the twists and turns in the fortunes of a radical movement of apocalyptic expectation, in which civil authorities, religious rivals, and faithless disciples pose constant dangers to Paul and his companions and in which the overall prospects of success often seem far from assured. Although the Pauline letters have been adopted as separate "books" of the New Testament and have been inter-preted for centuries as timeless theological essays, we must remember that each letter (and, in some cases, specific passages *within* individual letters) was composed in a particular historical context. Writing to various groups of his followers in documents that were meant to be read aloud to the assembled congregation, Paul never intended any of his letters to offer a general exposition of his gospel (he had presumably done that before—in person), but he composed them to include only those arguments that he believed would be most effective in dealing with questions or pressing disputes that arose at specific places and times, among specific groups of his followers.

As modern readers of Paul's letters, we are therefore catching only occasional snatches of ongoing dialogue between Paul and his commu-nities. And the modern scholar's task of reconstructing the nature of the relationship between Paul and his followers is made even more difficult by the general consensus that only seven of the fourteen letters ascribed to Paul in the New Testament (Romans, First and Second Corinthians, Gala-tians, First Thessalonians, Philemon, and Philippians) are his authentic compositions. The seven others (Second Thessalonians, Ephesians, Colossians, First and Second Timothy, Titus, and Hebrews) are believed—on the basis of clear differences in style and subject matter—to be the work of a *second* generation of Paul's followers and therefore of only indirect historical value for tracing Paul's career. It is thus only by examining the authentic letters of Paul (arranged in a chronological order suggested both by internal evidence and the general framework of the Book of Acts) and analyzing them against the historical events and archaeological remains in Greece and Asia Minor during the reigns of Claudius (41–54 C.E.) and Nero (54–68 C.E.) that we can begin to construct a dramatic new understanding of the gradual crystallization of Pauline Christianity.

HOW COULD A SINGLE MAN—with the help of only one or two companions—ever bring word of divine redemption to the population of a vast area that spanned mountains, oceans, and islands over thousands and thousands of square miles? How could he persuade the few truly righteous men and women scattered among the world's peoples that they must separate themselves from the ways of the wicked and await the impending climax of a divine drama that had been unfolding for thousands of years? He would do it by recognizing how Roman imperial rule manifested itself in each of the regions he visited—and by skillfully adapting the core images and ideals of the Jesus Movement to the specific cultural traditions of each province's population, he could organize a network of local movements of resistance and renewed communities.

Paul's earlier travels with Barnabas had carried him across the Taurus Mountains to the towns of Pisidian Antioch, Iconium, Derbe, and Lystra along the Via Sebaste, and it is not surprising that the Book of Acts 15:41 suggests that Paul returned there immediately after his break with Peter and Barnabas, this time with only a single companion—a man variously named Silas in Acts or Silvanus in Paul's letters and described as a "prophet" (15:32)—who seems to have been naturally inclined to sympathize with Paul's reliance on the Spirit over tradition or the scrupulous observance of Mosaic law. Arriving in the Lycaonian town of Lystra a second time, he gained the assistance of a young man named Timothy, whose reported circumcision (16:3) may suggest that he had been drawn into the Jesus Movement as the result of Antioch's earlier missionary campaigns. Yet Paul, Silas, and Timothy apparently did not tarry long or establish any new assemblies in this region; according to Acts they soon headed north "through the region of Phrygia and Galatia" (16:6), joining the traffic of traders, pilgrims, soldiers, and imperial officials already on the road. And while some scholars suggest that their subsequent route took them northwestward toward the Aegean and the cities of Macedonia, other scholars suggest that Paul and his companions proceeded due northward toward the scattered villages of the Galatian highlands to embark on a dramatically new missionary endeavor. And there is good reason to suppose that it was there in the remote and largely rural region of central Asia Minor that Paul's first independent assemblies of the "saints" arose.

Northern Galatia was not a place where members of the Jewish people had ever wandered. In contrast to the ancient trading cities of Cilicia, Syria, and Judea—and to the Romanized market towns of the Taurus region—the landscape of central Anatolia was an almost entirely unurbanized expanse of wheat fields and scattered villages of *Galatai*, "Gauls" or "Galatians," an isolated population of farmers and herders who spoke a language akin to Welsh and Gaelic and celebrated the memory of their heroic Celtic chieftains who had led them from their original European homeland several centuries before. Biblical tradition identified these people as the descendants of Noah's son Japhet—in particular, of Japhet's firstborn son Gomer. But among the Greeks and Romans, the Galatians were known only as a fierce and warlike northern people, who had migrated *en masse* from Europe to Asia Minor in the time of the early Hellenistic kings. The Galatians long clung to their ancestral habits, holding raucous communal feasts, providing support for the indigent among them, and gathering in village assemblies to debate and decide on matters of concern to the entire community. Only gradually did they abandon their raiding and occasional service as mercenaries to settle down in those parts of central Anatolia where the seasonal rains made agriculture possible. By that time, the Galatians' chieftains had succumbed to the allure of Greco-Roman culture, eventually becoming client kings of the Romans and adopting the lifestyles indistinguishable from those of the nobility of neighboring Hellenistic kingdoms and city-states. As a result, the majority of the Galatians were reduced to the status of tax- and tribute-paying peasants, surviving as best they could from what was left of the produce of their crops and herds. And by 25 B.C.E., with the death of the powerful Galatian king Amyntas, Rome moved quickly to annex this large and strategically important kingdom in the heart of Asia Minor, dispatching a high-ranking governor and experienced legionary forces to pacify and rule the newly created province of "Galatia."

No less than in Galilee or Judea, Roman rule brought far-reaching changes to the character of Galatia's economic and social life. Classical historian Stephen Mitchell has reconstructed the main outlines of an ominously familiar historical process: with imperial annexation and taxation, the rural population of Galatia became increasingly indebted to government officials, local aristocrats, and independent Roman entrepreneurs, or *negotiatores*, from whom they obtained cash for tax payments by selling off parcels of tribal land or pledging the produce of future harvests in return for immediate loans. The subsequent, deepening spiral of indebtedness and dispossession gradually transformed Galatia's landscape of scattered villages of herders and subsistence farmers into vast grain-growing estates owned by a new class of absentee landowners residing in the distant provincial capital of Ancyra—and managed by a corps of managers and tax collectors (usually former slaves of the great landlords) who increasingly controlled the lives of the Galatian peasantry.

Paul later recalled that as he, Silas, and Timothy passed from place to place throughout Galatia, God had provided vivid demonstrations of the Spirit, working miracles among the people he encountered (Gal. 3:2–5), which was the usual way of describing spontaneous healings, exorcisms, and speaking in tongues. Indeed, we can detect in Paul's Letter to the Galatians the memory of an initial period of rural enthusiasm strikingly reminiscent of the movement that had swept over Judea and Galilee. Paul later vividly described the deeply felt personal experience of many Galatians into whose hearts "God has sent the Spirit of his Son" and who responded by crying out "Abba! Father!" (Gal. 4:6). There is no reason to see in this text—as many commentators have done—merely a reference to recitation of the Lord's Prayer or a standardized baptismal formula. The Greek verb *krazein*, "to cry out" to heaven (used here and in the parallel passage in Rom. 8:15), conveys a sense of shouting or blurting out sounds through violent trance or Spirit possession, and suggests that Paul's mission to Galatia was not a sedate program of spiritual education—methodically converting a pagan population to the spirtual advantages of monotheism. It was, instead, a series of Spirit-filled demonstrations of enlivening power that convinced the Galatians to join a new movement and forswear the power of Greco-Roman paganism, whose official rituals and ideology of privilege kept them in chains. Paul implored the Galatians to abandon their "bondage to beings that by nature are no gods" and from "the weak and beggarly spirits" whose slaves they had become (Gal. 4:8–10).

Paul's work in the rural regions of Galatia must therefore be seen as the beginning of a renewal movement that was parallel to, yet clearly not synonymous with, the Renewal of Israel. The *ekklesiai*, or "assemblies," that Paul established in Galatia were a revival of traditional Galatian community life. His practical instructions to the Galatians to "be servants of one another" (5:13); "to walk by the Spirit and do not gratify the desires of the flesh" (5:16); "to have no self-conceit, no provoking of one another, no envy of one another" (5:26); and to "bear one another's burdens and so fulfill the law of Christ" (6:2) must be understood as practical ethics for impoverished tenant farmers, whose economic survival could be best brought about by community discipline and coordinated action—not the cold chaos of individualism. Paul's gospel, in its far more elaborate exposition that is merely hinted at in the letter, offered the Galatians a strategy of resistance, not merely a "religion" that could be neatly separated from other facets of life. It is crucial to recognize the specific political and economic regime to which Paul referred when he assured his Galatian followers that "for freedom Christ has set us free; stand fast therefore and do not submit again to a yoke of slavery" (Gal. 5:1).

WE DO NOT GET THE IMPRESSION from either Acts or the letters that Paul had a definite timetable or geographical limit for his mission. Paul presumably knew that he, Silas, and Timothy—with only the limited funds they brought with them from Antioch—could not survive on the road indefinitely. They would have to depend on their wits and on the generosity of those who had been touched by the Spirit to supply them with food and shelter. Indeed, the experience was apparently neither comfortable nor easy, for Paul later recalled that it was only because he was unable to travel due to "a bodily ailment" that he began to preach the gospel in Galatia, and his mission prospered only because the people of the region, taking him in as the result of his disability and offering him their hospitality, honored him "as an angel of God" (Gal. 4:13–14). Yet it was precisely this lack of a fixed itinerary that enabled him to see many of the differing faces of Roman rule in the eastern provinces and to recognize that his movement would have to be simultaneously global and local. In this insight would lie an important key to the subsequent expansion and development of early Christianity.

How they came to choose the province of Macedonia as their next missionary destination must remain a mystery—even though the Book of Acts, in its consistent literary aim of fitting the many events of Paul's career into a larger, divinely ordained framework, suggests that heavenly guidance, rather than more down-to-earth considerations, was decisive in determining their course. "And they went through the region of Phrygia and Galatia, having been forbidden by the Holy Spirit to speak the word in Asia. And when they had come opposite Mysia, they attempted to go into Bithynia, but the Spirit of Jesus did not allow them; so passing by Mysia, they went down to Troas. And a vision appeared to Paul in the night: a man of Macedonia was standing beseeching him and saying: 'Come over to Macedonia and help us.' And when he had seen the vision, immediately we sought to go on to Macedonia, concluding that God had called us to preach the gospel to them" (Acts 16:6–10).

At the time of Paul's arrival, the name "Macedonia" had a legendary reputation throughout the Greco-Roman world as the homeland of Alexander the Great and the founders of the great Hellenistic kingdoms, but once there, Paul and his companions confronted a social and political landscape unlike any they had experienced before. After more than a century of intermittent warfare and economic exploitation, Macedonia had become a largely devastated imperial province entirely subject to the whims and the instructions of the Roman governor, who resided in the port city of Thessalonica. The population of the outlying districts was clustered in villages around the few tiny "cities" established by the Roman authorities to ensure the security of the Via Egnatia, the vital east-west highway linking the Aegean with the Adriatic Sea. Only in the remote, mountainous regions of Upper Macedonia did *koina*, or ancient tribal leagues, still function. On the coastal plain and among the cities through which Paul traveled, the Macedonians' traditional ethnic identities and institutions had been almost completely pulverized.

The Book of Acts 16:11–40 offers an elaborate description of Paul's arrival and missionary work in the province of Macedonia: after sailing across the Aegean from the port of Troas in Asia Minor and disembarking at Neapolis, he and his companions made their way inland "to Philippi, which is the leading city of the district of Macedonia, and a Roman colony." Their subsequent adventures in the city were enacted in a completely urban landscape of householders, slave owners, city fathers, and imperial officers. Yet archaeological excavations at the site of Philippi have offered evidence that a strictly urban mission here was extremely unlikely; at the time of Paul's visit in 49 or 50 C.E., Philippi's enclosed urban area covered only a quarter of a square mile—hardly enough room for much more than a closely packed civic center area of forum, theater, baths, temples, and gymnasium. Moreover, intensive archaeological surveys and ancient tomb inscriptions in the vicinity have shown that Philippi's urban core was just the centerpoint of a complex network of villages, estates, hamlets, and townlets—in which urban and rural economies were closely intertwined. Yet throughout the entire province, the distribution of political rights and economic benefits of empire were profoundly unequal: not only were the newly arrived Roman colonists in the area exempt from direct taxation, they alone were entitled to serve as leaders of local governing bodies—overseeing the collection of taxes from the local peasant population, along with the repayment of loans and the payment of rents.

Membership in the Kingdom of God offered the disenfranchised people of this region a means to empowerment—and here, Paul ironically utilized models from the contemporary Macedonian environment to define the character of their newly formed communities. It is clear that Paul was a keen observer of local conditions in every region through which he traveled. And having recognized how the people of the towns and villages had been excluded from full participation in the civic affairs of the Roman colony of Julia Augusta Philippensis, he assured the members of the assemblies he formed in the region of Philippi that they could now regard themselves as first-class citizens in their own heavenly *politeuma*, or commonwealth (Phil. 3:20). Although local aristocrats and Roman officials held all power and influence through the laws of the Roman province, the Christian commonwealth of mutual support and cooperation would rise above all others, with the coming of their *soter*, or savior, the Lord Jesus Christ. In the meantime, they would have to prepare themselves by strengthening their communal bonds with one another, "standing firm in one spirit, striving side by side with a common mind for the faith of the gospel" (1:27). Paul's admonitions to "do nothing from selfishness or conceit" (2:3) and to "let each of you look not only to his own interests, but also to the interests of others" (2:4) can certainly be seen as timeless ethical ideals, but they can also—and, we suggest, *must* also—be seen in practical, political terms as a means of resistance to the "crooked and perverse generation" (Phil. 2:15) whose obsession with wealth, social status, and place in the pyramid of power of the empire were the core values of the Augustan Age.

As a practical step toward the realization of their own redemption, the followers of Paul at Philippi took upon themselves a voluntary economic commitment without which the subsequent progress of the movement would have been impossible. "You Philippians know," Paul later recalled in gratitude, "that in the beginning of the gospel, when I left Macedonia, no church entered into partnership with me in giving and receiving except you only" (Phil. 4:15). That *koinonia*, or "partnership," was in the form of financial sacrifice, with the shared resources of the community—the funds pooled by the citizens of the heavenly *politeuma*—to be used to further the work of the gospel on earth. A permanent organization had at last begun to take shape in Philippi under Paul's guidance, with the active involvement of local men and women like Epaphroditus, Clement, Syntyche, and Euodia—whom Paul termed "my fellow workers, whose names are in the book of life" (Phil. 4:3). And from Philippi onward, Paul's mission was not to be just a vague peregrination directed by the Spirit and supported by the kindness of strangers. It had become a self-consciously independent apocalyptic movement, dedicated to the ideal of a new social order. All of its members were expected to set aside a significant portion of their liquid assets for evangelism and social welfare, fully cognizant that they must bide their time and survive as a community—*within* the structures of power of the Roman Empire.

SOMETHING DRAMATIC HAPPENED in Thessalonica, something that caused Paul to depict the Risen Jesus in distinctly *imperial* imagery. Paul had set off from Philippi toward the capital of the province, intending to spread the word of the Kingdom to the very center of the Roman provincial administration, but upon arriving in Thessalonica, he discovered just how tight Caesar's grip was on the hearts and minds of the humble tradespeople, craftspeople, slaves, servants, and day laborers, who had gradually drifted into the city from the rural areas over the previous few decades to find places for themselves in the highly stratified urban economy.

There are indications in Paul's later Letter to the Thessalonians that the community he founded there was predominantly poor, hardly a representative cross-section of imperial society. Paul stressed the "extreme poverty" of the Macedonian believers (2 Cor. 8:2–4), and his specific exhortation to the members of the *ekklesia* at Thessalonica "to aspire to live quietly, to mind your own affairs, and to work with your hands" (1 Thess. 4:11) offers a suggestive clue that they were primarily laborers or artisans. The spiritual ground seems to have been prepared for the acceptance of Paul's gospel. A number of modern scholars have pointed out that the indigenous Macedonian cult of Cabirus, a local Dionysus-type figure worshipped in Thessalonica and environs, had obvious, if superficial, similarities to the image of the crucified and resurrected messiah of Galilee. Cabirus was a legendary hero, perfidiously murdered by his brothers and buried with symbols of royal power, who was expected to return someday to aid the downtrodden people of Thessalonica. As a working-class demigod often pictured hefting a blacksmith's hammer, his tales told of his great acts of magic performed on behalf of the needy, his power to restore fertility and sexual fulfillment, and his liberation of slaves. Yet during the early empire, Thessalonica's ruling elite had gradually incorporated the cult of Cabirus into the established civic ceremonies—and into the public celebration of their own power and prestige. The emptiness of this cult was obvious to those who joined Paul's movement. He later recalled "what a welcome we had among you, and how you turned to God from idols, to serve a living and true God, and to wait for his Son from heaven, whom he raised from the dead, Jesus who delivers us from the wrath to come" (1 Thess. 1:9–10).

The Book of Acts's account of Paul's mission in Thessalonica speaks only of public preaching and religious disputation, yet it seems clear that he quickly settled into a routine in the city, apparently finding a trade or other means of employment to support himself during his extended stay. "For you remember our labor and toil, brethren; we worked night and day, that we might not burden any of you, while we preached to you the gospel of God" (1 Thess. 2:9). Although there is no indication that Paul encouraged his Thessalonian followers actively to resist the institutions of power or consciously evade the payment of rents or taxes, their new way of life was certainly not conducive to cold Roman ideas of efficiency and profitability. Community was everything; personal status was a thing to be despised. "We exhort you, brethren," Paul would write to them shortly after his departure, "admonish the idle, encourage the fainthearted, help the weak, be patient with them all. See that none of you repays evil for evil, but always seek to do good to one another and to all" (1 Thess. 5:14–15). And here is the political significance of this movement: in establishing an alternative order, it defied the power of the hierarchy of tax collectors, officers, and local grandees.

The official worship of the emperor in Thessalonica—as in all other provincial cities—was a public expression not only of allegiance to Rome but of symbolic support for the entire structure of patronage and clientage on which it was based. Just at the time when Paul was making his way through Macedonia, the Emperor Claudius was making a decided change in his attitude toward his own reputed divinity. In a sharp turnabout from the policy of his earlier reign, when, for example, he sternly prohibited the people of Alexandria from building a temple in his honor, Claudius now began actively to promote his own worship in the provinces and accordingly adopted the characteristic Augustan title of "savior of the world." Although there is no record of Claudius ever having made an ostentatious imperial progress along the Via Egnatia to display his imperial splendor to the people of Macedonia, the images of royal grandeur that were used to awe the emperor's subjects were common features in public sculpture and other visual arts. Thus, as we learn from his own later Letter to the Thessalonians, Paul had begun to evoke a new image of Christ that posed a direct challenge to the standard imperial imagery. Christ's universal rule might still be hidden, but his imminent *parousia*, or "coming," would be far more impressive than any Roman triumph or military campaign.

More and more Paul came to express his understanding of Christ's power in the idiom of empire. Speaking of the expected day of judgment, he later wrote to the Thessalonians with unmistakable imperial imagery: "For the Lord himself will descend from heaven with a cry of command, with the archangel's call, and with the sound of the trumpet of God" (1 Thess. 4:16). Elsewhere in the letter Paul invited the members of the community to become the palace guard of this heavenly emperor, to put on "the breastplate of love and faith" and the "helmet of love and salvation" (1 Thess. 5:8). These images, initially drawn from Jewish apocalyptic imagery, were at the same time inextricably linked with the visual symbolism of Roman rule. No wonder that Paul and the new community he founded ran into intense hostility and "persecutions" in Thessalonica, for his movement was, at least in its rhetoric and imagery, contesting the legitimacy of Rome. The political stakes of such pointed apocalyptic agitation were enormous—precisely at this time of increasing official repression of unauthorized, "seditious" groups. In Rome itself, according to the later chronicle of Suetonius, Claudius had recently expelled some Jews from the city, because they "caused continuous disturbances at the instigation of Chrestus"—apparently a reference to another branch of the Jesus Movement that had established itself there. The political implications of Paul's preaching in Thessalonica must therefore have been clear to the Thessalonian authorities. Acts 17:6 has his accusers report to the *politarchs* of Thessalonica that "these men who have turned the world upside down have come here also," and in a sense that accusation was true. Paul was organizing a countersociety loyal to a world-conquering emperor whose name was *not* Caesar. And that was sedition against the Roman order, not merely a religious heresy of concern only to the city's Jews.

Paul's response was to press on toward the heart of the empire, ever more convinced that his movement must confront, not shy away from, the realities of Roman rule. Of his subsequent departure from Macedonia, we hear nothing in his own letters except for a short comment in First Thessalonians that he had spent some time "left behind at Athens alone" (3:1). As usual, the Book of Acts 17:10–15 offers exciting tales of evangelistic adventure, repressive violence, and daring escapes. We read of Paul's nighttime flight from Thessalonica, his brief ministry in the southern Macedonian town of Beroea (with its standard description of initial preaching in the local synagogue, followed by vindictive persecution by Jews). With Silas and Timothy remaining in hiding in Beroea, Paul made his way southward into the province of Achaia. And once there, he sent back instructions that Silas and Timothy should rejoin him as soon as possible. Even though he wanted to return to the community in Thessalonica, the danger was apparently too great. As he put it in First Thessalonians 2:18, "Satan hindered us." But by this time it apparently did not matter to him if he crossed geographical or political borders, for he was no longer seeking discrete or identifiable peoples to restore. His experiences since leaving Galatia had made it clear that in this "evil age" peoples were becoming hopelessly jumbled and placed at each other's throats, both through the structures of empire on a region-wide level and through the ubiquitous local institutions of political patronage and the realities of economic inequality.

The challenge for Paul was now to go further—to spread the message throughout all of the Roman Empire that the miracles he worked and the assemblies he established were not ends in themselves. And even as imperial arrogance and economic oppression intensified around them, Paul and his followers clung to the hope of imminent divine intervention. This was not merely an abstract spiritual metaphor or distant expectation but a vivid hope that they would soon witness the utter destruction of "this evil age." In a stunning mystical revelation, Paul had caught a vivid glimpse of that great moment of liberation, when Christ would return to earth and vanquish all hatred, evil, and suffering (1 Thess. 4:16–17). It would be a time of fearful vengeance, when Christ would "deliver the kingdom to God the Father after destroying every rule and every authority and power. For he must reign until he has put all his enemies under his feet" (1 Cor. 15:24–25). At a time of imperial expansion, economic injustice, and rising social tensions, Paul was beginning to forge an empire-wide movement of suffering and disenfranchised people who dreamed of being the beneficiaries, not the victims, of an all-powerful emperor.

BY THE AUTUMN of 50 C.E., in the scattered villages of the Galatian highlands, at weekly gatherings in the rural districts around the Macedonian town of Philippi, and among the workshops and close-packed houses of the provincial capital of Thessalonica, small communities of "saints" continued to gather for their regular common meals together, for their hymns and healing meetings, and for their joyous expectation of the coming of the Lord. It is likely that the rituals and expressions of these various *ekklesiai* differed dramatically from one another in their earliest stages of organization. The message and meaning of Paul's gospel would have had a vastly different significance to villagers who lived all their lives working the fields of vast Anatolian plantations; to Macedonian peasants tending fields within sight of the rising marble colonnades and temples of newly imperialized cities; or to the craftspeople and workers who depended for survival on the bustle and barter of the urban scene.

Differences of language, dialect, social class, and worldview would have prevented the members of these various assemblies from meshing easily together face-to-face in a single congregation, even if they had indeed accepted in principle Paul's teaching that in this new worldwide movement of God's elect "there is neither Jew nor Greek, there is neither slave nor free, there is neither male nor female" (Gal. 3:28). The cultural distinctiveness of the various communities would have tended to focus their hope and devotion on the imminent transformation of *local* conditions of poverty and oppression, weakening the possibility for a truly worldwide movement to arise. That is perhaps why the ritual focus on the figure of Jesus Christ began to take on overarching significance in Paul's movement—representing in personified form a complex, many-faceted constellation of values, symbols, and behavior that could in its *entirety* transcend cultural differences between Jews, Greeks, Galatians, and Macedonians and in its *specifics* offer distinct and culturally powerful images of renewal and resurrection to each group. Thus in some places in Paul's letters, Jesus Christ appeared as a crucified victim, in others as a self-sacrificing divine figure, and in other places—where the idiom of Roman power was more deeply ingrained—as a conquering general who would come to wreak vengeance on his enemies.

Paul's many-faceted image of Christ was thus dramatically different from the historical figure who had lived a full generation before in the remote Galilean tetrarchy of Herod Antipas and had ended his life in a passionate prophetic demonstration against the Jerusalem authorities. The Jesus Christ to whom the members of Paul's movement paid homage in their hymns and in their rituals was an almost abstract source of redemptive power, a universal protector and savior figure who would soon return on the clouds above as a triumphant redeemer of the faithful, who would usher in the end of the present, sinful world. The details that Paul provided about Jesus' pre-crucifixion life in Galilee are sketchy almost to the point of being unimportant. He related only that the earthly Jesus was a Jew "born of woman, born under the law" (Gal. 4:4) and shared in the royal heritage of the people of the ancient land of Judea, being "descended from David according to the flesh" (Rom. 1:3). Yet there is not the slightest indication that Paul elaborated much more to his followers about the teachings, travels, and healings of Jesus, or even that Paul himself had access to additional first-hand information through contact with the surviving kinsfolk and early followers of Jesus still living in the villages of Galilee and southern Phoenicia, and still fishing, still tilling the earth as peasants or tenant farmers, trying to keep the Spirit-inspired sayings and parables of Jesus alive in their memories.

Paul's only main source of first-hand information about the life of Jesus was the Twelve in Jerusalem. In any case, his deepest interest was not in the earthly Jesus but on his martyrdom and heavenly vindication: how "he died for our sins in accordance with the scriptures, that he was buried, that he was raised on the third day in accordance with the scriptures, and that he appeared to Cephas, then to the twelve" (1 Cor. 15:3–5). For Paul, the importance of the crucifixion was not as a tragic injustice or the sacrifice of a noble leader for a specific political cause. He interpreted it rather as an event of cosmic dimensions, a divine drama in which the political and spiritual fate of all the world's peoples was at stake.

For Paul, knowledge about Jesus Christ—and the continuing contact of the believers with the healing, redeeming power of the Holy Spirit—did not come primarily from memory or from recorded traditions but from the collective fervor of communities driven to seek escape from the pressures and tensions of life as it was currently lived. In the gatherings of the saints, where no one was required to shuffle, bow, or pay homage to any *human* ruler or patron, the gospel came "not only in word, but also in power and in the Holy Spirit and with full conviction" (1 Thess. 1:5), transforming the lives of infirm, tormented, and formerly powerless people in tangible ways. We have no means of assessing the extent, nature, or permanence of the physical cures and other miracles that these explosions of the Spirit effected among Paul's followers, but they seem to have sparked an active change in behavior and community feeling—seeing in Jesus Christ not merely a heavenly patron but, in his martyrdom, a model for emulation. "Do nothing from selfishness or conceit, but in humility count others better than yourselves. Let each of you look not only to his own interests, but also to the interests of others. Have this in mind among yourselves, which you have in Jesus Christ, who though he was in the form of God, did not count equality with God a thing to be grasped, but emptied himself in the form of a servant, being born in the likeness of men" (Phil. 2:3–7).

Yet this was not the gospel of docile submission but the foundation of a practical mode of behavior in which the dominant culture of Caesars, landlords, and grasping individuals could be partitioned off from the lives of the truly faithful—and eventually be destroyed. Paul lived in a specific historical context and traveled among particular regions. Understanding this, we can see that the vices he railed against—"immorality, impurity, licentiousness, idolatry, sorcery, enmity, strife, jealousy, anger, selfishness, dissension, party spirit, envy, drunkenness, carousing, and the like" (Gal. 5:19–21)—were the kinds of behavior that were all too common among the powerless subjects of the empire. Unless his followers abandoned them, they would remain helpless to effect or be part of any world-transforming change. In that sense, the image of Jesus offered a model of practical self-sacrifice in the cause of the economic and spiritual resurrection for communities that were being scourged, mocked, and dismembered by imperial rule.

The cross became the symbol both of Roman violence and of the faith of those who dared to resist its inevitability. No less than in Galilee and Judea, the crooked timber crosses set up on the outskirts of Macedonian towns and in the province of Galatia represented the ultimate terror that the empire could dispense for those whom the authorities branded as rebels, traitors, criminals, or runaway slaves. For most, the sight of disfigured bodies hanging from the timbers—losing their dignity even after death, with little hope of a decent burial—was more than enough to promote obedience and passivity toward a system in which the labor and dedication of the many supported the arrogance of the few. The earlier expressions of the Galilean and Judean Renewal Movement had a wide range of symbols and scriptural traditions about martyrdom in which the precise method of self-sacrifice for the People of Israel was less important than the fact of martyrdom itself. For Paul, the cross was vitally important as a way to transform a familiar cultural icon into its antithesis. Terror became hope when the cross was used as a symbol that bridged the cultural differences between the various subject peoples of the empire. Grim resignation became joyful anticipation when the grotesque method of execution used by the Romans became an omen of the impending salvation of the righteous and destruction of the wicked. As Paul later put it, had any of "the rulers of this age" understood that fact, "they would not have crucified the Lord of Glory" (1 Cor. 2:8). The ritual of baptism was now a sign of wholehearted identification with the figure of Christ for many different peoples. What was once a symbolic ceremony of immersion undertaken by people throughout Galilee and Judea to signify a personal commitment to covenantal renewal now became a symbol of personal transformation. "I have been crucified with Christ," Paul wrote to the Galatians. "It is no longer I who live, but Christ who lives in me" (2:20).

Thus by the autumn of 50 C.E., as Paul proceeded to the Achaian provincial capital of Corinth, his movement of assemblies of the saints scattered throughout Galatia and Macedonia represented something entirely new. Other apostles of the Jesus Movement were traveling among and preaching at centers of the Jewish Diaspora throughout the Roman Empire, calling Jews and Godfearing Gentiles alike to join them in the movement for the Renewal of Israel. But Paul's vision had already begun to shift away from a tendency to view human history as the interaction of discrete peoples to a struggle of like-minded individuals scattered in communities throughout the Mediterranean against the structures and social relations of violence and inequality. Although his assemblies were still quite distinct in their cultural traditions, language, and customs, he would attempt to forge them into a new kind of global community—a family of righteous brothers and sisters whom God had adopted—through their own expressions of desire to join God's Kingdom and live out that commitment through a new way of community life.

At the center of this new image of the sacred human family was Christ Jesus, no longer a martyred prophet of Israel but a transcendent figure (intentionally, if ironically, addressed in the contemporary language of patronage as *kyrios*, or "Lord"). This figure was the antithesis of the familiar reputation-conscious, submission-demanding patron on whom the political and economic hierarchy of the empire was based. Each of Paul's communities could find its deepest hopes and profoundest ideals fulfilled in the particular image of Christ that it cherished—all of which were progressively drifting away from the verifiable historical facts of Jesus' life. Yet this dehistoricized figure of Christ, in its powerful, adaptable response to local sensibilities and conditions, was no mere mystical vision. In its complexity and studied ambiguity, it held the new communities together. And in that sense—in the villages, towns, and cities of Galatia and Macedonia—a new kind of Christianity was born.

8

Spirits in Conflict

P AUL COULD NOT have chosen a better spot to breathe life into a
soulless city, for Corinth, by far the largest and most prosperous
city in the province of Achaia, was among the most modern and
heartless metropolises in the world. Built in the rubble of a famous classical
city that had been burned and looted by the Romans, Corinth drew its
wealth from the entire Mediterranean and its people from every land on
earth. Officially founded in 44 B.C.E. as the Roman colony of Laus Julia
Corinthiensis astride the narrow isthmus between the sea lanes of the
Adriatic and the Aegean, it was initially populated by a motley, hastily
conscripted community of freed slaves from Italy, Greece, Syria, Egypt,
and Judea—all having great ambition and nothing to lose. Within just a
few years, New Corinth's settlers' enormously profitable commerce at this
crossroads of the nations had brought thousands more eager settlers from
all over the Mediterranean and enormous personal wealth to a local ruling
class of self-made women and men. Yet at the time of Paul's arrival, the
jarring juxtaposition of the city's splendid marble temples, bustling commercial center, suburbs of opulent homes for its rich and famous—and its
crowded workshops, stinking industrial quarters, and seamy sailors' inns
and warehouses down by the docksides—gave the lie to the imperial
promise of prosperity for all. And Corinth's tense and profoundly unequal
network of person-to-person relationships would lead Paul to recognize
that the basic mechanisms of Roman patronage and power—played out

almost unconsciously on a day-to-day level in the city's streets, workshops, and private homes—were the chief obstacles to the establishment of the Kingdom of God.

Unlike the landmarks of Paul's earlier missionary travels, ancient Corinth has been extensively excavated, and the layout—at least of the city's civic center—in the Early Imperial Period is clear. The impressive forum at the heart of the city was filled with temples and shrines dedicated to the emperor and to various members of the Julio-Claudian family, placed alongside temples to the older Greek gods. New Testament scholars have produced imaginary itineraries to speculate on Paul's first impressions of the city (as he might have strolled through areas uncovered by the modern excavations). Yet understanding what happened to Paul in Corinth is more than a matter of sightseeing, far more than a matter of linking marble monuments with scriptural texts. What "life was like" in Roman Corinth invariably depended on who you were, how wealthy you were, and how high you had climbed on the social ladder. For unlike the situation in the smaller cities of Macedonia and towns of Galatia where imperial rule was superimposed on traditional social structures and communal identities, Corinth was a chaotic melange of dislocated, deracinated individuals, the most successful of whom had good reason to cast off unpleasant reminders of their former low status and ethnic identities. Whether they were by ancestry Jews, Greeks, Syrians, or Egyptians, their shared goal was now civic honor and material success through assimilation into the Roman order. If Corinth was a melting pot, the distinctiveness of its ingredients had largely been simmered away.

As he had already done in Galatia, Thessalonica, and Philippi, Paul impressed potential followers in Corinth not only with theology but with "demonstrations of the Spirit and of power" (1 Cor. 2:4)—namely, miraculous healings, exorcisms, and spirit possessions. And in time he succeeded in transforming the spontaneous energy and enthusiasm released in those initial encounters into the long-term faithfulness of stable congregations. From passing comments by Paul in his later letters to his Corinthian followers, it seems that the movement in Corinth slowly took the form of a network of small *ekklesiai*, or "assemblies," based in private households scattered throughout the city. That may have occurred before, in Philippi and perhaps in Thessalonica, but in the vastly larger city of Corinth, individual households—rather than extended kin-groups or villages—

seem to have become the main social units on which his movement was based. From scriptural sources, we know of a household congregation that gathered in the home of "a Jew named Aquila, a native of Pontus, and his wife Priscilla"; other assemblies met in the households of individuals named Crispus, Gaius, and Stephanas—who were the only Corinthians whom Paul recalled as having personally baptized (1 Cor. 1:14–16). We should not, however, assume that all of these heads-of-households were necessarily wealthy. Archaeological investigation of Roman domestic life has revealed that in large cities, even the most humble shopkeeper or craftsman gathered around him or her a tight-knit group of immediate family members, servants, and slaves. Households were nothing less than the basic building blocks of every Roman city. And it is thus important to see that the establishment of the household *ekklesiai* in Corinth represented yet another major development of the crystallizing culture of early Christianity— made possible by Paul's determination to adapt Roman social forms to the purposes of the Kingdom of God.

In the course of time, Paul became increasingly dependent on faithful co-workers and enthusiastic local supporters in Corinth, and in this respect, his activities in the city began to take on the character of a settled sect rather than a wandering ministry. The most important of Paul's co-workers were Priscilla and Aquila, whom Acts 18:2 describes as being newcomers to Corinth themselves. They had "lately come from Italy . . . because Claudius had commanded all the Jews to leave Rome." This enigmatic report of Priscilla and Aquila's expulsion from Rome has been associated by many scholars with the agitation caused among the Jewish community by the mysterious figure known as "Chrestus," and it had often been suggested that Priscilla and Aquila were refugee Christian activists from Rome. Indeed, nowhere in Acts or in Paul's own letters is the conversion or baptism of the couple by Paul recorded, and they seemed to have formed a close and lasting bond. There may also have been an economic factor in their collaboration: Acts 18:2–3 relates that since Paul, Priscilla, and Aquila all shared the trade of tentmaking, Paul joined their household not only to preach the gospel but also to support himself. Thus Paul's stay in Corinth over a span of approximately eighteen months—from the autumn of 50 until the summer of 52—was dramatically different from his earlier missionary efforts. Not only did he join forces with other Christian activists, he also became a permanent resident of Achaia's largest city, both preaching his gospel and earning a living for himself by direct participation in Corinth's bustling economy (cf. 1 Cor. 4:12).

Yet Paul was determined to maintain his position of leadership over all his assemblies, and soon after the start of his work in Corinth—perhaps in early 51 C.E.—he received disturbing news from Thessalonica, which, if not totally unexpected, reminded him of the unrelenting social pressures or "afflictions" that threatened the continued existence of the communities that he had founded during the previous three years. Paul had promised his newly baptized followers in Galatia and Macedonia that if they piously separated themselves from the evil ways of imperial society, they would all live to see the dawn of God's Kingdom, yet in the few months since his departure from Thessalonica, several faithful members of the community there had died. In grief and growing uncertainty the Thessalonians dashed off a letter to Paul, anxiously seeking answers to some basic questions: How could Paul explain the untimely death of righteous brothers and sisters? Would they now be deprived of a share in the Kingdom? And would the continued suffering and persecutions of the surviving members of the community at the hands of the city authorities—and perhaps even by their own non-Christian relatives—really be rewarded at the end of days? Paul's emotional response to these questions, known in the New Testament as The First Letter to the Thessalonians, is the earliest surviving text written by Paul, and it offers a revealing glimpse at one of his initial attempts to maintain the coherence of a movement whose assemblies were now spread over hundreds of miles.

In contrast to the individual character-building letters of the Epicurean and other philosophers addressed to specific disciples, Paul's focus was on the unity of his *entire* movement, in its praise of the Thessalonians for receiving "the word in much affliction, with joy inspired by the Holy Spirit, so that you became an example to all the believers in Macedonia and in Achaia" (1:6–7). Reviewing the ethical precepts by which they should keep their community together and remain apart from the dominant system of patronage and economic dependence ("to work with your hands as we charged you; so that you may command the respect of outsiders, and be dependent on nobody" [4:11–12]), Paul assured them that the deaths of their loved ones should not be a source of sorrow but rather of apocalyptic comfort and a continuing article of faith. For at the coming of the Lord, Paul wrote, "the dead in Christ will rise first; then we who are alive, who are left, shall be caught up together with them in the clouds to meet the Lord in the air; and so we shall always be with the Lord" (4:17). In terms of literary motifs and religious concepts, this letter of exhortation to the beleaguered faithful was similar to the assurances of resurrection that the author of the biblical Book of Daniel offered to the persecuted Jewish communities in pre-Maccabean times. But Paul now skillfully utilized the traditional promises to the righteous of Israel to maintain the solidarity of his followers among *other* peoples, adapting the language of resurrection and of intervention of heavenly forces to encourage their continued down-to-earth resistance to the political and economic status quo.

It is not without significance for the subsequent course of events that an aggressive new governor—a distinguished Roman named Lucius Iunius Gallio—arrived in Corinth in the spring of 51 C.E. Gallio is one of the few Roman officials mentioned in the Book of Acts whose historical existence can be independently verified: in addition to references to his political career in the writings of Tacitus, Dio Cassius, and Pliny the Elder, a fragmentary Latin inscription discovered in 1907 at Delphi underlines Gallio's active participation in Achaia's imperial development. This inscription also offers a vital chronological clue to the date of Paul's first missionary stay in Corinth, since its indication of date suggests that Gallio served a normal one-year term as proconsul from the spring of 51 C.E. to the spring of 52. We now know that Paul's movement in Corinth was founded precisely at a time when the institutions of empire in the province of Achaia were becoming more assertive. If we recognize Acts's account of Paul's encounter with Gallio in Corinth (18:12–17) as a heavily overwritten version of some dispute that eventually rendered him *persona non grata* in the city, we can once again recognize the primary political context of Paul's work. He was regarded as less of a Jewish heretic than as a rabblerouser of those who would oppose the Roman order. And as his continuing contacts with his "subversive" communities throughout the provinces of Achaia, Macedonia, and perhaps Galatia become more regular, it would be increasingly difficult for Paul to avoid the unwanted attention of the spies and informers of the imperial authorities. Though the Book of Acts blames Paul's departure from Corinth on Jewish hostility, the empire was clearly to become his most dangerous enemy in the coming years. Thus leaving Corinth sometime during the summer of 52 C.E. after eighteen months in Achaia, he set sail for another huge and prosperous Roman city on the shores of the Aegean, where he would seek to coordinate the efforts of all his communities in a grand demonstration against the empire's spiritual and social bankruptcy.

ONLY TWO OR THREE YEARS EARLIER, as he and his companions had made their way northwestward from Galatia, Paul had studiously avoided passing through the province of "Asia," along the western coast of Asia Minor. But now he chose that great strip of fertile farmland, winding river valleys, and prosperous coastal cities as the headquarters of what would become his longest and most embattled missionary endeavor— ultimately lasting for approximately two and a half years. Instead of setting off to spread the word of Christ among distant lands and strange peoples in the northern mountains and forests of Europe, Paul now headed back across the Aegean to continue his work among the cosmopolitan, Greek-speaking urban population of the eastern provinces of the empire, intensifying his efforts to maintain the solidarity of his communities. Arriving in the great city of Ephesus in company with Aquila, Priscilla, and other co-workers (who had all apparently pulled up roots and departed from Corinth), Paul established himself in the capital of the province of Asia, where the famous Temple of Artemis attracted pilgrims and tourists from all over the Mediterranean world.

Although we cannot be sure about the sequence of events of this phase of Paul's career (Acts 18:18–19:1 suggests that he began his work in Ephesus only after returning to Antioch for a long-delayed reunion visit and a return journey through "the countryside of Galatia and Phrygia"), it seems that Aquila and Priscilla soon established their own house-assembly in the city (1 Cor. 16:19) and Paul took up where he had left off in Corinth: preaching to urban audiences (and perhaps also, on occasion, to rural people in the vicinity, as suggested in Acts 18:23), performing works of spiritual power and continually organizing new household assemblies led by newly baptized followers. And just as he had earlier joined forces with Priscilla and Aquila upon his arrival in Corinth, so too he was now joined by an itinerant preacher identified in Acts 18:24 as an eloquent Alexandrian Jew named Apollos, who would ultimately reveal a quite different understanding of Christianity. But in the meantime, the work was flourishing in this new missionary field. Paul's old companion Titus from Antioch arrived to help with the propagation of the movement among the peoples of the neighboring regions—ultimately carrying Paul's gospel from Ephesus eastward, with new assemblies being established in the towns at the head of the Lycus Valley—Hieropolis, Laodicea, and Colossae.

Paul's efforts to spread the word of Christ—and a practical strategy of resistance to the powers-that-be—to the population of the inland valleys of Asia brought him to the very edge of the Galatian highlands where he had established his first independent assemblies four or five years before. And sometime fairly soon after his arrival in Ephesus, Paul learned of an unexpected source of opposition: some preachers of "a different gospel" were circulating among the Galatian assemblies, condemning Paul as a false teacher, and urging the Galatian assemblies to join themselves to the *genuine* Renewal Movement of the People of Israel. We have no precise information about the identity of these rivals, but from the details Paul reveals in his later letter to the Galatians, these opponents' Torah-observant version of the Jesus Movement is strikingly reminiscent of the guiding precepts of the "people from James" who visited the Antioch community.

Paul reacted in horror and outrage to the news of rival apostles (from the community that he had rejected) entering a region that he believed to be his exclusive mission field. More than that: Paul believed that these new, Torah-observant apostles would cause the Galatians untold damage. The idea that villagers of the Galatian highlands should abandon their own village traditions and adopt the festivals, laws, and ceremonies of Israel in order to gain a share in God's Kingdom struck Paul as a direct challenge to all the work that he had been carrying out for the previous years. Having grown to understand the economic and political plight of the Galatians during his sojourn among them, Paul believed that he knew far better than the newly arrived apostles how the Galatian peasantry could best survive under the new conditions of empire and so inherit—on their own terms—the Kingdom of God. In fear that some of his followers would be persuaded to abandon his own movement for the Antioch- and Jerusalem-centered Renewal of Israel, he dashed off a passionate letter of exhortation to those "foolish Galatians," appealing to keep their eyes on the prize that *they*, as Galatians, must strive to attain. This text, known as Paul's Letter to the Galatians, has long been viewed by Christian theologians as a thorough repudiation of particularist "Judaism," which is pictured as obsessed with self-justification by "meritorious works" and the hypocritical (if meticulous) observance of ritual laws. Yet we must keep our attention fixed not on the abstract, theological interpretation of this letter but its specific historical context at the time of its writing, around

53 C.E. Paul was here speaking to the Galatians only—and repudiating the value of Israel's Torah for *them*.

In Paul's eyes, the spectacle of Galatians following the Torah would be as incongruous and counterproductive as Judeans and Galileans suddenly feasting and carousing like Celtic warriors or adopting the peasant traditions of Galatia. Whatever he thought of his own Jewish tradition and its value for the People of Israel, Paul's Galatian gospel was meant to show the people of that region what he believed was the real meaning of God's promises *for them*. "For freedom Christ has set us free; stand fast therefore and do not submit again to a yoke of slavery. Now I, Paul, say to you that if you receive circumcision, Christ will be of no advantage to you" (5:1–2). Having witnessed the plight of the Galatian communities under their landlords and overlords, Paul insisted that the laws of Israel were an irrelevant tactic and a dangerous diversion. He had only scorn for those who were attempting to win away the assemblies he had established with such great effort: "As we have said before, so now I say again, if anyone is preaching to you a gospel contrary to that which you received, let him be accursed" (Gal. 1:9).

In his travels through Galatia and Macedonia, Paul had transformed the principle of creative sharing into a practical component of each member's Christian practice, encouraging each community to put aside at least some of its resources to further the work of the Kingdom of God. He had earlier urged the Galatians to "bear one another's burdens" (6:2), and he had been gratified by the material assistance that the Philippians had offered to him. Yet Paul now recognized that the vulnerability of his movement to outside pressures was the relative autonomy of each community of the Jesus Movement (both those that he had founded among the non-Israelites and those of Antioch and Jerusalem). What was now needed—he believed—was an unprecedented act of cooperation and sharing of resources that could help overcome the subjugation of *all* peoples. As he wrote to the Galatians, "There is neither Jew nor Greek, there is neither slave nor free, there is neither male nor female; for you are all one in Christ Jesus" (3:28). Thus was born the idea of a great act of movement-wide unity in the form of a collection to be raised by all of Paul's Galatian, Macedonian, and Achaian assemblies, working in unison for the material benefit of the Jerusalem community. The great collection, once raised, would expand each community's local horizons by being delivered to Jerusalem by a delegation of "saints" chosen as representatives of the assemblies of each province, proceeding to the Holy City of Jerusalem and fulfilling Isaiah's prophetic vision of a procession of righteous Gentiles to Zion at the End of Days. Its effect would be to demonstrate the commitment and the value of non-Israelites to the realization of God's Kingdom, and Paul hoped that it would also disarm the opposition of the Jerusalem- and Antioch-based apostles. Yet he had not expected that at the same time—back in Corinth—some serious new problems were surfacing that threatened to make Paul's idea of the collection a dead issue there.

PAUL'S EARLIEST HOUSE-ASSEMBLIES in Corinth—those saints he would later proudly call "the firstfruits of Achaia" (1 Cor. 16:15)— maintained their faith in the imminence of the Kingdom of God even after Paul's departure for Ephesus, and they would be the bulwark of his impending battle to defend his leadership. The Corinthian householders Crispus, Gaius, and Stephanas, whom Paul had personally baptized with their entire households (1 Cor. 1:14–16), represented the nucleus of an urban movement whose members readily accepted the challenge of surviving until the *parousia* in the midst of—and in the face of—the imperial economy. Although we do not know of the specific trades or crafts that any of the Corinthian households engaged in (with the exception of the "tentmakers" Aquila and Priscilla), it seems likely that each formed a viable, self-supporting economic unit. Paul later linked the householder Stephanas with individuals named Fortunatus ("Lucky") and Achaicus ("The Greek") (1 Cor. 16:17), whom some scholars have identified as Stephanas's freedmen or domestic slaves. But individual households could never be completely independent or autonomous in a large imperial city like Corinth. Economic life was conducted through complex networks of personal relationships that linked even the humblest craftsperson or day laborer to empire-wide channels of commerce and trade.

The key to that connection was the role of "patrons"—wealthy and prominent civic figures—who offered political favors and financial support to the various civic groups, trade associations, and religious cults through which contacts were made and business deals concluded. The economic aspect of this pattern of patronage is evident from the fact that the membership of many professional associations, or *collegia*, was limited to practitioners of certain trades or dealers in particular kinds of goods. In the Italian port cities of Ostia and Puetoli, for example, inscriptions provide evidence for *collegia* of dyers, glassmakers, sailors, winesellers, and grain dealers—among others—and there is little reason to doubt that in the Romanized imperial port city of New Corinth business was conducted along much different lines. In most cases, only freeborn Roman nobles of the senatorial or equestrian orders were entitled to become city magistrates or the esteemed patrons of professional *collegia* (with all the accordant status, political prestige, and economic power), yet in a polyglot city like Corinth, there were many ambitious, newly prosperous freedmen who avidly sought the prestige of being someone's patron and thereby gaining enhanced social status and economic power for themselves. As a result, the network of independent house-assemblies established by Paul in Corinth—consisting of a cluster of self-supporting households of various trades—may well have offered an attractive opportunity for patronage activities by a new class of upwardly-mobile urban saints.

Soon after Paul's departure from Corinth, new people seem to have joined the movement, and their behavior was an immediate cause for concern for Paul's original followers. Paul later recalled sending a letter to Corinth that pointedly instructed them to stand fast and not "associate with immoral men" (1 Cor. 5:9). That he was clearly not referring to the general pagan population among whom the members of the assemblies had to interact and do business is clear, since he emphasized that he did not mean "the immoral of this world, or the greedy and robbers or the idolators, since then you would need to go out of this world. But rather I wrote to you not to associate with any one who bears the name of brother if he is guilty of immorality or greed, or is an idolator, reviler, drunkard, or robber—not even to eat with such a one" (5:9–11). New Testament scholar John Chow makes a persuasive case for seeing these "immoral brethren" not merely as backsliding Christians but as a group of status-conscious, would-be patrons who offered both their nominal allegiance to the gospel of Christ and substantial financial support to the Corinthian Christians, in order to acquire their own loyal clients and enhance their social status—just as the pagan aristocrats and civic leaders of Corinth were accustomed to doing with the city's various trade organizations and cults.

It is ironic that so many New Testament scholars have noted the similarity of Paul's *ekklesiai* in Corinth to contemporary urban associations and *collegia*, but have failed to see that the increasingly close resemblance in form may actually have horrifed Paul. From the Corinthian correspondence, we gather that the *ekklesiai* in the city (like the *collegia*) were supported by the largess of wealthy patrons who provided the meeting place, food for communal banquets, and incidental expenses, and who received in return the political allegiance of the members or the pleasure of being continually lauded and placed at the head of the banquet table. That clearly was not Paul's intestion, for the very concept of patrons in the *ekklesiai* was perceived by Paul to be a direct affront to his own leadership.

Before long, some new apostles apparently arrived in the city, and they introduced a number of theological innovations that served to bolster the patrons' grip on the movement and undermine the community solidarity that Paul had sought to instill. The most important of these new arrivals was the mysterious "Apollos" (1 Cor. 3:5–9), who is also mentioned in the Book of Acts. As the preacher of an esoteric variant of the Jesus Movement, Apollos began to present Jesus not so much as a martyr but as a prophet of Sophia, or "Heavenly Wisdom," who offered the elect a mystical means of communication with God. Indeed, Apollos and other spiritualist apostles may have readily offered their services to the new patrons of the movement, preaching that the mystical, meditative quest for higher consciousness was an end in itself.

Some of the patrons of the Corinthian communities soon began to regard spiritual gifts as a sign of social status. For at a time when the practice of novel pagan cults and the mystical rites of new age ideologies of personal salvation were becoming popular as after-dinner diversions for upwardly-mobile Romans, prophetic ecstacy and speaking in tongues came to be seen by some people within the Christian assemblies of Corinth as potent weapons for spiritual oneupsmanship. We know from Paul's later writings that some assembly members now boasted that they had much more direct access to the Holy Spirit than others. In their direct contact with the divine source of all knowledge and wisdom, they came to believe that in a spiritual sense they were now "powerful," "rich," of "noble birth," and "kings." And their feeling of membership in that spiritual "aristocracy" of the movement convinced them that they would not have to wait for the *parousia* of Christ to reap a full measure of divine blessing.

Through the spiritualist teachings of Apollos and through their own experiences of heavenly enlightenment, many of the upwardly-mobile members of Paul's assemblies became convinced that their souls were immortal and they had been granted intimate communication with the Spirit of God. And if this "immortality" were considered to be an inner state of mind and all worldly actions now seen as utterly inconsequential, what difference did it make if the leaders of the Corinthian congregations carried on their lives outside the weekly meetings of the assemblies largely as before? Since access to influence and the prospects of economic success in the everyday world of imperial Corinth were available only to those who participated in the important civic ceremonies and religious festivals, what real difference could it make if they simply engaged in a patriotic charade? After all, Paul himself would agree with Apollos that pagan idols of bronze, marble, clay, or wood had "no real existence" (1 Cor. 8:4). If that was so, what possible harm could come to them from participating in the public worship of Aphrodite, Asclepius—or even Caesar—so long as they did not *really* believe? And what difference did it make if they continued to forge marriage connections with local aristocratic families, even to the extent of a son deciding to marry his own step-mother to further his own links to nobility? (cf. 1 Cor. 5:1) And why should successful householders be prevented from enforcing property rights over slaves and collecting their legal share of the income of their freedmen by filing suit in the city's lawcourts and aggressively pursuing financial advantage—even if those slaves and freedmen happened to be brothers and sisters in Christ? (cf. 1 Cor. 6:1–8).

Collective action of the community was no longer the main or even a primary motivation for a growing number of members of the Corinthian assemblies. In time, some of the more mystically-inclined members of the rank-and-file of the Corinthian assemblies abandoned normal community life for mystical contemplation of Sophia, the source of all wisdom—for whom Jesus was merely a conduit. And becoming adept at Apollos's meditative methods, the members who styled themselves *pneumatikoi*, or "spirituals," began to believe that the heavenly Sophia regularly communicated to them beatific visions and a sense of perfect blissfulness. They, too, came to believe that their immortal souls had come to possess *gnosis*, or enlightened knowledge, that set them apart from the rest of humanity. And this feeling of spiritual elitism led many—both men and women—to embrace Sophia as their heavenly "spouse."

For married members, that meant physical separation from their previous partners; for unmarried members of the assemblies, that meant renouncing any potential marriage or sexual relations and, in effect, maintaining a sort of spiritual "virginity." In either case, the normal life of the community was disrupted, and the quest for personal spiritual transformation brought on by intimate communion with Sophia seems to have become especially popular among some of the women in the movement at Corinth, who may have found spiritual celibacy an effective means of escape from their generally powerless position in Hellenistic-Roman society. Women of all classes, often being married at age twelve or thirteen to much older husbands (whose life expectancy was only about forty years), were expected to bear children for their first husband and remarry and bear more children for a new husband after their first husband's death. Legally dependent on the status of husbands and male relatives, they were confined with few rights, in virtual sexual bondage to the household whose daily operations they were expected to run. Yet now suddenly, by means of their new relationship with the heavenly Sophia—achieved through mystical contemplation of her emissary Jesus—some of the women members of Paul's assemblies felt they could attain exalted spiritual status and freedom from oppressive patriarchalism.

By the fall of 53 C.E., these unexpected developments had come to Paul's attention, even as he waged his struggle against the influence of the Antioch-based apostles over the assemblies in Galatia. Those of his Corinthian followers who remained faithful to the original ideals of the movement had become increasingly desperate, and as Paul prepared to address their questions with firm exhortation and proper scriptural citations, he received word from some members of the movement—whom he enigmatically identified in 1 Cor. 1:11 as "Chloe's people"—that open rivalry had broken out between the various factions of the Corinthian community. While the members of the households of Gaius, Crispus, and Stephanas had remained faithful to Paul and his original teachings, Chloe's people reported that others had shifted their allegiance to alternative systems of Christian belief. As if identifying their assemblies with their particular teachers, some insisted "I belong to Paul," while others boasted "I belong to Cephas," while yet others claimed that "I belong to Apollos" (1 Cor. 1:12). Things were clearly getting out of control among the saints of Achaia, and Paul believed that if the forces of patronage, individualism, and spiritual elitism were to remain unchallenged in the assemblies in Corinth, the very cornerstone of his movement would be destroyed.

AN ALL-OUT BATTLE with the Corinthian patrons was now inevitable; Paul had to do something at once to revive the shattered spirit of the

Corinthian assemblies. The crisis in Corinth moved Paul to action—and to the composition of one of his most important letters, now known as First Corinthians. Although the various issues discussed in this letter have long been interpreted as the abstract moral concerns of any cosmopolitan congregation tempted by human failings and the seductive attractions of godlessness all around them, they must primarily be assessed in their original historical context. Among Paul's main objects of concern were those women who had separated from their husbands—and whom Paul pointedly admonished to return to married life, since "a wife is bound to her husband as long as he lives" (1 Cor. 7:39). Feminist scholars have condemned this statement as evidence that Paul himself was blind to the patriarchal structures of Roman society—and, despite his earlier assurance to the Galatians that there was "neither male nor female" among the true followers of Jesus Christ (Gal. 3:28)—that he was unsympathetic to any challenge to the time-honored structures of inequality between women and men.

Yet even though he may not have been fully sympathetic to the plight of the "spiritual" women, Paul minced no words with the group he identified as his main opponents in Corinth: the small group of social climbers who were attempting to use their patronage of the Jesus Movement to boost their civic status—just as other Corinthian notables in the city utilized patronage of other associations and cults. In his important study of the Corinthian correspondence, New Testament scholar John Chow has shown that each of the subjects that Paul addresses—the dangers of ecstatic spirituality (1 Cor. 12–14); participation in sacrifices and banquets in pagan temples (1 Cor. 8–10); marriages of convenience or status (1 Cor. 5:1); class distinctions in Lord's Suppers (1 Cor. 11:19); and lawsuits between members filed in the secular lawcourts (1 Cor. 6:1–8)—are all acts that would be far more likely to be committed by a prosperous, status-conscious class of would-be "patrons" than the craftsmen, workers, and slaves who comprised the urban run of the mill. But Paul apparently did not believe that mere argumentation would be enough to turn the tide in the struggle; he sought to involve all the members of the Corinthian assemblies in his idea of the great collection—as a shared program of practical self-sacrifice.

Just as he had instructed the Galatians, the Corinthians were to take up a great collection for the saints in Jerusalem to demonstrate their willingness to give of their resources and support the movement as it struggled against the present evil order. Yet in Corinth, this project was not meant only as a grand demonstration of movement-wide sharing. The particular *way* in which the collection for Jerusalem was to be gathered in Corinth struck a blow directly at the hierarchy of status that the patrons had instituted there. Instead of relying on the contributions of a few wealthy members to support the endeavor, every member—no matter how humble—would be asked to contribute to the best of his or her ability, and in doing so, all would have an equal share. "On the first day of every week," Paul instructed the Corinthians at the close of the letter, "each of you is to put something aside and store it up, as he may prosper, so that contributions need not be made when I come" (1 Cor. 16:2).

Paul's counterattack against the domination of the Corinthian patrons seems to have been successful, at least initially. He had dispatched his colleagues Timothy and then Titus to Corinth to begin raising the collection and formulated plans to return to Corinth himself. Yet the ultimate victory of Paul and his supporters was neither secure nor inevitable, for the patron-leaders of the Corinthian assemblies had staked their prestige on their control of the movement and they would not give up without a fight. And sometime in the summer of 54, they gained the services of a new group of preachers and teachers whom Paul would later call "false apostles, deceitful workers, disguising themselves as apostles of Christ" (2 Cor. 11:13) to help them overcome the efforts of Paul. Although their names are never explicitly mentioned in any of Paul's letters, these men seem to have been widely respected and well connected with other leaders of the Renewal Movement (presumably in Antioch and Jerusalem), bearing "letters of recommendation" (2 Cor. 3:1) and emphasizing their status as "Hebrews," "Israelites," "descendants of Abraham," and "ministers [*diakonoi*] of Christ" (2 Cor. 11:22–23). Indeed, these terms of self-designation sound suspiciously like those that might have been used by the Torah-observant missionaries who had moved among the Galatians a year or so previously.

Now, in their efforts to establish their own spiritual authority in Corinth as definitive interpreters of the significance of Jesus' resurrection, they bitterly attacked Paul's teachings by impugning his credentials as an apostle and attempted to undermine his apostolic authority by accusing him of financial impropriety (2 Cor. 11:7–10) and deception, even extortion, in demanding contributions for the great "collection" that he was now raising, even among the most poverty stricken of Corinthian saints

(2 Cor. 12:14–18). This was not merely a theological dispute but a political struggle within the Corinthian community, for these new apostles had gladly accepted the financial support of the local patrons of the movement as Apollos and the other "spiritual" apostles had apparently done (cf. 1 Cor. 9:6). For Paul, *that* was the ultimate betrayal, for he believed that these "superlative apostles" had surrendered to the very structures of patronage and status that made Roman oppression possible. The spirit of privilege and individual puffery strutting in imperial finery seemed to him to be the ultimate evil—and Paul would later muse that since "Satan disguises himself as an angel of light," it was not unusual "that his servants also disguise themselves as servants of righteousness" (2 Cor. 11:14–15).

When word of the arrival of these "superlative apostles" reached Paul in Ephesus during the summer of 54 C.E., he dashed off another letter to Corinth (now preserved in 2 Cor. 2:14–6:13, according to the literary analysis of a number of scholars), in which he defended his own career as a lonely and independent apostle, repeatedly stressing the primacy of the Spirit over Torah observance as the key to the Kingdom of God. Here, too, his words must be understood not as a condemnation of Judaism *per se* but as a rhetorical exhortation to the Corinthians, in *their* specific historical situation. For what emerges from Paul's often dense and complex theological argumentation is his insistence that the real struggle of the righteous was no longer only between the People of Israel and the Roman Empire. The real enemy was the ethos of aggressive, possessive individualism—so highly prized in Roman society—that had percolated into even the most seemingly innocent social and religious structures of everyday life.

In First Corinthians 5–6, Paul had insisted that the faithful spurn the seductive appeal of the larger order of power and exploitation—of patrons and clients and obedience to the Roman order—and separate themselves from any who would surrender to its charms. A long-disputed passage of Paul's Corinthian correspondence (2 Cor. 6:14–7:1) would appear to fit precisely this crisis. In it, Paul warns his Corinthian followers: "Do not be mismatched with unbelievers, for what partnership have righteous and iniquity? Or what fellowship has light with darkness? What accord has Christ with Belial? Or what has a believer in common with an unbeliever?" (2 Cor. 6:14–7:1). Paul refused to retreat from the central element of his vision: whatever their specific national orientation, the saints must not allow themselves to be unwittingly assimilated into the social structures of imperial society.

Yet even a personal journey by Paul to Corinth in the autumn of 54 failed to turn the tide. In fact, this visit to Corinth was a humiliating disaster. From the few details that Paul provides in his subsequent writing, we can gather that at least one particular individual attacked and humiliated Paul in the presence of the assembled members of the movement (cf. 2 Cor. 2:1–5). Standing alone and facing the accusations of his opponents that he had attempted to perpetuate a massive swindle of the poor members of the congregations, Paul could not overcome the hostile setting of the meeting where his career and integrity was placed before a tribunal, in which the patrons (still sponsoring the gatherings and sitting at the head of the tables, backed by the "superlative apostles") served as both jury and judge. So when Paul returned to Ephesus after this "painful visit" to Corinth (2 Cor. 2:1), he deeply feared that the triumph of the patrons in Corinth— if left unchecked—could endanger his assemblies everywhere. In bitterness and with a sense of unbridled recrimination, he composed what he would later call his "letter of tears" (2 Cor. 10–13). His response to the ad hominem attacks on his apostolic competence was to list the trials and tribulations he had personally suffered over the years for the cause of the gospel—public whippings, beatings, stonings, shipwreck, robbery, humiliation, betrayal, exhaustion, sleeplessness, hunger, stress, and exposure to the cold (2 Cor. 11:23–32). And he emphasized again that his gospel had come not from men but from his own mystical visions of Paradise, in which he "heard things that cannot be told, which man may not utter" (2 Cor. 12:1–6). In Paul's eyes, those experiences were proof of his unique perception of the divine guiding power that commissioned him to speak in the name of the Risen and Returning Christ.

Now, in the "letter of tears," Paul warned the members of the Corinthian assemblies that they were flirting with disaster. The Corinthian patrons had by their arrogance proved themselves no longer to be brothers and sisters but agents of the imperial order, and little but God's direct intervention could save the movement that he had worked so hard to establish over the years. "Examine yourselves, to see whether you are holding to your faith," Paul implored them (2 Cor. 13:5). He could now clearly see that the campaign battle for the Kingdom of God was no longer to be waged on the battlefield of nations or in a contest of spiritual credentials. The battle must now be waged in the hearts and minds of righteous people throughout the empire who were in danger of being possessed by the evil spirits of power, status, and patronage.

AT THE VERY TIME when Paul found himself ousted from a position of authority in the Corinthian assemblies, great changes were sweeping the wider world that would ultimately have a decisive effect on the subsequent history of Christianity. By the autumn of 54 C.E., the fourteen-year reign of the Emperor Claudius was grinding to its inevitably chaotic conclusion, with court intrigues running rampant and the day-to-day affairs of state left increasingly in the hands of a close circle of former slaves. According to the Roman historian Tacitus, a series of bizarre omens indicated that great catastrophes were coming: "Standards and soldiers tents were set on fire from the sky. A swarm of bees settled on the pediment of the Capitoline temple. Half-bestial children were born, and a pig with hawk's claws." Suetonius added that the ominous portents included "the rise of a long-haired star, known as a comet," lightning that struck the tomb of Claudius's father, Drusus the Elder, and "an unusual mortality among magistrates of all ranks." These signs could not help but bring apprehension and uncertainty to the superstitious inhabitants of the city that considered itself to be the divinely decreed capital of the world. Indeed, the people of Rome were probably more relieved than surprised when, in October 54, the doddering Claudius was poisoned by his wife. A few days later, the newly deified Nero, Claudius's chubby seventeen-year-old successor, presided at a state funeral as the new emperor and world savior; stories soon began to circulate about Nero's miraculous infancy and childhood, in preparation for an eventual declaration of divinity for himself.

The Julio-Claudian dynasty had by this time become a parody of kingship, and growing foreign threats evoked a sense of repressive suspicion within. On the eastern border of the empire, the Parthians were again becoming aggressive, raiding the buffer state of Armenia and ousting Rome's compliant client king. The Judeans were becoming increasingly restless and causing tumults and public disorders. Throughout the empire, scapegoats were sought for the unfortunate turns of events, and hostile agents were believed to be lurking everywhere. In the province of Asia, the governor, Marcus Junius Silanus, was murdered by Nero's secret agents on suspicion of plotting against the new regime, and a widespread wave of official repression began. It is little wonder that at precisely this time of political uncertainty and fear of sedition, the leaders of the Jesus Movement in the province were identified as threats to the public order. And sometime in the fall of 54 C.E.—soon after Nero's accession—Paul was arrested with several of his co-workers and was imprisoned in Ephesus.

We cannot be sure about the charges lodged against him, but in a letter written soon afterward, Paul referred cryptically to "the affliction that came over us in Asia; for we were so utterly, unbearably crushed that we despaired of life itself" (2 Cor. 1:8). In another letter Paul pointedly mentioned his "imprisonment" and the success of his preaching "throughout the whole praetorian guard" (Phil. 1:13). The Book of Acts, in its extensive description of Paul's career in Ephesus, makes no mention of any imprisonment, but it does make much of a public uproar that brought about the effective end of Paul's ministry there. According to Acts, the local guild of silversmiths (who produced expensive souvenirs of the Great Temple of Artemis for foreign visitors and pilgrims to the city) fomented a riot against him, fearing that Paul's success in turning people away from the worship of the city's patron deity was threatening to destroy their livelihoods and posed the danger that "the Temple of the great goddess Artemis may come to nothing, and that she may even be deposed from her magnificence, she who all Asia and the world worship" (Acts 19:23–27). In later times, Christianity would indeed challenge and overcome the pagan cult of Artemis, and the story in Acts may well anticipate that later development. But for the purposes of more realistic historical reconstruction, it may be more reasonable to conclude that in the winter of 54–55 C.E.—in the tense period of transition between imperial regimes—Paul was rounded up as a potentially dangerous agitator against the Roman order and taken out of circulation lest he infect more malcontents with treasonous ideas. That was a capital offense in the eyes of the imperial administration, and Paul later remembered this as a time of darkness: "Indeed, we felt that we had received the sentence of death so that we would rely not on ourselves but on God who raises the dead" (2 Cor. 1:9).

The efforts of almost ten years of travel, preaching, and organizing seemed about to end in the isolation and helplessness of a Roman prison, and even though Paul had the company of fellow workers to comfort him, he was torn between wanting to be released so that he could continue his mission and accepting his fate as a holy martyr for Christ. As he wrote to the assembly in Philippi, "Christ will be honored in my body, whether by life or death. For to me to live is Christ, and to die is gain. If it is to be life in the flesh, that means fruitful labor for me. Yet which I shall choose I cannot tell. I am hard pressed between the two" (Phil. 1:20–23). Word of Paul's imprisonment had quickly spread back to the assemblies that Paul had established in Macedonia and the Philippians responded generously—as they always had—dispatching a prominent member named Epaphroditus with funds to bribe Paul's guards and buy him better rations, thereby lessening the privations he would have to suffer in jail.

By this time, the Philippians had distinguished themselves as among the most dedicated members of the movement, and in writing to thank them, Paul emphasized the principle that had become the centerpoint of his ideology. Far more than political agitation, class warfare, or zeal for national liberation, he had come to believe that a focused concentration on sacrifice and sharing—monetary sharing as well as spiritual selflessness— was the most potent and effective weapon that God's elect could possibly use against the forces of darkness they would all face until the *parousia* of Christ and Judgment Day. The Philippians' gift was therefore more than a generous gesture, it was an exercise in worship, "a fragrant offering, a sacrifice acceptable and pleasing to God" (4:18). And if the principle of selfless sharing were to be faithfully followed, Paul assured the Philippians, an earthly revolution would be effected both before and after Christ's return: "God will supply every need of yours according to his riches in glory in Jesus Christ" (4:19).

It is surely significant that one of Paul's prison letters—addressed to an individual named Philemon, rather than to an assembly—has been preserved as a distinct "book" of the New Testament even though it is only 335 words long. From the salutation at the top of the letter, we learn that Philemon was a householder who hosted an assembly (presumably in Ephesus) and whom Paul regarded as his "beloved fellow worker" (v. 1). Yet during the time that he had been imprisoned, Paul had given shelter to and apparently baptized a runaway slave named Onesimus who had belonged to Philemon. The ownership of a household slave—even for Christians— was hardly unusual in the urban milieu of the early empire, yet Paul now made an extraordinary demand. In sending Onesimus back to his lawful owner, he fervently requested that Philemon immediately offer Onesimus his freedom. More than that: in direct contradiction to the normal procedures of manumission—whereby the slave was required to purchase his freedom at considerable cost and pay a continuing share of his income to his owner-turned-patron—Paul begged Philemon to accept Onesimus "as a beloved brother" (v. 16) and asked that "if he has wronged you at all, or owes you anything, charge that to my account" (v. 18).

At stake in this request was Paul's newly focused social vision, which he maintained even as he languished in prison and his network of communities teetered on the verge of disintegration. To challenge the institution of slavery even among his most loyal supporters was, to his mind, the only effective way to strike a blow against Caesar. And even though the fate of his Galatian communities was now uncertain, Corinth seemed lost, and Macedonia might soon fall to his opponents, Paul had come to believe that in an age of patrons and clients, of power and exploitation, of status and possessions, only continual acts of radical self-sacrifice, modeled on the crucified figure of Jesus Christ, could renew and redeem the world.

9

Storming the Kingdom

A STUNNING MIRACLE took place during the winter of 54–55 C.E. as Paul languished in his prison cell in Ephesus and fervently prayed for God's intervention. The scattered communities of the saints that he had established across Macedonia, Galatia, Asia, and Achaia now joined together in an act of unprecedented unity that would leave its mark on Christian tradition for centuries to come. In the face of the power of patronage and the cold logic of everyday life in the Roman Empire, they threw themselves wholeheartedly into the great collection project that Paul had initiated among them, in an impressive, outward display of dedication to their shared conception of the Kingdom of God. In Corinth, in particular, the workers, tradespeople, and craftspeople, who had been shunted off to the ends of the banquet tables of the high and mighty, now rose up in symbolic revolt against the grandees and "superlative apostles" who had held the movement hostage to their own quest for personal prestige. Among Paul's other followers in villages throughout Galatia, in the workers' quarters of Philippi and Thessalonica, in Ephesus and the towns of the province of Asia, scattered communities now acted in concert. Every Sunday, as Christian brothers and sisters gathered to sing hymns of faith and thanksgiving to God, the clink of coins could also be heard. By gathering a great fortune from the members' often humble donations of coins, family heirlooms, and personal bangles and bracelets that might otherwise be rendered to the pagan gods or to Caesar, the "saints" of Paul's movement had undertaken a grand act of economic defiance to be delivered at Jerusalem which would capture attention of Jews and Gentiles the world over, both symbolizing and bringing on the Kingdom of God.

Events throughout the Mediterranean seemed to be moving toward a dramatic climax. The vast Mediterranean *imperium* established almost ninety years before by Augustus Caesar was about to undergo a life-threatening change. Steadily increasing economic pressure in the rural areas and teeming cities, combined with serious military threats from the East, would ultimately embolden the long-stilled forces of domestic dissent. And the greed and arrogance of the empire's new ruler—the spoiled, self-centered, seventeen-year-old Nero—was only one of the causes. Even though Nero's plump, pampered public image offered an unflattering contrast with the trim, soldierly statues of the deified Augustus, the causes of the coming crisis lay not so much in the changing personal style of the *princeps* as in the very structures of Roman imperialism. The effects of the bureaucratic centralization could be felt in the economic tensions and rural dissatisfaction throughout the empire as the network of patronage and power gradually expanded into every region and walk of life. The ever-higher burden of tax, tribute, and public construction meant that the wealth and well-being of local aristocracies was subject to increasing pressure and the increased cost of maintaining their lifestyles had to be borne by the peasants and the new waves of uprooted workers who streamed into the cities desperately seeking jobs. In the brave new world of Nero Caesar, the ruthless competition of individuals for economic survival and social status left little room for selfless altruism or communal philanthropy.

The collection for "the poor among the saints in Jerusalem" now being raised by the Galatian, Macedonian, and Achaian Christians was therefore meant to be both a practical and symbolic challenge to the dominant ethos. In withdrawing their material wealth from the potential grasp of the patron, merchant, land dealer, or tax collector and in giving it away to people with whom they had no blood kinship or political connection, the assemblies were demonstrating their commitment to the principle of radical self-sacrifice and focusing their exercise of that principle on effecting a particular social change. This project was far more ambitious than the injunction "to remember the poor," to which Paul had reportedly agreed at the Jerusalem conference so many years before (Gal. 2:10). The key term that Paul used for the assemblies' participation in the collection—*koinonia*, or "fellowship"—represented the same kind of active solidarity and economic sharing that was practiced in village communities according to age-old covenantal traditions, but now the scope was global. Paul's far-flung network of assemblies were now engaged in a coordinated act of *leitourgia* that emphasized their character as a worldwide movement of prophetic action. Although the Greek word *leitourgia*—whose English form is "liturgy"—is usually narrowly translated as religious or cultic activity, the term in antiquity referred to any political-economic service rendered for the common good by the citizens of a city, the subjects of a king, or the devotees of a god. It was an active demonstration of power. And in offering funds to help the communities of the saints in Judea survive without dependence on wealthy patrons or surrender to the normal economic networks of the empire, the collection for Jerusalem could be seen as a profound political act.

Had this effort been allowed to develop as a long-term project of financial redistribution, early Christianity's struggle against imperial society might have unfolded in quite a different way. But the fate of the assemblies' new-found unity and commitment to the collection project was soon to be transformed into a risky apocalyptic gamble. In the spring of 55 C.E., Paul was suddenly released from confinement in Ephesus and became convinced that the delivery of the collection to Jerusalem—under his leadership—would trigger a sequence of events culminating in the dawning of the Kingdom of God. Although we face complete historical silence on the precise circumstances of Paul's release from prison, his faithful co-workers Priscilla and Aquila seem to have had something to do with it. As he later wrote to the Romans (16:3–4), it was they "who risked their necks for my life." And as much as we might like to know more details about his flight from death row in the imperial prison (Were the charges against him dropped through skillful legal intervention? Did Priscilla and Aquila help him make a daring jailbreak?), his newfound freedom allowed him to reestablish his leadership over the various assemblies and begin a fateful new phase in his career. Arriving in Macedonia to find a gratifying scene of communities working in concert, he declared the success of the collection enterprise to be a manifestation of "God's righteousness" (2 Cor. 9:9) and praised it with the images of overflowing blessings and material well-being that had been associated by Isaiah (55:10) with the establishment of a new Covenant between God and the People of Israel. And after spending the rest of the summer of 55 in Macedonia, marshalling the communities and overseeing the election of representatives to accompany the delivery of the collection, Paul headed southward to Corinth, planning to embark for Jerusalem with a delegation of his followers, in order to be present in the Holy City at the time of the festival of Pentecost. And once there, he would alter the history and character of his movement in a way he could not possibly have predicted at the time.

THE SUCCESS of the collection effort in Galatia and in the cities of Macedonia, Achaea, and Asia—with faithful communities of former pagans actively demonstrating their absolute faith in God's providing power by *giving away* a significant portion of their wealth—was, in Paul's eyes, a world-transforming achievement. Although doubters might suggest that a few scattered village assemblies and a handful of house-churches in a handful of cities (probably not numbering more than a few hundred people) could hardly pose a realistic threat to the existence of the Roman Empire, Paul was not interested in the mundane logic of military balance. "For though we live in the world we are not carrying on a worldly war," he assured the Corinthians, "for the weapons of our warfare are not worldly but have divine power to destroy strongholds" (2 Cor. 10:3–4). His work in the eastern provinces of the empire seemed to be nearing completion, for despite the small numbers of his followers, he firmly believed that he had located all the potential heirs to the Kingdom, whose Spirit-filled response to his message signified their election by God. In the wide swath of lands around the eastern shores of the Mediterranean, where many of the descendants of Noah's son Japhet had settled—"from Jerusalem and as far round as Illyria"—Paul believed that he had fully preached the gospel of Christ (Rom. 15:19).

The delivery of the great collection to Jerusalem was a crowning achievement, but it was not to be the final one. As the prophet Isaiah had predicted, righteous representatives of *all* the peoples of the earth would someday gather in a great procession to bring offerings to Zion, to symbolize their worship of the one true God: "And the foreigners who join themselves to the Lord, to minister to him, to love the name of the Lord, and to be his servants, every one who keeps the Sabbath and does not profane it, and holds fast my covenant—these I will bring to my holy mountain, and make them joyful in my house of prayer; their burnt offerings and their sacrifices will be accepted on my altar; for my house shall be called a house of prayer for all peoples. Thus says the Lord God, who gathers the outcasts of Israel, I will gather yet others to him besides those already gathered" (Isa. 56:6–8). Paul had no doubt that through his own missionary efforts, Isaiah's ancient eschatological prophecy of Gentiles marching to Jerusalem bearing gifts was about to be fulfilled. Yet even as he arrived in Corinth and was greeted, even there, with a gratifying reception and an immediate, generous response in his appeal for contributions, he looked to even wider and more ambitious missionary fields. Far to the west, beyond the eastern Mediterranean, lay distant places and peoples that had not yet heard the good news of the redeeming sacrifice and imminent return of Jesus Christ. And Paul could plainly read in the concluding chapter of the Book of Isaiah that the final redemption of the righteous would not come before he had effected an ingathering of representatives of *all* the nations of the world.

Paul's younger contemporary Josephus noted in his encyclopedic historical work *Jewish Antiquities* that the descendants of Noah's son Japeth— among whom Paul had wandered in Galatia, Macedonia, Achaia, and Asia—had wandered as far as "Gadeira," or Cadiz, on the Iberian peninsula. Other traditions declared that Japeth's son Tubal was the ancestor of the Iberians and that Spain was the biblical land of Tarshish, settled by other descendants of Japhet, on the very edge of the known world. Thus Paul's mission would not be finished until he reached the Pillars of Hercules at the shore of the great world-encircling ocean. Did not the final chapter of the Book of Isaiah describe the boundaries of his ultimate mission to help bring on the redemption of the world? "For I know their works and their thoughts and I am coming to gather all nations and tongues; and they shall come and see my glory, and I will set a sign among them. And from them I will send survivors to the nations, to Tarshish, Put, and Lud who draw the bow, to Tubal and Javan, to the coastlands afar off, that have not heard my fame or seen my glory; and they shall declare my glory among the nations. And they shall bring all your brethren from all the nations as an offering to the Lord, upon horses, and in chariots, and in litters, and upon mules, and upon dromedaries, to my holy mountain Jerusalem, says the Lord" (66:18–20). Paul saw his commission as apostle not merely to "some" Gentiles, or "the" Gentiles wherever he found them, but to all the descendants of the family of Noah to the very Pillars of Hercules at the ends of the earth. Even though Paul had always acted alone—following personal revelations and relying on his own devices—in pressing forward with his missionary endeavors, he now needed allies to help maintain the communities he had already established and offer continuing support for his final missionary journey to Spain. The practical program of community solidarity and survival was slowly being replaced in Paul's mind by a far grander apocalyptic drama. And during the winter of 55–56 C.E., as he remained in Corinth preparing to deliver the proceeds of the collection to the "saints" in Jerusalem, his thoughts were drawn westward. In order to ensure the success of his upcoming journey to Tarshish, he composed a detailed appeal for help in that great enterprise to the members of the Jesus Movement in Rome.

Paul's Letter to the Romans—the longest of his epistles preserved in the New Testament—is also the most comprehensive explanation of his theology and historical outlook. While he had previously written letters to nurture and encourage assemblies that he had personally established, Paul now had different intentions in mind. He explicitly noted in the opening of the letter (1:10) that he had never visited the capital of the empire, and the distinctive form of address he used—"To all God's beloved in Rome, who are called to be saints" (1:7)—hints at a possible difference in organization from the *ekklesiai* or "assemblies" to which his own letters generally refer. Many modern commentators have suggested that Paul's Letter to the Romans was a "scholastic diatribe" or rhetorical composition about philosophical or theological issues written according to classical literary conventions, but as we have seen throughout our story, abstract philosophical and theological issues can rarely be separated from the larger political, economic, and cultural milieu in which Paul and the other members of the Jesus Movement lived their lives. And whatever resonance this document may later have had in the minds of theologians and church leaders, its historical significance must be related clearly and directly to the specific political challenges that Paul faced as he prepared to depart for Jerusalem and then set out—via Rome—for the distant western provinces of the Roman Empire.

If we read Paul's condemnation of the sins of the pagans (Rom. 1:18–32) as an attack on *all* systems of belief and social behavior that did not acknowledge the primacy of God and the divinely decreed balance inherent in Creation, we can see that he was condemning the scheming ambition and self-centered possessiveness that he believed had come to typify the age in which he lived. And in his denunciation of Torah-observing Jews who were nonetheless entangled in the inequities and violence of imperial society (2:13–29), he was not issuing a blanket condemnation of the traditions of Israel—as many Christian theologians have suggested. He was, rather, emphasizing how seductive and pervasive the habits of patronage and privilege could be when otherwise righteous people—both Gentile and Jew—did not firmly fix their attention on the necessity for self-sacrifice and total devotion to God. For Paul, total faith in God's saving power, as manifested in the suffering and crucifixion of Jesus Christ, was the ultimate political strategy for survival. To him, "sin" was both active participation in the regime of injustice and personal surrender to the pleasure of its material benefits. And in an uncompromisingly radical demand that few comfortable people—then or now—could ever accept, Paul sought to convince the members of the movement in Rome that the heart of their apocalyptic struggle was the battle against patronage, power, and privilege as it was symbolically manifest in the trappings of power and the rites of idolatry all over the world. But this was not a timeless ethical injunction. Paul was now growing impatient, and he appealed to the Roman community to help him immediately—to bring on the imminent Kingdom of God.

The gamble was enormous, for Paul was now risking all that he had accomplished on the outcome of his new plan. The heterogeneous mixture of Latin, Greek, and possibly Jewish names of people in Rome to whom Paul addressed greetings in the Letter to the Romans indicates that Paul already knew a whole network of people in the capital (Rom. 16:3–16), and he now called upon them to offer essential organizational and financial support. It is important to recognize that Paul was as deeply involved in the practical task of organizing an underground movement: one of the most important names that Paul mentions in the letter to Rome is a woman named Phoebe, identified as "the *diakonos* of the *ekklesia* at Cenchrae" (16:1–2), Corinth's eastern seaport. Her mention at the head of a long list of names—associated with the male form of the title for "deacon"—may indicate that hers was a special role and that Paul was introducing her to the Romans as his trusted associate, preparing the way for his mission to Spain. The phrase "welcome her in the Lord as is fitting for the saints and help her in whatever she may require from you" (16:2) seems to have signified Paul's request that she be welcomed in Rome with full hospitality and be assisted in certain business or legal transactions. Paul had apparently dispatched Phoebe to Rome while he was delivering the collection to Jerusalem, in order to set up the logistical base there for his coming mission to Spain. In fact, many scholars have assumed that Phoebe was the bearer of the letter to Rome.

Thus the plan was set: once Paul had completed his errand to Jerusalem, he would travel west to the far limits of the world to begin to bring on the final, fateful stage of human history. And now we come to what is perhaps the greatest ideological innovation in Paul's Letter to the Romans—with all its consequences for the future character of the institutionalized Christian Church. The passage in chapter 13:1–7 instructed that "every person be subject to the governing authorities. For there is no authority except from God, and those that exist have been instituted by God. Therefore he who resists the authorities resists what God has appointed, and those who resist will incur judgment. For rulers are not a terror to good conduct, but to bad. Would you have no fear of him who is in authority? Then do what is good and you will receive his approval, for he is God's servant for your good." Although a number of scholars have placed this passage in the context of tactical caution, its clear implications suggest temporary resignation to the rule of the powers-that-be. For Paul, God's redisposition of the powers was imminent and nothing should be done to endanger the crucial undertakings of the movement—"for salvation is nearer to us now than when we first believed" (13:11). Yet in pinning all his hopes on the power of a single demonstration of faithfulness by the leaders of the movement—directly confronting the authorities in Jerusalem—Paul was taking an enormous gamble. If Christ's *parousia* were to be somehow delayed, Paul's injunctions on good citizenship could merely become a code of continuing dutiful obedience to earthly powers, not the foundation of a visionary community of truly free women and men.

THE SPECTACLE of a grand delegation of Gentiles joining forces and wealth from the four corners of the eastern empire to provide both monetary and spiritual support for the beleaguered members of their movement in Jerusalem was meant to show the power already available to the Elect of God, but it would have an unexpectedly explosive outcome. For more than a century, the treasure caravans of the yearly half-shekel contributions from Jews the world over to the Jerusalem Temple had wound their way over mountains, down rivers, and across oceans to Jerusalem from the four corners of the diaspora. Yet that standard yearly offering, whose safe passage was secured by law and imperial decree since the time of Augustus, was possible only under the continued sufferance of Rome. From Paul's perspective—and the perspective of the assembly members who had contributed to the collection during the last year—*their* offering was authorized by no one but God. They therefore proceeded under what they believed to be God's protection. But Paul must also have recognized that at this time of tension and ethnic sensitivity, his arrival in Jerusalem at the head of a large delegation of uncircumcised, non-Torah-observant representatives of his Gentile assemblies could—and probably would—be seen as a provocative act.

Jerusalem was, after all, a city where mere entry into the inner courts of the Temple by Gentiles was a crime punishable by immediate execution. And with the crowds gathering in Jerusalem for Pentecost (or the "Festival of Weeks," Shavuot in Hebrew) in the late spring of 56 C.E., the Roman authorities and the Temple officials were ready for trouble. Just seven weeks before—at Passover—a mysterious prophet known only as "the Egyptian" had appeared with his followers on the Mount of Olives, posing as a new Joshua, and preaching to the people of Jerusalem that the day of deliverance was at hand. Roman forces quickly and violently dispersed the crowds that the Egyptian had gathered, but the prophet himself had escaped. He was still at large as Pentecost now approached and the Roman authorities were clearly nervous, fearing that the disturbances would be renewed if the would-be prophet returned to Jerusalem. There were, in addition, some even more pervasive dangers lying in wait for arriving prophets or reformers, since Jerusalem's political landscape had changed dramatically since Paul's last visit to the city, approximately a decade before. With the royal prestige of the Herodian family now reduced to lavish dinner parties, public philanthropy, and priestly appointments made by Agrippa's innocuous, thoroughly Romanized son Agrippa II, a fierce struggle for power had developed between a parade of successive Roman governors and incumbent High Priests.

The current Roman procurator was Felix, one of the late Emperor Claudius's powerful Greek freedmen, who had courted and won the hand of the Herodian princess Drusilla, thereby making his own infant son Agrippa a potential heir to the Judean throne. And the current High Priest, Ananias, son of Nedebaeus, was hardly less ambitious. He utilized his position as the chief executive officer of the vast Temple complex to enrich his family, bolster his political influence, and feed his growing hunger for power. Flavius Josephus later described Ananias's naked hunger for power: "Now the high priest Ananias daily advanced greatly in reputation and was splendidly rewarded by the goodwill and esteem of the citizens; for he was able to supply them with money." Josephus also reported that Ananias "had servants who were utter rascals and who, combining with the most reckless men, would go to the threshing floors and take by force the tithes of the priests; nor did they refrain from beating those who refused to give." In that respect, Ananias was hardly different from the wealthy high priests of the great pagan cults of Asia Minor or the respected urban nobles of Greece under the rule of the Romans, who cultivated the loyalty of obedient clients and crowds of urban rabble by skillfully wielding the carrot of public largess and the brutal stick of organized violence. There may indeed be some symbolic significance in a colorful tradition in the Babylonian Talmud (*Pesahim* 57a) that remembered Ananias as a great, greedy glutton who once consumed the meat of three hundred calves, three hundred barrels of wine, and a veritable mountain of fine squabs at a single meal.

Our only surviving description of Paul's journey to Jerusalem (Acts 20:3–26:30) evokes clear echoes of Jesus' last journey. It tells of Paul's sudden departure from Corinth (with his itinerary suddenly changed "when a plot was made against him by the Jews"); of his journey northward to spend a last Passover with the faithful assemblies of Macedonia; of the ominous omens and tearful farewells he received as he bade farewell to the leaders of all his communities as he made his way by ship down the western coast of Asia Minor and across to Phoenicia; and, finally, of his journey from Caesarea up to Jerusalem, where, after having been ominously warned that "the Jews at Jerusalem" shall "bind the man who owns this girdle and deliver him into the hands of the Gentiles" (Acts 21:11), he and his companions met an unfortunate—if not totally unexpected—fate. While the basic framework of this narrative, with its detailed listing of ports-of-call and names of the members of the large accompanying delegation, is suffused with a convincing air of historical plausibility, it completely avoids the central concern of the journey to Jerusalem. The delivery of the collection—which had occupied so much of Paul's time and energy for the previous year—is not even *mentioned* in the Acts account.

A number of modern scholars have speculated that the author of Acts neglected to mention the delivery of the collection by Paul and his followers because he was well aware of the unpleasant fact of its rejection by the Jerusalem community. The Jerusalem leadership was, after all, in a sensitive political position, living under both Roman domination and the domestic tyranny of rival priestly clans. For the twenty-six years since the crucifixion of Jesus, they had survived and maintained their faith in the Renewal of Israel through prophetic gifts, communal sharing of resources, and a studious refusal (after the executions of John and James and the exile of Peter during the reign of Agrippa I) to pose a direct, public challenge to the powers-that-be. In their faith in the coming divine judgment and in their pious, practical dedication to the Renewal of Israel through Torah-observance and honoring the memory of the martyred Jesus, they sought to effect a national revival of dedication to the Mosaic Covenant. The community's leader—James, the brother of Jesus—had gained great public respect for his righteousness and observance of the Law. The arrival in Jerusalem of Paul at the head of a Gentile delegation would therefore have been a highly provocative act in the explosive political atmosphere of the city, yet we have only Acts's highly idealized description to inform us of what went on at the first meeting between the Jerusalem leaders and Paul.

Acts relates that Paul was received with quiet respect and honor. "After greeting them, he related one by one the things that God had done among the Gentiles through his ministry. And when they heard it, they glorified God" (Acts 21:19–20). This is, of course, clearly incompatible with what we know of Paul's long-running battle with the Torah-observant branches of the movement led by "certain men" sent by James to Antioch (Gal. 2:12); with the preachers of the gospel of circumcision in Galatia (Gal. 5); with the "superlative apostles," apparently commissioned in Jerusalem, who made their appearance in Corinth (2 Cor. 11); and with the "evil-workers" who Paul feared would preach the necessity of circumcision in Philippi (Phil. 3:2). *They* knew exactly what Paul had been preaching and, having little patience for his radical, universal critique of patronage, saw it as a direct threat to Israel's national struggle against Rome. Thus it is understandable why the Acts account of Paul's initial meeting with the leaders of the Jerusalem community does not deal at all with the issue of the collection but digresses into a puzzling description of the expensive and involved purification ceremonies that James prescribed for Paul to counter the accusation that "you teach all the Jews who are among the Gentiles to forsake Moses, telling them not to circumcise their children or observe the customs" (Acts 21:21). If the Book of Acts was trying to ignore or hide something, it must surely have been what Paul himself expressly feared in Romans 15:31: the rejection of the collection by the leaders of the Jerusalem community and the sudden, violent termination of his mission to Jerusalem at the hands of the Roman and Temple authorities.

Because Paul's personal testimony ends with his Letter to the Romans—written on the eve of his departure from Corinth to Jerusalem—our only ancient source describing the violent climax of his Pentecost pilgrimage is the account in Acts 21:28–36, which relates Paul's near-lynching in the courtyard of the Temple on charges by "Jews from Asia" that "this is the man who is teaching men everywhere against the people and the law and this place; moreover he also brought Greeks into the temple, and he has defiled this holy place." The Book of Acts suggests the charge was false, but from the indications we have from his own letters, it would not be out of the realm of possibility that Paul would have mounted a prophetic demonstration in the Temple courtyards in which he condemned the High Priests of the Temple as those who called themselves Jews and boasted of their relation to God and yet were guilty of theft, adultery, and embezzlement. For "you who boast in the law," he had rhetorically announced in the Letter to the Romans, "do you dishonor the God by breaking the law?" (Rom. 2:23). Here at the center of the celebration of Law in Israel's Holy City—on the Festival of Weeks commemorating the giving of the Law from Sinai—Paul had a unique opportunity to preach his gospel in which the struggle against patronage and power was the primary commandment and in which the most powerful imperial authorities and leaders of the People of Israel stood accused. In these very days, he believed, the Holy Spirit had called the righteous sons of Japhet to send offerings to Zion—just as Isaiah had foretold would occur at the end of days. Surely the wicked would soon feel the pain of God's vengeance, and the righteous of all nations would inherit the Kingdom of God. The reaction to this heterodox preaching was expectable. Paul was quickly arrested by Roman guards and hustled off to prison. And a telling historical detail in the Acts account bolsters the possibility that he mounted a provocative demonstration in the Temple courtyards: Acts relates that he was initially mistaken by the arriving Roman security forces as the mysterious Egyptian prophet who had caused such a violent stir in Jerusalem just a few weeks before (Acts 21:38).

Paul's arrest in the Temple compound initiated a sequence of events that would determine the future character of his own assemblies and, indirectly, result in the virtual destruction of the Jerusalem community. Whether or not we take as an accurate quotation the words that Acts 22:1–21 places in Paul's mouth as he stood in Roman custody on the staircase between the Antonia and the Temple (so much like the set-piece speeches of Josephus's characters at times of national or personal crisis), it seems clear that Paul not only *did not* convert the people of Jerusalem to his gospel through the delivery of the collection, but he attracted the unwelcome attention of the high-priestly administration and the Romans toward both the Jerusalem community of the Jesus Movement and himself. Paul was imprisoned in the coastal city of Caesarea, and the right to judge his case became the subject of a bitter jurisdictional dispute between the procurator and the High Priest, resulting in Paul's extradition to face an imperial tribunal in Rome. And in 62 C.E., the incumbent High Priest Ananus, son of Ananus (a man whom Josephus described as "rash in temper and unusually daring") saw an opportunity to strike a blow against the local followers of Jesus. "And so he convened the judges of the Sanhedrin," Josephus reported, "and brought before them a man names James, the brother of Jesus who was called the Christ, and certain others. He accused them of having transgressed the law, and delivered them up to be stoned."

The grisly details of James's martyrdom in Jerusalem were long preserved in church tradition, even though his role as a great champion of the Renewal of Israel was not. According to the vivid, highly embellished account of the second-century C.E. church chronicler Hegesippus, James was summoned by "scribes and the Pharisees" and ordered to deny his faith in his late brother Jesus as the martyred redeemer of Israel. When he merely proclaimed his faith more fervently than ever, he was thrown from the high parapet of the Temple, stoned by an angry crowd, and then beaten to death. Yet Josephus relates that far from being accomplices in the bloody murder of a saintly figure, most Judeans reacted in horror to the High Priest's brutal grab for power: "Those who were considered the most fair-minded people in the city, and strict in their observance of the law, were most indignant at this." Even though the outrage was general among the people of Jerusalem and Ananus was deposed from power, the Jerusalem community of the Jesus Movement was never the same again. The realistic hope of joyfully establishing the Kingdom had been beaten out of them.

After the death of the towering figure of James, who had guided the community in Jerusalem for more than two decades, the community would slowly drift from its original ideal of establishing an egalitarian village-in-the-city toward a more conventional sectarian existence, governed along hereditary dynastic—rather than Spirit-inspired—lines. Even though James had been a blood relative of Jesus, his prestige within the movement seems to have been based on his charisma and great spiritual authority. With James's death, however, the movement in Jerusalem abandoned the uncompromising anti-monarchic fervor of its earlier days. According to a tradition preserved by Eusebius, a new leader for the Jerusalem community was chosen in a solemn conclave of the aging apostles and disciples of Jesus and the surviving members of Jesus' own family. The choice of Jesus' first cousin Symeon, son of Clopas, as the new leader of the Jerusalem community signified that earlier methods of selection (revelation, drawing by lot, or gift of the Spirit) had given way to a more conventional dynastic principle. A messianic royalty had now come to rule the utopian village-in-the-city. In Jerusalem at least, the original Galilean ideal of the kingless Kingdom was dead.

AND WHAT OF PAUL and his great, apocalyptic visions of changing the world? The Book of Acts provides an unforgettable adventure story of Paul's storm-tossed voyage in Roman custody westward from Judea to Italy, where he would finally receive the hearing before Nero that he sought. This account (chapters 27–28:11) is filled with fascinating details about winds, sailors, harbors, and seagoing vessels—and culminates in a thrilling tale of a sudden storm and Paul's shipwreck on the half-civilized island of Malta, where he spent several months performing signs and wonders among the natives until the arrival of more favorable weather allowed him and his entourage (still including the Roman officer who kept him in custody) to gain passage on an Alexandrian ship named *The Twin Brothers* to Italy. And after making two port calls at Syracuse and Rhegium, the passengers disembarked at the harbor of Puetoli and made their way toward Rome. The Book of Acts 28:14–16 describes Paul's subsequent overland journey as something of an imperial progress, with enthusiastic crowds of supporters greeting him along the way: "And the brethren there, when they heard of us, came as far as the Forum of Appius and Three Taverns to meet us. On seeing them Paul thanked God and took courage. And when we came into Rome, Paul was allowed to stay by himself, with the soldier that guarded him."

Not mentioned or even hinted at in the Acts account of Paul's arrival in Rome to face an imperial tribunal was the Emperor Nero's growing madness, which no one living at the time could possibly have ignored. For by the time of Paul's arrival in Rome—which has been dated by many scholars to the spring of 60 C.E.—the twenty-three-year-old Nero was becoming increasingly obsessed with his own visionary scheme of world redemption.

The chubby, primped, and spoiled *princeps* imagined, even insisted, that he was destined to be the savior figure who would usher in a restoration of classical Greek grace, beauty, and artistry everywhere throughout the vast empire that he ruled. Despite his repellent physical appearance (he possessed a protuberant belly, spindly legs, squat neck, and a body that was "pustular and malodorous," according to the Roman historian Suetonius), Nero fancied himself to be a Greek god in both flesh and spirit. In the musical, athletic, and poetic competitions that he entered (and always won through the cowering sycophancy of the judges), Nero imagined that he was helping to create through his own example an ideal realm of order, logic, and harmony. Of course this new Hellenic Eden existed only in his mind and was taken seriously only due to his subjects' fear of incurring imperial displeasure. "No one was allowed to leave the theater during his recitals, however pressing the reason," related Suetonius in his scathing account of Nero's excesses. "We read of women in the audience giving birth, and of men so bored with listening and applauding that they furtively dropped down from the wall at the rear, since the gates were kept barred, or shammed dead and were carried away for burial."

Yet there was a sweeping apocalyptic ideology behind Nero's madness, for the emperor truly believed that the new age about to dawn for the world must be ushered in by a stunning transformation. In a perverse parallel to Jewish eschatological visions of God's remaking of the Holy City of Jerusalem at the time of redemption, Nero fancied himself to be the empire's grand architect, designing symmetrical boulevards, temples, palaces, and open spaces of a New Rome that would replace the present twisting alleys, tumbledown shacks, and closely packed bazaars. Later, on a tour of the classical sites of Achaia, he stopped at Corinth and, with great ceremony, personally turned the first shovelful of earth for a canal to be dug through the isthmus between the Gulf of Corinth and the Aegean that would physically unite the empire's East and West. Nero imagined himself to be nothing less than the incarnated Apollo—spirit of majesty and divine order—appearing in public playing a lyre, with a wreath of laurel on his head and wearing, according to Suetonius, "a Greek mantle spangled with gold stars over a purple robe." Nero imagined that he was inaugurating a new age in which the old-fashioned taboos and regulations to which the people of Rome had been enslaved for centuries were to be superseded by a new code of universal enlightenment. He bathed his sweaty body in the once-sacred spring at the source of the Marcian Aqueduct; he married his

freedman Doryphorus in a spectacular public wedding; and he was reportedly "convinced that nobody could remain chaste or pure in any part of his
body, but that most people concealed their secret vices; hence if anyone
confessed to obscene practices, Nero forgave him all his other crimes." In
his own way he envisioned himself as a spirit-inspired prophet of *hellenismos*—and, unlike Paul and the many other would-be prophets and seers
that roamed throughout the Mediterranean doing miracles and propound-
ing their various gospels—he had the earthly power to make his dreams a
reality.

This was certainly not the kind of new world that Paul had envisioned
in his years of travel, preaching, healing, and community building throughout the empire. And it is hard to avoid the conclusion—if there is the least
bit of historical reliability to the Acts account that Paul was in Rome at this
very time—that Paul and the other members of the Jesus Movement in
Rome would have reacted passionately against the rule of this tyrannical,
megalomaniac emperor, who had his own twisted vision of the dawning of
a new age. We know little about Paul's personal situation or even the
character of the Roman assemblies, but from what we know of Paul's
thinking as expressed in his Letter to the Romans, he believed that the
culmination of history was indeed at hand. And in light of the miraculous
flexibility of apocalyptic logic—which unfailingly finds new omens and
signs of coming divine intervention in even the most horrible of earthly
disappointments and disasters—it is reasonable to assume that Paul and his
followers interpreted his arrest in Jerusalem and the loss of the collection as
powerful indications that the *parousia* of Christ was quickly approaching
and that a great, cleansing judgment would soon deliver punishment to the
wicked of the earth—"when sudden destruction will come upon them as
travail comes upon a woman with child, and there will be no escape" (1
Thess. 5:3). And in the language of the prophetic oracle from which Paul
drew so many of his images, that day of the vengeance of God was
envisioned as coming upon the world with sudden fury: "For behold, the
Lord will come in fire, and his chariots like the stormwind, to render his
anger in fury, and his rebuke with flames of fire" (Isa. 66:15).

But when the great purging cataclysm finally came, it came in a form
more terrifying than Paul or the Roman assemblies could ever have
dreamed. As mass catastrophe rather than selective judgment, they too
would be engulfed. And so it came to pass that sometime during the balmy,
breezy summer night of July 18, 64 C.E., flames erupted in one of the

closely packed shops near the Circus Maximus in the heart of the city. The cheap textiles, perfumes, oils, leather, and wooden goods on the shelves of the stalls in the marketplace provided explosive fuel for the fire. "Fanned by the wind," Tacitus reported in his famous account of the disaster, "the conflagration grew and swept the whole length of the Circus. There were no walled mansions or temples, or any other obstructions, which could arrest it. First, the fire swept violently over the level spaces. Then it climbed the hills—but returned to ravage the level ground again. It outstripped every countermeasure. The ancient city's narrow streets and irregular block encouraged its progress. Terrified, shrieking women, helpless old and young, people intent on their own safety, people unselfishly supporting invalids or waiting for them, fugitives and lingerers alike—all heightened the confusion. When people looked back, menacing flames sprang up before them or outflanked them. When they escaped to a neighboring quarter, the fire followed—even districts believed remote proved to be involved. Finally, with no idea where or what to flee, they crowded onto country roads, or lay in the fields. Some who had lost everything—even their food for the day—could have escaped but preferred to die. So did others, who had failed to rescue their loved ones. Nobody dared fight the flames. Attempts to do so were prevented by menacing gangs. Torches, too, were openly thrown in by men crying that they acted under orders. Perhaps they had received orders. Or they may just have wanted to plunder unhampered."

For six full days the conflagration continued, eventually burning out of its own accord. Ten of the fourteen districts of the city had been almost completely leveled; tens of thousands were dead, tens of thousands home-less. And almost immediately rumors began to spread that the emperor himself had ordered the conflagration so that his great architectural plans for a New Rome could be implemented with the least inconvenience. Nero may not have fiddled while Rome burned, but Suetonius recorded the hostile gossip that "Nero watched the conflagration from the Tower of Maecenas, enraptured by what he called 'the beauty of the flames'; then put on a tragedian's costume and sang *The Sack of Ilium* from beginning to end." But as the reconstruction work got under way and Nero announced plans for the construction of a massive Golden House for himself in the center of the city, he acted quickly to counter the rumors and gossip against him, finding the perfect scapegoats on whom to pin the blame. After all, hadn't that damnable sect of Middle Eastern immigrants and religious fundamentalists who called themselves Christians long warned that they would bring about the end of the world? Read from a hostile perspective, even the oracles of Isaiah could be read as a violent revolutionary tract. "For by fire will the Lord execute judgment, and by his sword, upon all flesh; and those slain by the Lord shall be many" (66:16). For hostile government agents and investigators, that kind of subversive talk would be more than enough to seal the Roman Christians' earthly fate.

The Roman historian Tacitus offers a glimpse of how a public persecution of a despised minority—presented as entertainment—could be used to divert popular hatred from the emperor: "Neither human resources, nor imperial munificence, nor appeasement of the gods eliminated sinister suspicions that the fire had been instigated. To suppress this rumor, Nero fabricated scapegoats—and punished with every refinement the notoriously depraved Christians (as they were popularly called). Their originator, Christ, had been executed in Tiberius's reign by the governor of Judea, Pontius Pilatus. But in spite of this temporary setback, the deadly superstition had broken out afresh, not only in Judea (where the mischief had started) but even in Rome. All degraded and shameful practices collect and flourish in the capital. First, Nero had self-acknowledged Christians arrested. Then on their information, large numbers of others were condemned—not so much for their incendiarism as for their anti-social tendencies. Their deaths were made farcical. Dressed in wild animals' skins, they were torn to pieces by dogs, or crucified, or made into torches to be ignited after dark as substitutes for daylight. Nero provided his Gardens for the spectacle, and exhibited displays in the Circus, at which he mingled with the crowd—or stood in a chariot, dressed as a charioteer."

This was the ruler whose personal justice—according to the Book of Acts—Paul had longed for when he demanded to have his case heard before Caesar in Rome. No wonder the Book of Acts concluded without mentioning Paul's ultimate fate; this was another unpleasant historical reality too painful for its larger theological agenda to include. The only source we have for Paul's final years is a eulogy preserved in the First Letter of Clement, written at Rome around the turn of the second century: "Through jealousy and strife Paul showed the way to the prize of endurance; seven times he was in bonds, he was exiled, he was stoned, he was herald both in the East and in the West, he gained the noble fame of his faith, he taught righteousness to all the world, and when he had reached the limits of the West he gave his testimony [*martyresas* = he "witnessed" in martyrdom] before the rulers, and thus passed from the world and was taken up into the holy place, the greatest example of endurance" (5:5–7). Eusebius preserved a more succinct tradition about Paul and the aged, former Galilean fisherman Peter. Their long personal journeys from the streets of Damascus and the dockside of Carpernaum were over: "It is recorded that in [Nero's] reign Paul was beheaded in Rome itself, and that Peter was likewise crucified, and the record is confirmed by the fact that the cemeteries there are still called by the names of Peter and Paul."

PAUL NEVER LIVED to greet the returning Christ at the time of the great Rapture, of being caught up "in the clouds to meet the Lord in the air" (1 Thess. 4:17). Neither is there any hard evidence that he founded any new assemblies after his arrest in Jerusalem and transfer to Rome. His personal energy was stilled and his voice silenced by the forces of repression who took their marching orders from a mad, sybaritic emperor. But the members of the communities he had established in Galatia, Macedonia, and Achaea—and the harried saints among the assemblies in Rome who had survived the Great Fire—lived on in confidence that the dawn of the Kingdom of God foretold and described by the ancient Hebrew prophets would, someday, arrive. In the meantime, they had to do what they could to put their lives back together, to provide food for their hungry children, and survive as best they could until they could make sense of the apparent failure of the great project of the collection for Jerusalem and the apparent triumph of Nero's depravity—and his embodiment as the archetypal "enemy of Christ" whose "god is the belly" and who "glory in their shame, with minds set on earthly things" (Phil. 3:19).

For the time being, at least, nothing had changed in the way life went on in the provincial cities of the empire—and for that matter, in Rome itself after the burned districts had been demolished and new market places and apartment houses were built. Wealth was still drawn upward through a system of power and patronage in which respect and a share in all crops, profits, and wages was claimed by landowners, tax officials, aristocrats, and upwardly-mobile entrepreneurs. The brothers and sisters in Christ in Corinth, Ephesus, Thessalonica, Philippi, and Galatia had no alternative but to go about their business, continuing to engage in trade and handcrafts in the busy markets of their cities, buying, selling, sizing up potential customers, and gaining the best prices for their services or finished products, in the hope of keeping themselves and their communities alive. Paul had already suggested in that troubling passage of Romans that they should keep a low public profile and "be subject to the governing authorities," paying all the taxes they demanded and giving "respect to whom respect is due" (13:1–7). Paul's own fate should have called that advice into question, but as a matter of survival for those brothers and sisters who preferred to wait for Christ's return to earth in glory rather than meet him in heaven as martyrs, they had to numb themselves to the injustice of their day-to-day lives.

Only in their joyful, Spirit-fired assemblies, in their regular gatherings to celebrate the Lord's Supper, in their material sharing among themselves, and in their solemn rituals of baptism to signify the rebirth of new members were they able to perfect a system of ceremony and ritual to survive spiritually in an imperial situation over which they ultimately had no control. With the bitter disappointment of the failure of the collection journey to Jerusalem slowly receding from the memories of the members of the main Pauline communities, the goal of the communities' existence had less and less to do with effecting down-to-earth political change. The crystallizing "religion," or Christianity—and here we can at last begin to speak of a religion, in its celebration of the vivid central image of the crucified Christ—offered a long-range method of dealing with the feelings of helplessness and dislocation that plagued so many subjects of the Roman Empire. Yet the movement that had begun as a quest for the Renewal of Israel by John the Baptist and Jesus—and various other latter-day Israelite prophets and apocalyptic movements in Roman-occupied Judea—now increasingly lost touch with its goal of forming a practical worldwide alliance against the forces of empire. The weekly meetings of the *ekklesiai*, the singing of hymns in honor of the crucified Jesus, and the ritualized reenactment of Christ's resurrection through baptism and the Lord's Supper became sacred ends in themselves.

As the days, weeks, months, and years passed with no change in the heavens or on the horizon, new understandings had to be developed for the meaning of salvation and the Kingdom of God. Paul had already transformed the central figure of the crucified Christ into an adaptable symbol of sacrificial commitment. His followers continued to believe that wickedness was neither natural nor inevitable and that God would some-how, sometime, somewhere ensure that the righteous meek would inherit the earth. That was also the hope of the Galilean peasantry among whom

Jesus of Nazareth had preached, healed, and wandered. Yet in the last days of the reign of Nero, no one could really be blamed for dismissing the tiny tribe of Christians as a cult of doomed dreamers and idealists. The empire could marshal enormous power and violence to ensure public docility and the appearance of order, even though, in the streets, temples, and marketplaces, the law of the jungle prevailed. The most famous leaders of the Jesus Movement had been discredited or crushed by the power of empire, and the scattered assemblies of Galatia, Macedonia, Achaia, and Asia were living an underground existence. The greatest miracle one could possibly imagine was that the dream of the Kingdom of God would survive at all.

10

The Triumph of Caesar

THE WORLD WOULD SOON be transformed almost beyond
recognition, as the long struggle of God's people against the
Roman Empire moved inexorably toward a dramatic new stage.
And one of the keys to the ultimate success of Christianity would—
ironically—be the violent destruction of the Jerusalem Temple and the
total devastation of the world in which Jesus and the first apostles had
lived. For the time being, Paul's assemblies held together in their towns,
villages, and cities and the great Christian community of Antioch continued to send its apostles of renewal into the hinterland. But in the birthplace
of the movement—the Land of Israel—a bloody struggle would soon
erupt to alter forever the fate of the entire Mediterranean world. The
warning signs should have been obvious to any open-eyed observer, but at
the time no one in a position of power seemed to notice or care. By the
twelfth year of the reign of Nero—in 66 C.E.—the once-peaceful hills and
valleys of the Galilee had become a simmering volcano, ready to explode
in violence and chaos, to destroy the palaces and strongholds of aristocratic privilege that had molded the region's history for more than a
hundred years. The region through which Jesus of Nazareth had led his
followers almost forty years earlier was still suffering from the ills of a
system of imperial patronage in which most peasants were sinking ever
deeper in debt—or had already become urban workers or tenant farmers—
and in which a Romanized urban nobility lived off their incomes from
industry and trade and looked westward, for guidance, to Rome.

In some Galilean villages, the sayings of Jesus were still remembered and perhaps even recited in assemblies of the faithful—in their call for separation, renewal, and the establishment of an egalitarian Kingdom of God. In other towns and villages, submission to the structures of Herodian and Roman power had become too deeply embedded to be challenged. Yet in the slums of Tiberias, in the salt-fish factories of Taricheae, and in hill country villages throughout the region, other, more impatient voices were calling for action. Roving bands of dispossessed farmers' sons, impoverished townspeople, and social misfits were collecting arms and calling for revolution, which they identified with the coming of the messianic age. Their primary targets were the property and the prestige of the great Herodian landowners and the prominent priestly clans. Yet this was by no means a unique situation among the countless peoples who had been brought under the rule of the Caesars. In Gaul, Spain, and Britain, popular dissatisfaction also simmered just beneath the surface, and the fervor for banditry of the poor-against-rich could, under the right conditions, ignite a conflagration that would engulf the entire empire.

As things turned out, the spark flared first in the crowded, angry streets of the Mediterranean port city of Caesarea Maritima, the administrative capital of the province of Judea—a place known by contemporaries as Judea's "Little Rome" and by modern archaeologists, seduced by the elegance of its promontory palace, theater, and impressive harbor, as "King Herod's Dream." But that dream had turned to a nightmare during decades of hatred and violence between the local Greek and Jewish communities who bitterly competed for the favor of Roman aristocrats and provincial officials, thereby obtaining lucrative contracts, commercial advantage, and public works jobs. The outbreak of open violence between Jews and Greeks in Caesarea soon after the accession of Nero brought matters to a head. Separate Greek and Jewish delegations departed for Rome to press their claims to the emperor, with the Jews seeking confirmation of their traditional grant of *isopolitea*, or equal rights in the life of the city, despite their refusal to worship the emperor or participate in Caesarea's pagan cults and ceremonies. At stake in this local conflict was an issue with enormous implications for minority rights throughout the empire: Could a distinct ethnic group like the Jews continue to live in the midst of a Greco-Roman city, maintaining their own distinctive customs and connections with the Jerusalem priesthood, yet still be considered loyal subjects of the empire?

The Apostle Paul—and some of the era's best known pagan writers and philosophers—had in their own ways attempted to address the problem of ethnic conflict and coexistence in the empire's major cities, but Nero, the psychopathic philhellene, solved the Caesarea case in a particularly brutal way. In the spring of 66 C.E. he issued a decree annulling the longstanding grant of equal civil rights to the Jews. That act, eliminating the independent economic—if not yet political or religious—rights of the Jews would have repercussions far wider than Nero or his closest advisers could ever have imagined. It created an explosive situation in which an otherwise insignificant neighbors' quarrel could change the course of history. And so it happened on one Sabbath morning in May 66, that a young Greek— eager to taunt the newly humbled Jews of the city—sat down in a narrow alley leading to one of the local synagogues and began to sacrifice birds according to a pagan rite. With the arrival of the Jewish worshippers, angry words led to blows and scattered fistfights led to city-wide rioting. And the violence that soon erupted all over the Land of Israel would finally bring on the climactic act in the century-long drama between the People of Israel and the emperors of Rome.

The Holy City of Jerusalem soon became the focal point of rebellion. The current and particularly brutal Roman procurator, Gessius Florus, proceeded with troops to Jerusalem and sent soldiers into the Temple compound to confiscate by force seventeen talents (more than 700 kilograms of precious metal, apparently silver) to pay the overdue tax levies owed by the people of Judea to the imperial treasury. When a public demonstration against this brutal violation of the sanctity of the Temple arose in the streets of Jerusalem, Florus gave free reign to his soldiers— many of them recruited from the poor Greek neighborhoods of Caesarea—to give vent to their anti-Jewish hatred by killing, raping, and looting Jerusalem's markets and residential neighborhoods. Street battles quickly spread throughout the city and, according to Josephus, "many of the peaceable citizens were arrested and brought before Florus, who had them first scourged and then crucified." The members of the upper priesthood and the Herodian royal family, though shocked and deeply shaken, urged calm and a respectful appeal to Nero. But for many Judeans, the time for accommodation was over. A rebel faction gained strength in Jerusalem, gaining control of the Temple compound and—for the first time since the victories of the Maccabees over the Hellenistic armies of Antiochus more than two centuries before—foreign troops were driven from the Holy City of Jerusalem with the panicked flight of Florus and his troops.

King Agrippa II and his entourage were expelled from the city under a shower of stones and curses. And in an unmistakable demonstration of their new resolve for independence, some of the younger, more radical priests in the Temple declared their allegiance to God rather than Caesar by discontinuing the daily sacrifice for the well-being of the emperor that had been a part of the Temple ritual since the time of Herod the Great.

We have no source to inform us how the members of the Jerusalem community of the Jesus Movement reacted to the violence, the excitement, and the anticipation of Judea's imminent liberation during the summer and early autumn of 66 C.E. But they could not have been unaffected by the building revolutionary fervor: in August, the radical priests and the *sicarii*, or "knifemen," gained control of the Temple and set fire to the opulent residences of the former High Priest Ananias and the Herodian royal family. They then, according to Josephus, "eager to destroy the money-lenders' bonds and to prevent the recovery of debts, in order to win over a host of grateful debtors and to cause a rising of the poor against the rich," put the Public Record Office to the torch. Violence, so long utterly unsuccessful and counterproductive in resisting the rule of the Romans, now suddenly seemed to have miraculous power to liberate the People of Israel. And for many Judeans, the clear proof of God's divine assistance came in the autumn, when a large legionary force led by the governor of Syria, Cestius Gallus, was decimated by Judean guerrillas in its panicked retreat after a brief foray to rebel-held Jerusalem. Judean and Perean peasant rebels attacked the Hellenistic cities and neighboring Greek villages they had long seen as their oppressors and rivals. In Galilee, a village leader named John of Gischala mounted raids against neighboring territories, and the fishermen and urban poor of Tiberias, led by Jesus, son of Sapphias ("the ringleader of the sailors and the destitute class," according to Josephus), stormed, looted, and burned the opulent palace built almost fifty years before by Herod Antipas. And as its gilded roof buckled and collapsed in rivulets of molten gold leaf and heat-cracked marble, the rebels quickly carried off its furniture, ornaments, and other treasures to their own poor lakefront neighborhoods.

THIS WAS CERTAINLY not the world of classical order and artistic beauty that the Emperor Nero envisioned as he traveled with his retinue through the ancient shrines of Achaia, competing (always successfully) in numberless athletic competitions and poetic displays. When word came from the East of the setbacks suffered by Roman legions in that damnably barbaric province of Judea, he turned to a gruff, boorish old soldier named Titus Flavius Vespasianus to restore Elysian serenity to his empire again. Vespasian was a bald, bull-necked career military officer, who had commanded legions in Germany and in Britain and had proved his mettle in a no-nonsense term in office as proconsul of the province of Africa. And even though he had recently incurred Nero's displeasure by falling asleep during one of the emperor's interminable poetry readings, Vespasian was given command of the Judean operations in February 67, and with three full legions at his disposal—together with auxiliary support from the armies of the client kings Antiochus of Commagene, Sohaemus of Edessa, Malichus II of Nabatea, and Judea's own Agrippa II—he launched a brutal scorched-earth campaign of destruction and enslavement, intended to extinguish Judea's tendency for stiff-necked rebellion once and for all.

The Galileans were the first to bear the brunt of the Roman fury. Many Galileans had spent the spring and summer of 67 preparing to defend their towns and villages against the expected onslaught of the Romans, directed—if not always wisely or effectively—by the completely inexperienced thirty-year-old "general" named Josephus, who had been sent out from Jerusalem to lead the regional defense. But with the arrival of Vespasian in the autumn, the Galilean towns and villages were systematically overrun and leveled. It mattered little that at the first serious engagement between Jewish and Roman forces, at the town of Jotapata, General Josephus defected to the Roman side. By the autumn, the human landscape of Galilee was changed forever and the world that Jesus and his earliest followers had known became just a memory. Towns and villages across the region were burned and leveled, and tens of thousands of men, women, and children—even those who played no active part in the rebellion—were hacked, burned, or beaten to death. Tiberias surrendered. Permanent Roman garrisons were established. And at the salt-fish industrial town of Taricheae (where the fishermen of the Sea of Galilee had brought their hauls since even before the time of Jesus), General Vespasian held a victor's tribunal. According to Josephus, more than 30,000 Galilean prisoners of war were sold into slavery; twelve hundred elderly and infirm captives (having no market value) were executed; and "six thousand of the most robust" young people of the region were sent off as imperial slaves to

Achaia—where Nero still tarried—to undertake the backbreaking labor of digging his visionary Corinthian Canal.

With the panicked flight of Galilean survivors and refugees to rebel-held Jerusalem, Vespasian led his armies southward in the spring of 68 C.E., ravaging the coastal plain, Samaria, the Jordan Valley, and the rich farm-land of Idumea, enclosing Jerusalem and the heartland of Judea in an ever-tightening noose. Back in Rome, the Julio-Claudian Dynasty—stretching all the way back to the days of Julius Caesar—was collapsing from within, weighed down by Nero's own madness, greed, and arrogance. Ever since the Great Fire, Nero had been squandering unimaginable sums on his megalomaniac plans to rebuild Rome and make the entire empire an ornament to his own sense of elegance and grandeur. As the flames of rebellion flickered in the East, unrest spread just beneath the surface of the daily life of imperial Rome. In 65, a court conspiracy against Nero led by the senator Gaius Calpurnius Piso had been exposed and averted at the last moment. Yet the ensuing reign of terror—with the torture and murder of dozens of Rome's leading citizens, not to mention those unfortunate plebe-ians and slaves swept up in the net of suspicion—only made matters worse. And by the spring of 68, as Nero triumphantly returned from his tour of Greece and his general Vespasian rampaged through Judea, rebellion flared in another flashpoint of imperial rule. In distant Gaul, the native-born governor Gaius Julius Vindex raised the banner of Gallic independence, scornfully declaring that the present emperor was nothing more than a second-rate zither player who should be immediately removed. An even more serious threat soon came from Spain, at the far western end of the empire, where the Christian apostle Paul had once dreamed of fulfilling Isaiah's prophecy. The anti-Neronian resistance was headed by a cantan-kerous old nobleman named Servius Sulpicius Galba, who called for the empire's return to the stern Augustan ideals of his distant youth.

At first, Nero played the role of an unshaken, if unstable, dictator determined to cling on to the reins of power at any cost. Suetonius later reported that Nero, on hearing the news of the spreading rebellion, threatened to depose and execute all his army commanders and provincial governors; to poison the entire Senate at a banquet; or even to let wild beasts loose in the streets of Rome to discourage all seditious activity. Yet these fantasies came to nothing. By June 68—just at the time when Vespasian was completing his mopping-up operations in Judea and enjoy-ing the spectacle of bound prisoners being tossed in the Dead Sea and merely bobbing on the surface—Nero was driven to a complete break-down. Pursued by a detachment of rebel cavalry as he fled in panic from Rome into the countryside, he stabbed himself to death, declaring, "Such a great artist dies with me!"

Nero's successor Galba proved to be no more of a savior and even less of an artist. As just another arrogant aristocrat who had been raised to believe that the fruits of the empire were his private property, he quickly alienated his fellow senators, the army, the provinces, and the people of Rome. Political chaos continued through the succeeding months (later to become famous as "The Year of the Four Emperors")—as Galba, then Nero's boyhood friend Marcus Salvius Otho, and yet another imperial pretender named Aulus Vitellius ousted each other in quick sequence to claim the throne for themselves. Rome's future was held hostage to the same bloody competition between rivals that had, a century before—in the wake of Julius Caesar's assassination—led to all-out civil war. And just as his nephew Octavian had emerged in the midst of empire-wide chaos to ascend to the throne and proclaim the dawn of a grand era of peace and prosperity, so a new savior was now to come again.

How ironic it was that the old Judean prophecies that had been used for centuries as the basis for national independence would now be adopted to imperial ends. In a stunning, revisionist interpretation of the same apoca-lyptic prophecies of messianic redemption that occupied the hopes and dreams of Jewish rebels, Dead Sea sectarians, and the visionaries of the Jesus Movement, Josephus, the Jewish turncoat who had defected to the Romans at the battle of Jotapata in Galilee, claimed to have been the first to see that the biblical prophecies of a world-conquering messiah arising in Judea applied to none other than Titus Flavius Vespasian. In time, other claimants arose to offer similar predictions of Vespasian's glorious future: Rabban Yohanan Ben Zakkai, who would later go on to found the Great Rabbinic Academy at the seaside town of Yavne; the pagan priests of Mount Carmel; and the votaries of the Egyptian god Serapis in Alexandria. The truth was that people throughout the eastern provinces of the empire were tired of suffering and dying for the greed of rival aristocrats and they longed for a plain-spoken savior to put things right again. After being acclaimed as Rome's legitimate emperor by his own soldiers, Vespasian also won the allegiance of all the client kings of the region—Sohaemus of Edessa, Antiochus of Commagene, and Agrippa II and his sister Berenice of the Herodian dynasty. According to Tacitus, "all the provinces washed by the sea, as far as Asia and Achaia, and the whole expanse of country inland towards Pontus and Armenia, took the oath of allegiance." The dynastic principle of imperial succession among the heirs of the divine Augustus had given way to the coronation of the prototypical self-made man.

And there was one other history-making change worth remarking: before departing for Alexandria and Rome to assume his imperial duties, Vespasian entrusted his elder son Titus Flavius Vespasianus with the task of bringing the revolt of the Judeans to a close. With the new era for the Flavian family dawning, the continued rebellion of imperial subjects was unseemly, and Titus—himself a methodical and experienced general— took command of the Roman legions and auxiliary forces already in Judea and prepared to mount a final siege to capture the Jews' Holy City of Jerusalem. By the spring of 70 C.E., the city was crowded with refugees and riven by conflicts between competing rival leaders, but the shared hope that God would finally intervene in the earthly course of their battle with the Romans steeled the determination of a hard core of resisters, even as thousands within the walls died of hunger, disease—and thousands more fled the city to be killed as they ran; to be crucified for the Roman soldiers' entertainment; or to become helpless prisoners of war. By May, after breaking through the city's outer lines of fortifications, Titus's forces erected siege works around the city and by August were poised to overrun the Temple compound. With the priests and remaining population still awaiting divine redemption—despite the conditions of famine, disease, and continual Roman sorties—Titus resolved to end the rebellion in a brutal and definitive way. While the temples and central cult places of other conquered peoples had been allowed to stand (after the demonstration of appropriate obeisance to the superiority of Rome and precedence of the imperial cult), such a thing was clearly not possible with the God of Israel.

Thus on the ninth day of the Hebrew month of Av—at the end of August in the year 70 C.E.—the Temple of Jerusalem was stormed and, after thorough plunder, destroyed to its very foundations. By the end of September, the last pockets of Jewish resistance in the Upper City had been stilled. Titus then ordered that the entire city of Jerusalem be leveled, leaving only three towers of its once-vast Herodian fortifications standing, "in order to indicate to posterity," according to Josephus, "the nature of the city and of the strong defenses which had yet yielded to Roman prowess." Vespasian and Titus together celebrated a great triumph in Rome the following spring to mark the end of rebellion against the Roman order, with the trophies of war, including the great golden menorah of the Jerusalem Temple, carried by the victorious troops. And as a grim and cruel substitution for the annual half-shekel contribution that Jews the world over had contributed to the Jerusalem Temple, Vespasian ordered that all Jews now be required to pay a special tax (in the same amount) to the treasury of the Capitoline Jupiter in Rome. The question reportedly posed to Jesus in Jerusalem some forty years earlier had been decisively answered: tribute must now be rendered only to Caesar. With the Temple destroyed and both Judea and Galilee in ruins, there was no longer any easy way to render tribute to God.

THE DAY OF VENGEANCE had come and gone and there was hardly one stone left on another in the once-magnificent city of Jerusalem. Yet neither the Risen Jesus Christ nor any other messianic figure had descended to earth to destroy the evil rulers and greedy oppressors who had for so long threatened the people of God. Though some groups in Judea and throughout the diaspora clung to the hope that the present misfortunes—reaching unimagined depths of suffering and national humiliation—were merely a necessary prelude to the final arrival of divine intervention, most of the survivors were forced to face the grim realities created by the Roman victory. The same conditions of debt and dispossession that had caused so much suffering in the preceding decades now continued much as before. Only the creditors' and landlords' names had changed. The lands and urban property owned by Judean priests and nobles suspected of participation in the revolt were now subject to confiscation and sale to the aristocrats or entrepreneurs of the surrounding Hellenistic city-states. And the demands of the new landlords and creditors on the surviving Judean and Galilean rural population were compounded by their need to come up with an additional quantity of coin or produce to pay the annual "Jewish tax." Where was God at this time of tribulation? Could the conquest of the Land of Israel be a sign of divine wrath, not promise? How could the People of Israel possibly survive?

Without a Temple, without viable national leadership, without the tens—possibly hundreds—of thousands of Judean, Galilean, and Perean men, women, and children killed or sold off into slavery, the surviving village communities of the Land of Israel and the scattered communities of

Jews throughout the diaspora were suddenly left on their own. The humbling of the priestly aristocracy in Jerusalem might have been viewed with righteous satisfaction by those who had long condemned their greed and temporal ambitions, but the discontinuance of the age-old rituals of Temple worship, festival celebration, and purification ceremonies created a situation where new methods of worship and sanctification had to be devised. And in the larger picture of Jewish adaptation and adjustment to the catastrophe of revolt and destruction, the reactions of the scattered followers of the various branches of the Jesus Movement in the Land of Israel went almost unnoticed at first. At a time when a group of Jewish sages led by Rabban Yochanan Ben-Zakkai established themselves in the Roman-occupied town of Jamnia (better known in Hebrew as Yavne) on the Mediterranean coast and began to formulate new structures for the way of life that would eventually become Rabbinic Judaism, a process of creative, if painful, soul searching was beginning to go on within the Jesus Movement as well.

There was no longer a single center, not even a central symbolic focus for Christian speculations about the next stage in the divine drama: whatever spiritual authority the Jerusalem community of the movement may have continued to possess after the death of James, the "pillars" and elders of the Jesus Movement in Jerusalem seem to have disappeared without a trace in the maelstrom of revolt, violence, and siege. The church historian Eusebius preserved a tradition that "the members of the Jerusalem church, by means of an oracle given by revelation to acceptable persons there, were ordered to leave the city before the war and settle in a town in Perea called Pella." This tradition of the flight of a Judean group to a neighboring Greek city at the time of intense Greek-Jewish violence is now considered historically questionable by many scholars, but even if there is no factual basis for a flight across the Jordan, it is undeniable that precisely at the same time that other Jewish groups were reorganizing their national life and establishing new religious and legal institutions, scattered branches of the Jesus Movement were themselves trying to come to terms with the catastrophe.

Just as the first destruction of the Jerusalem Temple by the Babylonians had been the crucible in which a refined and restored Israel ultimately endured in righteousness to merit God's forgiveness and return to the Land of Promise, the saints of the early Christian communities believed that their survival of the day of vengeance signified their election as the righteous remnant of Israel. While the rabbis of Yavne struggled to adapt the observance of the Torah to an era without a Temple, the various branches of the Jesus Movement—both those who saw themselves as members of the Jewish People and those who envisioned a future redemption for all the world's people—sought quite different explanations for the awesome turn of events that brought an end to the national institutions of Israel. And here we at last come to the emergence of the texts now known as "the Gospels," those four stylized Greek biographies of Jesus attributed to Matthew, Mark, Luke, and John that were eventually chosen—from among the many variant gospels that apparently circulated among early Christian communities—to become the first four books of the New Testament. Beginning to circulate in something resembling their present forms in the closing decades of the first century, they are not only literary classics and core scriptures of Christianity, but these texts also provide precious evidence about the self-perception and worldview of various Christian communities in the decades that followed the fall of Jerusalem and the rise of the Flavian dynasty.

IN THE VILLAGES of southern Syria and Phoenicia that had not been directly touched by the scorched-earth campaigns of the horrible autumn of 67—and where the Renewal Movement initiated by Jesus and his first generation of followers still lingered—an explanation was needed for why the promises to the faithful members of the People of Israel, which seemed so close to fulfillment with the outbreak of the revolt against the Romans, did not materialize. In the eyes of at least one group of Jesus' followers, the fault was placed at the feet of the political and cultic leaders of the Jewish nation—and, for that matter, with the leaders of the Jesus Movement who had abandoned their Galilean roots to establish their center in Jerusalem. This is the outlook adopted by the Gospel of Mark— whose allusions to the (apparently recent) destruction of the Temple have many modern scholars date its composition to a time not long after 70 C.E. For centuries, church tradition held that the Gospel of Mark was written in Rome following the fall of Jerusalem by the figure known as "John Mark" from Jerusalem who accompanied Paul and Barnabas on their early missionary journeys (Acts 12:25). Yet a growing number of scholars now see its many accurate details about Near Eastern peasant life and its familiarity with the geography of Jesus' ministry as evidence that it was the product of a Greek-speaking Jesus community in the agricultural districts of

Phoenicia, southern Syria, or the Decapolis. And if we read "Mark" as a coherent narrative, written in the specific historical context of the Roman repression of the revolt in Judea—without reducing it to context-less theological components or doctrines such as "Christology" and "discipleship"—we may be able to see how a particularly creative member of one Jesus community sought to make sense of the catastrophes that had so recently befallen the People of Israel and how he, she, or they insisted that the Kingdom of God was precisely what Jesus had preached it to be: a movement of community renewal and liberation among the towns and villages of southern Syria and Galilee.

In spite of the speculation that had gone on in the preceding decades about messiahs (Herodian, heavenly, priestly, royal, and even Roman), the author or authors of this gospel had little sympathy for traditions of messianic royalty. Looking back on the ministry of Jesus from the perspective of the Flavian period, the Gospel of Mark skillfully portrayed Jesus as a divinely inspired prophet and teacher who stood the royal, imperial understanding of the messiah on its head. Even though the lordly title "messiah," or *Christos*, in Greek, had become virtually part of Jesus' name to the Greek-speaking members of the movement, the Jesus of the Gospel of Mark stubbornly refused to act the part of a royal messiah, except to mock it and condemn the very concept. Mark's narrative showed Jesus to be a traditional, Spirit-filled prophet figure performing healings, exorcisms, and miracles in the manner of ancient Israelite prophets, a figure whom contemporaries readily identified as either Elijah or John the Baptist come back to life. Thus the titles "Messiah" and "Son of God" suddenly took on a new, ironic meaning for those who read or listened to recitations from the Gospel of Mark. In it, Jesus was a peasant "messiah," a willfully powerless "messiah," a "messiah" who had only contempt for the earthly splendor of Herod's Temple, a martyred "messiah" who scorned—and even kept secret—his divine mission even as earthly rulers eagerly attached messianic epithets to their names.

The communities who cherished this new biography of Jesus harbored painfully mixed feelings about Jesus' inner circle of disciples—and those feelings were expressed in one of Mark's most significant subplots, in which the Twelve were accused of being seduced by their own ambition for power. Despite Jesus' explanation to the disciples of the mystery of the Kingdom of God (4:10–34) and his commission to them to extend his work of renewal through exorcisms and preaching repentance (6:7–13), they seem unable to understand that Jesus is *not* talking about conventional political power: at a crucial point in the story, when Jesus is on his way to Jerusalem for his fateful confrontation with the rulers, James and John boorishly request positions of prestige for themselves, to which Jesus answers bluntly that in his movement whoever wishes to be a "great one" must be the servant of all (10:35–45). Thereafter in the story, particularly following the Last Supper, the disciples again demonstrate their lack of devotion, with the leading figures of Peter, James, and John falling asleep in Gethsemane during Jesus' agonizing vigil (14:37–42); Judas betraying Jesus to the Temple authorities (14:43–46); Peter denying his relationship to Jesus when questioned (14:66–71); and all Twelve simply disappearing once Jesus is taken off for trial. These vivid anecdotes and unforgettable scenes must be seen not necessarily as journalistic reporting but as the powerful expression of at least one branch of the Jesus Movement that the Twelve, no less than the national leaders, were obsessed with individual political power and not sufficiently focused on the kingless Kingdom of God.

The Kingdom that the Gospel of Mark envisioned would not be established in the cities, with their forums, temples, and palaces built at such great cost and embellished with such extravagance. It would be one in which the demons called "Legion," coldhearted landowners, arrogant te-trarchs, and tribute to Caesar, would have no part. It is surely significant at the end of Mark's story—after the disciples have fled for their lives in the aftermath of the crucifixion—that women play leading roles. The "two" Marys and Salome who, having followed Jesus in Galilee and up to Jerusa-lem, become the only witnesses to the empty tomb. The mysterious, angelic figure whom they find in the tomb and who announces the resur-rection of Jesus informs these faithful women that the Galilean fishermen and peasants who considered themselves the true disciples of Jesus had utterly missed the boat. "Do not be amazed," the young man told them, when they saw that the tomb was empty, "you seek Jesus of Nazareth, who was crucified. He is risen, he is not here; see the place where they laid him. But go tell his disciples and Peter that he is going before you to Galilee; there you will see him as he told you" (16:6–7). The *real* work remained to be done in the villages and towns where the movement started. And now that Jerusalem had been destroyed, the Gospel of Mark underlined the point that the Kingdom movement must go on in the villages and towns of Galilee and the hillcountry regions beyond.

IN JUDEA, where the Temple lay in ruins and the House of Herod had fallen forever, an otherworldly vision of cosmic redemption arose. The possibility for practical action to restore the earthly fortunes of the faithful was limited. The oppressive presence of the Tenth Legion in the rubble of Jerusalem and in its outlying garrisons throughout Judea; the expropriation of significant tracts of agricultural land by the imperial authorities; and the loss of central leadership with the disappearance of the Jerusalem community of the movement left a spiritual vacuum for the disheartened followers of Jesus in Judea. Though the Gospel of John was attributed by later church tradition to John, the son of Zebedee (who may have also been the figure referred to as Jesus' "beloved disciple"), and long thought by scholars and commentators to be the most otherworldly, spiritual, and "un-Judean" of the gospels, there are some intriguing indications that it may actually represent a direct literary response to the changing Judean political reality. Its identification of Jesus as the pre-existing, eternal Logos, or "word" of God (1:1), and its attempt to lift the believer above the mundane aspects of life into eternal life and to an eventual heavenly home in "the many mansions" of "my Father's house" (14:2) may have been the internalizing ideology of a separatist group standing resolutely apart from those other strands of the movement and of the Jewish people who were prepared, out of necessity or compulsion, to make compromises with the imperial powers-that-be. In recent years, especially since the discovery of the literature of the Dead Sea Scrolls with its passionate commitment to sectarian separation from corrupt society—as an expression of intense opposition to the established parties and politics of Judea—the mystical withdrawal expressed in the Gospel of John no longer appears quite so ethereal or resolutely nonpolitical as it once might have seemed.

While modern biblical scholars have often read the Gospel of John as a document addressed to a community that had been expelled from "the synagogue" or the mainstream of Judaism, it is now becoming clear that in the chaotic and uncertain decades after the fall of Jerusalem, there was no organized "Judaism," either centralized or localized, that could impose on widely scattered groups such unequivocal discipline. In fact, the modern scholarly concentration on the attempt to trace the evolution of abstract

Christian theology (as if it could be studied without reference to the specifics of social and political conflict in post-conquest Judea) has been responsible for perpetuating the traditional misreading of the Gospel of John as sharply anti-Jewish, in a modern anti-Semitic sense. There is no question that the passages in John and the other gospels which attack the *Ioudaioi*— "Judeans" or "Jews"—as hostile to Jesus and unfaithful to their own heritage have been used for centuries as the basis for anti-Semitic hatred and violence. But the term *Ioudaioi* in John appears in many instances specifically to mean the Judean authorities, the Judean rulers and insiders, or what the other gospels refer to as "the high priests, scribes, and elders." And once we discern that the fundamental conflict in John is not between "the Jews" and the believers in Jesus, but between a shaken post-war community of the Jesus Movement and those leaders whom it considered responsible for the great catastrophe, its historical context begins to emerge. Unlike Mark, which views Jerusalem as a distant arena where urban tensions and political conflicts get in the way of village renewal, "John" focuses strongly on Judea and places itself in direct and continuing opposition to the Temple hierarchy. In contrast to Mark (and Matthew and Luke) who has Jesus concentrate his ministry in Galilee and in the surrounding northern regions—and make only one, final journey to Jerusalem—John has Jesus moving regularly back and forth between Jerusalem and Galilee, making several pilgrimages to the Temple, and gathering a following in the south as well as in the north and, in fact, conducting his ministry primarily in Judea.

Yet in John, there is no clear hope of a drastic change in the political affairs of Judea. There is no mention of the *parousia* of Christ or future resurrection of believers. Jesus' sole mission was his crucifixion and exaltation as a martyr (as stated explicitly in 12:32–33), which served as an epoch-making event for his followers in Jerusalem. Indeed, it is significant that most of the post-resurrection appearances of Jesus described in the Gospel of John take place in Jerusalem (20:14–29), and a number of scholars have suggested that his appearance to the Galilean disciples "by the Sea of Tiberias" (21:1–19) rightfully belongs to a cycle of miracle stories that took place during his earthly ministry. Yet whether John's community was restricted to Judea—or whether it also included Galileans—its unifying principle and vision of the Kingdom of God was not village renewal among peasants but communal solidarity among a spiritual brotherhood and sisterhood of the oppressed wherever they lived.

After insisting through the prologue of chapter 1 and in the discourses of chapters 2–11 that all aspects of higher spiritual life were *in* Jesus or now *were* Jesus, John explained in the "farewell discourses" of chapters 14–17 that this higher spiritual life is based on love shared between God, Jesus, and the disciples. The Kingdom of God as envisioned by the Gospel of John is a state of intentional secession from imperial life. "My kingdom is not of this world," Jesus tells Pilate in this gospel. "If my kingship were of this world, my servants would fight, that I might not be handed over to the Jews; but my kingship is not from this world" (18:36). And despite the continuing contention of many New Testament scholars that such statements represent spiritual escape from mundane political and economic realities, it is possible to see such expressions as powerful responses to empire. The undeniably vivid anti-imperial imagery of the Book of Revelation, attributed to the Apostle John and most likely written by one of his persecuted followers on the island of Patmos in the distant Aegean in the mid-90s, offers the same kind of prophetic resistance expressed some six centuries earlier as the exiles of Israel mourned the destruction of their Temple by the waters of Babylon.

IN YET ANOTHER AREA of the reborn Flavian Empire—in the northern districts of the province of Syria around the capital of Antioch—there arose yet another distinctive variant of the Jesus Movement, this one gradually incorporating the symbolic trappings and political realities of kingship into its understanding of Jesus Christ and of its own role in the post-war world. A growing consensus of scholars suggests that the Gospel of Matthew was composed in Antioch during the early Flavian period (sometime shortly after 80 C.E.), and its tone, style, and reinterpretation of earlier sources and traditions offers evidence of a concern with institutional structure and spiritual authority. If the Gospel of Mark urged a regional revival of the Renewal Movement among the villages in Galilee and if the Gospel of John urged faithful solidarity for self-segregating Judean communities, the Gospel of Matthew offered a practical, organizational charter for the reconstitution of the Davidic dynasty of Israel. At the very time when Emperor Vespasian was commissioning vast public works projects in the provinces of Asia, Galatia, and Syria to improve the roads and seaports and overseeing legislation that would tie the East ever more firmly to the rest of the empire, the Gospel of Matthew portrays Jesus as an alternative emperor, laying out a programmatic renewal of Israel—in explicit opposition both to the law codes of the (now destroyed) Jerusalem Temple and to the earthly laws of the Roman Empire.

In sharp contrast to the community represented by "Mark," who saw Jesus as a suffering peasant anti-messiah, and in contrast to the sympathizers of "John," who pictured Jesus as the heavenly intercessor for a spiritual elite, "Matthew" described Jesus as a genuine royal messiah from the outset, a new king for a new Israel. Archaeological remains and contemporary Latin inscriptions testify to the unprecedented extent of the public works projects undertaken in Antioch by the Flavian emperors, and it can be no mere coincidence that the Antioch Christian community came to acknowledge the stability and prosperity that could be brought about by the beneficent guidance of royal rule. In Matthew, Jesus is born as the messiah, explicitly and dramatically in opposition to Herod and the Herodian tyranny (2:6), and he displays a royal character throughout his public ministry. At the "triumphal entry" of Jesus into Jerusalem, his royal pedigree is explicitly acclaimed: the crowds shout "Hosanna to son of David! Blessed is he who comes in the name of the Lord!" (21:9). Indeed, in Matthew's concern for genealogy—so characteristic of a period in which the legitimacy of imperial sucession was an issue of concern throughout the empire—Jesus is from the outset declared to be not only of the royal lineage of the David but also a direct descendant of the Patriarch Abraham (1:1–17). His followers were now heirs to God's promises of land, peoplehood, *and* eternal royalty.

A new vision of the movement was arising in which Antioch—and later, Rome—would replace Jerusalem to become the most influential center of the messianic age. The very structure of the Gospel of Matthew suggests that attempts were being made to consolidate formerly independent traditions: in its use of material from both the "Q" Sayings Gospel (still apparently circulating in oral form among rural villages) and the Gospel of Mark (perhaps composed, as we have suggested, in one of the Greek-speaking towns of Phoenicia or southern Syria), inconsistencies of tradition were reconciled and a shared ritual and constitution were formed. Matthew restructured the story line of Mark's gospel into five books of narrative sections, interspersed with social and ethical instruction, creating far more than an inspirational tract for an existing movement but a holy scripture in its own right. First and foremost was the outline of the new covenant presented in the Sermon on the Mount in chapters 5–7—given by Jesus in his role of a new "Moses" on the mountain—including, among other precepts, a guide for local cooperation (5:38–42) and a system of welfare (6:2). In essence, the Gospel of Matthew served as the lawcode and handbook of a network of communities who saw themselves as the true inheritors of the Kingdom of God, whose trappings consisted of an ironic combination of Davidic tradition and the present-day power of the Flavian dynasty.

Yet the leadership of the Antioch community had to struggle against serious competition from the crystallizing rabbinic movement *within* the People of Israel, which was also putting forth its claim to be the authoritative interpreter of the tradition of Israel. In their attempts to renew the solidarity of the People of Israel without the central institution of the Temple, the rabbis traveled widely throughout much of the Mediterranean, answering legal questions, handing down rulings, offering instruction in new rituals and customs, and slowly establishing the authority and priority of the Academy of Sages at Yavne among Jewish communities throughout the diaspora. Again and again throughout the Gospel of Matthew, the "scribes and the Pharisees" of Jesus' time appear as villains, pictured in garb and demeanor more appropriate to that of the rabbis and sages of early Rabbinic Judaism than that of the scribes and retainers of Herodian Galilee. Jesus explicitly warns his disciples that they are not to follow the ways of those who "do all their deeds to be seen by men; for they make their phylacteries broad and their fringes long, and they love the place of honor at feasts and the best seats in the synagogues, and salutations in the market places, and being called rabbi by men. But you are not to be called rabbi, for you have one teacher, and you are all brethren" (23:5–8). The bitterness of that struggle between early Christians and the rabbis can also be perceived in Matthew's fierce condemnation of the Temple establishment. In Jesus' lament over the tragic fate of Jerusalem (23:37–24:2) and in the ugly—and utterly unrealistic—scene of the people of Jerusalem eagerly, bloodthirstily taking the responsibility for Jesus' execution upon themselves and their children (27:25), Matthew attempts to show his readers how the Judeans have forfeited their claim to be beneficiaries of the divine promises, leaving the followers of Jesus in the role of the only legitimate heirs.

Thus by the closing decades of the first century, the followers of Jesus and the followers of the rabbis had apparently reached a decisive parting of the ways. Though no single Christian "church" had yet emerged and no single orthodoxy had been agreed upon, the scattered Christian communities had gradually come to accept the verdict of history, at least as had been determined by the furious might of Vespasian and Titus's legions in their brutal suppression of the Judean Revolt. The conquered Land of Israel, ruined Jerusalem, the destroyed Temple, and the ethnic descendants of the nation of Israel had all—in their eyes—lost a special claim to salvation. And from this time onward, they fervently believed, the fulfillment of the divine plan would be accomplished through a Kingdom of Heaven reserved for Christians alone.

11

Keeping the Faith

ITHIN SEVENTY-FIVE YEARS of the crucifixion of Jesus in
Jerusalem, the signs of the Kingdom were unmistakable wherever the assemblies of the saints gathered. The most important
rituals of every Christian's life—baptism, Lord's Supper, and collection—
now and then interspersed with fresh infusions of the Holy Spirit from
traveling teachers and prophets—seemed to gird the assemblies scattered
throughout the eastern Mediterranean for the part they believed they were
destined to play in the establishment of the Kingdom of God on earth. As
the years wore on and the Roman Empire refused to vanish, the passion and
rage against immorality and injustice were turned increasingly inward. The
churches continued to help the weak and the powerless, and the widows,
orphans, and destitute strangers among them, and over time, they gradually developed permanent ecclesiastical structures and officers to oversee
and regulate the day-to-day lives of the communities. Bishops and deacons
became permanent figures of authority in many congregations, figures to
whom respect and honor were to be accorded as a matter of course. Indeed,
by the early second century, the Kingdom of God was increasingly seen as
an entirely spiritual state of grace accessible only through the increasingly
regularized discipline and rituals of the church—and through the obedient
spirituality of individual Christian sisters and brothers who were urged to
be "attuned to their bishop like the strings on a harp."

For many churches, the Roman Empire was no longer the main enemy but rather the earthly environment in which Christianity would have to exist peacefully until the second coming of Christ. Indeed, so pervasive was the eventual acceptance of empire that the image of Christ was slowly transformed from that of an alternative king to that of a *model* emperor—presiding over a shadow government in heaven and showing by example how things should be done on earth. A new generation of Christian leaders accepted and creatively adapted the main elements of the dominant imperial milieu to their own spiritual ends. Composing a series of letters in the name of Paul—strikingly different in language and style from the earlier Pauline epistles—they focused the attention of the scattered assemblies of saints on a Kingdom of God that existed primarily in another, purely spiritual realm.

"Set your minds on things that are above, not on things that are on earth," the faithful were instructed in the Letter to the Colossians. "For you have died, and your life is hid with Christ in God" (3:2–3). In contrast to Paul's own career of struggle against a succession of earthly opponents, the Letter to the Ephesians concluded that "we are not contending against flesh and blood, but against the principalities, against the powers, against the world rulers of this present darkness, against the spiritual hosts of wickedness in the heavenly places" (6:12). The rule of the Caesars was no longer seen as the main "enemy of the cross" or obstacle to salvation. With the rise of the Flavians and the reform of imperial administration, the concept of universal kingship—far from being despised or resisted—became the dominating metaphor for peace on earth and good will toward men.

There would be countless reinterpretations, revisions, and transformations in the character of Christian belief as it developed and spread throughout the eastern Mediterranean and across North Africa and Europe in the turbulent centuries of persecution, martyrdom, schism, and imperial politics that followed. As we have stressed throughout our story, the theological evolution of Christianity cannot be neatly separated from the political, economic, and cultural struggles of its believers and opponents in any particular period or place. Christianity—the formalized religion based on the movement begun by Jesus and continued in dramatically different forms after his crucifixion—was and is a dynamic social phenomenon with many branches, many intentions, and many distinct perceptions of the world. And in concluding our narrative, we must point to one particularly crucial literary achievement that enabled the far-flung movement to overcome its natural centrifugal tendency to disintegrate into countless, local ideological sub-groups, each with its own vision of Jesus, his message, and its implication for their relations to the powers-that-be.

At the beginning of the second century, somewhere in the Aegean basin—presumably in one of the cities of Achaia, Macedonia, or Asia where the memories of Paul's career were maintained and cherished—a member of one of the Pauline communities composed a brilliant two-volume history of the Jesus Movement in which many of the pre-existing traditions and narratives were skillfully woven together to achieve a single effect. Prior to the composition of this two-part text—now known to us as the Gospel of Luke and the Book of Acts (both works dedicated in their opening verses to a patron named Theophilus)—the stories and sayings of Jesus and the Epistles of Paul circulated freely. No one was expected to know them all. The concluding verses of the Gospel of John expressed that situation succinctly, after offering its own version of Jesus' life: "There are also many other things which Jesus did; were every one of them to be written, I suppose that the world itself could not contain the books that would be written" (21:25). Yet the author we call "Luke"—who was long identified with Paul's companion mentioned in Philemon, v. 23—had a different intention. His goal was to write a definitive account of the birth and growth of the movement, from Galilee to Rome, from Jesus to Paul, with a single perspective and a single conclusion about the place of Christianity in world history. "Inasmuch as many have undertaken to compile a narrative of the things which have been accomplished among us, just as they were delivered to us by those who from the beginning were eyewitnesses and ministers of the word, it seemed good to me also, having followed all things closely for some time past, to write an orderly account for you, most excellent Theophilus, that you may know the truth concerning the things of which you have been informed" (1:1–4).

Weaving together imperial history, earlier gospels, collections of sayings, and anonymous eyewitness accounts, Luke-Acts represented a powerful appeal for a unified, universal Christian identity. The author attempted to show how the earthly ministry and resurrection of Jesus was unmistakable proof that God's blessing had been transferred from the People of Israel to the faithful Christian subjects of the Roman Empire. All the events of salvation were related to imperial chronology: Jesus' Nativity took place at the time of a world-wide census decreed by Augustus (Luke 2:1); the ministry of John the Baptist was synchronized with the reign of Tiberius

(Luke 3:1); and the activity of the church at Antioch was linked to events in the reign of Claudius (Acts 11:28).

Equally significant were the roles played by Roman provincial officials who remained conspicuously neutral or even expressed sympathy with the movement: most notable among them were Pontius Pilate in Jerusalem (Luke 3:1); the converted centurion Cornelius (Acts 10:1); the proconsul Sergius Paulus on Cyprus (Acts 13:7); Gallio in Corinth (Acts 18:12); and the procurators Felix (Acts 23:24) and Festus (Acts 25:1) in Caesarea; and the eminently reasonable client king Agrippa II and his sister Berenice (Acts 25:13). Many scholars have suggested that Luke-Acts, with its repeated accusations against the evil and perfidy of "the Jews" and its repeated expressions of appreciation for the fairness of Roman rulers and impartiality of Roman justice, was written to prove to the imperial authorities that the new religion of Christianity was utterly harmless and did not represent a seditious threat to the current order of things. Other scholars, notably Paul Walaskay, have suggested a reverse understanding: that Luke's two-volume story of the rise of Christianity was written to convince a Christian readership that *they* had nothing to fear from the continued existence of the empire, which would, in fact, facilitate, not hinder, the coming of the Kingdom of God.

Here, after all, was a brilliant new epic that did not contest Rome's power but skillfully utilized its soaring imperial imagery. The story of the omen-rich birth of the world savior, adored by the humble shepherds and praised by the angels who heralded a new era of peace and prosperity, offered a familiar literary opening that was routinely used in the personality cults of the emperors. And in order to make it clear that Jesus was neither a political rebel nor a fiery prophet of disgruntled peasants, Luke portrayed him as a mild-mannered ethical teacher, who offered sermons and pithy sayings aimed at the individual. In his incorporation of large chunks of the "Q" Sayings gospel (in contrast to Matthew's more selective weaving of the sayings into his narrative), Luke characterized Jesus as a down-to-earth sage of the people—a country prophet of the type that urban audiences, comfortably far from the earth and the sounds and smells of the barnyard, have always enjoyed. And it is no wonder that some modern scholars have identified Jesus as a "Cynic" teacher in the Hellenistic tradition, for that is precisely how "Luke," himself apparently raised in an urbanized Hellenistic environment, so skillfully characterized him. Moreover, Luke-Acts depicted Paul as a Roman citizen—despite Paul's own silence on the matter—and showed him being treated with respect by Roman officials and soldiers (Acts 22:25–29); possessing the legal right to appeal his unjust imprisonment directly to the emperor (25:11); ultimately being allowed to preach about the Kingdom of God and teach about Jesus Christ in Rome itself (28:31).

Of course this was stretching the historical facts, but by Luke's time, a full half-century later, the capriciousness and brutality of Roman imperial rule as Paul had experienced it seems to have become a thing of the past. Even if there were no longstanding church tradition about Paul's martyrdom (and continuing veneration for his tomb by the members of the Roman community), it would have been difficult for anyone who had actually *lived* at the time of mad Nero to take seriously the happy ending of the Book of Acts that pictures Paul in Rome "preaching the kingdom of God and teaching about the Lord Jesus Christ quite openly and unhindered" (28:31). But the Gospel of Luke and the Book of Acts was a decisive turning point in the evolving Christian image of the Kingdom of God. As a rollicking, inspirational adventure novel, it eventually gained a far wider audience than the stately Latin cadences of Vergil, Horace, and Ovid in their celebration of the *auctoritas* and *gravitas* of the ideal king. Luke's colorful, vivid, down-to-earth narrative represented a literary achievement that no Augustan historian or philosopher ever equalled: the transformation of a local movement of resistance into a universal ideology of redemption for the empire's vast underclasses of hard-pressed and overworked children, women, and men.

BY THE FOURTH CENTURY C.E.—with the the gradual eclipse of official paganism and with the Emperor Constantine's adoption of Christianity as the official religion of the Roman Empire—even the outward form and trappings of the movement were dramatically altered. The vast population of the empire's villages and cities learned to pay homage to the sign of the cross as a royal as well as religious symbol and accept the discipline imposed by imperially sanctioned bishops, deacons, and priests. Indeed, the organization of the churches and hierarchy of ecclesiastical officials eventually became so closely connected to the structure of empire that the Kingdom of God increasingly merged with the Kingdom of Men. Towering basilicas and, later, cathedrals rose in the central squares of major cities, providing awe-inspiring stage settings for the announcement of imperial edicts and the coronations of kings. The power of the state became intertwined with the power of the Church Triumphant, and the original social message of the movement was all too often lost. Yet even then, some of the original values endured. A Greek text known as the Didache, or "The Teaching of the Twelve Apostles," was circulating widely, offering the faithful a guide to righteous living in the time remaining before the coming of the Kingdom of God. This text was known to Bishop Eusebius of Caesarea in the early fourth century at the time he composed his great *History of the Church* and was highly praised by his contemporary Bishop Athanasius of Alexandria, who characterized it as a work of supreme importance for righteous Christians. Yet all traces of it were lost in the succeeding centuries. How ironic it was therefore that in 1873, just at a time when the modern archaeological exploration of the Holy Land and the other lands of the Roman Empire was beginning, Bishop Philotheos Bryennios of Nicomedia in northwestern Turkey announced the discovery of a manuscript text of the long-lost Didache in a church library in Istanbul.

This new-found text offered a sudden insight into the world of the early Christians at a time before the great institutions of power and ecclesiastical splendor had entirely overwhelmed the character of Christian community life. The document began with a sermon on the choice between Two Ways that every man, woman, and child living in the world of Caesars, violence, and power inevitably faced. One way was the Way of Life, which could be gained by a simple prescription: "Thou shalt love first the Lord thy Creator and secondly thy neighbor as thyself; and thou shalt do nothing to any man that thou wouldst not wish to be done to thyself." Closely following sayings of Jesus that would later also appear prominently in the Gospel of Matthew, those who would follow the Way of Life were instructed to observe a rigorous code of nonviolent resistance, communal solidarity, and economic sharing that directly confronted the ills of patronage. They were to bless anyone who cursed them, pray for their enemies, and "if someone strikes you on the right cheek, turn the other one to him as well" (1:3). Humility, chastity, and generosity were to be the marks of a righteous person. "Never turn away the needy; share all your possessions with your brother, and do not claim that anything is your own" (4:8).

The Way of Death, on the other hand, was a continuing temptation, to be found in the everyday reality Christians found all around them in both the individual and public spheres: "murders, adulteries, lusts, fornications, thefts, idolatries, witchcraft, sorceries, robberies, perjuries, hypocrisies, duplicities, deceit, pride, malice, self-will, avarice, foul language, jealousy, insolence, arrogance, and boastfulness; persecutors of good men, hating truth, loving a lie, not perceiving the reward of righteousness, not cleaving to the good nor to righteous judgment, wakeful not for that which is good but for that which is evil—from whom gentleness and forbearance stand aloof; loving vain things, pursuing a recompense, not pitying the poor man, not toiling for him that is oppressed with toil, not recognizing Him that made them, murderers of children, corrupters of the creatures of God, turning away from him that is in want, oppressing him that is afflicted, advocates of the wealthy, unjust judges of the poor, altogether sinful. Flee, my children, from all this!" (5:1–2).

The Didache was a handbook for a movement of both rural and urban communities, who still saw themselves as a Renewed Israel or a continuation of the historical Israel of the villages, for the faithful were instructed "to take the first products of your winepress, your threshing-floor, your oxen and your sheep, and give them as first-fruits to the prophets, for nowadays it is they who are your High Priests" (13:3). Even the prayers to be recited at the Eucharist directly addressed the "God of David" and appealed to the traditions of Israel. Raising the chalice to thank God "for the holy vine of David, which thou hast made known through thy servant Jesus," they were instructed to declare that just "as this broken bread, once dispersed over the hills, was brought together and became one loaf, so may thy ekklesia be brought together from the ends of the earth into thy kingdom." And before offering the obligatory apocalyptic expectations of the "end" and "the Lord coming on the clouds of Heaven," the text warned the faithful that "in the last days of the world false prophets and deceivers will abound, sheep will be perverted and turned into wolves, and love will change to hate, for with the growth of lawlessness, men will begin to hate their fellows and persecute and betray them" (16:3–4). The original struggles of the Christian movement were preserved not only in the gospels' images of the rural Jesus and his followers traveling through the hills and valleys of the Galilee but in the continuing challenges faced by living communities. That was why the discovery of the Didache and the subsequent rise of New Testament archaeology were so revealing. They provided a sudden bridge to a long-forgotten world of villages and struggling farmers who were responsive to the message of the historical Jesus. They revealed what a great gulf lies between our time and his.

The Galilee that Jesus knew during his brief life and ministry in the first century was undergoing great social change and upheaval. It was a time and a place where the passion of prophetic pronouncements and the hyperbole of apocalyptic rhetoric often obscured their down-to-earth implications— at least to our secularized, rationalized modern sensibilities. The quest of the earliest followers of Jesus was to reassert the value of their own lives and cherished traditions without allowing themselves and their children to become helpless pawns in a new order of the world. Were we to try to identify that kind of struggle in our own era, it might be found among rural people in underdeveloped regions who stubbornly refuse to acknowledge the superiority of agribusiness over small-scale family farming. Or it might be found in the Spirit-filled faith of storefront churches among the illegal aliens crowded into cities—who are there not because they naturally want to live in tenements and on street corners but because the great tides of economy and change have destroyed the traditional lives of their home-lands and set them adrift in a hostile and often frightening world.

The movement that began with Jesus of Nazareth was primarily con-cerned with the way that people could somehow resist exploitation by the rich and powerful, without either surrendering their traditions or resorting to violence. Likewise, the Apostle Paul—in his wide-ranging travels throughout the lands and peoples of the Eastern Empire—engaged in a career of confrontation with the forces of patronage and empire and died in the attempt. Time and again over the succeeding centuries the same struggle would be waged. Whether in the heretical Christian sects of Asia Minor, the mystical brotherhoods of the Middle Ages, the radical religious groups of the Reformation, the utopian communities of nineteenth-century America, or the visionary, idealistic political movements of the present, the quest for the Kingdom of God lives on. To many scholars, the often-failed protests of common people are merely footnotes to the mainstream history of Christianity, which is traced through the official chronicles of church councils and the respectful biographies of church leaders and kings. Cer-tainly the words and deeds of the rich and famous should not be ignored or neglected, but they are only part of a great, complex mosaic of social and religious change.

If the quest for the Historical Jesus and the archaeology of the world of the earliest Christians can offer us any lesson about the roots and birth-pangs of a movement that became one of the world's great institutionalized religions, it is that those who today fancy themselves to be faithful fol-lowers of Jesus should be constantly reminded of the painful struggle of the saints against Caesar in which the Christian faith was born. Christianity's historic origins do not lie in an abstract concern with isolated issues of individual ethics but in a dedication to resist the idolatry of power embodied by the Roman Empire. Jesus of Nazareth offered desperate Galileans and Judeans a path to village revival; Paul of Tarsus sought to provide fragmented, aimless communities of Galatians, Greeks, and Macedonians a way to achieve the same ideals. The Church, in its pomp and in its splendor, may have inherited the earthly Kingdom. Yet as Paul sternly warned the scattered assemblies that he established among the Galatian peasants in their highland villages, in the towns and rural districts of Macedonia, and in the crowded streets of Ephesus and Corinth, power and personal grandeur are sinful illusions. And he passionately believed that only those down-to-earth saints who faithfully challenged the pretensions of earthly kings and patrons—and battled the private fears, weaknesses, and selfishness that enabled injustice and suffering to flourish—were destined to inherit the Kingdom of God.

TIMELINE 1: The Life and Times of Jesus of Nazareth

DATE	SCRIPTURAL EVENTS	JUDEAN HISTORY	GALILEAN HISTORY	IMPERIAL HISTORY
10		Herod the Great, client king 37–4 B.C.E.		Augustus, emperor 27 B.C.E.–C.E. 14
5	Birth of Jesus c. 4 B.C.E.	Death of Herod Accession of Archelaus Messianic revolts 4 B.C.E.	Herod Antipas, tetrarch 4 B.C.E.–C.E. 39 Revolt of Judas 4 B.C.E.	
- B.C.E.				
0				
- C.E.			Rebuilding of Sepphoris	
5		Archelaus deposed Census in Judea 6 C.E.		
		ROMAN PREFECTS: Coponius 6–9 C.E.		
10		Marcus Ambivulus 9–12 C.E.		
		Annius Rufus 12–15 C.E.		
15		Valerius Gratus 15–26 C.E.		Tiberius, emperor 14–37 C.E.
20			Founding of Tiberias c. 18–20 C.E.	
25				
	Ministry of John the Baptist Jesus' Galilean Ministry	Pontius Pilate 26–36 C.E.	Marriage to Herodias Execution of John the Baptist c. 29 C.E.	
30	Jesus to Jerusalem			

TIMELINE 2: The Career of Paul

DATE	SCRIPTURAL EVENTS	TEXTS COMPOSED	JUDEAN HISTORY	IMPERIAL HISTORY
30	Crucifixion of Jesus			Tiberius, emperor 14–37 C.E.
-	Community of Twelve			
-	established in Jerusalem			
-	Conflict of "Hebrews" and			
-	"Hellenists"			
35	Paul in Damascus receives "call" c. 34 C.E.		Pilate deposed 36 C.E.	
-	To Arabia c. 34–37 C.E.		Joseph Caiaphas deposed 36 C.E.	
-	Visit with the Jerusalem		Herodian– Nabatean War	Gaius Caligula, emperor
-	Community c. 37 C.E.		37 C.E.	37–41 C.E.
-	To Syria and Cilicia		Antipas deposed 39 C.E.	
40	Paul joins Antioch Community		Agrippa I, tetrarch	
-	c. 40 C.E.		Agrippa I, king 41–44 C.E.	Claudius, emperor
-	"First Missionary Journey" with Barnabas to		Campaign against followers of Jesus in	41–54 C.E.
-	Cyprus, Pamphylia, and		Jerusalem	
-	southern Galatia c. 43 C.E.		Death of Agrippa	
45			Direct Roman rule over Judea resumes	
-				
-	Jerusalem Council, Conflict at Antioch		Ananias ben Nedebaeus, high priest	
-	c. 48 C.E.		47–59 C.E.	
-	To Galatia c. 49 C.E.		Ventidius	Disturbances at
49			Cumanus,	Rome instigated
	To Macedonia c. 49–50 C.E.		procurator 48–52 C.E.	by "Chrestus" c. 49 C.E.

DATE	SCRIPTURAL EVENTS	TEXTS COMPOSED	JUDEAN HISTORY	IMPERIAL HISTORY
50	To Corinth 50–52 C.E.			
-	To Ephesus 52–55 C.E.	1 Thessalonians c. 51 C.E.		
-	Opposition in Galatia	Galatians c. 53 C.E.	Antonius Felix, procurator 52–60 C.E.	
-	Crisis in Corinth			
-	"Visit of Tears" to Corinth	1 Corinthians c. 54 C.E.		Nero, emperor 54–68 C.E.
55	Imprisonment in Ephesus	2 Corinthians c. 54 C.E.		
-	Collection Project	Philippians c. 54 C.E.		
-	Visit and Arrest in Jerusalem spring 56 C.E.	Philemon c. 54–55 C.E.		
-	Imprisonment in Caesarea c. 56–60 C.E.	Romans c. 55–56 C.E.		
-	Hearing before Festus and Agrippa II; Transfer to Rome for Trial c. 60 C.E.		Porcius Festus, procurator 60–62 C.E.	
60			Ananus ben Ananaus, high priest	
-				
-	Paul's martyrdom (?) c. 62 C.E.		Martyrdom of James 62 C.E.	Fire in Rome 64 C.E.
-			Albinus, procurator 62–64 C.E.	Persecution of Christians in Rome
-			Gessius Florus, procurator 64–66 C.E.	Nero tours Greece
65				Galba, emperor 68–69 C.E.
-			Outbreak of Revolt	Otho, emperor 69 C.E.
-			Vespasian arrives autumn 67 C.E.	Vitellius, emperor 69 C.E.
-				
-			Revolt crushed	Vespasian, emperor 69–79 C.E.
70			Sack of Jerusalem	

Bibliographical Notes

Prologue: Searching for Jesus

For surveys of recent archaeological finds from first-century Galilee and Judea and their relation to the New Testament, see Finegan, *The Archaeology of the New Testament: The Life of Jesus;* Arav and Rousseau, *Jesus and His World;* Horsley, *Galilee;* and Wilkinson, *Jerusalem.* Material evidence of early Christianity in other parts of the Greco-Roman world is presented in Finegan, *The Archaeology of the New Testament: The Mediterranean World;* Snyder, *Ante Pacem;* and McRay, *Archaeology and the New Testament.* The general archaeological and historical situation has been presented in concise and highly readable form in Shanks, *Christianity and Rabbinic Judaism,* and summarized in Silberman, "Searching for Jesus" and "The World of Paul."

Some of the most significant recent advances in the study of the economic and social history of the Roman world have been achieved through the use of regional archaeological survey, as presented, for example, in Barker and Lloyd, *Roman Landscapes,* and Alcock, "Roman Imperialism." For a sampling of other recent archaeological approaches to the social history of the Roman Empire, see Greene, *The Archaeology of the Roman Economy;* Wallace-Hadrill, *Houses and Society;* and Alcock, *Graecia Capta.* For innovative interpretations of the political ideology of Roman imperial culture as manifest in its art and monuments, see Price, *Rituals and Power,* and Zanker, *The Power of Images.*

Most studies of Jesus and Paul and of Judaism and early Christianity tend to pay relatively little attention to the internal political dynamics of the Roman Empire, since they see the phenomena as primarily "religious." Convenient synopses of recent views of the Historical Jesus can be found in Borg, *Jesus in Contemporary Scholarship;* Chilton and Evans, *Studying the Historical Jesus;* and

Witherington, *The Jesus Quest*. Among the studies of Jesus and early Christianity, Richard Horsley frames *Jesus and the Spiral of Violence* with a broad sketch of the "imperial situation," and John Dominic Crossan provides brief sketches of social relations in the Roman Empire in *The Historical Jesus*. Georgi, *Theocracy*, and Elliott, *Liberating Paul*, are important steps toward consideration of the career of Paul in relation to the imperial cultural context. The works of Robert Eisenman—among them, *James the Brother of Jesus* and *The Dead Sea Scrolls and the First Christians*—are valuable for their emphasis on the impact of Rome on Judean society and the role of religious rhetoric in anti-Roman resistance.

Chapter 1: Heavenly Visions

Among the most frequently cited works on the sociology and history of early Christian communities are Frend, *The Rise of Christianity;* Lane-Fox, *Pagans and Christians;* Malherbe, *Social Aspects;* Thiessen, *The Social Setting;* and Meeks, *The First Urban Christians*. Pliny's correspondence with Trajan about the legal status of the Christians in Bithynia-Pontus can be found in Pliny, *Epp.* 10.96, 97, on which Sherwin-White has provided a solid historical commentary in his edition of *The Letters of Pliny*. On the persecution of Christians at the hands of imperial authorities and voluntary martyrdom of early Christians, the classic treatment is that of Frend, *Martyrdom and Persecution*, but see also Tabor and Droge, *The Noble Death*, for a wider historical context.

In *Augustan Culture*, Galinsky presents a description and interpretation of many facets of the ideology of empire at the outset of the principate. Millar organizes a vast array of sources on these subjects in *The Emperor in the Roman World*. For a basic treatment of imperial art and architecture, see Zanker, *The Power of Images*.

Among New Testament scholars, Georgi has focused on the "eschatological" orientation of the new imperial ideology in "Who Is the True Prophet?" For a collection of literary and inscriptional evidence of Roman imperial practices that are pertinent to the New Testament, see Wengst, *Pax Romana and the Peace of Jesus Christ*. For particularly striking Christian reactions to Roman imperial practices, see Schüssler Fiorenza, *The Book of Revelation: Justice and Judgment;* Bauckham, "The Economic Critique of Rome in Revelation 18";* and Friesen, *Twice Neokoros*.

On the political and religious situation of Jews in the Hellenistic world and under the Roman Empire, see Safrai and Stern, *The Jewish People;* Smallwood, *The Jews Under Roman Rule;* and Feldman, *Jew and Gentile*. Archaeological material on the social and economic aspects of earliest Israelite history is provided in Finkelstein, *The Archaeology of the Israelite Settlement*, and Finkelstein and Na'aman, *From Nomadism to Monarchy*. Gottwald's pioneering work on early Israel, *The Tribes of Yahweh*, though a frequent target for criticism, still offers a refreshing viewpoint on the ideological dimension of Israelite history and material culture change.

The political and social background of Israelite and Judean prophecy has been explored by Chaney, "Bitter Bounty";* Gottwald, *All the Kingdoms of the Earth;* and

Peckham, *History and Prophecy*. For the development of early apocalyptic and messianic thought, see Hanson, *The Dawn of Apocalyptic;* Collins, *The Apocalyptic Imagination;* and Stone, *Scriptures, Sects, and Visions.* That the expectation of a single "messiah" was neither widespread nor uniform in its characteristics among first-century Jews is one of the principal points of Horsley and Hanson, *Bandits, Prophets, and Messiahs;* Neusner, Green, and Frerichs, *Judaisms and their Messiahs;* and Collins, *The Scepter and the Star,* which delineates a wide variety of messianic archetypes.

The definitive Hebrew biography of Herod the Great by Schalit, *Herod the King,* is yet to be translated into English. Other good shorter treatments of Herod in general and the Herodian dynasty can be found in Avi-Yonah, *The World History of the Jewish People,* and Smallwood, *The Jews under Roman Rule.* For socio-political studies, see Richardson, *Herod: King of the Jews and Friend of the Romans,* and Gabba, "The Finances of King Herod." For a summary of the massive construction projects of Herod the Great, see Netzer, "Herod's Building Program," and his reports on the excavations at Jericho, Herodium, and Masada in E. Stern, *The New Encyclopedia of Archaeological Excavations.* For details on the Herodian Temple and its decoration, see Mazar, *The Mountain of the Lord.*

Josephus's accounts of Herod's death, the accession of Archelaus, and the popular insurrections in every major district and their vicious suppression by Varus are described in *Jewish War* 2.55–79 and *Jewish Antiquities* 17.271–98. For the wider sociological implications of these events, see Fenn, *The Death of Herod.* The distinctive form of the popular revolts after the death of Herod (and their parallels in later Judean revolts) was brought out in Horsley and Hanson, *Bandits, Prophets, and Messiahs,* and in Horsley, *Jesus and the Spiral of Violence.* Because many modern scholars, like ancient imperial authorities, often underestimate the depth of popular resistance against imperial rule, the latter has received little critical attention. For a modern perspective, see Hobsbawm, *Primitive Rebels;* for comparative perspectives of popular resistance in other provinces of the empire, see Dyson's important articles, "Native Revolts" and "Native Revolt Patterns."

For historical background on the Nativity stories and a discussion about the probable date of the birth of Jesus, see Meier, *Marginal Jew,* vol. 1; Brown, *The Birth of the Messiah;* and Horsley, *The Liberation of Christmas.* The historical reliability of the early Christian traditions about Bethlehem as the site of the Nativity are discussed in Taylor, *Christians and the Holy Places.*

Chapter 2: Remaking the Galilee

The principal textual sources for the reign of Herod Antipas, tetrarch of Galilee and Perea, are collected and discussed in Hoehner, *Herod Antipas.* For general background on the delicate political position of client rulers of all ranks under the early empire, see Braund, *Rome and the Friendly King.* The economy and society of Hellenistic-Roman Galilee is explored in Horsley, *Galilee.* The results of the excavations at Sepphoris are summarized in Meyers, "Roman

Sepphoris": scholarly debate continues on the question of whether the city's theater should be dated to the time of Herod Antipas's rebuilding. In any case, ample evidence exists for the rebuilding and expansion of the city in the time of Antipas. The fish-salting industry in Magdala-Taricheae is briefly mentioned in Applebaum, "Economic Life in Palestine." More suggestive are archaeological remains from Magdala, documented in Corbo, "La Citta Romana di Magdala" and "Piazza e Villa Urbana a Magdala," which are connected with industrial-type installations. See also the discussion of a mosaic with fishing motifs in Reich, "A Note." The larger pattern of manufacturing and sale of salt-fish and fish sauces throughout the Roman Empire is described in Curtis, *Garun and Salsamentum*, with references. A narrative account of the excavation of a first-century fishing boat just off the coast of Magdala can be found in Wachsmann, *The Sea of Galilee Boat*.

On the conflict between Antipas and the Galilean peasantry generally, particularly his economic exploitation of the peasant producers in order to fund his massive building programs and political ambitions, see Horsley, *Galilee*. The impact of taxation throughout the empire is explored in Hopkins, "Taxation and Trade."

The traditional material culture of Israelite highlanders of the Iron Age is analyzed in Stager, "Archaeology of the Family," and Hopkins, *The Highlands of Canaan*. Only recently have archaeologists begun to focus on the character of Galilean villages in particular: see Horsley, "Archaeology and the Villages of Upper Galilee," with a reply by Meyers, "An Archaeological Response." Some suggestive archaeological evidence of the process of the gradual "industrialization" of the Galilean olive oil industry is presented in Aviam, "Large-scale Production."

Horsley's earlier treatments of the pressures on peasant life in Palestine can be found in *Bandits, Prophets, and Messiahs* and *Liberation of Christmas*. Basic background on the anthropology of peasant societies can be found in Wolf, *Peasants*, and Scott, *The Moral Economy of the Peasant*. The tradition of resistance that is cultivated by villagers in traditional societies all over the world is explored in Scott, *Weapons of the Weak* and *Domination and the Arts of Resistance*.

Goodman's perceptive analysis of the causal connection between economy and political conflict in Judea during the first century is set out at length in *The Ruling Class of Judea* and in his earlier article, "The First Jewish Revolt: Social Conflict and the Problem of Debt," and by Horsley, *Sociology and the Jesus Movement*. The archaeological remains of "manor houses" throughout Judea—structures that may represent a material correlate to the economic changes in agricultural production charted by Goodman—have been documented by Hirschfeld, "Changes in Settlement Patterns." Alcock, *Graecia Capta*, traces a parallel phenomenon in Roman Greece.

Among the earliest modern attempts to place John the Baptist in historical perspective are Eisler, *Messiah Jesus and John the Baptist;* Enslin, *Christian Beginnings;* and Kraeling, *John the Baptist*. Hollenbach provides a thorough and judicious critical analysis of the fragmentary evidence in "Social Aspects" and in his entry "John the Baptist" in the *Anchor Bible Dictionary*. Meier devotes a lengthy discussion of texts pertinent to John the Baptist in *A Marginal Jew*, vol. 2. See also Murphy-O'Connor, "John the Baptist and Jesus," and Webb, *John the Baptizer*.

For critical treatments of the popular, Moses- and Elijah-like prophets contemporary with John the Baptist and Jesus, see Horsley's essays "'Like One of the Prophets of Old': Two Types of Popular Prophets at the Time of Jesus" and "Popular Prophetic Movements at the Time of Jesus: Their Principal Features and Social Origins," and Gray, *Prophetic Figures in Late Second Temple Jewish Palestine*.

The story of Antipas and Herodias is told by Josephus in *Antiquities* 18.109–112. Although Hoehner, *Herod Antipas*, deals with the marriage, there is need for a scholarly study of Herodias in her own right. Cf. Ilan, *Jewish Women*. On the messianic ideology of the Hasmoneans, see Eisenman, *Maccabees, Zadokites, Christians, and Qumran*. The only major study of Herod that takes seriously into account the "messianic" aspect of his program and ideology is Schalit, *King Herod*, but see also the suggestions of Wirgin, "A Note on the 'Reed' of Tiberias" and "On King Herod's Messianism."

The politics and economy of the Nabatean kingdom in early imperial times has been studied by Millar, *The Roman Near East*, and Bowersock, *Roman Arabia*. For a cultural and archaeological perspective, see Zayadine, *Petra and the Caravan Cities*. The historicity of the gospel accounts of John's execution at Machaerus and the Herodian-Nabatean War are examined in Hoehner, *Herod Antipas*, and Tatum, *John the Baptist*.

One of the few critical treatments of the relationship between John the Baptist and Jesus is that of Paul Hollenbach, "The Conversion of Jesus: From Jesus the Baptizer to Jesus the Healer." Meier provides an exhaustive discussion of the gospel texts pertinent to Jesus' relation to John in *A Marginal Jew*, vol. 2.

Chapter 3: Faith Healer

For the human landscape of first-century Capernaum, see the accessible summary of archaeological explorations in Laughlin, "Capernaum: From Jesus' Time and After." For the latest analysis of the results of the excavations (with slightly differing interpretations), see Tsaferis, "Capernaum," and Loffreda, "Capernaum." The chronology of Jesus' Galilean ministry and its beginning in either Capernaum or Nazareth is analyzed in Meier, *Marginal Jew*, vol. 2. The difficulty of constructing a precise chronology of Jesus' ministry is stressed in Crossan, *The Historical Jesus*, and Meier, *Marginal Jew*, vol. 1.

The stories of Jesus' healings and exorcisms were virtually ignored as "miraculous" and beyond the canons of historical reason by New Testament scholars earlier in this century, but have been taken more seriously in the last few decades. Recent investigations have drawn upon clinical psychology, medical anthropology, comparative ethnography, and the social history of ancient Palestine to provide a credible context in which to understand the likely healing and exorcism practices of Jesus, the typical stories about them in the gospels, and their significance for his ministry. For a general background, see Kee, *Medicine, Miracle, and Magic*. For the ministry of Jesus in particular, see Hollenbach, "Jesus, Demoniacs, and Public Authorities"; Horsley, *Jesus and the Spiral of Violence*; Crossan, *Historical Jesus*; Meier, *Marginal Jew*, vol. 2; Smith, *Jesus the Magician*; Twelftree, *Jesus the Exorcist*; and most suggestively (though perhaps without a clear enough connection to the political-economic context of first-century Galilee) Davies, *Jesus the Healer*. The classic discussion of the relationship between physical and psychological disorders and the imperial situation can be found in Fanon, *The Wretched of the Earth*.

On the wider implications of the Dead Sea Scrolls text 4Q521 as a messianic document, see Wise and Tabor, "The Messiah at Qumran."

For a fuller argument that Jesus' practices and teachings can be understood in both a concrete and social-political sense—with the principal theme of "the Kingdom of God" meaning basically a Renewal of Israel—see Horsley, *Jesus and the Spiral of Violence*. For further development of the idea that Jesus' ministry included a renewal of the Mosaic Covenant as the traditional basis of village life and a mission modeled on the traditions of Elijah and Elisha, see Horsley, *Sociology and the Jesus Movement* and "Q and Jesus." The recent interpretation of Jesus and his followers as "Cynic"-like itinerant vagabonds (as depicted in Mack, *The Lost Gospel*, and Crossan, *Historical Jesus*, among others) is based on the isolation of Jesus' sayings as "aphorisms" in a way that projects an unrealistic, unhistorical mode of communication upon Jesus. Criticism of the Cynic interpretation of Jesus and gospel traditions can be found in Betz, "Jesus and the Cynics"; Horsley, *Sociology and the Jesus Movement*; and Tuckett, "A Cynic Q?"

That Jesus spoke as prophet, in oracles of judgment as well as deliverance, much as had John the Baptist, has been sacrificed by the recent emphasis on the (unhistorical) dichotomy between "apocalyptic" and "sapiential." Jesus is seen primarily as prophet by Sanders, *Jesus and Judaism*, and Horsley, *Jesus and the Spiral*, with their picture now supplemented by the implications of Davies, *Jesus the Healer*. Although Crossan worked closely with the typology of groups and leaders developed by Horsley in *Bandits, Prophets, and Messiahs* and several articles, he does not apply it to Jesus of Nazareth, opting for the (historically questionable) role of a peasant "sage." Assuming that the so-called "action" or "signs" prophets active in Judea at the time of Jesus were acting out roles modeled after Moses and Elijah, they would have pronounced oracles as well as served as popular leaders.

On the vilification of Jesus as a "friend of toll-collectors and sinners," see Horsley, *Jesus and the Spiral*, to which can be compared the interpretation of "sinners" in Sanders, *Jesus and Judaism*. Saldarini, *Pharisees, Scribes, and Sadducees*, is the most extensive discussion of the Pharisees in the sociological role of "retainers" for the Temple establishment. For the suggestion that "the Herodians" would have been the parallel "retainers" of Antipas based in Tiberias and Sepphoris, see Rowley, "Herodians."

Virtually no attention has been paid to the possible historical relation between Jesus and Antipas. For a suggestive exploration of the Markan story of John's arrest and execution as displaying "local color" and a certain historical verisimilitude, see Theissen, *The Gospels in Context*. For the sequence of the events as presented by the evidence of the gospels and Josephus, see Hoehner, *Herod Antipas*. Our approach here is to place Jesus' public ministry and Antipas's likely reaction in broader historical context.

The likely ambivalence of many Galileans toward the Jerusalem Temple and its cultic and fiscal demands upon the people is explored in Horsley, *Galilee*, which challenges the perception of Galilean loyalty to the Temple emphasized previously by Freyne, *Galilee*.

Chapter 4: Power and Public Order

The administration of the province of Judea by the various Roman governors is comprehensively detailed in Smallwood, *The Jews under Roman Rule*, and discussed in standard handbooks such as Safrai and Stern, *The Jewish People in the First Century*, and the revised edition of Schürer, *The History of the Jewish People*. The provincial policy of Tiberius is analyzed in Levick, *Tiberius the Politician*, and the general political background of his era is described in the still classic article by Marsh, "Roman Parties in the Reign of Tiberius." For the administration of Pilate, in particular, see Lémonon, *Pilate*, and Schwartz, "Josephus and Philo on Pontius Pilate." The inscription from Caesarea was first published by Frova, "L'inscrizióne di Ponzio Pilato."

There is considerable debate among New Testament scholars regarding the historical value of the gospel narratives of Jesus' last week in Jerusalem. The massive recent study by Brown, *The Death of the Messiah*, is relatively trusting of the historicity of the canonical gospel narratives (including certain problematic aspects of traditional Christian attitudes toward "the Jews'" responsibility for the death of Jesus). Crossan's book *Who Killed Jesus?* offers a far more critical interpretation. Among shorter recent critical reviews of many of the complex literary-historical and theological issues aroused by the Passion Narratives see Mack, *A Myth of Innocence*, and Koester, *Ancient Christian Gospels*. Horsley, "The Death of Jesus," reviews twentieth-century scholarly treatment of several key issues. Partly because the literary-critical and theological issues are so deeply entangled with traditional religious beliefs, critical studies of the Passion Narratives have rarely devoted much attention to the wider historical context of Jesus' climactic journey to and activity in Jerusalem—thus our emphasis here.

For a discussion of the heightened tension between the Judeans and their Roman rulers at festival time, see Horsley and Hanson, *Bandits, Prophets, and Messiahs*, and Horsley, *Jesus and the Spiral*, which points out that prophetic parody as a means of popular protest was a tradition strongly rooted in Israelite prophetic tradition. The studies of the urban "mob" in Hobsbawn, *Primitive Rebels*, and Rudé, *The Crowd in History*, and studies of popular protests in nineteenth-century America (as in Davis, "The Career of Colonel Pluck") are suggestive of the widespread use of parodies of power as public political spectacles.

For a comprehensive survey of the archaeology of Jerusalem in the Herodian Period, see Mazar, *Mountain of the Lord*, and the articles by Avigad and Geva within the entry "Jerusalem: The Second Temple Period" in Stern, *New Encyclopedia*. The classic work on the Temple and its related services is Jeremias, *Jerusalem in the Time of Jesus*, but see also Safrai, "The Temple and the Divine Service."

Sanders, *Jesus and Judaism*, argues that Jesus' prophetic sayings and actions against the Temple were only part of a broader divine plan to rebuild the Temple. Horsley, *Jesus and the Spiral*, argues, to the contrary, that the rebuilding of the Temple is not a prominent motif in the traditional prophetic or apocalyptic scheme of the Renewal of Israel, with much of the contemporary literature from Judea being critical of the existing Temple and calling for the deposition and punishment of the priestly hierarchy. To the extent that texts like the Dead Sea Temple Scroll speak of a "new" Temple, they should probably be seen as primarily condemnatory, rather than reformist. Fuller argument for this interpretation of the prophetic oracles and parables of Jesus in Jerusalem can be found in Horsley, *Jesus and the Spiral*, and Crossan, *Historical Jesus*.

The excavation of the Upper City of Jerusalem and the residences of the priestly aristoracy are described by Avigad, *Discovering Jerusalem* and *The Herodian Quarter*. The "Caiaphas" ossuary was first published by Greenhut, "The 'Caiaphas' Tomb." Goodman definitively deals with the political and economic position of the priestly aristocracy in *The Ruling Class of Judea*, but see also Stern, "Aspects of Jewish Society."

For various accounts of the "trial" of Jesus and its historicity, see Brown, *Death of the Messiah*; Crossan, *Who Killed Jesus?*; and Hoehner, *Herod Antipas*. Jesus, son of Ananias, described in Josephus, *Jewish War* 6: 300–309, is highlighted as a principal example of an individual "oracular prophet" in Horsley's typology of popular leaders and movements in first-century Judea in *Bandits, Prophets, and Messiahs*. On the political dimension of Jesus' parables of the wicked tenants and the coin, see Horsley, *Spiral of Violence*.

Hengel provides a good —if also gruesome —sketch of the punitive, torturous Roman form of execution for provincial rebels, low-status criminals, and slaves in *Crucifixion in the Ancient World and the Folly of the Message of the Cross*. For the latest archaeological assessment, see Zias and Sekeles, "The Crucified Man."

Chapter 5: Preaching the Word

For the reactions of Jesus' followers to the horror of the crucifixion—and their impact on the crystallization of later tradition—see Crossan, *Who Killed Jesus?* An analysis of the "Yehohanan" Tomb was first published by Tsaferis, "Jewish Tombs." The revised conclusions on the manner of death are detailed in Zias and Sekeles, "The Crucified Man." On the Church of the Holy Sepulchre and the archaeological debates about the historical authenticity of its site, see Coüasnon, *The Holy Sepulchre*, and Taylor, *Christians and the Holy Places*. The topography of first-century

Jerusalem and its fortification system has been reconstructed in Bahat, *Illustrated Atlas*, and Wilkinson, *Jerusalem*.

The theorized origins of rural communities of the "Jesus Movement" and background of the "Synoptic Sayings Source," or "Q" Sayings Gospel, have received intensive examination and wide-ranging interpretation in recent decades. On the earliest history of the Galilean Jesus Movement, see also Mack, *Myth of Innocence*, and Crossan, *The Historical Jesus*. Perhaps the most balanced critical analyses of literary traditions from this period can be found in Jacobson, *The First Gospel*, and Kloppenborg, *The Formation of Q*. The clear implications of Kloppenborg's analysis is that this "gospel" is not a collection of sayings but a series of speeches or discourses, and is not particularly "sapiential" but rather "prophetic" in character, as Horsley points out in *"Logoi Propheton? Reflections on the Genre of Q."* The scholars comprising the "Q Seminar" tend to believe that Q can be divided into distinct literary strata, the earliest of which is comprised basically of sapiential sayings and that the Historical Jesus must therefore have been a "sage." That perception lies behind the increasingly frequent scholarly description of Jesus as a wisdom teacher and of his earliest followers as itinerant Cynic-like vagabonds, as in some of Crossan's observations in *Historical Jesus*. Most "Q" scholars, however, would not go as far as Mack, *The Lost Gospel*, in his sketch of Q's Jesus as a Cynic philosopher of a type common throughout the Graeco-Roman world.

An alternative, prophetic interpretation of "Q" is offered by Horsley, "Q and Jesus" and "Social Conflict in the Synoptic Sayings Source Q," which emphasize the prophetic tone of the social conflict evident in Q. For fuller elaboration on the interpretation of Q offered here, see Horsley, *Sociology and the Jesus Movement* and "Q and Jesus." We believe that Mack's interpretation of the Q-people in *The Lost Gospel* as countercultural pranksters falters for a number of reasons, not least of which is its ahistorical reconstruction of the extent and pervasiveness of Hellenization in Galilee in the first century.

An excellent review of scholarship on the so-called "pronouncement stories" and chains of miracle stories in and behind the Gospel of Mark is provided by Mack, *A Myth of Innocence*. For some recent conflicting views on the ethnic and religious self-perception of Galileans in the first century and their relationship with the ruling authorities, see Freyne, *Galilee*, and Horsley, *Galilee*.

On the domestic development projects and international fame of Herod Antipas, see Hoehner, *Herod Antipas*. An important contribution to the chronology of Antipas's reign and that of his brother Philip can be found in Strickert, "Coins of Philip."

Because literary sources relating to the membership and activities of the Twelve and the establishment of the Jerusalem community of the Jesus Movement are so meager and overlaid with later interpretation, the reconstruction of the specific historical situation is particularly difficult. An early attempt to understand the distinctive character of the Jerusalem community of the Jesus Movement was Brandon, *The Fall of Jerusalem*. Among more recent attempts, see Hengel, *Between Jesus and Paul* and *Acts and the Earliest History of Christianity*, and

Schwartz, *Studies in the Jewish Background*. A wide range of articles on the historical and archaeological background is provided in Bauckham, *The Book of Acts in Its Palestinian Setting*. The "Commentary" in Lüdemann, *Earliest Christianity According to the Tradition in Acts*, is conspicuously accepting of the Lukan historical tradition.

The classic description of economic life in first-century Jerusalem—Jeremias, *Jerusalem in the Time of Jesus*—should be supplemented by Applebaum, "Economic Life," and the more recent, archaeologically based data in Mazar, *Mountain of the Lord;* Avigad, *Discovering Jerusalem;* and the articles on Jerusalem in the Second Temple Period in the *Encyclopedia of Archaeological Excavations*. See also Broshi, "The Role of the Temple."

The traditional Israelite background of organized "charity" in the provision of food for the destitute is explored in Seccombe, "Was There an Organized Charity in Jerusalem before the Christians?" and, more indirectly, in the discussion of the role of community officials such as the *gabbaim* and *parnasim* of the local assembly (*synagōgē/ knesset*) of Galilean villages in Horsley, *Galilee*. The biblical precedents for such "social welfare" were, of course, the provisions for grain to be left in the fields for gleaning; the sabbatical nonplanting of the fields so that the poor could harvest the wild growth; the sabbatical cancellation of debt; and the third tithe. How such Israelite covenantal economics, seen in texts such as Leviticus 25, compare with the mechanisms for keeping the constituent households of villages viable that were standard in peasant societies can be seen in Scott, *The Moral Economy of the Peasant*. For other examples of the general phenomenon of communal pooling of resources in first-century Judea, see Capper, "The Palestinian Context."

Hengel offers a solid, critical start to approaching the historical reality of the "Hellenists" through the narratives in the Book of Acts in *Between Jesus and Paul* and *Acts and the History of Earliest Christianity*. The long-standing need for a critical challenge to the standard interpretation of the "Hellenists" and Stephen in particular, in the context of an emerging progressive universalistic "Hellenistic" Christianity over against the narrow Law-oriented "Jewish" Christianity, has now been addressed in Hill, *Hellenists and Hebrews*, which argues that there is little basis for assuming a serious theological split between two factions within the Jerusalem community of Jesus' followers. Significant is the fact that the Book of Acts labels as "Hellenists" both those who oppose Stephen as well as those who are appointed to be *diakonoi*, or "deacons," with him.

In his commentary on *I Maccabees* in the Anchor Bible series, Goldstein includes an incisive discussion on the significance of the rarely used term *ioudaismos*, arguing that it simply cannot be taken as a reference to a discrete religion known as "Judaism," but rather to a wider movement or political ideal. A critical analysis of II Maccabees can be found in Doran, *Temple Propaganda*. For the wider background of the diaspora communities in the Greco-Roman world, see Hengel, *Judaism and Hellenism;* Collins, *Between Athens and Jerusalem;* and the still-classic work of Tcherikover, *Hellenistic Civilization and the Jews*. Feldman, *Jew and Gentile*, and Mendels, *The Rise and Fall of Jewish Nationalism*, highlight some of the militant, political aspects of *ioudaismos*.

The precise date and origins of the earliest belief that Jesus was "the" or "a" messiah (*Christos*, in Greek) remains a contested issue among scholars, partly because it emerged so suddenly and lacked any obvious precedent or point of departure in the biblical messianic traditions in which such a "confession of faith" of a crucified messiah could have arisen. The problem is discussed in Collins, *The Scepter and the Star*. Reconstructions of an early (yet fully articulated) "Christ cult"— as suggested in Mack, *Who Wrote the New Testament?*—seem weakly based. We believe that the most credible background must be sought in variations and elaborations on traditions of martyrdom, as suggested in Tabor and Droge, *A Noble Death*; Williams, *Jesus' Death*; and Seeley, *The Noble Death*. The initial conviction may have been that Jesus was a martyr for the cause of the Kingdom of God and had been vindicated or rewarded by God for his personal suffering and sacrifice— through being exalted after death to abide in the presence of God in heaven, from where he would subsequently "appear" to his faithful followers in visions and auditions.

Chapter 6: Reviving the Nations

For the character of early activities of the members of the Jesus Movement in the diaspora, see Hengel, *Between Jesus and Paul*; Gager, *Kingdom and Community*; Meeks, *The First Urban Christians*; Theissen, *The Social Setting*; Malherbe, *Social Aspects*; and Georgi, "The Early Church." The issue of "Godfearers" and their connection with diaspora communities is extensively discussed in Feldman, *Jew and Gentile*. For opposing views on the character of proselytism among Jewish communities, see Georgi, *The Opponents of Paul* (which sees it as a common and pervasive phenomenon), and Goodman, *Mission and Conversion* (which sees the phenomenon as relatively rare among Jewish communities in the first century). The relationship of Gentiles to the fulfillment of biblical prophecy is analyzed in Donaldson, "Proselytes or 'Righteous Gentiles,' " and related to the method of diffusion of the Jesus Movement in Frederikson, *From Jesus to Christ*.

The problematics of Paul's biography are explored by Hengel, *The Pre-Christian Paul*; Jewett, *A Chronology of Paul's Life*; Lüdemann, *Paul*; and Murphy-O'Connor, *Paul*. A concise and incisive analysis of Saul/Paul's activity in Damascus can be found in Frederikson, *From Jesus to Christ*, which places his activities in the historically plausible context of inter-communal discipline. For various perspectives on the political and philosophical dimensions of Paul's "conversion," see Elliott, *Liberating Paul*; Sanders, *Paul*; Segal, *Paul the Convert*; and Boyarin, *Radical Jew*.

On the ecstatic, visionary aspects of Paul's conversion against the background of apocalyptic prophecy, see Stendahl, *Paul Among Jews and Gentiles*, which insists that Paul's decisive experience must be understood as "call rather than conversion." Studies that class Paul's experience as a visionary ascent to heaven in the manner of Ezekiel and other prophets include Tabor, *Things Unutterable*, and Himmelfarb, *Ascent to Heaven*. Rowland, *The Open Heaven*, offers a somewhat broader historical social context. Both Beker, *Paul the Apostle*, and Schoeps, *Paul*, insist on the apocalyptic orientation of Paul's thinking. Elliott, *Liberating Paul*, opens up to scholarly review the previously underestimated or ignored political roots and thrust of Paul's apocalyptic perspective.

Apart from Paul's own cryptic autobiographical references in Galatians 1:17 and 2 Corinthians 11:32, there are no additional details of Paul's time in "Arabia" or his run-ins with the officers of the Nabatean king. The outbreak and outcome of the Nabatean-Herodian war and its far-reaching political implications are discussed in Hoehner, *Herod Antipas*.

Standard treatments of the activities of Jesus' followers in Antioch, where they were first called "Christians," are presented by Brown and Meier, *Antioch and Rome*, and Meeks and Wilken, *Jews and Christians in Antioch*. Hengel analyzes the decisive move to proselytizing the Gentiles in *Acts and the History of Earliest Christianity*. The definitive history of Antioch in the early imperial period (with an excursus on the earliest Christian community) can be found in Downey, *A History of Antioch*. The internal workings and conflicts of the Antioch community are discussed in Taylor, *Paul, Antioch, and Jerusalem*. A pioneering (if now dated) study of some of the sites of the early missionary work of the Antioch community is Ramsay, *The Cities of Saint Paul*. For archaeological remains, see also Finegan, *The Archaeology of the New Testament: The Mediterranean World*.

Schwartz, *Agrippa I: The Last King of Judea*, offers a critical analysis of Agrippa I's life and career in the context of Roman and Judean political history. It is curious that even though the Book of Acts depicts Agrippa I as playing an important role in the early history of the Jesus Movement, modern New Testament scholars pay relatively little attention to political events and figures such as Agrippa. Schwartz, however, underlines the political dimensions of the activities of the Jerusalem Christian community. See also his *Studies in the Jewish Background*. An earlier, but essentially similar, reading of the political situation can be found in Brandon, *The Fall of Jerusalem*.

The circumstances surrounding the so-called "Apostolic Council" have been widely discussed and variously interpreted. Some critical discussions can be found in Hengel, *Acts and the History of Earliest Christianity*; Achtemeier, *The Quest for Unity*; Georgi, *Remembering the Poor*; and Taylor, *Paul, Antioch, and Jerusalem*. A somewhat different view of the council in Jerusalem and its aftermath is offered in Hill, *Hellenists and Hebrews*, and Hann, "Judaism and Jewish Christianity in Antioch." The importance of James's role in the Jerusalem community is highlighted in Brandon, *Fall of Jerusalem*, and in several of the essays in Bauckham, *The Book of Acts*. Eisenman, *James the Brother of Jesus*, offers an incisive and provocative analysis of the figure of James and his historical context in Roman-ruled Judea. No less important, he attempts to reconstruct the political character of the movement in Jerusalem.

Regarding the approximate date of the Jerusalem Council, we generally follow Jewett's reconstruction of the sequence of events in Paul's career (*A Chronology of Paul's Life*), but depart significantly from his reconstruction by having the Council *precede* Paul's striking out on his own to Galatia, Macedonia, and Greece.

Chapter 7: Assemblies of the Saints

For background on the various regions through which Paul traveled, see Mitchell, *Anatolia* (for Galatia); Pandermalis and Papazoglu, "Macedonia Under the Romans" (for Philippi and Thessalonica); Alcock, *Graecia Capta* (for Achaia); and Trebilco, "Asia," and Koester, *Ephesos* (for Asia). Each of these regional studies integrates archaeological and historical background. An important analysis of the function of the imperial cult in the larger political life of this region can be found in Price, *Rituals and Power*. For a general administrative and cultural history, see Magie, *Roman Rule*.

There have been countless attempts to reconcile the information Paul provided in his own letters with that contained in the Book of Acts. For general introductions to the Book of Acts, its style and its historical value, see, among many, Walaskay, *'And So We Came to Rome'*; Hengel, *Acts and the History of Earliest Christianity*; and Hemer, *The Book of Acts*. On its literary genre, see Tiede, *Prophecy and History*; Pervo, *Profit with Delight*; and Aune, *The New Testament in Its Literary Environment*.

For recent scholarly discussions of the authenticity of Paul's various letters and their date of composition, see Jewett, *A Chronology*, and Lüdemann, *Paul*. Our adaption of the accepted chronologies can be found in the chronological chart placed after the main body of the text in this book. For general historical background of Paul's independent mission, see Elliger, *Paulus in Griechenland*, and Gill and Gempf, *The Book of Acts*. Among the most widely read discussions of Paul's theology are Sanders, *Paul and Palestinian Judaism*; Davies, *Paul and Rabbinic Judaism*; and, in an earlier generation, Bultmann, *New Testament Theology*, and Schweitzer, *The Mysticism of Paul the Apostle*. As mentioned in the text, we avoid a synthetic description of Pauline "theology," preferring to analyze a progressive, historically contextualized series of re-interpretations.

On the debate between the "North Galatian" and "South Galatian" theories of Paul's itinerary after leaving Antioch, see Betz, *Galatians* (for North), and the original conclusions of the nineteenth-century explorer, Ramsay, *A Historical Commentary* (for South). As mentioned in the text, we find the Northern Hypothesis more compelling in the general historical context of the times. The importance of the traditional Jewish (biblically based) understanding of historical "geopolitics" of the nations for Paul—and a determining factor in his decision to proceed to the heartland of Galatia as a prophetic commission to preach redemption among the descendants of the biblical Japhet—is stressed in the recent study by Scott, *Paul and the Nations*. First-century Jewish traditions discussed there identify the Galatians as the descendants of Gomer, the firstborn son of Japhet.

Cautious and critical historical analysis of Paul's Letter to the Galatians is necessary before using it as a source for Paul's mission there. This approach is exemplified by Gaventa, "Galatians 1 and 2: Autobiography as Paradigm," and Martyn, "Events in Galatia." In addition to textual analysis of Paul's letter, fuller acquaintance with the history of Galatia, Phrygia, Pisidia, and Lycaonia, in such works as Magie, *Roman Rule*; Levick, *Roman Colonies*; and Mitchell, *Anatolia*, is necessary before attempting to reconstruct either Paul's activities in the area or the subsequent institution of the "Pauline" assemblies there.

Those acquainted with the early history of Roman rule in Judea and Galilee will be impressed by the closeness of the parallels to Roman rule in Galatia, which would have been dramatically different from that in the somewhat more "urbanized" areas around Philippi and Thessalonica, and particularly that of Corinth, which are the central focus of Meeks, *The First Urban Christians*. As we stress in the text, the situation in Galatia was one of an almost entirely agrarian area undergoing dramatic changes in land tenure and crop production, as described in Mitchell, *Anatolia*. Indeed, Lull's discernment through Paul's later Letter to the Galatians of the importance of concrete manifestations of the Spirit among the Galatians, in *The Spirit in Galatia*, becomes all the more revealing when we also take into consideration the association of such phenomena in peasant societies under stress all over the world—as indicated by such diverse sources as Fanon, *The Wretched of the Earth*, and Scott, *Weapons of the Weak*.

Elliott, *Liberating Paul*, emphasizes that Paul intended through his preaching for his communities to embody alternative social relations, not merely individual ethics. Strelan, "Burden-Bearing and the Law of Christ," suggests some of the ways that Paul's ethical injunctions to the Galatians may have had tangible historical effects.

For an important examination of the methodology that should be used in assessing the historical background of Paul's mission in Philippi—and indeed his other activities described in the Book of Acts—see White, "Visualizing the 'Real' World." An excellent example of the kind of literary analysis necessary before utilizing Paul's Letter to the Philippians as a historical source is Stowers, "Friends and Enemies in the Politics of Heaven." Recent archaeological work in the region of Philippi with regard to its human lanscape in the early Roman period is summarized in Papazoglu, "Le territoire" and *Les villes*, and Pelekanidis, "Excavations." More specific studies on history, religion, and material culture in first-century Philippi include Bormann, *Philippi*; Abrahamsen, "Women at Philippi"; and Reumann, "Contributions of the Philippian Community to Paul and to Earliest Christianity."

Thessalonica and Paul's First Letter to the Thessalonians have received a great deal of scholarly attention in the last decade or so, particularly in the major studies by Jewett, *The Thessalonian Correspondence*; Malherbe, *Paul and the Thessalonians*; and the cautionary rhetorical-critical study by Smith, *Comfort One Another*. Recent archaeological discoveries in Thessalonica are summarized by Koester and Hendrix, *Archaeological Resources*. For the first-century urban plan of the city, see

Vickers, "Toward the Reconstruction of the Town Planning of Roman Thessaloniki."

The official pagan cults of Thessalonica were systematically described in Edson, "Cults of Thessalonica." Hendrix, "Beyond 'Imperial Cult,'" examined the Thessalonian honors to the emperor and imperial family and made some qualifications of the conclusions reached in Price, *Rituals and Power*. On the Cabirus cult in Thessalonica, see Jewett, *The Thessalonian Correspondence*, and Donfried, "The Cults of Thessalonica and the Thessalonian Correspondence." A recent article by John Barclay, "Thessalonica and Corinth: Social Contrasts in Pauline Christianity," attempts to reconstruct the political conflict touched off by Paul's mission by linking it to the social and economic situation of Paul's followers.

Elliott offers a provocative, political interpretation of the image of the crucified Christ for the members of the early assemblies in *Liberating Paul*. See also, Judge, "Paul as a Radical Critic of Society."

Chapter 8: Spirits in Conflict

The literature on Roman Corinth and Paul's Corinthian correspondence is vast. Wiseman, "Corinth and Rome," provides a comprehensive summary history and survey of archaeological explorations. For examples of the considerable scholarly debate that has recently arisen on the cultural character of the city, see Engels, *Roman Corinth*, and Gill, "Corinth: A Roman Colony." The results of archaeological surveys in the area around Corinth and other regions of Roman Greece have been summarized and analyzed in Alcock, *Graecia Capta*.

Murphy-O'Connor's article "The Corinth that Saint Paul Saw," and his book *St. Paul's Corinth*, and Furnish, "Corinth in Paul's Time" offer selected archaeological finds matched with passages from Paul's Corinthian correspondence and Acts. Yet see the cautionary article by Oster, "Use, Misuse, and Neglect of Archaeological Evidence," for a critical review of the common use of excavated remains to verify or explicate Paul's Corinthian correspondence.

A careful and concise treatment of Paul's association and collaboration with Priscilla and Aquila, based on their occupation as "tentmakers," can be found in Hock, *The Social Context of Paul's Ministry*. On the institution and composition of the house-church, see Meeks, *The First Urban Christians*, and White, *Building God's House*. The recent methodological experiment by Barton, "Paul's Sense of Place," is also highly suggestive.

Stowers, *Letter Writing in Greco-Roman Antiquity*, places the purpose, forms, and functions of Paul's letters in their broad cultural-historical context, indicating the differences as well as similarities to ordinary letter writing by the Greco-Roman elite. On the date and historical context of First Thessalonians, see Jewett, *The Thessalonian Correspondence*. On the sense of community Paul hoped to solidify through his letter, see Malherbe, "God's New Family in Thessalonica."

The evidence for dating Gallio's term as proconsul of Achaia is the peg on which all chronology of the Pauline mission hangs. See particularly the critical discussion by Jewett, *A Chronology of Paul's Life*, and Georgi's discussion of chronology in *Remembering the Poor*. Although we rely heavily on Jewett, we do not follow his dating of the beginning of Paul's work at Ephesus—after a brief journey back to Jerusalem. We see no convincing evidence of such a side trip and prefer to assume that Paul proceeded directly across the Aegean to Ephesus from Corinth. As will be seen, Paul's later (and final) journey to Jerusalem seems to have occurred after an absence of many years. Beker, *Paul: Apostle to the Gentiles*, lays out a precise reconstruction of the sequence of events in Ephesus.

For an illuminating collection of essays on the archaeology and history of Ephesus and their relation to early Christianity, see Koester, *Ephesos*. Its importance as a cultic center for the eastern provinces is examined in Oster, "Ephesus," and its social history in the early imperial period is analyzed in White, "Urban Development and Social Change."

Regarding the description of the figure known as "Apollos," mentioned in Acts 18:24–19:7, in Ephesus and its relation to the figure mentioned in Paul's Corinthian correspondence as an eloquent Hellenistic Jewish teacher of wisdom from Alexandria, see Pearson, "Hellenistic Jewish Wisdom Speculation and Paul," and Horsley, "Wisdom of Word and Words of Wisdom" and " 'How Can Some of You Say, 'There is no Resurrection of the Dead?' " These articles are based on a critical analysis of the conflict between Paul's position and that apparently taught in Corinth by Apollos.

On the opposition in Galatia and for interpretations of Paul's ensuing Letter to the Galatians, see Howard, *Paul: Crisis in Galatia*; Boyarin, *Radical Jew*; and Betz, *Galatians*. However, as mentioned, most scholars who have dealt with this issue have not paid enough attention to the specific political and economic milieu of first-century Galatia. The most penetrating analysis of the form and meaning of Paul's collection project (which apparently began in Galatia) is provided in Georgi, *Remembering the Poor*.

The issue of the "social status" of the "early Christians" in Corinth as elsewhere has been perhaps the principal concern of recent social analyses of early Christian literature, as in Theissen, *The Social Setting*, and Meeks, *First Urban Christians*. Chow's *Patronage and Power* now replaces Theissen's studies and makes more precise and convincing the points and comments of Meeks on the patronal "house-church" infra-structure of the overall Corinthian assembly. For a fuller examination of the institution as a pervasive social structure and a mode of personal relationship, see the essays in Wallace-Hadrill, *Patronage in the Ancient World*, particularly Johnson and Dandeker, "Patronage: Relation and System," and Braund, "Function and Dysfunction." Wallace-Hadrill, *Houses and Society*, provides an insightful examination of the relationship between these social structures of patronage and archaeological remains. An important sociological portrait of the upwardly-mobile classes in Roman cities (of the type that might have risen to leadership in the Corinthian communities) is offered in D'Arms, *Trade and Social Standing*.

How the Corinthians may have responded to the teaching of Apollos has been explored by Pearson, *The Pneumatikos-Psychikos Terminology*; Thisleton, "Realized Eschatology"; and articles on First Corinthians by Horsley, "Gnosis in Corinth" and "Pneumatikos versus Psychikos." The more recent rhetorical criticism of First Corinthians, such as Mitchell, *Paul and the Rhetoric of Reconciliation*, reinforces the necessity of discerning the specific "rhetorical situation" in Corinth that lies behind the letter. Indeed, the recognition that the Corinthians' religious language and orientation was similar to and perhaps derived from Hellenistic Jewish devotion to Sophia/Logos makes unnecessary the hypothesis of "Gnosticism" in Corinth, drawn from later Christian Gnostic literature.

The classic treatment of Logos, or Wisdom-mysticism, as expressed in the writings of Philo of Alexandria is Goodenough, *By Light, Light*. It is possible to get a general flavor of Hellenistic Jewish wisdom-devotion by reading chapters 6–10 of the apochryphal book *The Wisdom of Solomon* (composed probably in Alexandria in the first century B.C.E.). For other varieties of Hellenistic Jewish piety, see Collins, *Between Athens and Jerusalem*. Horsley, "Spiritual Marriage with Sophia," draws a parallel between the wisdom-devotion in *The Wisdom of Solomon*, Philo, and among the Therapeutrides of Egypt and that of the Corinthians as addressed in First Corinthians. For examinations of the impact of Sophia-wisdom on the women of the Corinthian community and in the formative period of Christian origins, see Schüssler Fiorenza, *In Memory of Her* and *Jesus*, and Kraemer, *Her Share of the Blessings*.

Several other interpretations of the beliefs of the Corinthian community that Paul addresses in First Corinthians (such as Wire, *Corinthian Women Prophets*) sketch a similar picture except that they see the Corinthians as focused not directly on Sophia/Lady Wisdom but on Christ conceived in terms of Wisdom. The recent commentary by Fee, *The First Epistle to the Corinthians*, offers a response to the understanding of the Corinthian spirituals articulated by Horsley and Pearson, from a more conservative exegetical viewpoint.

Paul's response to the Corinthians is examined in Horsley, " 'How Can Some of You Say?' " Mitchell, *Paul and the Rhetoric of Reconciliation*, shows Paul's response is loaded with political language, reinforcing the impression that his overriding concern is that the community hold together—under his authority. Chow, *Power and Patronage*, emphasizes that much of the behavior that is so severely criticized by Paul can be seen as typical of a Romanized aristocracy. For a discussion of the identity of the "superlative apostles" and their relationship with the Corinthian community, see Georgi, *The Opponents of Paul*.

Georgi, *Remembering the Poor*, offers a detailed reconstruction of the events between Paul and the Corinthians, while Chow, *Patronage and Power*, reconstructs Paul's correspondence and argumentation in politically charged, anti-patronal terms. An alternative reconstruction can be found in Becker, *Paul: Apostle to the Gentiles*.

On the accession of Nero and the disintegration of the Julio-Claudian dyanasty, see Griffin, *Nero*. The historicity of the "riot of the silversmiths" in

Ephesus is discussed in Trebilco, "Asia." For a reconstruction of the physical conditions of Paul's various periods of imprisonment, see Rapske, *The Book of Acts and Paul in Roman Custody* (which, however, places the Onesimus incident in Caesarea). Koester, "Ephesos in Early Christian Literature," presents the main arguments for placing this period of imprisonment in Ephesus. Georgi, *Remembering the Poor*, analyzes the ideology of giving as manifested by the Philippians' gift to Paul. For the context of Paul's appeal for continued faithfulness, see Mearns, "The Identity of Paul's Opponents at Philippi." On the Letter to Philemon, see Petersen, *Rediscovering Paul*, and Hock, "A Support for His Old Age."

It is important to stress that the institution of patronage that Paul condemned in Corinth and in the particular case of Philemon was not merely an urban phenomenon, but formed the basic structure of economic exploitation throughout the Roman world. That is perhaps why Paul's focus on the patron-client relationship (and its paradoxical anti-type in the relationship of the believer to the "non-patronly" patron Christ) was so powerful. For other distinctive varieties of patronage relevant to the Pauline movement in predominantly agrarian areas such as Galatia and Macedonia, see Garnsey and Woolf, "Patronage of the Rural Poor," and Hopwood, "Bandits, Elites, and Rural Order."

Chapter 9: Storming the Kingdom

Our principal source for reconstructing the progress of the collection is Georgi, *Remembering the Poor*, which combines analysis of the purpose and rationale of Paul's collection project with careful consideration of issues of chronology and critical analysis of the sources. In an important concluding section of the book, Georgi characterizes the collection as a demonstration against economic greed and possessiveness. We prefer to make the background motivation more specific: while Georgi discusses highly generalized economic concepts, we believe that the structure of imperial patronage—extending downward from Rome to the humblest subject of the empire—is the reality that the collection is meant to contest. See Wallace-Hadrill, *Patronage in Ancient Society*.

The prophetic-apocalyptic dimension of the collection is explored in Donaldson, "Proselytes or 'Righteous Gentiles.' " For an explanation of Paul's sense of satisfaction—and closure—in having preached the gospel "from Jerusalem and as far round as Illyria," see Scott, *Paul and the Nations*, and Aus, "Paul's Travel Plans," which discusses the geographical dimensions of the biblical tradition of Japhet's descendants—and their possible implications for understanding Paul's plans to proceed from the eastern Mediterranean to Spain.

There is an intriguing possibility that Paul's sudden sense of apocalyptic urgency in undertaking the journey to Jerusalem and then proceeding immediately to the West may have been influenced by calendrical considerations, in particular the completion of a sabbatical cycle of years. On this subject, see Wacholder, "The

Calendar of Sabbatical Cycles" and "Chronomessianism." According to his calcu-
lations, the year 55–56 C.E.—in which we believe Paul's last journey to Jerusalem
occurred—was a sabbatical year. Other formative events in the history of the Jesus
Movement that apparently took place during sabbatical years (according to this
chronology) are the appearance of John the Baptist (27/28); Paul's "conversion"
(34/35); the coronation and death of Agrippa I (42/43); and the Jerusalem Council
and beginning of Paul's independent mission (48/49). As we will see, other
important events—James's and Paul's martyrdom (62/63) and the destruction of
the Temple in Jerusalem (69/70)—also took place during sabbatical years. Although Wacholder deals only with the appearance of John the Baptist and the
hypothesized date for the birth of Jesus in his scheme, he provides abundant
evidence of the importance of sabbatical cycles in the public consciousness of the
Jewish people during the first century.

In recent years, a steady stream of books has chipped away at standard
theological readings of Paul's Letter to the Romans. Elliott, *Liberating Paul*, has built
on important earlier studies such as Stendahl, *Paul Among Jews and Gentiles*; Beker,
Paul the Apostle; Williams, *Jesus' Death as Saving Event*; Gaston, *Paul and the Torah*; and
Gager, *The Origins of Anti-Semitism*. Most recently, Stowers, *A Rereading of Romans*,
offers a revisionist interpretation closely in touch with ancient Greek and Roman
rhetorical forms. Stowers's "rereading," moreover, is highly amenable to our attempt to place Paul's Letter to the Romans in historical political context.

On the possible identification of the list of names in Romans 16 as members of
the various Jesus assemblies in Ephesus—rather than in Rome—see Koester,
"Ephesos," with bibliography. The scholarly consensus, however, maintains that
these people were residents of Rome, even if a few might originally have come
from Ephesus.

Events and principal personalities in Jerusalem during the years following the
death of Agrippa are extensively described in Smallwood, *Jews Under Roman Rule*,
and Horsley, "High Priests." The power struggles that gradually resulted in open
revolt against Rome are covered critically and comprehensively by Goodman, *The
Ruling Class of Judaea*. The appearance of the "Egyptian prophet" is discussed in
Horsley and Hanson, *Bandits, Prophets, and Messiahs*, and Wacholder, "Chronomessianism." For a provocative reconstruction of the career of Ananias, see Wise, "The
Life and Times of Ananias Bar Nedebaeus."

Even critical commentaries on the Book of Acts tend to be relatively trusting
of the general historical reliability of the reported sequence of events. The most
influential of these commentaries is Haenchen, *The Acts of the Apostles*. Lüdemann,
Earliest Christianity, focuses explicitly on sorting out "history" from "tradition." The
possibility of an open clash between the Jerusalem community and Paul being later
intentionally obscured by the author of Acts is explored in Brandon, *The Fall of
Jerusalem*, and examined in great detail in the provocative study by Eisenman, *James
the Brother of Jesus*.

The reported arrest and trial of Paul in Jerusalem and Caesarea is discussed in

Rapske, *The Book of Acts*, which generally affirms the historicity of its details. Walasky, *'And So We Came to Rome,'* offers a more critical appraisal of the later historical context of the narrative. On the impact of these events on the subsequent life of the Jerusalem community, see Brandon, *The Fall of Jerusalem*, and Hill, *Hellenists and Hebrews*.

Rapske, "Acts, Travel, and Shipwreck," discusses Paul's journey to Rome, with extensive bibliography. For the archaeological and textual background to Paul's reported Roman imprisonment, see Rapske, *Paul in Roman Custody*. On the "messianic" ideological dimensions of Nero's philhellenism, see Alcock, "Nero at Play?" Tacitus, *Annals*, is the primary source for the accounts of the Great Fire and the subsequent persecution of the Christians of Rome. A recent survey of the speculation about Paul's apparent martyrdom can be found in Beker, *Paul the Apostle*.

The basic source for the life of the assemblies after Paul's death is reconstructed in Meeks, *The First Urban Christians*. As we have argued, however, the movement was not strictly "urban" and included many rural communities.

Chapter 10: The Triumph of Caesar

The phenomenon of "social banditry" in Roman Judea was treated by Horsley, *Bandits, Prophets, and Messiahs*, with bibliography. On the situation in Galilee, in particular, see Horsley, *Galilee*. For an analysis of other movements of native revolt throughout the empire at about the same time, see Dyson, "Native Revolts" and "Patterns of Native Revolts."

The eruption of violent conflict in Caesarea and the interrelated events in Jerusalem and greater Judea are recounted by Josephus in *Jewish War* 2.285–344. The history and archaeology of Caesarea is examined by Levine, *Roman Caesarea;* the wider context of official, intellectual, and popular attitudes toward Jews and Judaism in the early empire is explored by Gager, *The Origins of Anti-Semitism*. Rappaport, "The Land Issue," highlights the underlying economic tensions that fueled the ethnic tensions.

The initial phase of the revolt in Jerusalem, through the attack on the Roman garrison, is narrated by Josephus in *Jewish War* 2.405–456 and is fully analyzed by Goodman, *The Ruling Class*. Horsley focused on the sicarii as a distinctive group of retainers turned terrorists, with comparative perspective, in "The Sicarii: Ancient Jewish Terrorists." They are clearly not to be identified with the "Zealots," who were a coalition of brigand bands from northwest Judea, who formed when Judean peasants were driven out of their villages by the scorched-earth tactics of the advancing Roman army.

In his seven-book *Jewish War*, Josephus provides an extensive account of the great revolt against Rome, which erupted simultaneously in Jerusalem and in the countryside in the summer of 66 C.E. While his attribution of motives to the actors involved may be highly unreliable and his account of his own role as the Jerusalem-designated military-governor of Galilee exaggerated in the extreme, he could not have gotten away with gross inventions of particular events, since other participants survived who could contradict him. For recent assessments of Josephus's historical role and historical reliability, see Cohen, *Josephus in Galilee and Rome*; Rajak, *Josephus*; and Bilde, *Flavius Josephus*.

A critical reconstruction of events in Galilee in 66–67, particularly the regional divisions and the rivalry between the northern Galilean strongman John of Gischala and Josephus for control of affairs in Galilee, is attempted in Horsley, *Galilee*. The wider conflict, including the massacres of Jews in the Hellenistic cities surrounding Judea and Galilee, is recounted by Josephus in *Jewish War* 2.457–480.

For the collapse of the Julio-Claudian dynasty, see Griffin, *Nero*. On the extended, bloody struggles over the imperial succession in 69, see Nicols, *Vespasian and the Partes Flavianae*, and Greenhalgh, *The Year of the Four Emperors*.

Rebecca Gray, *Prophetic Figures*, provides a recent critical analysis of Josephus's account of his miraculous escape from a besieged city and prophecy of Vespasian becoming world-ruler. For the remarkable parallels of Josephus's prophecy with the legend of Yohanan ben Zakkai's miraculous escape and prophecy, see Alon, "Rabban Johanan B. Zakkai's Removal to Jabneh." The political implications of the Roman decision to destroy the Jerusalem Temple are explored by Goodman, *The Ruling Class*.

For the reorganization of political, economic, and religious life in Judea after the Revolt, see Goodblatt, "The Jews of Eretz-Israel," and Alon, *The Jews in Their Land*. The confiscation of the property of the Judean aristocracy is discussed in Goodman, *The Ruling Class*, and suggested by the archaeological material in Hirschfeld, "Manor Houses."

The crystallization of Rabbinic Judaism is surveyed in Cohen, *From the Maccabees to the Mishnah*; Schiffman, *From Text to Tradition*; and Alon, *The Jews in Their Land*.

For conflicting theories on the development of the various strands of the Jesus Movement after the fall of Jerusalem, see—among many recent works—Mack, *Who Wrote the New Testament?*; Frederikson, *From Jesus to Christ*; Brown and Meier, *Antioch and Rome*; Pagels, *The Origin of Satan*; the essays in Robinson and Koester, *Trajectories Through Early Christianity*; and Sanders, *Jewish and Christian Self-Definition*.

The emergence of the gospels has been extensively documented by Koester, *Christian Gospels*, and their background has been explored in Aune, *The New Testament in Its Literary Environment*. The wider cultural and political milieu—in addition to the religious—has been masterfully reconstructed by Frederikson, *From Jesus to Christ*. For representative views of the members of the Jesus Seminar on this subject, see Funk, Hoover, et. al., *The Five Gospels*. For a conservative perspective, see Johnson, *The Writings of the New Testament*.

Among the most suggestive of recent treatments of the Gospel of Mark in historical social context are Myers, *Binding the Strong Man*, and Mack, *Myth of Innocence*. The date and place of authorship is analyzed by Marcus, "The Jewish War and the *Sitz im Leben* of Mark," who contests the traditional Roman hypothesis of Markan origins.

Recent thinking on the historical social context of the Gospel of John has been specially influenced by Martyn, *History and Theology in the Fourth Gospel*. In the Gospel of John, perhaps even more than in the other gospels, we are dealing with the continuing development of a literary tradition, as explored by Koester, *Ancient Christian Gospels*. With critical tools one can move behind the existing text of John to the self-definition of a branch of the Jesus Movement perhaps based in Judea, as in Robinson, *The Priority of John*, and Hendricks, *A Discourse of Domination*. On the parallelism of the concepts of light and darkness between the Dead Sea Scroll literature and the Gospel of John, see Flusser, *Judaism and the Origins of Christianity*. The best treatments of the Book of Revelation are still Schüssler Fiorenza, *The Book of Revelation: Justice and Judgment*, and Yarbro Collins, *Crisis and Catharsis*. For a recent study that suggests that the Book of Revelation was a direct response to the revivified Flavian cult of the emperors, see Friesen, *Twice Neokoros*.

A reconstruction of the historical development of the community in Antioch after 70 C.E. is proposed by Brown and Meir, *Antioch and Rome*, who follow the hypothesis of the Antiochene origins for the Gospel of Matthew. For the text itself, Saldarini, *Matthew's Christian-Jewish Community;* Balch, *Social History;* and Overman, *Matthew's Gospel and Formative Judaism* examine Matthew's Gospel and community in historical social context. The material background for Antioch in the Flavian period is described in detail in Downey, *A History of Antioch*, and more generally in Millar, *The Roman Near East*.

Chapter 11: Keeping the Faith

The regularization and institutionalization of Christian practice in the age of the Apostolic Fathers is detailed in Frend, *The Rise of Christianity*. For internal ideological developments, see Meeks, *The Moral World of the First Christians* and *The Origins of Christian Morality*. Some basic texts of this period are collected in Stamforth, *Early Christian Writings*. The quotation about the obedience of Christian brothers and sisters comes from *First Clement*.

Among many recent studies of how the deutero-Pauline letters help assimilate the movement to the dominant patriarchal imperial order, see Schüssler Fiorenza, *In Memory of Her*. Koester surveys the deutero-Pauline literature in *Introduction to the New Testament*.

The wider "world" as well as the narrative of Luke-Acts has attracted many good studies in recent years. The articles of Robbins, "The Social Location" and "Luke-Acts," combine a clear sense of the narrative rhetoric with the concrete social-cultural situation of Luke's two-volume history of the Christian movement. Among the variant assessments of the political orientation and purpose of Luke-Acts, Walaskay, '*And So We Came to Rome,*' argues that the author is attempting to persuade Christians of the benefits of empire, while Esler, *Community and Gospel*, views Luke's history as primarily a legitimation of Christianity in the imperial context.

For accounts of the gradual expansion of Christianity, see MacMullen, *Christianizing the Empire*, and Lane-Fox, *Pagans and Christians*.

The Didache, "The Teaching of the Twelve Apostles," which contains much material that overlaps or parallels the Jesus traditions in the gospels, has recently received social analysis that deepens the previous literary analysis. See particularly, Draper, "Social Ambiguity" and *The Didache in Modern Research*.

Bibliography

Abrahamsen, Valerie. "Women at Philippi: The Pagan and Christian Evidence." *Journal of Feminist Studies in Religion* 3 (1987): 17–30.

Achtemeier, Paul J. *The Quest for Unity in the New Testament Church.* Philadelphia: Fortress Press, 1987.

Alcock, Susan E. *Graecia Capta: The Landscapes of Roman Greece.* Cambridge: Cambridge University Press, 1993.

———. "Nero at Play?: The Emperor's Grecian Odyssey." Pp. 98–111 in *Reflections of Nero: History, Culture, Representation,* eds. Jás Elsner and Jamie Masters. Chapel Hill, NC: University of North Carolina Press, 1994.

———. "Roman Imperialism in the Greek Landscape." *Journal of Roman Archaeology* 2 (1989): 5–34.

Alon, Gedaliah. *The Jews in Their Land in the Talmudic Age.* Cambridge, MA: Harvard University Press, 1994.

———. "Rabban Johanan B. Zakkai's Removal to Jabneh." Pp. 269–313 in *Jews, Judaism, and the Classical World.* Jerusalem: Magnes Press, 1977.

Applebaum, Shimon. "Economic Life in Palestine." Pp. 631–700 in *The Jewish People in the First Century,* vol. 2, eds. Shmuel Safrai and Menachem Stern. Philadelphia: Fortress Press, 1974.

Arav, Rami, and Rousseau, John J. *Jesus and His World.* Minneapolis: Fortress Press, 1995.

Aune, David E. *The New Testament in Its Literary Environment.* Philadelphia: Westminster Press, 1987.

Aus, Roger D. "Paul's Travel Plans and the 'Full Number of Gentiles' in Rom. XI: 25." *Novum Testamentum* 21 (1979): 232–262.

Aviam, Mordechai. "Large-scale Production of Olive Oil in Galilee." *Cathedra* 73 (1994): 26–35. [In Hebrew]

Avigad, Nahman. *Discovering Jerusalem*. Nashville: Thomas Nelson, 1983.

──────. *The Herodian Quarter in Jerusalem*. Jerusalem: Keter, n.d.

Avi-Yonah, Michael, ed. *The World History of the Jewish People: The Herodian Period*. Jerusalem: Massada Publishing Co., 1975.

Bahat, Dan. *The Illustrated Atlas of Jerusalem*. New York: Simon and Schuster, 1989.

Balch, David L., ed. *Social History of the Matthean Community: Cross-Disciplinary Approaches*. Minneapolis: Fortress Press, 1991.

Barclay, John M. G. "Thessalonica and Corinth: Social Contrasts in Pauline Christianity." *Journal for the Study of New Testament* 47 (1992): 49–74.

Barker, Graeme, and Lloyd, John. *Roman Landscapes: Archaeological Survey in the Mediterranean Region*. London: British School at Rome, 1991.

Barton, Stephen. "Paul's Sense of Place: An Anthropological Approach to Community Formation in Corinth." *New Testament Studies* 32 (1986): 225–246.

Bauckham, Richard, ed. *The Book of Acts in Its Palestinian Setting*. Grand Rapids, MI: Eerdmanns, 1995.

──────. "The Economic Critique of Rome in Revelation 18." Pp 47–90 in *Images of Empire*, ed. Loveday Alexander. Sheffield: Sheffield Academic Press, 1991.

Beker, J. Christiaan. *Paul the Apostle: The Triumph of God in Life and Thought*. Philadelphia: Fortress Press, 1980.

Betz, Hans-Dieter. *Galatians: A Commentary on Paul's Letter to the Churches in Galatia*. Philadelphia: Fortress Press, 1979.

──────. "Jesus and the Cynics: Survey and Analysis of a Hypothesis." *Journal of Religion* 74 (1994): 453–75.

Bilde, Per. *Flavius Josephus between Jerusalem and Rome: His Life, His Works, and Their Importance*. Sheffield: Journal for the Study of the Old Testament Press, 1988.

Borg, Marcus J. *Jesus in Contemporary Scholarship*. Valley Forge: Trinity Press International, 1994.

Bormann, Lukas. *Stadt und Christengemeinde zur Zeit des Paulus*. Leiden: E. J. Brill, 1995.

Bowersock, Glen. *Roman Arabia*. Cambridge, MA: Harvard University Press, 1983.

Boyarin, Daniel. *A Radical Jew: Paul and the Politics of Identity*. Berkeley: University of California Press, 1994.

Brandon, S. G. F. *The Fall of Jerusalem and the Christian Church*. London: Society for Promoting Christian Knowledge, 1951.

Braund, David. "Function and Dysfunction: Personal Patronage in Roman Imperialism." Pp. 137–152 in *Patronage in the Ancient World*, ed. Andrew Wallace-Hadrill. London: Routledge, 1989.

──────. *Rome and the Friendly King: The Character of Client Kingship*. New York: St. Martin's Press, 1984.

Broshi, Magen. "The Role of the Temple in the Herodian Economy." *Journal of Jewish Studies* 38 (1987): 31–37.

Brown, Raymond E. *The Birth of the Messiah: A Commentary on the Infancy Narratives in Matthew and Luke*. Garden City, NY: Doubleday, 1977.

————. *The Death of the Messiah: From Gethsemane to the Grave: A Commentary on the Passion Narrative in the Four Gospels*. 2 vols. New York: Doubleday, 1994.

Brown, Raymond E., and Meier, John P. *Antioch and Rome: New Testament Cradles of Christianity*. New York: Paulist Press, 1983.

Bultmann, Rudolf. *The Theology of the New Testament*. New York: Charles Scribner's Sons, 1951.

Capper, Brian. "The Palestinian Context of the Earliest Christian Community of Goods." Pp. 323–356 in *The Book of Acts in Its Palestinian Setting*, ed. Richard Bauckham. Grand Rapids, MI: Eerdmanns, 1995.

Chaney, Marvin L. "Bitter Bounty." Pp. 15–30 in *Reformed Faith and Economics*, ed. Robert L. Stivers. Lanham, MD: University Press of America, 1989.

Chilton, Bruce, and Evans, Craig A. eds. *Studying the Historical Jesus: Evaluations of the State of Current Research*. Leiden: E. J. Brill, 1994.

Chow, John K. *Patronage and Power: A Study of Social Networks in Corinth*. Sheffield: Journal for the Study of the Old Testament Press, 1992.

Cohen, Shaye J. D. *From the Maccabees to the Mishnah*. Philadelphia: Westminster Press, 1987.

————. *Josephus in Galilee and Rome: His Vita and Development as a Historian*. Leiden: E. J. Brill, 1979.

Collins, John J. *The Apocalyptic Imagination*. New York: Crossroad, 1984.

————. *Between Athens and Jerusalem: Jewish Identity in the Hellenistic Diaspora*. New York: Crossroad, 1983.

————. *The Scepter and the Star: The Messiahs of the Dead Sea Scrolls and Other Ancient Literature*. New York: Doubleday, 1995.

Corbo, Virgilio. "La Citta Romana di Magdala." Pp. 355–378 in *Studia Hierosolymitana in onore del P. Bellarmio Bagatti*, eds. Emmanuele Testa, Ignacio Mancini, and Michele Piccirillo. Jerusalem: Franciscan Printing Press, 1976.

————. "Piazza e Villa Urbana a Magdala." *Liber Annus* 28 (1978): 232–240.

Coüasnon, C. *The Holy Sepulchre*. London: Oxford University Press, 1974.

Crossan, John Dominic. *The Historical Jesus: The Life of a Mediterranean Jewish Peasant*. San Francisco: HarperSanFrancisco, 1991.

————. *Who Killed Jesus? Exposing the Roots of Anti-Semitism in the Gospel Story of the Death of Jesus*. San Francisco: HarperSanFrancisco, 1995.

Curtis, Robert I. *Garun and Salsamenta: Production and Commerce in Materia Medica*. Leiden: E. J. Brill, 1991.

D'Arms, John H. *Commerce and Social Standing in Ancient Rome*. Cambridge, MA: Harvard University Press, 1981.

Davies, Stevan L. *Jesus the Healer: Possession, Trance, and the Origins of Christianity*. New York: Continuum, 1995.

Davies, W. D. *Paul and Rabbinic Judaism: Some Rabbinic Elements in Pauline Theology*. New York: Harper and Row, 1967.

Davis, Susan G. "The Career of Colonel Pluck: Folk Drama and Popular Protest in Early Nineteenth-Century Philadelphia." Pp. 487–501 in *Material Life in Amer-*

ica, 1600–1860, ed. Robert Blair St. George. Boston: Northeastern University Press, 1988.

Donaldson, Terence. "Proselytes or 'Righteous Gentiles'? The Status of Gentiles in Eschatological Pilgrimage Patterns of Thought." *Journal for the Study of the Pseudepigrapha* 7 (1990): 3–27.

Donfried, Karl P. "The Cults of Thessalonica and the Thessalonian Correspondence." *New Testament Studies* 31 (1985): 336–56.

Doran, Robert. *Temple Propaganda: The Purpose and Character of 2 Maccabees.* Washington, D.C.: Catholic Biblical Association of America, 1981.

Downey, Glanville. *A History of Antioch in Syria.* Princeton: Princeton University Press, 1961.

Draper, Jonathan. *The Didache in Modern Research.* Leiden: E. J. Brill, 1996.

———. "Social Ambiguity and the Production of Text: Prophets, Teachers, Bishops, and Deacons and the Development of the Jesus Tradition in the Community of the Didache." Pp 284–312 in *The Didache in Context: Essays on Its Text, History and Transmission*, ed. C. N. Jefford. Leiden: E. J. Brill, 1995.

Dyson, Steven L. "Native Revolts in the Roman Empire." *Historia* 20 (1971): 239–74.

———. "Native Revolt Patterns in the Roman Empire." *Aufstieg und Niedergang der Römischen Welt* II.3 (1975): 138–175.

Edson, Charles. "Cults of Thessalonica." *Harvard Theological Review* 41 (1948): 153–204.

Eisenman, Robert. *The Dead Sea Scrolls and the First Christians.* New York: Element, 1996.

———. *James the Brother of Jesus: Recovering the True History of Early Christianity.* New York: Penguin, 1997.

———. *Maccabees, Zadokites, Christians, and Qumran.* Leiden: E. J. Brill, 1983.

Eisler, Robert. *Messiah Jesus and John the Baptist.* Lincoln, UK: Dial Press, 1931.

Elliger, Winfried. *Paulus in Griechenland: Philippi, Thessaloniki, Athen, Korinth.* Stuttgart: Katholisches Bibelwerk, 1978.

Elliott, Neil. *Liberating Paul: The Justice of God and the Politics of the Apostle.* Maryknoll, NY: Orbis Books, 1994.

Engels, David. *Roman Corinth: An Alternative Model for the Classical City.* Chicago: University of Chicago Press, 1990.

Enslin, Morton. *Christian Beginnings.* New York: Harper, 1938.

Esler, Philip F. *Community and Gospel in Luke-Acts: The Social and Political Motivations of Lucan Theology.* Cambridge: Cambridge University Press, 1987.

Fanon, Franz. *The Wretched of the Earth.* New York: Grove Press, 1963.

Fee, Gordon D. *The First Epistle to the Corinthians.* Grand Rapids, MI: Eerdmans, 1987.

Feldman, Louis H. *Jew and Gentile in the Ancient World: Attitudes and Interactions from Alexander to Justinian.* Princeton, NJ: Princeton University Press, 1993.

Fenn, Richard K. *The Death of Herod: An Essay in the Sociology of Religion.* New York: Cambridge University Press, 1992.

Finegan, Jack. *The Archaeology of the New Testament: The Life of Jesus and the Beginning of the Early Church.* Princeton, NJ: Princeton University Press, 1992.

――――. *The Archaeology of the New Testament: The Mediterranean World of the Early Christian Apostles.* Boulder, CO: Westview Press, 1981.

Finkelstein, Israel. *The Archaeology of the Israelite Settlement.* Jerusalem: Israel Exploration Society, 1988.

Finkelstein, Israel, and Na'aman, Nadav, eds. *From Nomadism to Monarchy.* Washington: Biblical Archaeology Society, 1994.

Flusser, David. *Judaism and the Origins of Christianity.* Jerusalem: Magnes Press, 1988.

Fox, Robin Lane. *Pagans and Christians.* New York: Knopf, 1987.

Fredriksen, Paula. *From Jesus to Christ: The Origins of the New Testament Images of Jesus.* New Haven: Yale University Press, 1988.

Frend, W. H. C. *Martyrdom and Persecution in the Early Church.* Oxford: Basil Blackwell, 1965.

――――. *The Rise of Christianity.* Philadelphia: Fortress Press, 1984.

Freyne, Sean. *Galilee from Alexander the Great to Hadrian: A Study of Second Temple Judaism.* Wilmington, DE: Michael Glazier, 1980.

Friesen, Steven. *Twice Neokoros: Ephesus, Asia, and the Cult of the Flavian Imperial Family.* Leiden: E. J. Brill, 1993.

Frova, Antonio. "Le Inscrizione di Ponzio Pilato a Cesarea." *Reconditi* 95 (1961): 419–434.

Funk, Robert W., Hoover, Roy W., eds. *The Five Gospels.* New York: Macmillan, 1993.

Furnish, Victor Paul. "Corinth in Paul's Time—What Can Archaeology Tell Us?" *Biblical Archaeology Review* 14:3 (May/June 1988): 14–27.

Gabba, Emilio. "The Finances of King Herod." Pp. 160–168 in *Greece and Rome in Eretz Israel,* eds. Aryeh Kasher, Uriel Rappaport, and Gideon Fuks. Jerusalem: Yad Izhak Ben-Zvi, 1990.

Gager, John G. *Kingdom and Community: The Social World of Early Christianity.* Englewood Cliffs, NJ: Prentice-Hall, 1975.

――――. *The Origins of Anti-Semitism: Attitudes Toward Judaism in Pagan and Christian Antiquity.* New York: Oxford University Press, 1983.

Galinsky, Karl. *Augustan Culture: An Interpretive Introduction.* Princeton: Princeton University Press, 1996.

Garnsey, Peter, and Woolf, Greg. "Patronage of the Rural Poor in the Roman World." Pp. 117–136 in *Patronage in the Ancient World,* ed. Andrew Wallace-Hadrill. London: Routledge, 1989.

Gaston, Lloyd. *Paul and the Torah.* Vancouver, BC: University of British Columbia Press, 1987.

Gaventa, Beverly. "Galatians 1 and 2: Autobiography as Paradigm." *Novum Testamentum* 28 (1986): 309–26.

Georgi, Dieter. "The Early Church: Internal Jewish Migration or New Religion? *Harvard Theological Review* 88 (1995): 35–68.

——. *The Opponents of Paul in Second Corinthians*. Philadelphia: Fortress Press, 1986.

——. *Remembering the Poor: The History of Paul's Collection for Jerusalem*. Nashville: Abingdon, 1992.

——. *Theocracy in Paul's Praxis and Theology*, Trans. David E. Green. Minneapolis: Fortress Press, 1991.

——. "Who Is the True Prophet?" Pp. 100–126 in *Christians Among Jews and Gentiles: Essays in Honor of Krister Stendahl on His Sixty-fifth Birthday*, eds. George Nickelsburg and George W. MacRae. Philadelphia: Fortress Press, 1986.

Gill, David W. J. "Corinth: A Roman Colony in Achaea." *Biblische Zeitschrift* 37 (1993): 259–264.

Gill, David W. J., and Gempf, Conrad. *The Book of Acts in Its Greco-Roman Setting*. Grand Rapids, MI: Eerdmans, 1994.

Goldstein, Jonathan A. *I Maccabees*. Anchor Bible vol. 41. Garden City, NY: Doubleday, 1976.

Goodblatt, David. "The Jews of Eretz-Israel in the Years 70–132 CE." Pp. 155–84 in *Judea and Rome: Revolts of the Jews*, ed. Uriel Rappaport. Tel Aviv: Am Oved, 1983. [In Hebrew]

Goodenough, Erwin R. *By Light, Light: The Mystic Gospel of Hellenistic Judaism*. New Haven: Yale University Press, 1935.

Goodman, Martin. "The First Jewish Revolt: Social Conflict and the Problem of Debt." *Journal of Jewish Studies* 33 (1982) 418–27.

——. *Mission and Conversion: Proselytizing in the Religious History of the Roman Empire*. Oxford: Clarendon Press, 1994.

——. *The Ruling Class of Judaea: The Origins of the Jewish Revolt against Rome A.D.* 66–70. Cambridge: Cambridge University Press, 1987.

Gottwald, Norman, K. *All the Kingdoms of the Earth: Israelite Prophecy and International Relations in the Ancient Near East*. New York: Harper and Row, 1964.

——. *The Tribes of Yahweh*. Maryknoll, NY: Orbis Books, 1979.

Gray, Rebecca. *Prophetic Figures in Late Second Temple Jewish Palestine: The Evidence from Josephus*. Oxford: Oxford University Press, 1993.

Greene, Kevin. *The Archaeology of the Roman Economy*. Berkeley: University of California Press, 1986.

Greenhalgh, P. A. L. *The Year of the Four Emperors*. London: Wiedenfeld and Nicolson, 1975.

Greenhut, Zvi. "The 'Caiaphas' Tomb in North Talpiyot, Jerusalem." *Atiqot* 21 (1992): 63–71.

Griffin, Miriam T. *Nero: The End of a Dynasty*. London: Batsford, 1984.

Haenchen, Ernst. *The Acts of the Apostles: A Commentary*. Philadelphia: Westminster Press, 1971.

Hann, Robert R. "Judaism and Jewish Christianity in Antioch: Charisma and Conflict in the First Century." *Journal of Religious History* 14 (1986–7): 341–360.

Hanson, Paul. *The Dawn of Apocalyptic*. Philadelphia: Fortress Press, 1979.

Hemer, Colin J. *The Book of Acts in the Setting of Hellenistic History*. Tübingen: J. C. B. Mohr, 1989.

Hendricks, Obery M. *A Discourse of Domination: A Socio-rhetorical Study of the Use of Ioudaios in the Fourth Gospel*. Maryknoll, NY: Orbis Books, forthcoming.

Hendrix, Holland L. *Thessalonians Honor Romans*. Ph.D. diss., Harvard University, 1984.

Hengel, Martin. *Acts and the History of Earliest Christianity*. Philadelphia: Fortress Press, 1980.

————. *Between Jesus and Paul*. Philadelphia: Fortress Press, 1983.

————. *Crucifixion in the Ancient World and the Folly of the Message of the Cross*. Philadelphia: Fortress Press, 1977.

————. *Judaism and Hellenism: Studies in Their Encounter in Palestine during the Early Hellenistic Period*. Philadelphia: Fortress Press, 1974.

————. *The Pre-Christian Paul*. Philadelphia: Trinity Press International, 1991.

Hill, Craig C. *Hellenists and Hebrews: Reappraising Division within the Earliest Church*. Minneapolis: Fortress Press, 1992.

Himmelfarb, Martha. *Ascent to Heaven in Jewish and Christian Apocalypses*. Oxford: Oxford University Press, 1993.

Hirschfeld, Yizhar. "Changes in Settlement Patterns of the Jewish Rural Populace Before and After the Rebellions Against Rome." *Cathedra* 80 (1996): 3–18. [In Hebrew]

Hobsbawm, Eric J. *Primitive Rebels: Studies in Archaic Forms of Social Movement in the 19th and 20th Centuries*. New York: W. W. Norton and Company, 1965.

Hock, Ronald F. *The Social Context of Paul's Ministry: Tentmaking and Apostleship*. Philadelphia: Fortress Press, 1980.

————. "A Support for His Old Age: Paul's Plea on Behalf of Onesimus." Pp. 67–81 in *The Social World of the First Christians*, eds. L. Michael White and O. Larry Yarbrough. Minneapolis: Fortress Press, 1995.

Hoehner, Harold W. *Herod Antipas*. Cambridge: Cambridge University Press, 1972.

Hollenbach, Paul W. "The Conversion of Jesus: From Jesus the Baptizer to Jesus the Healer." *Aufstieg und Niedergang der Römischer Welt* 2.25.1 (1982): 196–219.

————. "Jesus, Demoniacs, and Public Authorities: A Socio-historical Study." *Journal of the American Academy of Religion* 99 (1981): 567–588.

————. "John the Baptist." Pp. 887–899 in *The Anchor Bible Dictionary*, vol. 3, ed. David Noel Freedman. New York: Doubleday, 1992.

————. "Social Aspects of John the Baptizer's Preaching Mission in the Context of Palestinian Judaism." *Aufstieg und Niedergang der Römischer Welt* 2.19.1 (1979): 850–75.

Hopkins, David. *The Highlands of Canaan: Agricultural Life in the Early Iron Age*. Sheffield: Almond, 1985.

Hopkins, Keith. "Taxation and Trade in the Roman Empire (200 BC–AD 400)." *Journal of Roman Studies* 70 (1980): 101–125.

Hopwood, Keith. "Bandits, Elites, and Rural Order." Pp. 171–188 in *Patronage in the Ancient World*, ed. Andrew Wallace-Hadrill. London: Routledge, 1989.

Horsley, Richard A. "Archaeology and the Villages of Upper Galilee: A Dialogue with Archaeologists." *Bulletin of the American Society of Oriental Research* 297 (1995): 15–16, 26–28.

――――. "The Death of Jesus." Pp 395–422 in *Studying the Historical Jesus: Evaluations of the State of Current Research*, eds. Bruce Chilton and Craig A. Evans. Leiden: E. J. Brill, 1994.

――――. *Galilee: History, Politics, People*. Valley Forge, PA: Trinity Press International, 1995.

――――. "Gnosis in Corinth: 1 Corinthians 8:1–6." *New Testament Studies* 27 (1980): 32–51.

――――. "High Priests and the Politics of Roman Palestine." *Journal for the Study of Judaism* 17 (1986): 23–55.

――――. " 'How Can Some of You Say That There Is No Resurrection of the Dead?': Spiritual Elitism in Corinth." *Novum Testamentum* 20 (1978): 203–231.

――――. *Jesus and the Spiral of Violence: Popular Jewish Resistance in Roman Palestine*. San Francisco: Harper and Row, 1987.

――――. *The Liberation of Christmas: The Infancy Narratives in Social Context*. New York: Crossroad, 1989.

――――. " 'Like One of the Prophets of Old': Two Types of Popular Prophets at the Time of Jesus." *Catholic Biblical Quarterly* 47 (1985): 435–63.

――――. "Logoi Propheton? Reflections on the Genre of Q." Pp 195–209 in *The Future of Early Christianity: Essays in Honor of Helmut Koester*, eds. Birger Pearson et al. Minneapolis: Fortress Press, 1991.

――――. "Pneumatikos versus Psychikos: Distinctions of Status Among the Corinthians." *Harvard Theological Review* 69 (1976): 269–288.

――――. "Popular Prophetic Movements at the Time of Jesus: Their Principal Features and Social Origins." *Journal for the Study of the New Testament* 26 (1986): 3–27.

――――. "Q and Jesus: Assumptions, Approaches, and Analyses." *Semeia* 55 (1991): 175–209.

――――. "The Sicarii: Ancient Jewish Terrorists." *Journal of Religion* 59 (1979): 435–58.

――――. "Social Conflict in the Synoptic Sayings Source Q." Pp. 37–52 in *Conflict and Invention: Literary, Rhetorical, and Social Studies on the Sayings Gospel Q*, ed. John S. Kloppenborg. Valley Forge, PA: Trinity Press International, 1995.

――――. *Sociology and the Jesus Movement*. New York: Crossroad, 1989.

――――. "Spiritual Marriage with Sophia." *Vigiliae Christianae* 33 (1979): 30–54.

――――. "Wisdom of Word and Words of Wisdom in Corinth." *Catholic Biblical Quarterly* 39 (1977): 224–239.

Horsley, Richard A., with Hanson, John S. *Bandits, Prophets, and Messiahs: Popular Movements in the Time of Jesus*. San Francisco: Harper and Row, 1987.

Howard, George. *Paul: Crisis in Galatia, A Study in Early Christian Theology*. Cambridge: Cambridge University Press, 1979.

Ilan, Tal. *Jewish Women in Greco-Roman Palestine*. Tübingen: J. C. B. Mohr, 1995.

Jacobson, Arland D. *The First Gospel: An Introduction to Q*. Sonoma, CA: Polebridge Press, 1992.

Jeremias, Joachim. *Jerusalem in the Time of Jesus*. London: Society for Promoting Christian Knowledge, 1969.

Jewett, Robert. *A Chronology of Paul's Life*. Philadelphia: Fortress Press, 1979.

————. *The Thessalonian Correspondence: Pauline Rhetoric and Millenarian Piety*. Philadelphia: Fortress Press, 1986.

Johnson, Luke Timothy. *The Writings of the New Testament: An Interpretation*. Philadelphia: Fortress Press, 1986.

Johnson, Terry, and Dandeker, Chris. "Patronage: Relation and System." Pp.219–238 in *Patronage in the Ancient World*, ed. Andrew Wallace-Hadrill. London: Routledge, 1989.

Judge, E. A. "Paul as Radical Critic of Society." *Interchange* 16 (1974): 191–203.

Kee, Howard Clark. *Medicine, Miracle, and Magic*. Cambridge: Cambridge University Press, 1986.

Kloppenborg, John S. *The Formation of Q: Trajectories in Ancient Wisdom Collections*. Philadelphia: Fortress Press, 1987.

Koester, Helmut. *Ancient Christian Gospels: Their History and Development*. Philadelphia: Trinity Press International, 1990.

————. "Ephesos in Early Christian Literature." Pp. 119–140 in *Ephesos: Metroplis of Asia*, ed. Helmut Koester. Valley Forge, PA: Trinity Press International, 1995.

————. *Ephesos: Metropolis of Asia*. Valley Forge, PA: Trinity Press International, 1995.

————. *Introduction to the New Testament*. 2 vols. Philadelphia: Fortress Press, 1982.

Koester, Helmut, and Hendrix, Holland. *Archaeological Resources for New Testament Studies*. Valley Forge, PA: Trinity Press International, 1995.

Kraeling, Carl H. *John the Baptist*. New York: Charles Scribner's Sons, 1951.

Kraemer, Ross Shepard. *Her Share of the Blessings: Women's Religions Among Pagans, Jews, and Christians in the Greco-Roman World*. New York: Oxford University Press, 1992.

Lane-Fox, Robin. *Pagans and Christians*. New York: Alfred A. Knopf, 1987.

Laughlin, John C. H. "Capernaum: From Jesus' Time and After." *Biblical Archaeologist* 56 (1993): 54–61.

Lémonon, Jean-Pierre. *Pilate et le gouvernment de la Judée: Textes et monuments*. Paris: J. Gabalda, 1981.

Levick, Barbara. *Roman Colonies in Southern Asia Minor*. Oxford: Clarendon Press, 1967.

————. *Tiberius the Politician*. London: Thames and Hudson, 1976.

Levine, Lee I. *Roman Caesarea: An Archaeological-Topographical Study*. Jerusalem: Institute of Archaeology, Hebrew University, 1975.

Loffreda, Stanislao. "Capernaum." Pp. 416–419 in *The Oxford Encyclopedia of Archae-ology in the Near East*, ed. Eric M. Meyers. New York: Oxford University Press, 1997.

Lüdemann, Gerd. *Earliest Christianity According to the Tradition in Acts: A Commentary*. Minneapolis: Fortress Press, 1989.

———. *Paul, Apostle to the Gentiles: Studies in Chronology*, trans. E. Stanley Jones. Philadelphia: Fortress Press, 1984.

Lull, David. *The Spirit in Galatia*. Missoula: Scholars Press, 1980.

Mack, Burton L. *The Lost Gospel: The Book of Q and Christian Origins*. San Francisco: HarperSanFrancisco, 1993.

———. *A Myth of Innocence: Mark and Christian Origins*. Philadelphia: Fortress Press, 1988.

———. *Who Wrote the New Testament? The Making of the Christian Myth*. San Francisco: HarperCollins, 1995.

MacMullen, Ramsay. *Christianizing the Roman Empire, AD 100–400*. New Haven: Yale University Press, 1984.

McRay, John. *Archaeology and the New Testament*. Grand Rapids, MI: Baker Book House, 1991.

Magie, David. *Roman Rule in Asia Minor*. Princeton: Princeton University Press, 1950.

Malherbe, Abraham J. "God's New Family in Thessalonica." Pp. 116–125 in *The Social World of the First Christians*, eds. L. Michael White and O. Larry Yarbrough. Minneapolis: Fortress Press, 1995.

———. *Social Aspects of Early Christianity*. Philadelphia: Fortress Press, 1983.

———. *Paul and the Thessalonians*. Philadelphia: Fortress Press, 1987.

Marcus, Joel. "The Jewish War and the *Sitz im Leben* of Mark." *Journal of Biblical Literature* 111 (1992): 441–462.

Marsh, Frank Burr. "Roman Parties in the Reign of Tiberius." *American Historical Review* 31 (1925–26): 233–250.

Martyn, J. Louis. "Events in Galatia." Pp. 160–179 in *Pauline Theology*, vol. 1, ed. Jouette M. Bassler. Minneapolis: Fortress Press, 1991.

———. *History and Theology in the Fourth Gospel*. New York: Harper and Row, 1967.

Mazar, Benjamin. *The Mountain of the Lord*. Garden City, NY: Doubleday, 1975.

Mearns, Chris. "The Identity of Paul's Opponents at Philippi." *New Testament Studies* 33 (1987): 194–204.

Meeks, Wayne A. *The First Urban Christians: The Social World of the Apostle Paul*. New Haven: Yale University Press, 1983.

———. *The Origins of Christian Morality*. New Haven: Yale University Press, 1993.

Meeks, Wayne, and Wilken, Robert. *Jews and Christians in Antioch in the First Four Centuries of the Common Era*. Missoula, MI: Scholars Press, 1978.

Meier, John P. *A Marginal Jew: Rethinking the Historical Jesus*. 2 vols. New York: Doubleday, 1991, 1994.

Mendels, Doron. *The Rise and Fall of Jewish Nationalism*. New York: Doubleday, 1992.

Meyers, Eric M. "Roman Sepphoris in the Light of New Archaeological Evidence and Recent Research." Pp. 321–35 in *The Galilee in Late Antiquity*, ed. Lee I. Levine. New York: Jewish Theological Seminary of America, 1992.

———. "An Archaeological Response to a New Testament Scholar." *Bulletin of Oriental Research* 297 (1995): 17–25.

Millar, Fergus. *The Emperor in the Roman World (31 BC–AD 337)*. London: Duckworth, 1977.

———. *The Roman Near East 31 BC–AD 337*. Cambridge: Harvard University Press, 1993.

Mitchell, Margaret M. *Paul and the Rhetoric of Reconciliation: An Exegetical Investigation of the Language and Composition of 1 Corinthians*. Tübingen: J. C. B. Mohr, 1991.

Mitchell, Stephen. *Anatolia: Land, Men, and Gods in Asia Minor*. Oxford: Clarendon Press, 1993.

Murphy-O'Connor, Jerome. "The Corinth That Saint Paul Saw." *Biblical Archaeologist* 47 (1984): 147–159.

———. "John the Baptist and Jesus: History and Hypotheses." *New Testament Studies* 36 (1990): 359–74.

———. *Paul: A Critical Life*. Oxford: Clarendon Press, 1996.

———. *St. Paul's Corinth: Texts and Archaeology*. Wilmington, DE: Michael Glazier, 1983.

Myers, Ched. *Binding the Strong Man: A Political Reading of Mark's Story of Jesus*. Maryknoll, NY: Orbis Books, 1988.

Netzer, Ehud. "Herod's Building Program." Pp. 169–173 in *The Anchor Bible Dictionary*, vol. 3, ed. David Noel Freedman. New York: Doubleday, 1992.

Neusner, Jacob, Green, William Scott, and Frerichs, Ernest. *Judaisms and Their Messiahs*. Cambridge: Cambridge University Press, 1987.

Nicols, John. *Vespasian and the Partes Flavianae*. Wiesbaden: Steiner, 1978.

Oster, Richard E. "Ephesus as a Religious Center under the Principate." *Aufstieg und Niedergang der Römischen Welt* 2.18.3 (1990): 1661–1728.

———. "Use, Misuse and Neglect of Archaeological Evidence in Some Modern Works on 1 Corinthians." *Zeitschrift für die Neutestamentliche Wissenschaft* 83 (1992): 52–73.

Overman, J. Andrew. *Matthew's Gospel and Formative Judaism: The Social World of the Matthean Community*. Minneapolis: Fortress Press, 1990.

Pagels, Elaine. *The Origins of Satan*. New York: Random House, 1995.

Pandermalis, D., and Papazoglou, Fanoula. "Macedonia Under the Romans." Pp. 192–221 in *Macedonia: 4000 Years of Greek History and Civilization*, ed. M. B. Sakellariou. Athens: Ekdotike Athenon, 1983.

Papazoglou, Fanoula. "Le territoire de la colonie de Philippes." *Bulletin du correspondance hellénique* 106 (1982): 89–106.

———. *Les villes de Macedoine à l'epoque Romaine*. Athens: Ecole Française d'Athénes, 1988.

Pearson, Birger. "Hellenistic Jewish Wisdom Speculation and Paul." Pp 43–66 in *Aspects of Wisdom in Judaism and Early Christianity*, ed. Robert L. Wilken. Notre Dame, IN: Notre Dame University Press, 1975.

―――. *The Pneumatikos-Psychikos Terminology in 1 Corinthians*. Missoula: Scholars Press, 1973.

Peckham, Brian. *History and Prophecy: The Development of Late Judean Literary Traditions*. New York: Doubleday, 1993.

Pelekanidis, Stylianos. "Excavations in Philippi." *Balkan Studies* 8 (1967): 123–126.

Pervo, Richard I. *Profit With Delight: The Literary Genre of the Acts of the Apostles*. Philadelphia: Fortress Press, 1987.

Petersen, Norman R. *Rediscovering Paul: Philemon and the Sociology of Paul's Narrative World*. Philadelphia: Fortress Press, 1985.

Price, S. R. F. *Rituals and Power: The Roman Imperial Cult in Asia Minor*. Cambridge: Cambridge University Press, 1984.

Rajak, Tessa. *Josephus: The Historian and His Society*. London: Duckworth, 1983.

Ramsay, William Mitchell. *The Cities of St. Paul: Their Influence on His Life and Thought*. London: Hodder and Stoughton, 1908.

―――. *A Historical Commentary on St. Paul's Letter to the Galatians*. New York: G. P. Putnam, 1900.

Rappaport, Uriel. "The Land Issue as a Factor in Inter-ethnic Relations in Eretz-Israel During the Second Temple Period." Pp. 80–86 in *Man and Land in Eretz-Israel in Antiquity*, eds. Arieh Kasher, Aaron Oppenheimer, and Uriel Rappaport. Jerusalem: Yad Izhak Ben Zvi, 1986. [In Hebrew]

Rapske, Brian. "Acts, Travel, and Shipwreck." Pp. 1–47 in *The Book of Acts in Its Greco-Roman Setting*, eds. David W. J. Gill and Conrad Gempf. Grand Rapids, MI: Eerdmans, 1994.

―――. *The Book of Acts and Paul in Roman Custody*. Grand Rapids, MI: Eerdmans, 1994.

Reich, Ronny. "A Note on the Roman Mosaic at Magdala on the Sea of Galilee." *Liber Annus* 41 (1991): 455–458.

Reumann, John. "Contributions of the Philippian Community to Paul and to Earliest Christianity." *New Testament Studies* 39 (1993): 438–57.

Richardson, Peter. *Herod: King of the Jews and Friend of the Romans*. Columbia, SC: University of South Carolina Press, 1996.

Robbins, Vernon K. "The Social Location of the Implied Author of Luke-Acts." Pp. 305–332 in *The Social World of Luke-Acts: Models for Interpretation*, ed. Jerome H. Neyrey. Peabody, MA: Hendrickson, 1991.

―――. "Luke-Acts: A Mixed Population Seeks a Home in the Roman Empire." Pp. 202–221 in *Images of Empire*, ed. Loveday Alexander. Sheffield: Sheffield Academic Press, 1991.

Robinson, James, and Koester, Helmut. *Trajectories Through Early Christianity*. Philadelphia: Fortress Press, 1971.

Robinson, John A. T. *The Priority of John*. London: Society for Promoting Christian Knowledge, 1985.

Rowland, Christopher. *The Open Heaven: A Study of Apocalyptic in Judaism and Early Christianity*. New York: Crossroad, 1982.

Rowley, H. H. "The Herodians in the Gospels." *Journal of Theological Studies* 41 (1940): 14–27.

Rudé, George. *The Crowd in History*. New York: Wiley, 1964.

Safrai, Shmuel. "The Temple and the Divine Service." Pp. 284–337 in *The World History of the Jewish People: The Herodian Period*, ed. Michael Avi-Yonah. Jerusalem: Massada Publishing Co., 1975.

Safrai, Shmuel, and Stern, Menachem, eds. *The Jewish People in the First Century*. Philadelphia: Fortress Press, 1974.

Safrai, Ze'ev. *The Economy of Roman Palestine*. New York: Routledge, 1994.

Saldarini, Anthony J. *Matthew's Christian-Jewish Community*. Chicago: University of Chicago Press, 1994.

———. *Pharisees, Scribes, and Sadducees in Palestinian Society: A Sociological Approach*. Wilmington, DE: Michael Glazier, 1988.

Sanders, E. P. *Jesus and Judaism*. Philadelphia: Fortress Press, 1985.

———. ed. *Jewish and Christian Self-Definition*. 3 vols. Philadelphia: Fortress Press, 1980-82.

———. *Paul and Palestinian Judaism: A Comparison of Patterns of Religion*. Philadelphia: Fortress Press, 1977.

Schalit, Avraham. *Herod the King: The Man and His Work*. Jerusalem: Mosad Bialik, 1964. [In Hebrew]

Schiffman, Lawrence. *From Text to Tradition: A History of Second Temple and Rabbinic Judaism*. Hoboken, NJ: Ktav, 1991.

Schoeps, Hans-Joachim. *Paul: The Theology of the Apostle in the Light of Jewish Religious History*, trans. Harold Knight. Philadelphia: Westminster Press, 1961.

Schürer, Emil. *The History of the Jewish People in the Age of Jesus Christ*. 3 vols., revised by Geza Vermes, Fergus Millar, Matthew Black, and Martin Goodman. Edinburgh: Clark, 1973–87.

Schüssler Fiorenza, Elisabeth. *The Book of Revelation: Justice and Judgment*. Philadelphia: Fortress Press, 1985.

———. *Jesus: Miriam's Child, Sophia's Prophet*. New York: Continuum, 1994.

———. *In Memory of Her: A Feminist Reconstruction of Christian Origins*. New York: Crossroad, 1988.

Schwartz, Daniel R. *Agrippa I: The Last King of Judea*. Tübingen: J. C. B. Mohr, 1990.

———. "Josephus and Philo on Pontius Pilate." *The Jerusalem Cathedra* 3 (1983): 26–45.

———. *Studies in the Jewish Background of Christianity*. Tübingen: J. C. B. Mohr, 1992.

Schweitzer, Albert. *The Mysticism of Paul the Apostle*. London: A. and C. Black, 1931.

Scott, James C. *Domination and the Arts of Resistance*. New Haven: Yale University Press, 1990.

———. *The Moral Economy of the Peasant: Subsistence and Rebellion in Southeast Asia*. New Haven: Yale University Press, 1976.

————. *Weapons of the Weak: Everyday Forms of Peasant Resistance*. New Haven: Yale University Press, 1985.

Scott, James M. *Paul and the Nations: The Old Testament and Jewish Background of Paul's Mission to the Nations with Special Reference to the Destination of Galatians*. Tübingen: J. C. B. Mohr, 1995.

Seccombe, David. "Was There an Organized Charity in Jerusalem before the Christians?" *Journal of Theological Studies* 29 (1978): 140–143.

Seeley, David. *The Noble Death: Graeco-Roman Martyrology and Paul's Concept of Salvation*. Sheffield: Journal of the Study of the New Testament Press, 1990.

Segal, Alan. *Paul the Convert: The Apostolate and Apostasy of Saul the Pharisee*. New Haven: Yale University Press, 1990.

Shanks, Hershel, ed. *Christianity and Rabbinic Judaism: A Parallel History of Their Origins and Early Development*. Washington, D.C.: Biblical Archaeology Society, 1992.

Sherwin-White, Adrian. N. *The Letters of Pliny: A Historical and Social Commentary*. Oxford: Clarendon Press, 1966.

Silberman, Neil Asher. "Searching for Jesus." *Archaeology* 47:6 (November/December 1994): 30–40.

————. "The World of Paul." *Archaeology* 49:6 (November/December 1996): 30–36.

Smallwood, E. Mary. *The Jews under Roman Rule from Pompey to Diocletian*. Leiden: E. J. Brill, 1976.

Smith, Abraham. *Comfort One Another: Reconstructing the Rhetoric and Audience of 1 Thessalonians*. Louisville, KY: Westminster/John Knox, 1995.

Smith, Morton. *Jesus the Magician*. San Frnacisco: Harper and Row, 1978.

Snyder, Graydon F. *Ante Pacem: Archaeological Evidence of Church Life Before Constantine*. Macon, GA: Mercer University Press, 1985.

Stager, Lawrence E. "The Archaeology of the Family in Ancient Israel." *Bulletin of the American Schools of Oriental Research* 260 (1985): 1–35.

Stamforth, Maxwell, trans. *Early Christian Writings*. London: Penguin Books, 1968.

Stendahl, Krister. "The Apostle Paul and the Introspective Conscience of the West." *Harvard Theological Review* 56 (1963): 199–215.

————. *Paul Among Jews and Gentiles*. Philadelphia: Fortress Press, 1976.

Stern, Ephraim. *The New Encyclopedia of Archaeological Excavations in the Holy Land*. New York: Simon and Schuster, 1993.

Stern, Menahem. "Aspects of Jewish Society: The Priesthood and Other Classes." Pp. 561–630 in *The Jewish People in the First Century*, eds. Shmuel Safrai and Menachem Stern. Philadelphia: Fortress Press, 1974.

Stone, Michael. *Scriptures, Sects, and Visions: A Profile of Judaism from Ezra to the Jewish Revolts*. Philadelphia: Fortress Press, 1980.

Stowers, Stanley. "Friends and Enemies in the Politics of Heaven: Reading Theology in Philippians." Pp. 105–121 in *Pauline Theology I: Thessalonians, Philippians, Galatians, Philemon*, ed. Jouette M. Bassler. Minneapolis: Fortress Press, 1991.

————. *A Rereading of Romans: Justice, Jews, and Gentiles*. New Haven: Yale University Press, 1994.

————. *Letter Writing in Greco-Roman Antiquity.* Philadelphia: Westminster Press, 1986.

Strelan, John G. "Burden Bearing and the Law of Christ: A Re-examination of Galatians 6:2." *Journal of Biblical Literature* 94 (1975): 266–276.

Strickert, Fred. "The Coins of Philip." Pp. 165–189 in *Bethsaida*, eds. Rami Arav, and Richard A. Freund. Kirksville, MO: Thomas Jefferson University Press, 1995.

Tabor, James D. *Things Unutterable: Paul's Ascent to Paradise in Its Greco-Roman, Judaic, and Early Christian Contexts.* Lanham, MD: University Press of America, 1986.

Tabor, James D., and Droge, Arthur J. *A Noble Death: Suicide and Martyrdom among Christians and Jews in Antiquity.* San Francisco: HarperSanFrancisco, 1992.

Tatum, W. Barnes. *John the Baptist and Jesus: A Report of the Jesus Seminar.* Sonoma, CA: Polebridge Press, 1994.

Taylor, Joan E. *Christians and the Holy Places: The Myth of Jewish Christian Origins.* Oxford: Clarendon Press, 1993.

Taylor, Nicholas H. *Paul, Antioch, and Jerusalem: A Study in Relationships and Authority in the Earliest Church.* Sheffield: Journal for the Study of the Old Testament Press, 1992.

Tcherikover, Victor A. *Hellenistic Civilization and the Jews.* Philadelphia: Jewish Publication Society, 1959.

Theissen, Gerd. *The Gospels in Context: Social and Political History in the Synoptic Tradition.* Minneapolis: Fortress Press, 1991.

————. *The Social Setting of Pauline Christianity: Essays on Corinth.* Philadelphia: Fortress Press, 1982.

Thisleton, Anthony C. "Realized Eschatology in Corinth." *New Testament Studies* 24 (1978): 510–526.

Tiede, David Lenz. *Prophecy and History in Luke-Acts.* Philadelphia: Fortress Press, 1980.

Trebilco, Paul. "Asia." Pp. 291–363 in *The Book of Acts in Its Greco-Roman Setting*, eds. David W. J. Gill and Conrad Gempf. Grand Rapids, MI: Eerdmans, 1994.

Tsaferis, Vassilios. "Capernaum." Pp. 291–296 in *The New Encyclopedia of Archaeological Excavations in the Holy Land*, ed. Ephraim Stern. New York: Simon and Schuster, 1993.

————. "Jewish Tombs at and Near Giv'at ha-Mivtar." *Israel Exploration Journal* 20 (1970): 18–32.

Tuckett, Christopher M. "A Cynic Q?" *Biblica* 70 (1989): 349–76.

Twelftree, Graham H. *Jesus the Exorcist: A Contribution to the Study of the Historical Jesus.* Tübingen: J. C. B. Mohr, 1993.

Vickers, Michael. "Toward the Reconstruction of the Town Planning of Roman Thessaloniki." Pp. 239–251 in *Ancient Macedonia I*, ed. Basil Laourdas. Thessaloniki: Institute for Balkan Studies, 1970.

Wacholder, Ben Zion. "The Calendar of Sabbatical Cycles During the Second

Temple and Early Rabbinic Period." *Hebrew Union College Annual* 44 (1973): 153–196.

———. "Chronomessianism: The Timing of Messianic Movements and the Calendar of Sabbatical Cycles." *Hebrew Union College Annual* 46 (1975): 201–218.

Wachsmann, Shelly. *The Sea of Galilee Boat.* New York: Plenum Press, 1995.

Walaskay, Paul W. *'And So We Came to Rome': The Political Perspective of St. Luke.* Cambridge: Cambridge University Press, 1983.

Wallace-Hadrill, Andrew. *Houses and Society in Pompeii and Herculaneum.* Princeton: Princeton University Press, 1991.

———, ed. *Patronage in the Ancient World.* London: Routledge, 1989.

Webb, Robert L. *John the Baptizer and Prophet: A Socio-historical Study.* Sheffield: Journal for the Study of the Old Testament Press, 1991.

Wengst, Klaus. *Pax Romana and the Peace of Jesus Christ.* Philadelphia: Fortress Press, 1987.

White, L. Michael. *Building God's House in the Roman World: Architectural Adaption among Pagans, Jews, and Christians.* Baltimore: Johns Hopkins University Press, 1990.

———. "Urban Development and Social Change in Imperial Ephesos." Pp. 27–79 in *Ephesos: Metropolis of Asia,* ed. Helmut Koester. Valley Forge, PA: Trinity Press International, 1995.

———. "Visualizing the 'Real' World of Acts 16: Toward Construction of a Social Index." Pp. 234–261 in *The Social World of the First Christians,* eds. L. Michael White and O. Larry Yarbrough. Minneapolis: Fortress Press, 1995.

Wilkinson, John. *Jerusalem as Jesus Knew It.* London: Thames and Hudson, 1978.

Williams, Sam K. *Jesus' Death as Saving Event: The Background and Origins of a Concept.* Missoula: Scholars Press, 1975.

Wire, Antionette Clark. *The Corinthian Women Prophets: A Reconstruction Through Paul's Rhetoric.* Minneapolis: Fortress Press, 1990.

Wirgin, Wolf. "On King Herod's Messianism." *Israel Exploration Journal* 11 (1961): 153–154.

———. "A Note on the 'Reed' of Tiberias." *Israel Exploration Journal* 18 (1969): 248–249.

Wise, Michael. O. "The Life and Times of Ananias Bar Nedebaeus and His Family." Pp. 51–102 in *Thunder in Gemini and Other Essays on the History, Language, and Literature of Second Temple Palestine.* Sheffield: Journal for the Study of the Old Testament Press, 1994.

Wise, Michael O., and Tabor, James D. "The Messiah at Qumran." *Biblical Archaeology Review.* 18:6 (November/December 1992): 60–65.

Wiseman, James. "Corinth and Rome I: 228 B.C.—A.D. 267." *Aufstieg und Niedergang der Römischen Welt* 2.7.1 (1979): 439–548.

Witherington, Ben. *The Jesus Quest.* Downers Grove, IL: InterVarsity Press, 1995.

Wolf, Eric R. *Peasants.* Englewood Cliffs, NJ: Prentice-Hall, 1966.

Yarbro Collins, Adela. *Crisis and Catharsis: The Power of the Apocalypse.* Philadelphia: Westminster Press, 1986.

Zanker, Paul. *The Power of Images in the Age of Augustus*. Ann Arbor: University of Michigan Press, 1988.

Zayadine, Fawzi, ed. *Petra and the Caravan Cities*. Amman: Department of Antiquities, 1990.

Zias, Joseph, and Sekeles, Eliezer. "The Crucified Man from Giv'at ha-Mivtar: A Reappraisal." *Israel Exploration Journal* 35 (1985): 22–27.

Index